A PRACTICAL GUIDE TO INTERNATIONAL ARBITRATION IN LONDON

Related titles:

Arbitration Law Handbook
by Ben Horn & Roger Hopkins
(2007)

Arbitration Act 1996
3rd edition
by Robert Merkin
(2005)

Arbitration Law
by Robert Merkin
(2004)

International Arbitration: A Handbook
3rd edition
by Phillip Capper
(2004)

So You Really Want to be an Arbitrator?
by Mark Cato
(1999)

Introduction to Arbitration
by Harold Crowter
(1998)

A PRACTICAL GUIDE TO INTERNATIONAL ARBITRATION IN LONDON

BY

HILARY HEILBRON Q.C.

informa

LONDON
2008

Informa Law
Mortimer House
37–41 Mortimer Street
London W1T 3JH
law.enquiries@informa.com

an Informa business

First published 2008

British Library Cataloguing in Publication Data
A catalogue record for this book
is available from the
British Library

ISBN 978–1–84311–729–2

Text set in 10/12pt Plantin
by Interactive Sciences Ltd, Gloucester
Printed in Great Britain by
MPG, Bodmin, Cornwall

Printed on paper sourced from sustainable sources

For my Father,

who, as a retired general medical practitioner,
knows little about international arbitration in London,
but aged 102, still has time to learn!

PREFACE

This book was conceived to fill a gap. There are many books on international arbitration law and several specifically relating to English arbitration law, but most tend to address the subject in detail and are largely aimed at a specialist audience. Yet with the proliferation of international arbitration there are many lawyers who are newcomers to the field who need to know about international arbitration in London. How do such lawyers advise a client who suddenly appears in their office with a contract containing a London arbitration clause? What should they do next, tactically and otherwise? What does the process involve? How do they avoid the pitfalls?

Those not necessarily familiar with international arbitration include litigation or trial lawyers, in-house corporate counsel and other external lawyers both in England and elsewhere in the world, for international arbitration, as its name implies, is a global form of dispute resolution. This is the audience to whom this book is primarily addressed, although it is hoped that the book will also be useful to those who already practise international arbitration, but are less familiar with arbitrating in London, as well as to transactional lawyers considering drafting London arbitration clauses. It provides a relatively short, but comprehensive, overview with the emphasis on practical issues, buttressed by reference to the statutory framework of the Arbitration Act 1996 and the attitude of the English courts.

I am most appreciative of all those who have given me help and support with this project, but particular thanks are due to Peter Butler, Freehills, Sydney; Professor Robert Merkin; Victoria Ophield; Klaus Reichert, Brick Court Chambers; and Jessica Westwood. Any errors are, of course, the author's alone. Finally, I would like to thank the late and much missed Sir Michael Kerr, one of the doyens of the subject, who spurred me into the direction of a more active involvement in international arbitration alongside my practice in commercial litigation, for which encouragement I remain especially grateful.

CONTENTS

Preface vii
Table of Cases xv
Table of Legislation, Conventions and Rules xix
Introduction xxiii

1. SOME RELEVANT ASPECTS OF THE ENGLISH LEGAL SYSTEM AND PRACTICE
   Introduction 1
   The court system 1
   The split profession and its relevance to international arbitration 2
   Civil procedure 3
   The Arbitration Act 1996 4
   European Community law 5

2. OVERVIEW OF THE ADVANTAGES AND DISADVANTAGES OF INTERNATIONAL ARBITRATION COMPARED WITH OTHER FORMS OF DISPUTE RESOLUTION
   Introduction 7
   Enforcement 7
   Privacy and confidentiality 9
   Cost and delay 9
   Choice of the tribunal 10
   A neutral forum 10
   Forum shopping 10
   Additional parties and other claims 12
   Precedent and certainty of result 12
   Flexibility of the process 13
   Other forms of dispute resolution 13

3. UNDERSTANDING ARBITRATION CLAUSES
   Introduction 15
   The basic essentials of an arbitration clause 16
   Arbitral institution, independent rules or ad hoc 17
   The tribunal 19
   The seat of the arbitration 20
   The applicable law 21
   The language 23
   Time limits and pre-conditions to commencement of arbitration 23

Additional possible exclusions and inclusions 23
Defective or pathological arbitration clauses 24

4. THE SCOPE OF THE ARBITRATION CLAUSE
Introduction 25
Whether the dispute is covered by the clause 26
Set-offs and counterclaims 27
The parties to the arbitration agreement 27
Non-signatories and third parties 28
Assignees and insurers 29
States 30
Consolidation and concurrent hearings 31
Other issues relating to parties 32
How the parties should approach such issues 32
Availability of remedies 33

5. CHOOSING THE TRIBUNAL AND THE LEGAL TEAM
Introduction 35
Choosing the tribunal 35
The ten criteria for nominating an arbitrator 35
Finding out about English arbitrators 38
Choosing the legal team 39

6. ACTIVITY AND CONSIDERATIONS PRIOR TO COMMENCING AN ARBITRATION
Introduction 41
The appointment of an emergency arbitrator or expedited tribunal 42
Applications to the English court before the tribunal is fully constituted 42
Applications for a stay of court proceedings 44
Multi-tier clauses and alternative dispute resolution 46

7. FIRST STEPS IN THE PROCESS
Introduction 47
Starting the arbitration 47
The response and reply 49
Appointing the tribunal 49
Challenges to the arbitrator 51
Arbitrators' tenure 52
Matters for agreement between the parties 52
Advance costs and deposits 53

8. ACTIVITY AND CONSIDERATIONS FOLLOWING THE FORMATION OF THE TRIBUNAL
Introduction 55
Initial general communications and directions by the tribunal 55
Non-participating parties 56
Terms of Reference 57

Bifurcation and preliminary issues 57
Security for costs 59
Preservation of evidence and other interlocutory applications 59
An order limiting recoverable costs and other protective measures as to costs 60
Exclusion of recourse to the courts 61

9. JURISDICTION
Introduction 63
The autonomy of the arbitration agreement 63
The effect of delay in raising jurisdictional issues 64
The powers of the tribunal 65
The powers of the court prior to an award 66
Applications to the court for determination of a preliminary point of jurisdiction 66
Application to the court by a respondent for a declaration or injunction 67
Appeals and challenges to the award 67

10. DIRECTIONS AND TIMETABLE
Introduction 69
Further written statements or submissions 70
Disclosure issues between the parties 71
Disclosure from third parties 72
Expert evidence 73
Witnesses of fact 75
Other common directions 75
Ensuring compliance 79

11. APPLICATIONS TO THE COURT PRIOR TO THE HEARING
Introduction 81
Procedure 81
Injunctions, including freezing orders, relating to London arbitration 84
Other provisional measures 85
Section 44(6) of the 1996 Act 86
Preliminary points of law 86
Anti-suit injunctions to restrain foreign proceedings and anti-arbitration injunctions 87
Aiding foreign arbitrations 88

12. ONGOING ISSUES AND PREPARING FOR THE HEARING
Introduction 91
Common issues and problems 91
Procedural orders and hearings 93
Provisional awards 94
Costs and charges 94
Court applications 95

Hearing preparation 95
Initiatives from the tribunal 97
Protection as to costs 97
Mediation 98

13. HEARINGS
Introduction 101
Miscellaneous matters 101
Written submissions 102
Opening statements 102
Oral evidence 102
Experts 104
Applicable law 104
Final submissions 104
Privacy and confidentiality 104

14. AWARDS
Introduction 107
Remedies 107
Assessing damages 108
Form and contents of awards 109
Partial awards 110
Costs 110
Settlements 111
Communicating the award to the parties 111
Confidentiality 111

15. CHALLENGES TO AN AWARD AND APPEALS GENERALLY
Introduction 115
Section 67 of the 1996 Act (jurisdiction) 115
Section 68 of the 1996 Act (serious irregularity) 117
Section 69 of the 1996 Act (appeal on point of law) 119
Challenges and appeals generally 121
Appeals to the Court of Appeal 122

16. ENFORCEMENT OF AN ENGLISH OR FOREIGN AWARD
Introduction 123
Enforcement under section 66 of the 1996 Act 124
Recognition and enforcement of New York Convention awards 124
Procedure 126
Ancillary measures 126
States 128

17. INVESTMENT TREATY ARBITRATION
Introduction 131
Justiciability 131
Enforcement 132

Appendices

A. Arbitration Act 1996 133
B.1 Index to Comparison of the Rules of the LCIA, ICC, ICDR and UNCITRAL 191
B.2 Index of the LCIA, ICC, ICDR and UNCITRAL Rules in numerical order 196
B.3 Comparison of the Rules of the LCIA, ICC, ICDR and UNCITRAL 200
C.1 CPR Part 62: Arbitration Claims 269
C.2 CPR Part 62 Practice Direction (and forms N8, N8A, N8B and N15) 280
D. The Admiralty and Commercial Courts Guide—Sections F and O 293
E. IBA Rules on the Taking of Evidence in International Commercial Arbitration 325
F. The Chartered Institute of Arbitrators: Protocol for the Use of Party-Appointed Expert Witnesses in International Arbitration 333
G. The New York Convention 339

Glossary 345

Index 347

TABLE OF CASES

A *v.* B [2007] EWHC 54 (Comm) 45, 87
ABB AG *v.* Hochtief Airport GmbH & Anor [2006] EWHC 388 119
Aectra Refining and Manufacturing Inc. *v.* Exmar NV [1994] 1 W.L.R. 1634 27
AEGIS *v.* European Reinsurance Company of Zurich [2003] UKPC 11; [2003] 1 W.L.R. 1041 ... 31, 112, 113
AIG Capital Partners Inc. & anor *v.* Kazakhstan & ors [2005] EWHC 2239 (Comm) 130, 132
Al Wahab, The, *see* Amin Rasheed Shipping Corp *v.* Kuwait Insurance Co.
Ali Shipping Corp *v.* Shipyard Trogir [1999] 1 W.L.R. 314 .... 112, 113
American Cyanamide Co. *v.* Ethicon Ltd [1975] A.C. 396 85
AMR Amin Hamza El Nasharty *v.* J Sainsbury plc [2007] EWHC 2618 (Comm) 45, 64
Amin Rasheed Shipping Corp *v.* Kuwait Insurance Co. (The Al Wahab) [1984] A.C. 50 23
Andrew Owusu *v.* Nugent B. Jackson (t/a Villa Holidays Ball-Inn Villas) & ors [2002] EWCA Civ 877 11
Angelic Grace, The, [1995] 1 Lloyd's Rep. 87 87
ASM Shipping Ltd of India *v.* TTMA Ltd of England [2006] EWCA Civ 1341 122
Assimina Maritime Ltd *v.* Pakistan Shipping Corp and HR Wallingford Limited [2004] EWHC 3005 (Comm) 72, 86
AT&T Corp and another *v.* Saudi Cable Co. [2000] 2 Lloyd's Rep. 127 52
Athena, The, *see* Sea Trade Maritime Corp *v.* Hellenic Mutual War Risks Association (Bermuda) Limited
Athletic Union Constantinople *v.* National Basketball Association (No. 2) [2002] EWCA Civ 830 122
Atlantic Emperor, The, *see* Marc Rich & Co. *v.* Societa Italiana Impianti PA

Babanaft International Co. SA *v.* Bassatne [1990] Ch. 13 85
Baytur SA *v.* Finagro Holding SA [1991] 4 All E.R. 129 30
Beximco Pharmaceuticals Ltd & ors *v.* Shamil Bank of Bahrain E.C. [2004] EWCA Civ 19 21
BLCT (13096) *v.* J Sainsbury plc [2003] EWCA Civ 884 122
BNP Paribas & ors *v.* Deloitte & Touche LLP [2003] EWHC 2874 (Comm) 71, 72

C *v.* D [2007] EWCA Civ 1282 .... 22, 45, 87, 112
Calderbank *v.* Calderbank [1976] Fam. 93 98
Cetelem SA *v.* Roust Holdings Ltd [2005] EWCA Civ 618 .... 43, 72, 85, 86, 122
CGU International Insurance plc and others *v.* AstraZeneca Insurance Co. [2006] EWCA 1340 122
Channel Tunnel Group Ltd and another *v.* Balfour Beatty Construction Ltd and ors [1993] 2 W.L.R. 262 45
Charles M Willie and Co. (Shipping) Ltd *v.* Ocean Laser Shipping Ltd (The Smaro) 1999 1 Lloyd's Rep. 225 32
CMA CGM SA *v.* Beteiligungs-Kommanditgesellschaft MS Northern Pioneer Schiffahrtgesellschaft mbH & Co. & ors [2002] EWCA Civ 1878 119
Czech Republic *v.* European Media Ventures SA [2007] EWHC 2851 (Comm) 117, 131

Dadourian Groupo Int. Inc. *v.* Simms & ors [2006] EWCA Civ 399 85
Dardana Ltd *v.* Youkos Oil Co. [2002] EWCA Civ 543 126
David Wilson Homes Limited *v.* Survey Services Limited (in liquidation) and David Jonathan Marshall [2001] EWCA Civ 34 (C.A.) 16
Davinder Singh Virdee *v.* Amritpal Singh Virdi [2003] EWCA Civ 41 122
Demco Investments & Commercial SA & ors *v.* SE Banken Soesakring Holding Aktiebolag [2005] EWHC 1398 121

Department of Economics, Policy & Development of the City of Moscow *v.* Bankers Trust Co. & ors [2004] EWCA Civ 314 112
Derby & Co. Ltd *v.* Weldon [1990] Ch. 65 85
Dow Chemical ICC 4131/1982 29
DST *v.* Rakoil [1987] 2 Lloyd's Rep. 246 125

Econet Satellite Services Ltd *v.* Vee Networks Ltd (formerly Econet Wireless Nigeria Ltd) [2006] EWHC 1664 (Comm) 27
Econet Wireless Ltd *v.* Vee Networks & ors [2006] EWHC 1568 43
Elektrim SA *v.* Vivendi Universal and ors [2007] EWHC 571 (Comm) 84, 87, 88
Electrosteel Castings Ltd *v.* Scan-Trans Shipping and Chartering SDN BHD [2002] EWHC 1993 (Comm) 28
Essex County Council *v.* Premier Recycling Ltd [2006] EWHC 3594 (TCC) 119
Esso Australia Resources Ltd *v.* The Honourable Sidney James Plowman (1995) 183 C.L.R. 10 112
Exfin Shipping (India) Ltd Mumbai *v.* Tonali Shipping Co. Ltd Mumbai [2006] EWCA 1090 (Comm) 27

Fiona Trust & Holding Corp & ors *v.* Yuri Primalov & ors [2007] EWCA Civ 20 .... 16, 26, 44, 67
Front Comor, The, *see* West Tankers Inc. *v.* (1) Ras Riunione Adriatica Di Sicurta SpA (2) Generali Assicurazione Generali SpA

Gasser GmbH *v.* MISAT Srl (Case G116/02) [2003] ECR I-14693 .... 11, 88
Gater Assets Ltd *v.* Nak Naftogaz Ukrainiy [2007] EWCA Civ 988 127
Gidrxslme Shipping Co. Ltd *v.* Tantomar-Transportes Maritimos Lda [1995] 1 W.L.R. 299 127
Glidepath BV & ors *v.* John Thompson & ors [2005] EWHC 818 (Comm); [2004] EWHC 2234 (QB) 43, 72
Golden Strait Corp *v.* Nippon Yusen Kibishka Kaisha [2007] UKHL 12 108

Halpern & another *v.* Halpern & ors [2007] EWCA Civ 291 21
Hassneh Insurance Co. of Israel and ors *v.* Steuart J Mew [1993] 2 Lloyd's Rep. 243 113
Henry Boot Construction (UK) Ltd *v.* Malmaison Hotel (Manchester) Ltd [2001] 1 Q.B. 388 122
Hobbs Padgett & Co. (Reinsurance) Ltd *v.* JC Kirkland Ltd [1969] 2 Lloyd's Rep. 547 16
Holloway and another *v.* Chancery Mead Ltd [2007] EWHC 2495 (TCC) 46

Intermet FZCO & ors *v.* Ansol Ltd & ors [2007] EWHC 226 88
Investors Compensation Scheme Ltd *v.* West Bromwich Building Society [1998] 1 W.L.R. 896 25
Ipco (Nigeria) Ltd *v.* Nigerian National Petroleum Corp [2005] EWHC 726 .... 125, 126, 127

Jay Bola, The, *see* Schiffahrtsgesellschaft Detlev Von Appen GmbH *v.* Voest Alpine Intertrading GmbH
Jordan Nicolov, The, *see* Montedipe SpA *v.* JTP-RO Jugotanker

Kanoria & ors *v.* Guinness & Anor [2006] EWCA Civ 222 .... 125, 126
Kazakhstan *v.* ISTIL Group Inc. [2007] EWCA Civ 471 117
Kershaw Mechanical Services Ltd *v.* Kendrick Construction Ltd [2006] EWHC 727 120
Konkola Copper Mines plc *v.* Coromin [2005] EWHC 898 (Comm) and EWCA Civ 5 12

Laker Airways Inc. *v.* (1) FLS Aerospace Ltd (2) Stanley Jeffrey Burnton [2000] 1 W.L.R. 113 37
Lesotho Highlands Development Authority *v.* Impregilo SpA & ors [2005] UKHL 43 .... 108, 118

Marc Rich & Co. *v.* Societa Italiana Impianti PA (The Atlantic Emperor) [1991] ECR I-3855 88
Messier-Dowty Ltd & anor *v.* Sabena SA & ors [2000] 1 W.L.R. 2040 11
Metal Distributors (UK) *v.* ZCCM Investment Holdings plc [2005] EWHC 156 (QB) 27
Minmetals Germany GmbH *v.* Ferco Steel Ltd [1999] C.L.C. 647 125
Montedipe SpA *v.* JTP-RO Jugotanker (The Jordan Nicolov) [1990] 2 Lloyd's Rep. 11 30

Nigel Peter Albon *v.* Naza Motor Trading SDN BHD & another [2007] EWHC 665 (Ch); [2007] EWHC 1879; [2007] EWCA Civ 1124 .... 45, 64, 83, 89
Nisshin Shipping Co. Ltd *v.* Cleaves & Co. Ltd [2003] EWHC 2602 (Comm) 29

Nobel Assurance and ors *v.* Gerling-Kinzern General Insurance Co. [2007] EWHC 253 (Comm) 88
North Range Shipping Ltd *v.* Seatrans Shipping Co. [2002] EWCA Civ 405 122
Northern Star Systems & ors *v.* Fielding & ors [2005] EWHC (Ch) 1638 96

Occidental Exploration & Production Co. *v.* Republic of Ecuador [2005] EWCA Civ 1116 131
Owusu *v.* Jackson [2002] EWCA Civ 877 (C.A.) 11

Padre Island (No. 2), The [1990] 2 Lloyd's Rep. 191 30
Penwith District Council *v.* VP Developments Ltd [2007] EWHC 2544 (TCC) 119
Peterson Farms Inc *v.* C & M Farming Ltd [2002] EWHC 121 (Comm) 29
Premium Nafta Products Limited and ors *v.* Fili Shipping Company Limited and ors [2007] UKHL 40 .... 16, 26, 44, 64, 67

Reliance Industries Ltd *v.* Enron Oil and Gas India [2002] 1 Lloyd's Rep. 645 119
Republic of Ecuador *v.* Occidental Exploration & Production (No. 2) [2006] EWHC 345 (Comm) 117
Rosseel NV *v.* Oriental Commercial Shipping (UK) Ltd & ors [1990] 1 W.L.R. 1387 127

Sayyed Mohammed Musawi *v.* RE International (UK) & ors [2007] EWHC 2981 (Ch) 21
Schiffahrtsgesellschaft Detlev Von Appen GmbH *v.* Voest Alpine Intertrading GmbH (The Jay Bola) [1997] 2 Lloyd's Rep. 279 .... 29, 87
Scott *v.* Avery (1856) 25 LJ Ex 308 .... 46, 121
Sea Trade Maritime Corp *v.* Hellenic Mutual War Risks Association (Bermuda) Limited (The Athena) [2006] EWHC 2530 (Comm) 16
Sempra Metals Ltd (formerly Metallgesellschaft Limited) *v.* Her Majesty's Commissioners of Inland Revenue and another [2007] UKHL 34 108
Smaro, The, *see* Charles M Willie and Co. (Shipping) Ltd *v.* Ocean Laser Shipping Ltd
Smith *v.* Pearl Assurance Co. Ltd [1939] 1 All E.R. 95 32
Starlight Shipping Co. & another *v.* Tai Ping Insurance Co. Ltd, Hubei Branch and ors [2007] EWHC 1893 (Comm) 72, 82, 84, 87
Surefire Systems *v.* Guardian ECL Ltd [2005] EWHC 1860 (TCC) 119
Sumukan Ltd *v.* Commonwealth Secretariat [2007] EWCA Civ 1148; [2007] EWCA Civ 243 .... 49, 119, 120, 122
Sun Life Assurance Co. of Canada & ors *v.* The Lincoln National Life Insurance Co. [2004] EWCA Civ 1660 113
Svenska Petroleum Exploration AB *v.* (1) Government of the Republic of Lithuania (2) AB Geonafta [2006] EWCA Civ 1529 .... 30, 129, 130

Tajik Aluminium Plant *v.* Hydro Aluminium and another [2005] EWCA Civ 1218 72
Taylor Woodrow Holdings Ltd & another *v.* Barnes & Elliott Ltd [2006] EWHC 1693 (TCC) 58, 86
Through Transport Mutual Insurance Association (Eurasia) Limited *v.* New India Assurance Association Company Limited [2004] EWCA (Civ) 1598 87
Torch Offshore LLC & Anor *v.* Cable Shipping Inc [2004] EWHC 787 118
Turner *v.* Grovit (Case G159/02) [2004] ECR I-3565 88

Universal General Insurance Co. *v.* Group Josi Reinsurance Co. SA (Case C-412/98) [2000] 3 W.L.R. 1625 11

Vale do Rio Navegação SA & anor *v.* Shanghai Bao Steel Ocean Shipping Co. Ltd (t/a Baosteel Ocean Shipping Co.) and anor [2000] 2 Lloyd's Rep. 1 .... 67, 82
Viking Insurance Co. *v.* Edward George Rossdale and ors, unreported, 1 August 2001 89

West Tankers Inc. *v.* (1) Ras Riunione Adriatica Di Sicurta SpA (2) Generali Assicurazione Generali SpA *sub nom* The Front Comor [2005] EWHC 343 (Comm); [2007] UKHL 4 ..... 5, 11, 29, 87, 88
Whiting *v.* Halverson [2003] EWCA Civ 403 16

TABLE OF LEGISLATION, CONVENTIONS AND RULES

Administration of Justice Act 1920 8
Arbitration Act 1698 4
Arbitration Act 1950 4
Arbitration Act 1975 4
Arbitration Act 1979 4
Arbitration Act 1996—
s. 2 5
(1) 4
(2) 123
(2)–(5) 4
(2) 20, 44
(3) 20
(5) 22
s. 3 .... 5, 21, 24, 52
s. 4(1)–(2) 5
(1)–(3) 17
(3), (5) 5, 24, 52
(5) 21, 24
s. 5 .... 16, 20
s. 6 16
(1) 26
(2) 16
s. 7 .... 5, 22, 24, 28, 44, 52, 63–64
(7) 43
s. 8 .... 5, 24, 32, 52
s. 9 .... 44, 45, 66, 67
(3) 44
(4) 44
(5) 46
s. 12 48
(2) 23
(3) 23
(5) 23, 47
s. 13(1), (4) 47
s. 14 47
(1) 47
ss. 14–18 .... 5, 24, 52
s. 15 .... 20, 35
(3) 19, 24
s. 16 .... 19, 49
(7) 24
s. 17 .... 19, 49
s. 18 .... 19, 49
(3) 52
s. 19 .... 19, 49
ss. 20–22 56
ss. 20–23 .... 5, 24, 52
s. 23 52

Arbitration Act 1996—*cont.*
s. 23(4) 16
s. 24 52
(2) 5, 24
s. 25 .... 5, 24, 52, 52
s. 26(2) 5, 24, 52
s. 27 .... 5, 24, 52
s. 28(1) 51, 54
(5) 51, 54
s. 29 55
s. 30 .... 5, 24, 44, 52, 63
(1) 116
(2) 116
ss. 30–31 32
s. 31(1) 33
(1)–(3) 65, 116
s. 32 .... 32, 66–67, 122
(5) 67
(6) 68
s. 33 .... 55, 93
s. 34 .... 61, 97
(1) 5, 69
(2)(d) 71
ss. 34–36 .... 5, 24, 53
s. 35 .... 24, 331
s. 37 74
(1) 5, 24, 53
s. 38 .... 61, 84
(1) 56, 59, 84, 103
(3) 59
(4) 59
(5) 103
(6) 59
ss. 38–39 .... 5, 24, 53
s. 39 .... 59, 81, 84, 94
s. 41(2) 92
(3) 92
(4) 101
(5) 59, 84, 92
(6) 59, 60
(7) 84, 92
ss. 41–42 .... 5, 24, 53, 93
s. 42 .... 60, 61, 80, 84, 92, 93
s. 43 .... 72, 88, 95, 103
s. 44 .... 53, 42, 61, 72, 81–82, 85–89, 122
(1) 84
(1), (2), (3), (6) 43
(2)(e) 84

Arbitration Act 1996—*cont.*
s. 44(4) 87
(6) 81, 86
ss. 44–45 .... 5, 24
s. 45 .... 53, 56, 61, 86, 122
s. 46 22
(1)(a) 21
(1)(b) 21
(2) 21
(3) 21–22
ss. 46–55 53
s. 47 110
s. 48 107
s. 49 108
s. 50 .... 107, 122
s. 51 111
s. 52 109
s. 56(1) 111
s. 57 .... 5, 24, 53, 110, 116, 118, 120
s. 58 .... 5, 24, 53, 110
(1) 17
s. 60 .... 98, 110
s. 61 110
ss. 61–65 .... 5, 24, 53
ss. 63–64 110
s. 65 .... 60, 98
s. 66 .... 66, 123, 124, 126, 127
(4) 123
s. 67 .... 25, 32, 36, 66, 115–117, 118, 119, 121, 131
(1) 116
(3) 117
(4) 117
s. 68 .... 36, 117–119, 121
(1) 118
(2) 117
(2)(b) 118
(3) 118
(4) 118
s. 69 .... 5, 23, 37, 53, 61, 119–121, 122
(1) 119
(2) 119, 120
(3) 120
(4) 119
(6) 120
(7) 120
(8) 121
s. 70(2) 32, 116, 117, 118
(3) 32, 116, 118, 120
(4)–(5) 116, 117
(6) 121
(6)–(7) 116, 118, 120
(8) 117, 118
s. 71 121
s. 72 .... 32, 44, 66, 67, 116
(2) 117, 118
s. 73 .... 32, 124
(1) 65
(2) 65

Arbitration Act 1996—*cont.*
ss. 76–79 .... 5, 24, 53
s. 78(3) 118, 120
s. 79 .... 49, 79
(1) 116, 118, 120
s. 81(1) 123
(b) 16
s. 82 .... 26, 44
(1) 37, 63, 86, 116, 119
(2) 29, 87
s. 100(2) 21
ss. 100–103 123
ss. 100–104 66
s. 101 126
ss. 101–104 124–126
s. 102 126
s. 103(2) 129
(b) 21
(f) 127
(3)(d) 25
(4) 126
(4) 127
s. 104 123
Schedule 1 .... 5, 52, 61
Arbitration (International Investment Disputes) Act 1966—
s. 1(2) 132
s. 2 132
Arbitration Rules of the Arbitration Institute of the Stockholm Chamber of Commerce—
Art. 20 18
Arbitration Rules of the Singapore International Arbitration Centre (SIAC Rules 2007)—
Art. 18 18
Charging Orders Act 1979—
ss. 1, 2 128
CIArb Protocol 70, 73
Arts 4, 5, 7.4, 8 75
Art. 8 96
Civil Jurisdiction and Judgments Act 1982 8
Civil Procedure Rules (CPR) 3–4, 13
Part 1.1 4
6.20 89
6.20(5) 83
8 132
23 85
25 85
25.12–13 121
52.3 126
62 .... 82, 85
62.2(1) 82
62.3–4 82
62.4(2) 82
62.5 .... 82, 83
62.6 82
62.8 83
62.10 83

Civil Procedure Rules (CPR)—*cont.*
Part 62.18 126
62.21 132
72 127
73 128
74 .... 8, 132
Contracts (Applicable Law) Act 1980 22
Contracts (Rights of Third Parties) Act 1999—
ss. 1, 8 29
Council Regulation (EC) No. 44/2001 .... 8, 11, 82
European Convention on Human Rights 1950—
Art. 6 .... 117, 119
European Convention on State Immunity 130
Evidence (Proceedings in Other Jurisdictions) Act 1975—
s. 1(a) 89
Foreign Judgments (Reciprocal Enforcement) Act 1933 8
Hague Convention on Recognition and Enforcement of Foreign Judgments in Civil and Commercial Matters 8
IBA Rules on Conflicts of Interest 37, 50
IBA Rules of Evidence 36, 73
Arts 3, 9 71
Art. 4(5) 95
Art. 4(8) 103
Art. 4(11) 103
Art. 5 96
ICC Rules 18, 21, 27, 41, 48, 105, 119
Art. 2(iii) 110
Art. 2.1(b) 27
Art. 5.5 27
Art. 6.2 .... 63, 65, 67
Art. 6.3 .... 56, 67
Art. 6.4 64
Art. 7 51
Art. 7.4 51
Art. 8.4 49
Art. 9.1 50
Art. 9.5 50
Art. 10.2–2 49
Art. 11.1–3 51
Art. 12.1–4 52
Art. 12.2 52
Art. 12.3–4 52
Art. 12.5 52
Art. 15.2 55
Art. 15.3 27
Art. 17.1 22
Art. 17.2 22
Art. 17.3 21
Art. 18 57
Art. 18.4 69
Art. 19 .... 57, 93
Art. 20.1 38
Art. 20.4 74
Art. 20.5 .... 97, 103
ICC Rules—*cont.*
Art. 20.6 77
Art. 20.7 71
Art. 21.2 101
Art. 21.3 105
Art. 23 59
Art. 24 38
Art. 24.1–2 107
Art. 26 111
Art. 27 109
Art. 28.1–2 111
Art. 28.6 .... 58, 61, 119
Art. 29 110
Art. 30 56
Art. 31 110
Art. 31.3 110
Art. 32 79
Art. 33 65
Art. 33.1–4 53
ICDR Rules 18, 38, 48
Art. 7 51
Art. 8.1–3 51
Art. 9 51
Art. 10 52
Art. 11.1 52
Art. 11.2 52
Art. 15 65
Art. 16.1–2 55
Art. 21 59
Art. 23 56
Art. 25 65
Art. 26.2 56
Art. 28.1–28.3 22
Art. 28.3 21
Art. 29 111
Art. 31 110
Art. 37 42
ICSID (International Centre for the Settlement of Investment Disputes) Convention Regulations and Rules 131–132
Art. 53 132
Art. 54(1) 132
Art. 54(3) 132
Art. 55 132
Law of Property Act 1925—
s. 136 30
LCIA Rules 18, 21, 27, 38, 48, 97, 119
Art. 1.2 47
Art. 4.7 79
Art. 5 51
Art. 5.5 50
Art. 6.1–6.3 50
Art. 7.2 49
Art. 8.1–2 49
Art. 9 42
Art. 10.1–2 52
Art. 10.3–4 51
Art. 11 52
Art. 12.1–2 52

LCIA Rules—*cont.*
Art. 14.1(i), (ii) 55
Art. 14.3 56
Art. 15.8 56
Art. 19.1 77
Art. 19.3 .... 80, 97
Art. 19.4 105
Art. 20.4 103
Art. 21 74
Art. 21.1(a) 93
(b) 79
(c) 79, 97, 103
(f) 97
(g) 107
(h) 31
Art. 22.2 .... 58, 61
Art. 22.3 22
Art. 22.4 21
Art. 23 65
Art. 23.2 65
Art. 23.4 .... 58, 61, 67
Art. 24.1–3 53
Art. 24.3 .... 53, 56
Art. 25 59
Art. 26.5 111
Art. 26.7 110
Art. 26.8 111
Art. 26.9 .... 58, 61, 119
Art. 27 110
Art. 28 110
Art. 28.3 110
Art. 30.1 .... 53, 105, 112
Art. 32.1 65
Art. 32.2 56
Limitation Act 1980—
s. 5 47
LMAA (London Marine Arbitrators Association) Terms 18
Lugano Convention 2007 .... 8, 11
Money Laundering Regulations 2003 102
New York Convention on the Recognition and Enforcement of Foreign Arbitral Awards 1958 .... 8, 9, 20, 66, 123, 124, 132
Art. II(1), (2) 17
Art. V 9
(1)(a) 21
Proceeds of Crime Act 2002 102
Rome Convention 22
Art. 1 22
(2)(d) 22
Rome Convention—*cont.*
Art. 2 22
Art. 4 22
State Immunity Act 1978—
ss. 1, 13 129
s. 2(1) 128
(2), (7) 128
s. 3 129
(1)(a), (2) 128
(b), (2) 129
(3) 128
s. 6 129
s. 9 .... 30, 129, 139
ss. 13, 14 130
s. 13(1)–(3) 85
s. 14(2) 129
Supreme Court Act 1981—
s. 37 121
(1) 84, 87, 88
Swiss Rules of International Arbitration—
Art. 1(2) 18
Art. 4 31
Art. 42 42
Third Parties (Rights Against Insurers) Act 1930 30
UNCITRAL (UN Commission on International Trade Law) 4, 5, 18, 27, 35, 48, 75, 105, 119, 131
Arts 6–8 .... 17, 49
Art. 9 51
Art. 10.1–2 51
Arts 10–12 51
Art. 11.1–3 51
Art. 12.1–2 51
Art. 13.1–2 52
Art. 14 52
Art. 15.1 55
Art. 16.1 21
Art. 17 59
Art. 19.3 27
Art. 21 65
Art. 24.1 95
Art. 26 59
Art. 28 56
Art. 30 65
Art. 31.2 56
Art. 32.1 110
Art. 32.1–32.3 22
Art. 33.2 21
Art. 34 111
Arts 38, 40 110
Art. 41.1–5 53

INTRODUCTION

"*Why, Sir, you find no man, at all intellectual, who is willing to leave London. No, Sir, when a man is tired of London, he is tired of life; for there is in London all that life can afford.*"

Samuel Johnson

"*International arbitration may be defined as the substitution of many burning questions for a smouldering one.*"

Ambrose Bierce

There is a frequent misconception among those not familiar with international arbitration that it is no more than a variant of litigation. This misconception has become more marked as arbitration has increased as the dispute resolution method of choice of corporations and states. International arbitration has developed a body of law and practice of its own across the divide of national systems of law, both civil and common law. This can differ from the national system of law of the place designated by the parties for the arbitration. However, national systems of law are still necessary to support the process, as arbitrators' powers do have limitations.

London is one of the leading centres for international arbitration, a position which is enhanced by the increasing recognition of London as probably the foremost financial centre in the world. International arbitration taking place in London is underpinned by the Arbitration Act 1996. Arbitration is "a structured but informal process"[1] where familiarity with what it entails, as with all dispute resolution forums, is advantageous. This book seeks to take a pragmatic look at how to run an international arbitration where the seat of the arbitration is London. It considers these issues not only from the perspective of the arbitral process, but also from that of the inter-relationship of this process with the support given by the English courts. Some of the issues are common to all international arbitrations: others are peculiarly English.

The book considers the progress of an arbitration on a stage-by-stage basis from first sight of an arbitration clause to ultimate enforcement, examining the tactical, procedural and legal issues that arise for consideration at each stage. It explores the role and attitude of the English courts and of the relevant

1. The late Sir Michael Kerr, former judge of the Court of Appeal and President of the London Court of International Arbitration ("LCIA").

English principles of law and English court practice indicating when such applications should be made and how they should be approached. As some issues are relevant to more than one stage of the arbitral process, and are hence referred to more than once, the book contains internal cross-referencing to enable a reader who selects a specific stage of the process or specific topic to consider any such issue in the wider context of the whole arbitration. Additionally, a few issues, such as jurisdiction, are also considered as separate topics.

The issues covered are wide-ranging from the relatively elementary to the more complex. They include such basic matters as understanding the specific language sometimes used in international arbitrations and the appointment of arbitrators; more controversial issues such as the diverse approaches to disclosure of documents; and legal issues from challenges to arbitrators, to jurisdictional issues and enforcement. There are also references to the ambit of the English court's assistance in respect of arbitrations where the place of arbitration is not London.

While the main thrust of the book is directed towards international commercial arbitration, much of its contents are equally applicable to investment treaty arbitration. Accordingly, there is included a brief chapter on this topic at the end of this book, but the number of instances where the seat of an investment treaty arbitration is London has historically been limited. At Appendix B there is a comparative table of three sets of rules of arbitral institutions most likely to be used in London, namely the ICC, the LCIA, the ICDR as well as the UNCITRAL Rules together with related indices.

It assumes some basic legal knowledge on the part of the reader, but unusual terms are explained in the text and there is also a Glossary.

The book is not intended to be a treatise on international arbitration law, but a manageable and introductory guide intended for those lawyers less familiar with the process of international arbitration, whether practising in England or abroad (hence the inclusion of chapter 1), and particularly where the arbitration is London-based. The book accordingly seeks to set out the principles with limited reference to authorities. It aims instead to give a pragmatic perspective on the more common issues confronting those arbitrating in London.

Inevitably there is some subjective selection as to what is included, with the emphasis being on the practical aspects of running an arbitration in London rather than esoteric issues. Accordingly, the book does not pretend to cover every arbitral issue. To do so would considerably lengthen the book and defeat its purpose. However, the book, together with its appendices, should enable any lawyer to deal effectively with an international arbitration in London from first intimation of a claim to ultimate enforcement. The law is stated as at 31 December 2007.

CHAPTER 1

SOME RELEVANT ASPECTS OF THE ENGLISH LEGAL SYSTEM AND PRACTICE

INTRODUCTION

This chapter is principally directed to those who are not familiar with the English legal system and its practices and procedure. It focuses on five separate aspects of the English legal system and practice by way of background to the other chapters in this book, namely:

- the court system;
- the split profession and its relevance to international arbitration;
- civil procedure;
- the Arbitration Act 1996; and
- European Community law.

THE COURT SYSTEM

When a foreigner thinks of the English courts he or she pictures a barrister in a wig and gown and a sense of Dickensian grandeur. Nothing could be further from the truth, certainly for those involved in international arbitration. The English Commercial Court, where all applications concerning commercial international arbitration are heard, is a part of the High Court. It is a forward-thinking business court whose innovative processes have led the way in reforming court practices more generally. Its judges are specially chosen for their experience in commercial matters and arbitration and are of the highest calibre. Wigs and gowns are dispensed with in the Commercial Court. All matters, whether interim applications or full hearings, are handled by the assigned High Court judges themselves. In big cases a specific judge is assigned to the case throughout. There is a Commercial Courts Guide dealing with the procedure, to which reference shall be made in this book as appropriate. Applications, particularly if urgent, can be heard relatively quickly.

The Commercial Court is predominantly an international court and the Commercial Court judges are experienced at handling cases and applications involving foreign parties. The latest formal survey carried out in 2004–5 indicated that the number of claims where at least one claimant and one defendant originated from outside the United Kingdom constituted about

50% of all claims issued in the Commercial Court. The number of claims where at least one claimant or one defendant emanated from outside the jurisdiction constituted about 80% of all claims issued in the Commercial Court.

Arbitration applications concerning construction cases are heard in the Technology and Construction Court, another specialist court. This court similarly has its own specialist procedures. However, the procedure in respect of applications concerning arbitration is largely the same whether the application is made to the Commercial Court or the Technology and Construction Court. This book concentrates on the former.

Appeals to the Court of Appeal can be heard only with the permission of the original court or the Court of Appeal. In the arbitral context, appeals to the Court of Appeal under the Arbitration Act 1996 are rare. It is the almost invariable practice for an appellate tribunal hearing a commercial case, or one concerning international arbitration, to include at least one member of the court with detailed expertise in the area of law. Appeals to the House of Lords on matters of international arbitration are extremely rare and can only take place with either the permission of the Court of Appeal or of the House of Lords.

THE SPLIT PROFESSION AND ITS RELEVANCE TO INTERNATIONAL ARBITRATION

The legal profession in England and Wales, unlike, for example, in the United States, is split into barristers and solicitors. Successful senior barristers usually become Queen's Counsel, a process known as taking silk after the silk gown which a Queen's Counsel wears. A Queen's Counsel is akin to being a consultant in the medical profession. Queen's Counsel deal with the larger and more complicated cases often with a junior barrister(s) to assist. Historically only barristers had rights of audience in the higher courts. The position has changed and solicitors can now become solicitor-advocates. This enables them to appear in the High Court and a few have been made Queen's Counsel. However, advocacy work in the higher courts is still predominantly carried out by barristers.

Barristers or counsel work in sets of chambers, i.e. groups of barristers usually working in the same areas of law and sharing administrative expenses and facilities. Traditionally barristers' chambers were housed in the Inns of Court, but now many barristers' chambers are in modern or modernised buildings with all the up-to-date technology. Barristers in a set of chambers are not partners with each other, but are self-employed. Barristers employ clerks to look after their practices, and to fix their diaries and their fees, although some barristers now do some of this directly themselves. Previously barristers could only be instructed by solicitors, but there have been considerable changes in recent years. Barristers can be instructed directly by foreign lawyers, professional organisations, in-house corporate counsel and even by the lay public. This is particularly relevant in the context of international arbitration (see below). However, if the matter is before an English court an English solicitor has to appear on the court record.

Solicitors work in partnerships sharing profits and losses. Their firms range in size from sole practitioners to a couple of partners to many hundreds of partners, from local high street firms to global firms with offices throughout the world. Firms of solicitors usually deal with a large range of legal services but with increasingly specialised departments, although some firms concentrate exclusively on specific areas of law such as criminal law. London also houses the London offices of a substantial and growing number of foreign legal firms, particularly from the United States.

There are a number of solicitors, foreign lawyers practising in London and barristers who specialise or practise in international arbitration, some exclusively, others as part of their overall commercial practice. Several legal firms, both English and international, have specific international arbitration sections, others have specialists within their dispute resolution departments. Many of these do their own advocacy before tribunals and, if they are solicitor-advocates, sometimes also before the courts: others instruct barristers for these tasks.

The Bar similarly includes those who have international arbitration expertise. They advise on the subject, appear before arbitral tribunals throughout the world including, of course, London, and appear in the English courts. Barristers acting in international arbitration in either an advisory or advocacy capacity can be instructed directly by a foreign lawyer (whether based in London or abroad) or in-house corporate counsel or an English solicitor. It is not infrequent in international arbitration, particularly if the matter is complex, to have a mixed team of lawyers including a Queen's Counsel to undertake or share the advocacy and to give advice.

London has a large selection of experienced international arbitrators with a wide variety of legal and specialist expertise which include barristers (especially Queen's Counsel), retired judges, solicitors and foreign lawyers practising from London, as well as non-legal experts who also sit as arbitrators.

CIVIL PROCEDURE

Civil procedure in England underwent a revolution in 1998 with the implementation of reforms promulgated by Lord Woolf, the former Master of the Rolls and Lord Chief Justice. Its aim was to wrest control of the procedure away from the parties into the hands of the judges and to exert some constraints on time wasting and escalating costs. The procedure is set out in the Civil Procedure Rules (the "CPR") and accompanying Practice Directions (see Appendix C). The over-riding objective of the CPR is to ensure that the court deals with cases fairly and expeditiously and in a way which is proportionate to the amount involved and the importance of the case.[1] A further change in procedure has been the increasing emphasis on mediation. This duopoly of reforms has led to a reduced number of English cases reaching trials in the courts.

A frequent error of those unfamiliar with international arbitration is to cite before an international tribunal sitting in London the CPR as authority for some point, such as the width of disclosure of documents. The CPR has no direct relevance to international arbitration or to the procedure before tribunals conducted in London. The only relevance of the CPR in international arbitration relates to the procedure for bringing arbitration-related applications to the court, though sometimes some of the rules can provide inspiration for arbitration practice in a particular instance.

THE ARBITRATION ACT 1996

One year short of the third centenary of the first English Arbitration Act,[2] the Arbitration Act 1996 (the "1996 Act") came into force[3] providing a modern approach to international arbitration. The gestation period had been lengthy and at times controversial, with a growing demand to replace the then existing legislation[4] with a statute which provided a less interventionist approach from the English courts. Following lengthy deliberation by the Departmental Advisory Committee (the "DAC") established by the Department of Trade and Industry, and considerable consultation with the arbitration community, a new statute was born. Unlike other jurisdictions it was not based on the Model Law,[5] but was a compromise of some of the Model Law's provisions with other provisions adjusted to suit the English position. It has recently celebrated its tenth anniversary and the overall verdict is that it has been a success, although some would have liked it to have gone further.

The 1996 Act applies to all arbitration, domestic and international, irrespective of the law of the agreement, provided that the seat of the arbitration is England and Wales or Northern Ireland.[6] It also contains some limited provisions to aid international arbitration where the seat of the arbitration is outside England and Wales or Northern Ireland.[7] In the context of this book and international arbitration, reference shall be made to London rather than to the wider jurisdictional ambit of the 1996 Act, unless the context otherwise requires.

1. CPR Part 1.1.
2. The Arbitration Act 1698.
3. On 31 January 1997.
4. The Arbitration Acts of 1950, 1975 and 1979.
5. Agreed by the United Nations Commission on International Trade Law ("UNCITRAL") and adopted by the United Nations in June 1985.
6. Sections 2(1) and 4(4) of the 1996 Act.
7. Section 2(2)–(5) of the 1996 Act.

The 1996 Act, which is set out in full at Appendix A, contains both mandatory and non-mandatory provisions.[8] It gives precedence to party autonomy over the process, subject to the various mandatory provisions of the 1996 Act. This enables the parties, by agreement, to provide for how the process is to be conducted.[9] Such agreement is regularly accomplished by agreeing to the rules of an arbitral institution or to an independent set of rules such as the UNCITRAL Rules, but can also be achieved on an ad hoc or one-off basis as well. The 1996 Act also enables the court to intervene in a limited number of instances. It confirms the right of the tribunal to decide all procedural and evidential matters, absent agreement by the parties.[10] The 1996 Act therefore recognises the consensual nature of the arbitral process and the fact that it derives from private agreement. Nonetheless, disputing parties, although they have agreed to an arbitration agreement, are not always willing to compromise. Additionally, sometimes the respondent takes no part in the arbitration for a whole variety of reasons. It is then for the tribunal, or in limited circumstances the court, to fill in the gaps.

The 1996 Act is founded on the following "*general principles*" and has to be construed accordingly. These are that[11]:

"*(a) the object of arbitration is to obtain the fair resolution of disputes by an impartial tribunal without unnecessary delay or expense;*

(b) the parties should be free to agree how their disputes are resolved, subject only to such safeguards as are necessary in the public interest; [and]

(c) in matters governed by this Part the court should not intervene except as provided by this Part."

EUROPEAN COMMUNITY LAW

European Community law is part of English law. Arbitration is, however, excluded from the EC Regulation (otherwise known as the Brussels Regulation) "*on jurisdiction and the recognition and enforcement of judgments in civil and commercial matters*" which applies to all Member States of the European Community. The normal rules concerning which Member State is seized of the case, therefore, do not apply and arbitration matters are left to the supervising national courts. However, the issue is a contentious one and the House of Lords have recently referred a case to the European Court on the issue of the English court's ability to grant anti-suit injunctions to prevent proceedings in a Member State in breach of an arbitration agreement.[12]

8. Section 4(1)–(2) and Schedule 1 to the 1996 Act sets out the mandatory provisions. The following sections' provisions are subject to the parties' agreement and are non-mandatory, namely: sections 3, 4(3) and (5), 7, 8, 14–18, 20–23, 24(2), 25, 26(2), 27, 30, 34–36, 37(1), 38–39, 41–42, 44–55, 57, 58, 61–65, 69, 76–79. See chapter 3, chapter 7 page 52 and Appendix A for more detail.

9. Section 4(3) and (5) of the 1996 Act. The parties can also agree the applicable law of the agreement: section 4(5) of the 1996 Act.

10. Section 34(1) of the 1996 Act.

11. Section 2 of the 1996 Act.

12. *West Tankers Inc.* v *RAS Riunione Adriatica di Sicurta SPA & ors* [2007] UKHL 4. See also chapter 11 pages 87–88.

CHAPTER 2

OVERVIEW OF THE ADVANTAGES AND DISADVANTAGES OF INTERNATIONAL ARBITRATION COMPARED WITH OTHER FORMS OF DISPUTE RESOLUTION

INTRODUCTION

International arbitration and litigation have traditionally been the principal methods of cross-border dispute resolution, but they are not the only means of resolving disputes. Multi-tier clauses are, for example, an increasingly popular option. These provide for negotiation or a non-binding form of dispute resolution such as mediation as an optional or mandatory prerequisite to embarking upon litigation or arbitration. Another form of clause is an option to the parties to elect arbitration at the time of the dispute with a fall-back of litigation failing such exercise. This chapter gives an overview of the pros and cons of international arbitration as against litigation. Other forms of dispute resolution are also discussed. The following topics are considered:

- enforcement;
- privacy and confidentiality;
- cost and delay;
- choice of the tribunal;
- a neutral forum;
- forum shopping;
- additional parties and other claims;
- precedent and certainty of result;
- flexibility of the process; and
- other forms of dispute resolution.

ENFORCEMENT

Success in court or arbitration can be a pyrrhic victory if that success cannot be translated into an enforceable result. The ultimate aim of most claimants is to secure payment of sums due to them, whether as damages or a debt. The corresponding desire of some respondents is to resist paying any claim successfully brought against them. Lack of an effective international enforcement procedure can play into the hands of the latter at the expense of the former.

Various treaties provide for enforcement and recognition of judgments. The EC Regulation[1] for instance provides for a simple form of recognition and enforcement of judgments between Member States of the European Union. The Administration of Justice Act 1920 and the Foreign Judgments (Reciprocal Enforcement) Act 1933 are also relevant to recognition and enforcement of judgments in England.[2] However, at a global level, bilateral and other treaties relating to enforcement are limited, with many countries not being parties to such treaties.[3] Enforcement of court judgments can thus cause insuperable problems for successful parties.

One of the great advantages of international arbitration is that enforcement is relatively straightforward as a result of the New York Convention, which celebrates 50 years in existence in 2008. Most trading nations of the world are signatories to the New York Convention.[4] The New York Convention provides for mandatory recognition and enforcement with only narrow grounds on which an award can be challenged at this stage. These are set out in Article V of the New York Convention which provides as follows:

> "*Article V*
>
> *1. Recognition and enforcement of the award may be refused, at the request of the party against whom it is invoked, only if that party furnishes to the competent authority where the recognition and enforcement is sought, proof that:*
>
> *(a) The parties to the agreement referred to in article II were, under the law applicable to them, under some incapacity, or the said agreement is not valid under the law to which the parties have subjected it or, failing any indication thereon, under the law of the country where the award was made; or*
>
> *(b) The party against whom the award is invoked was not given proper notice of the appointment of the arbitrator or of the arbitration proceedings or was otherwise unable to present his case; or*
>
> *(c) The award deals with a difference not contemplated by or not falling within the terms of the submission to arbitration, or it contains decisions on matters beyond the scope of the submission to arbitration, provided that, if the decisions on matters submitted to arbitration can be separated from those not so submitted, that part of the award which contains decisions on matters submitted to arbitration may be recognized and enforced; or*
>
> *(d) The composition of the arbitral authority or the arbitral procedure was not in accordance with the agreement of the parties, or, failing such agreement, was*

1. Council Regulation (EC) No. 44/2001 and the original Lugano Convention have been incorporated into English law by the Civil Jurisdiction and Judgments Act 1982 as amended. The Lugano Convention was concluded between EU Member States and Members of the European Free Trade Association ("EFTA"). The Lugano Convention has been replaced by a new Lugano Convention signed on 30 October 2007. This applies between the European Community and Switzerland, Norway and Iceland.
2. The procedure for recognition and enforcement of judgments in England is set out in Part 74 of the CPR and the accompanying Practice Direction.
3. The Hague Convention on Recognition and Enforcement of Foreign Judgments in Civil and Commercial Matters would considerably alleviate the problems if it were to be taken up by the major trading states in the world.
4. Currently 142 countries.

not in accordance with the law of the country where the arbitration took place; or

(e) *The award has not yet become binding, on the parties, or has been set aside or suspended by a competent authority of the country in which, or under the law of which, that award was made.*

2. Recognition and enforcement of an arbitral award may also be refused if the competent authority in the country where recognition and enforcement is sought finds that:

(a) *The subject matter of the difference is not capable of settlement by arbitration under the law of that country; or*

(b) *The recognition or enforcement of the award would be contrary to the public policy of that country."*

The New York Convention is set out in full at Appendix G. The Article V grounds are essentially replicated in the 1996 Act (see chapter 16 at pages 124–126).

PRIVACY AND CONFIDENTIALITY

Save in very exceptional situations where national security or highly sensitive commercial information is disclosed, litigation takes place in public and potentially in the full glare of media publicity. Not only can the process, as well as the result, impact on the business of one or more of the parties, but litigation also exposes individuals to unnecessary stress and publicity. Arbitration, on the other hand, takes place in private and confidentiality largely attaches to all information relating to it. For a fuller discussion on privacy and confidentiality in arbitration see chapter 13 pages 104–105 and chapter 14 pages 111–113.

COST AND DELAY

There is an increasing concern that international commercial arbitration is becoming as costly as litigation and not significantly quicker as a result. There is always a balance that needs to be achieved between speed and cost, on the one hand, and a fair and just result, on the other. However, the scope for curtailing excess in arbitration exists and effective arbitrators will strive to do this in various ways as set out later in this book. Additionally, there are three significant factors which militate against delay. First, the limited scope for intervention by national courts of most countries as the process proceeds; secondly, the absence of an appeal from an arbitral award save in very circumscribed circumstances; and thirdly, a speedy and effective enforcement procedure. It is, therefore, important when choosing the seat of an arbitration to ascertain not only whether or not there is in place an effective arbitration statute in that country, but also the attitude of the judges to intervention in the process and appeals from awards. Some national courts intervene more readily than others in the process or on appeal.

CHOICE OF THE TRIBUNAL

Apart from the extremely rare occasions when an arbitration clause names one or more arbitrators, the composition of the arbitral tribunal is unknown at the time of the dispute. In international arbitration parties can nominate, or at least have some input into, the appointment of the arbitrator(s) (see chapter 5 page 35 and chapter 7 pages 49–51) and this can be an advantage. When parties face litigation, on the other hand, they have no input in the choice of judge who is to try their case. In some jurisdictions, such as England, cases will be assigned to judges with relevant specialist knowledge, but this is not always so in other countries with less sophisticated judicial systems.

A NEUTRAL FORUM

Judicial systems similarly vary in their procedure and legal approach to cases and in the quality of their judges. A foreign party not familiar with the procedures and judicial system of a local court may feel at a disadvantage against an opponent from such a jurisdiction, even if this is not the case. Thus, in an age of widening globalisation there is an increasing reluctance to entrust disputes to the national courts of a country of which the opposing party is unfamiliar. This has been a trigger for the increasing use of international arbitration as a neutral forum for the hearing of disputes and London is a particularly popular venue because of its long tradition of arbitration. In international arbitration the tribunal is frequently composed of arbitrators of different nationalities from the parties.

FORUM SHOPPING

Forum shopping and consequent satellite litigation to determine which national courts have jurisdiction over the dispute is a particular risk with litigation involving parties from more than one country. In the absence of an exclusive jurisdiction or non-exclusive jurisdiction clause (and even then there is no absolute certainty), there is always a risk that the choice of jurisdiction of the claimant will be challenged on *forum non conveniens* grounds or parties will seek to litigate simultaneously in two jurisdictions. This leads to extra expense and delay. Such problems arise to a much lesser extent with international arbitration and, provided that the arbitration clause is clear, it will be much more difficult for parties to enlist the aid of the courts to oust the jurisdiction of the tribunal. Courts of most jurisdictions are more likely to intervene to compel parties to arbitrate in such circumstances (see chapter 6 pages 44–45 and chapter 11 pages 87–88).

Mention should be made of the special position relating to Europe where the EC Regulation "*on jurisdiction and the recognition and enforcement of judgments in civil and commercial matters*"[5] applies. This can cause difficulties for parties involved in litigation, particularly now that the membership of the European Union is large and increasing in size. This book is not the place to set out the implications of the EC Regulation in any detail, but a few salient points are worth bearing in mind. As explained in chapter 1, the EC Regulation does not apply to arbitration, although in the light of recent European case law, the position is not wholly clear.[6]

In the context of a European party, practical problems in relation to litigation covered by the EC Regulation, which can be avoided by the use of arbitration,[7] include:

i. Where a defendant is domiciled in a contracting country (or if a corporation has its seat there), then even if the claimant is domiciled outside the European Union, for example in the United States, proceedings must be brought in the defendant's country of domicile.[8] This can mean that a claim has to be brought in the country of the corporation's head office, even though that head office had no involvement in the case.
ii. The chronological approach to jurisdiction. Once legal proceedings are lodged in a European jurisdiction, that court becomes the court first seized and must deal with any contest in relation to jurisdiction, even if the alternative ground is covered by the EC Regulation and this points to another jurisdiction.[9] This can cause delay if the courts of the country concerned are dilatory, as some are.
iii. A party cannot rely on the doctrine of *forum non conveniens* as this does not apply if the defendant is domiciled within the EU and is sued under Article 2, i.e. in his place of domicile.[10] Either the EC Regulation applies if the competing jurisdictions are within the EU or the contracting country is precluded from staying an action in

5. EC Regulation 44/2001. See also the Lugano Convention and the new Lugano Convention and fn. 1.

6. The House of Lords have recently referred to the European Court the question of the court's ability to grant an anti-suit injunction in respect of proceedings in a Member State on the ground that such proceedings are in breach of an arbitration agreement: *West Tankers Inc.* v *RAS Riunione Adriatica di Sicurta SPA & ors* [2007] UKHL 4. See also chapter 11 pages 87–88.

7. Negative declarations are a useful way of resolving the matter where the position is clear. See e.g. *Messier-Dowty Ltd & anor* v *Sabena SA & ors* [2000] 1 W.L.R. 2040.

8. *Universal General Insurance Co.* v *Group Josi Reinsurance Co. S.A.* (Case C-412/98) [2000] 3 W.L.R. 1625.

9. *Gasser GmbH* v *MISAT Srl* (Case G116/02) [2003] ECR I–14693.

10. *Andrew Owusu* v *Nugent B. Jackson (t/a Villa Holidays Ball-Inn Villas) & ors* [2002] EWCA Civ 877.

favour of a non-contracting country if jurisdiction is properly found.[11]

iv. Defendants and third parties from non-contracting states can be brought into the action, using the initial proceedings as an anchor. When the non-contracting country defendant or third-party then seeks to challenge its inclusion on *forum non conveniens* grounds, the court has to reconcile the inconsistency between the EC Regulation concerning the initial defendant and the problem of parallel proceedings if it allows the other defendant's case to be heard elsewhere.

ADDITIONAL PARTIES AND OTHER CLAIMS

It is relatively easy to add an additional defendant or third party in court proceedings. This is not the case with arbitration, which is a consensual process. A tribunal only has jurisdiction over the parties to the arbitration agreement. Consent or a provision in any applicable arbitral rules would be needed to confer such jurisdiction on a tribunal. This issue is discussed in chapter 4 pages 27–30. Similarly consolidation or consecutive hearings are normally not feasible in arbitration (see chapter 4 page 31).

PRECEDENT AND CERTAINTY OF RESULT

There is no precedent in international commercial arbitration.[12] Awards are not published.[13] The limited number of appeals means that the body of law available is restricted. Nonetheless, application of a national law to a dispute provides a constraint on uncertainty. In contrast the use of transnational law or equity clauses with their emphasis on justice and fairness enhances the uncertainty.[14] The amount of an award of damages, on the other hand, is even less predictable, although such awards have to be based on the facts and any applicable law. Such lack of precedent in arbitration coupled with the negligible opportunity of overturning a result emphasises the importance of choosing the right tribunal for a case.

11. The European Court has not yet decided if the doctrine of *forum non conveniens* would apply if jurisdiction was sought to be founded upon another Article of the Regulation, but it is likely that it will as it is the logical corollary to their decisions. However, the English courts have opined that the doctrine of *forum non conveniens* does still apply to an exclusive jurisdiction clause giving jurisdiction to a non-contracting state subject to discretionary factors: *Konkola Copper Mines plc* v *Coromin* [2005] EWHC 898 (Comm) and EWCA Civ 5.

12. "Arbitral Precedent: dream, necessity or excuse?", The Freshfields' Lecture 2006 by Gabrielle Kaufmann Kohler.

13. The ICC does publish a selection of awards suitably redacted. In contrast investment treaty awards are published.

14. See chapter 3 pages 21–23.

Litigation, on the other hand, is usually based on precedent and the hierarchy of the courts, although assessment of damages is less predictable. Thus, lower courts cannot over-rule higher ones. Moreover, the opportunity for appeal, even where permission or leave is required, is much greater. Nonetheless, litigation can have advantages where there are issues of legal principle involved, particularly where it is desired to change or develop the law or where it is necessary to establish a precedent for other similar cases, neither of which options are generally available in arbitration.

FLEXIBILITY OF THE PROCESS

In most jurisdictions litigation is conducted in accordance with specified procedural rules. In England the relevant rules are the Civil Procedure Rules. While the case management aspects of these rules do give judges some flexibility to control the process, similar rules in other jurisdictions may not. International arbitration, on the other hand, gives the parties the opportunity of agreeing their own procedure subject to certain restraints whether under the national supervisory law, any applicable sets of rules or the arbitration clause. It also provides arbitrators with the ability to tailor the procedure to the matter in hand and to reduce costs and delay. Essentially arbitration provides a much more flexible procedure which can be adjusted to meet the facts of each particular case and is not hide-bound by court rules.

OTHER FORMS OF DISPUTE RESOLUTION

There are a variety of other forms of dispute resolution apart from litigation and arbitration. Some can be binding such as expert determination. Others are not binding unless agreement is reached. These alternative forms of dispute resolution or ADR are becoming increasingly common. Some jurisdictions mandate such a process, others encourage it and others are neutral. Parties can seek non-binding opinions, mini-trials, mediation and a whole host of variants. The common thread is that these processes involve a neutral facilitator.

The most common of these is mediation. Like the other methods this is a confidential process.[15] Parties can exchange their views freely without prejudice to the outcome and in the knowledge that if the mediation fails, these views will not be put before an arbitrator or judge. Mediations are not binding unless a settlement agreement is reached. Resolving a dispute by mediation is quicker and cheaper than other forms of dispute resolution.

15. Although there are signs that in particular cases this confidentiality is susceptible to being eroded.

The presence of the key personnel of the respective parties who are involved in the dispute is really essential to the process and ensures that a commercial rather than a legalistic approach is taken. Even if a full settlement of the dispute is not reached the mediation can often provide a catalyst for narrowing the issues to be resolved by the courts or arbitration. Another most valuable benefit is that, unlike either the court or arbitration, there is no restriction on what can be included in the overall settlement, so that business considerations leading to commercial solutions can replace or reduce monetary compensation. Courts and arbitrators can only give the basic remedies, usually of damages. ADR and mediation is further discussed in chapter 6 at page 46 and chapter 12 at pages 98–99.

CHAPTER 3

UNDERSTANDING ARBITRATION CLAUSES

INTRODUCTION

Towards the end of many international contracts, there appears, almost as an afterthought, an arbitration clause. One can visualise clients after many long hours of drafting and negotiation being advised by their respective lawyers to insert a dispute resolution clause into the contract, a breakdown of relations probably being the last thing on any client's mind in the euphoria of a successfully concluded business deal. Yet parties do break contracts and a means of resolving the consequent issues that arise is essential.

The problem with scant attention frequently being given to the arbitration clause is that a poorly drafted or defective clause, referred to as a "*pathological arbitration clause*"[1] can cause many unnecessary difficulties. This and the following chapter therefore consider the principal questions that need to be asked when faced with an international arbitration clause in a contract or when considering including one in a contract. Although many of the issues would receive the same answer in most jurisdictions, the text below deals with the position where the seat of the arbitration is London and the process is subject to the 1996 Act. Similarly, the comments relate to clauses governed by English law, unless otherwise stated. The following issues are addressed in this chapter:

- the basic essentials of an arbitration clause;
- arbitral institution, independent rules or ad hoc;
- the tribunal;
- the seat of the arbitration;
- the applicable law;
- the language;
- time limits and pre-conditions to commencement of arbitration;
- additional possible exclusions and inclusions; and
- defective or pathological arbitration clauses.

Other issues relevant to the scope of the arbitration clause, namely the nature of the claims covered and the parties to it, are dealt with in chapter 4.

1. The name was apparently given to such clauses by Frederick Eisemann in 1974 when he was Secretary General of the ICC International Court of Arbitration.

THE BASIC ESSENTIALS OF AN ARBITRATION CLAUSE

The first pre-requisite to an arbitration clause under the 1996 Act is that it should be in writing.[2] This is provided for in section 5 of the 1996 Act. This is fairly broadly defined and covers: (a) a written agreement; (b) an exchange of written communications; (c) an agreement evidenced in writing; (d) an agreement which need not be in writing, for example, an oral agreement or one formed by conduct, by reference to written terms[3] provided, of course, that the arbitration clause is otherwise incorporated; or (e) an agreement arising from the uncontested written submissions of a party in arbitral or legal proceedings, but only where there is a response: silence is insufficient.

Writing is widely defined to include "*recorded by any means*" and thus, for example, extends to an e-mail exchange. A party's signature is not necessary, although desirable, particularly to minimise disputes as to who are parties to the arbitration clause. Such writing is also essential for enforcement under the New York Convention.[4]

General words are sufficient to incorporate by reference an arbitration clause forming part of standard terms and which are found in another document, even if the party is unaware of the arbitration clause. However, in certain exceptional two-contract cases such as charterparty/bills of lading cases, where the parties are different in each contract, the incorporation has to be by way of some express reference to arbitration or the clause itself.[5]

It is also necessary to determine whether or not the clause is an arbitration clause. There are various possible dispute resolution clauses that can be inserted into a contract. The most common are: an exclusive or non-exclusive jurisdiction clause relating to the courts; a mediation clause; an expert determination; an expert's non-binding opinion; an arbitration clause; or a combination of these. Sometimes the parties agree hybrid clauses or multi-tier clauses, for example, that the parties must first try to mediate their differences before resorting to arbitration. This is a question of construction of the relevant clause according to its applicable law (see below).

Section 6 of the Arbitration Act 1996 defines an arbitration agreement as: "*. . . any agreement to submit to arbitration present or future disputes (whether they are contractual or not).*" Thus, a clause referring a dispute in the classic formula to "*a person acting as an expert and not as an arbitrator*" would clearly not be an arbitration clause. However, it is not always necessary for the clause to say in terms that the disputes are to be referred to an "*arbitrator*" or to "*arbitration*", provided that there is "*an agreement to refer disputes to a person other than the court who is to resolve the dispute in a manner binding on the parties to the*

2. Section 81(1)(b) of the 1996 Act does preserve any rule of law as to the effect of an oral arbitration agreement and section 23(4) seems to confirm that writing is not necessary for the parties to terminate an arbitration agreement. This could for instance be by conduct.

3. For example, Bills of Lading or General Terms and Conditions.

4. Article II(1) and (2).

5. *Sea Trade Maritime Corporation* v *Hellenic Mutual War Risks Association (Bermuda) Limited (The Athena)* [2006] EWHC 2530 (Comm) and section 6(2) of the 1996 Act.

agreement".[6] Nor is it apparently essential for the clause to state that the result is to be binding if the clause is otherwise an arbitration clause. In such cases the 1996 Act will fill in the gap by virtue of section 58(1), which provides that "*unless otherwise agreed by the parties, an award made by the tribunal pursuant to an arbitration agreement is final and binding on the parties and on any persons claiming through or under them.*"

An agreement which gives the parties an election or option to arbitrate or uses the word "*may*" rather than "*shall*" becomes a binding arbitration clause once that mechanism is triggered.[7] Parties can also decide to have existing disputes resolved by arbitration even if their agreement makes no prior provision for such a resolution of the dispute. Such agreements are sometimes called submission agreements or ad hoc agreements.

ARBITRAL INSTITUTION, INDEPENDENT RULES OR AD HOC

It is important also to consider whether or not the parties have provided any procedural framework for their arbitration by reference to a set of rules or whether it is an ad hoc clause silent on institutional involvement or procedural issues.[8] There are four possibilities: first, the clause can provide for the application of the rules of an arbitral institution which will mean that the institution then acts as appointing authority and its procedural rules apply. Secondly, the arbitration clause refers to an appointing authority without additionally providing for any procedural rules to be incorporated. Thirdly, the clause refers to a set of rules such as the UNCITRAL Rules, without providing for an appointing authority.[9] Fourthly, the clause is silent both as to appointing authority and procedural rules.

6. *David Wilson Homes Limited* v *Survey Services Limited (in liquidation) and David Jonathan Marshall* [2001] EWCA Civ 34 (CA). The clause " . . . *any dispute or difference arising hereunder between the Assured and the Insurers shall be referred to a Queen's Counsel of the English Bar to be mutually agreed between the Insurers and the Assured or in the event of disagreement by the Chairman of the Bar*" was held to be an arbitration clause. In *Hobbs Padgett & Co. (Reinsurance) Ltd* v *J C Kirkland Ltd* [1969] 2 Lloyd's Rep. 547 the reference in an agreement for the dissolution of a reinsurance brokerage to "*suitable arbitration clause*" was held to amount to an arbitration clause, the reference to suitability being an objective test and the missing details capable of being inserted by the courts under the then statutory regime if agreement could not be reached by the parties.

7. See e.g. *Whiting* v *Halverson* [2003] EWCA Civ 403; *Fiona Trust & Holding Corporation & ors* v *Yuri Primalov & ors* [2007] EWCA Civ 20 affirmed on other points in *Premium Nafta Products Limited and ors* v *Fili Shipping Company Limited and ors* [2007] UKHL 40.

8. Section 4(1)–(3) of the 1996 Act.

9. Articles 6–8 of the UNCITRAL Rules provide for the parties to designate an appointing authority if they cannot agree on appointing the tribunal with a default designation if they cannot agree on an appointing authority.

A reference to the rules (preferably to the current rules) of one of the arbitral institutions such as the ICC (the "ICC Rules"),[10] the LCIA ("the LCIA Rules"),[11] the ICDR (the "ICDR Rules")[12] or to a recognised set of rules unattached to an appointing authority such as the UNCITRAL Arbitration Rules (the "UNCITRAL Rules")[13] makes for clarity. These rules then become part of what the parties have agreed for the purpose of the 1996 Act. A recognised set of rules provides a procedural framework which facilitates the smooth and speedy progress of an arbitration. In the absence of a reference to a body of rules in the arbitration agreement, parties should at the time of the dispute consider whether or not they wish to incorporate either their own agreed procedural rules, or the rules of an arbitral institution or of a recognised independent set of rules such as the UNCITRAL Rules, or a modified version of one of them. Similarly, if a set of rules which is not attached to an arbitral institution applies or is agreed, consideration may also want to be given to designating a separate appointing authority, which could be any number of institutions not necessarily an arbitral institution, or even someone in an official capacity such as the president of a professional body.

Although there are administrative costs associated with using an arbitral institution,[14] the use of an arbitral institution together with a specified set of rules (which need not be those of the institution) has advantages. It provides administrative back-up and assistance with such matters as the appointment of the tribunal, challenges to arbitrators and collection of fees. Most arbitral institutions provide model forms of arbitration clauses for incorporation which can be adapted as necessary. Further references to the impact of the various rules appear throughout this book according to the relevant context. Additionally at Appendix B there is set out a comparison, together with relevant indices, of the four sets of procedural rules which are most likely to be used in an international commercial arbitration held in London, namely the LCIA, ICC, ICDR Rules (attached to arbitral institutions and hence also covering appointments) and the independent UNCITRAL Rules (which is not attached to any arbitral institution). Whilst reference is most frequently made to these sets of rules in this book, arbitrations are also conducted in London according to the many other sets of rules that are in use in the international arbitral world.[15]

10. International Chamber of Commerce.
11. London Court of International Arbitration.
12. The International Centre for Dispute Resolution.
13. Set of arbitral rules drafted by the UN Commission on International Trade Law, but not connected to any arbitral administering institution.
14. Some institutions such as the ICC provide for arbitrators and institutional charges to relate to the value of the claim. Others such as the ICC or ICDR provide time-costed charges. Most institutions also provide for a non-refundable registration fee.
15. Examples include: in the context of shipping arbitrations LMAA (London Maritime Arbitrators Association) Terms. Other rules relating to international commercial arbitration, such as the Swiss Rules of International Arbitration (Article 1(2)); the Arbitration Rules of the Arbitration Institute of the Stockholm Chamber of Commerce (Article 20); and the Arbitration Rules of the Singapore International Arbitration Centre (SIAC Rules 2007) (Article 18) enable parties to choose London as a seat.

THE TRIBUNAL

Allied to the question of the procedural framework is the critical issue of the make-up of the tribunal and how it is to be appointed. Tribunals consist of either a sole arbitrator or a panel of three, either and more frequently comprising a chair or presiding arbitrator and two co-arbitrators. On rare occasions an umpire and two arbitrators are appointed, the umpire's role usually being to act as the sole decision maker only if the other two arbitrators disagree.

There are an almost unlimited number of permutations as to the composition of an arbitral tribunal. Sole arbitrators can be nominated jointly by the parties and in default by an arbitral institution or by the chair or president of a professional organisation, or they can be nominated and appointed directly by an arbitral institution. Panels can be nominated by each party whose nominated arbitrators in turn jointly choose the chair. Alternatively, the panel or the chair alone can be chosen by an arbitral institution. The arbitral institution can also nominate and appoint an arbitrator where a party defaults in nominating one. Sometimes the clause will set out specific qualifications for the arbitrator such as that he or she is a Queen's Counsel, or has a technical qualification, or is or is not of a particular nationality. Occasionally a specific named arbitrator or arbitrators are set out in the arbitration clause usually with a default appointment procedure. Relevant considerations relating to the nomination and appointment of arbitrators are dealt with in more detail in chapter 5 pages 35–38 and chapter 7 pages 49–51. An improperly constituted tribunal can lead to jurisdictional challenges (see chapter 9).

If no provision as to the number of arbitrators is made in the arbitration clause, whether expressly or by reference through incorporation of a set of rules, the 1996 Act provides a fall-back position of a sole arbitrator to be appointed jointly by the parties.[16] The 1996 Act also provides a procedure for choosing the tribunal if and to the extent that similarly this has not been agreed by the parties.[17] There is further a statutory default procedure with an option to apply to the court in certain circumstances where the parties fail to effect the relevant appointments to the tribunal and the agreement makes no provision for such default.[18]

In complex arbitrations there is undoubtedly an advantage in having a three-person tribunal. Panels take their deliberations very seriously and the presence of three people can act as a check on an otherwise erroneous view—three heads are usually better than one. In choosing the composition of a tribunal one needs to bear in mind that, save in extremely limited circumstances, there is no second chance or appeal. The main disadvantage with a three-person tribunal is delay, particularly if the three arbitrators are all busy and come from different parts of the world. As a generalisation, to which there are always

16. Section 15(3) of the 1996 Act.
17. Sections 16 and 19 of the 1996 Act.
18. Sections 17, 18 and 19 of the 1996 Act.

exceptions, an arbitration with a sole arbitrator tends to be speedier and less costly.

THE SEAT OF THE ARBITRATION

Most of the provisions of the Arbitration Act 1996 apply only to arbitrations where the seat of the arbitration is in England or Wales or Northern Ireland. Although, therefore, the jurisdiction of the 1996 Act covers these three regions, in practical terms international arbitrations are almost invariably held in London. Accordingly, references hereafter shall, unless the context otherwise requires, simply be to London.

There may be occasions, such as prior to the formation of a tribunal or even after its formation, where in order to support the process, the court may have to act where no seat has been designated or determined. In such a case the court may do so where there is a connection with the jurisdiction provided that the court is satisfied that it is appropriate to do so.[19] The English court also assists international arbitral tribunals where the seat is outside the jurisdiction by certain supportive measures, such as securing the attendance of witnesses, provided it is appropriate to do so.[20] Orders for a stay of English legal proceedings and for the enforcement of awards will also be granted even if the seat is outside the jurisdiction.[21] These issues are dealt with in subsequent chapters.

The juridical seat or location of the arbitration is different from the venue of the hearings. For convenience of all concerned hearings may be convened at places other than the seat of the arbitration.[22] The law of the seat does not have to be the same as the applicable law of the contract or the law of the arbitration agreement, although in the absence of an express provision the seat can be a guide to determining the law of the contract as a whole.

The seat has a fourfold importance. First, it determines the national supervisory jurisdiction, the ("*lex arbitri*") and its scope, which in London means the 1996 Act. Secondly, the law of the seat is often, but not necessarily, the same as the procedural law or curial law. If the seat of the arbitration is England it is likely that the procedural law will be English because of the mandatory provisions of the 1996 Act, otherwise there would be two procedural laws. Nonetheless, if the parties do specify a procedural law, this can be accommodated subject to the mandatory provisions. Thirdly, it may be relevant to the law of the arbitration clause or even the applicable law of the contract (see below). Finally, the seat may be relevant to issues of enforcement, such as questions of validity under the New York Convention as incorporated into the 1996 Act. This treats an arbitration award as made at the seat

19. Section 2(4) of the 1996 Act.
20. Section 2(3) of the 1996 Act and see in particular chapter 11.
21. Section 2(2) of the 1996 Act and see sections 5 and 15.
22. In some jurisdictions such as Stockholm in Sweden, this may cause problems, but it should not do so in respect of an arbitration whose seat is London.

of the arbitration and its validity is judged by that law in the absence of any indication of law in relation to the arbitration agreement by the parties.[23]

There are three alternative ways of ascertaining the seat of an arbitration. The first and clearest is for the parties to set it out in the arbitration clause or agree it once the dispute has arisen. It is not necessary, although preferable, to use the word "seat". A reference to London will suffice in most cases. The second is by reference to rules of an arbitral institution, for example, under the LCIA Rules the default seat is London and under the ICC Rules the ICC Court will designate a seat if the parties have not done so.[24] The third option is for the tribunal to do so, if so authorised by the parties.[25]

THE APPLICABLE LAW

It is important to distinguish between the applicable law of the contract, i.e. the law according to which the merits of the claim are to be determined[26] and the law of the separate arbitration agreement. In the context of the former, which in turn may be relevant to the latter, it is necessary first to determine whether or not there is any express provision as to the applicable law of the contract. The law of the contract is the substantive law not the conflicts of laws rules of the country concerned.[27] The 1996 Act also permits the arbitral tribunal to decide the dispute "*in accordance with such other considerations as are agreed by them or determined by the tribunal*".[28] Instead of providing for a national law, the contract may expressly entitle a tribunal to act, for example, as an "*amiable compositeur*" or to decide the case "*ex aequo et bono*"[29] or even to apply Sharia law[30] or transnational law, or some other non-municipal body of law.[31] However, if the parties to an arbitration want a form of rules which is not a national law to apply, then they must set this out in the agreement.[32]

In the absence of an express provision as to the applicable law, the matter is determined by the tribunal. Section 46(3) of the 1996 Act provides that "*if and to the extent that there is no such choice or agreement, the tribunal shall apply the law*

23. Article V(1)(a) of the New York Convention and sections 100(2) and 103(2)(b).

24. See e.g. Articles 16 of the LCIA Rules, 14 of the ICC Rules, 16 of the UNCITRAL Rules, and 13 of the ICDR Rules.

25. Section 3 of the 1996 Act and see e.g. Article 16.1 of the UNCITRAL Rules.

26. Sections 4(5) and 46(1)(a) of the 1996 Act.

27. Section 46(2) of the 1996 Act.

28. Section 46(1)(b) of the 1996 Act.

29. Such "equity clauses", which are relatively rare, enable arbitrators to decide the arbitration on a basis other than law.

30. *Beximco Pharmaceuticals Ltd & ors* v *Shamil Bank of Bahrain E.C.* [2004] EWCA Civ 19.

31. *Halpern & another* v *Halpern & ors* [2007] EWCA Civ 291 and *Sayyed Mohammed Musawi* v *RE International (UK) Ltd & ors* [2007] EWHC 2981 (Ch).

32. See e.g. Articles 22.4 of the LCIA Rules, 17.3 of the ICC Rules, 33.2 of the UNCITRAL Rules, and 28.3 of the ICDR Rules.

determined by the conflict of laws rules which it considers applicable".[33] Therefore, where the seat is London, there is no automatic presumption that English conflicts rules apply: it is a matter for the tribunal to determine. Arbitral rules reflect a similar principle and will be taken into account by the tribunal if applicable.[34] The law in this context would appear to be a specific system of law. Issues other than the law of the contract may also need resolution, for example, the law applicable to the constitution and internal management of a corporation. Moreover, given that the parties are frequently foreign, the applicable law as well as the conflicts rules, may be found ultimately to be a law other than English law.

When, on the other hand, English conflicts rules are relevant, then in the context of most, but not all, contractual obligations, the provisions of the Rome Convention would apply, as England is a contracting party to the Rome Convention.[35] Article 1 of the Rome Convention applies "*to contractual obligations in any situation involving a choice between the laws of different countries*". The Rome Convention would be relevant even if the connection is not with another Convention state such as the United States.[36] Under the Rome Convention only a national law can be applied.[37] The issue would be determined by reference to the country with which the contract "*is most closely connected*".[38]

While it is common to find a law of the contract designated in the agreement, it is much rarer to see a specific provision for the law of the arbitration agreement. However, the arbitration agreement is a distinct agreement separate from the main agreement, statutorily recognised as such[39] and hence subject to an independent law. The law of the arbitration agreement is important for a variety of reasons, including issues of interpretation of the arbitration clause, its validity and ultimately the jurisdiction of the tribunal. The 1996 Act does not lay down any guidance on the determination of the law of the arbitration clause. Section 46 refers to rules applicable to the substance of the dispute. In the absence of an express law governing the arbitration clause it is determined by reference to the law with which it has its closest and most real connection. This is more likely to be the seat of the arbitration than the law of the underlying contract.[40]

The Rome Convention does not apply to arbitration, i.e. the independent arbitration agreement.[41] Thus, any conflicts according to English conflicts rules would need to be determined by reference to the common law. In

33. Section 46 of the 1996 Act is not a mandatory provision.
34. See e.g. Articles 22.3 of the LCIA Rules, 17.1 & 17.2 of the ICC Rules, 32.1–32.3 of the UNCITRAL Rules, and 28.1–28.3 of the ICDR Rules.
35. The Contracts (Applicable Law) Act 1980.
36. Article 2 of the Rome Convention.
37. Article 4 of the Rome Convention.
38. Article 4 of the Rome Convention. For a more detailed consideration of English conflicts rules in this context see e.g. chapters 16 and 32 of Dicey, Morris & Collins, *The Conflict of Laws*, (14th edn).
39. Sections 7 and 2(5) of the 1996 Act and see chapter 9 pages 63–65.
40. *C* v *D* [2007] EWCA Civ 1282, a case concerning the Bermuda Form.
41. Article 1(2)(d) of the Rome Convention.

practice this is not likely to make much difference in most cases, but the law has to be the law of a country.[42] Whether in turn that national law, for example, France, recognises transnational law is a separate matter.

THE LANGUAGE

A well-drafted arbitration clause will provide for the language of the arbitration. This is a relevant factor when parties come from different countries and the arbitration is held in a third country with arbitrators of different nationalities. It would be rare to have an arbitration in London conducted other than in English, but it can happen.

TIME LIMITS AND PRE-CONDITIONS TO COMMENCEMENT OF ARBITRATION

It is advisable to look carefully for any time limits relating to the commencement of an arbitration or any prior pre-conditional steps, as the English court's ability to grant an extension of time is circumscribed. Such a step can only be taken after exhausting any available arbitral process for obtaining an extension of time.[43] The rules of arbitral institutions usually provide for extensions of time. The court can only extend time on such terms as it thinks fit if satisfied: "*(a) that the circumstances are such as were outside the reasonable contemplation of the parties when they agreed the provision in question, and that it would be just to extend the time, or (b) that the conduct of one party makes it unjust to hold the other party to the strict terms of the provision in question.*"[44]

Any extension given by the court will not affect the operation of any limitation period.[45] Further, even if time limits are not relevant, parties often agree to go through forms of negotiation or mediation before invoking the arbitration clause. Such clauses are known as multi-tier clauses (see chapter 6 page 46).

ADDITIONAL POSSIBLE EXCLUSIONS AND INCLUSIONS

There are a host of other matters additional to those set out above which parties can include in the arbitration agreement. It is advisable to consider these to the extent that they are not already included in any applicable rules of an arbitral institution or other independent body such as UNCITRAL. These include confidentiality clauses, exclusion of rights of appeal (section 69 of the

42. *Amin Rasheed Shipping Corp* v *Kuwait Insurance Co. (The Al Wahab)* [1984] A.C. 50, 61–62.
43. Section 12(2) of the 1996 Act.
44. Section 12(3) of the 1996 Act.
45. Section 12(5) of the 1996 Act.

1996 Act), provision for consolidation and multiple parties (sections 35 and 16(7) of the 1996 Act), issues relating to sovereign immunity, and provision for post-reference disputes. Reference is made in more detail to such issues in context during the course of this book. Agreement can also be made on any of the other matters covered by the following non-mandatory provisions of the 1996 Act, namely: sections 3, 4(3) and (5), 7, 8, 14–18, 20–23, 24(2), 25, 26(2), 27, 30, 34, 36, 37(1), 38–39, 41–42, 44–55, 57, 58, 61–65 and 76–79. Most of these relate to procedural issues and are dealt with more fully in chapter 7 pages 52–53.

DEFECTIVE OR PATHOLOGICAL ARBITRATION CLAUSES

Arbitration clauses vary in complexity, certainty and clarity. A vague or incomplete arbitration clause can lead to one party trying to litigate rather than arbitrate to be met perhaps by an application to stay the litigation (see chapter 6 pages 44–45); it can give rise to jurisdictional challenges before a tribunal (see chapter 9) and ultimately it may lead to court intervention or enforcement problems. If there are gaps in the arbitration clause it may be possible to fill them by agreement of the parties, or by the tribunal by reference to other terms in arbitral rules, or by the court, for example, the appointment of a sole arbitrator where there is no agreement as to the number of arbitrators.[46] In the past where such issues have come before the English courts, judges have striven to avoid rendering vague arbitration clauses unenforceable whenever possible, even if parts of the clause other than the agreement to arbitrate are uncertain.

Defective or pathological clauses occur all too frequently. While they provide fertile ground for law students, they also provide considerable problems for lawyers advising their clients. Defects take two forms: first, as to whether the wording amounts to an arbitration clause and secondly, if it does, what are its terms? Examples have been given earlier in this chapter of the former. As to the latter the permutations are endless. Such clauses can wrongly identify arbitral institutions or identify non-existent rules or institutions, fail to specify a country as a seat, fail to make provision for the appointment of arbitrators, or otherwise omit important aspects of an enforceable arbitration clause. Hence, it is always advisable to be as specific as possible when drafting such clauses.

46. Section 15(3) of the 1996 Act.

CHAPTER 4

THE SCOPE OF THE ARBITRATION CLAUSE

INTRODUCTION

The scope of the arbitration clause is probably the most critical issue to consider once it is established that an arbitration agreement exists. If either the claims made are outside the terms of the clause or the parties involved in the dispute are not parties to the arbitration clause, then jurisdictional issues arise which may derail the arbitral process. Jurisdictional issues as to the scope of an arbitration clause can also lead to attempts to bring the matter before the English courts and/or can impact on later attempts to enforce an award.[1] While some procedural aspects of jurisdiction are dealt with later in this chapter jurisdictional issues are covered more generally in chapter 9.

Determining the scope of an arbitration clause is a matter of construction of the arbitration clause under the applicable law of that contract. English law, unlike some other foreign laws such as French law, does not contemplate any delocalised law and so questions of transnational law cannot be used as an aid to construction.[2] English law looks to the contractual matrix at the time the contract was entered into and seeks to ascertain what the parties intended using an objective standard.[3] Prior negotiations are irrelevant.

The issues that arise are dealt with under the following heads:

- whether the dispute is covered by the clause;
- set-offs and counterclaims;
- the parties to the arbitration agreement;
- non-signatories and third parties;
- assignees and insurers;
- states;
- consolidation and concurrent hearings;
- other issues relating to parties;
- how the parties should approach such issues; and
- availability of remedies.

1. See e.g. sections 67 and 103(2)(d) of the Arbitration Act 1996.
2. See chapter 3 pages 21–23.
3. See e.g. *Investors Compensation Scheme Ltd* v *West Bromwich Building Society* [1998] 1 W.L.R. 896 for a useful guide as to the principles of construction relating to the meaning of words.

WHETHER THE DISPUTE IS COVERED BY THE CLAUSE

A refreshing and pro-arbitration approach to construction of such clauses under English law has recently been laid down by the English courts, both in the Court of Appeal and the House of Lords, in the *Premium Nafta* case (previously known as the *Fiona Trust* case), after one of the many parties. The case concerned in part an arid dispute as to the extent of the phrases "*arising under*" and "*arising out of*". The context was whether an issue relating to the validity of an arbitration clause, arising from an allegation that the contract was procured by bribery, fell within an arbitration clause and hence the jurisdiction of the arbitrators. The House of Lords affirmed the statement of Longmore L.J. in the Court of Appeal, where he commented that:

> "*For our part we consider that the time has now come for a line to be drawn and a fresh start made at any rate for cases arising in an international commercial context. Ordinary businessmen would be surprised at the nice distinctions drawn in cases and the time taken up by argument in debating whether a particular case falls within one set of words or another very similar set of words . . . As it seems to us any jurisdiction or arbitration clause in an international commercial contract should be liberally construed.*"[4]

The House of Lords went on to conclude that there should be no difference between the two phrases, Lord Hoffmann adding:

> "*In my opinion the construction of an arbitration clause should start from the assumption that the parties, as rational businessmen, are likely to have intended any dispute arising out of the relationship into which they have entered or purported to enter to be decided by the same tribunal. The clause should be construed in accordance with this presumption unless the language makes it clear that certain questions were intended to be excluded from the arbitrator's jurisdiction.*"

It is to be hoped that other familiar words and phrases such as "*all*" or "*any*" differences, disputes or claims or a qualification of "*in relation to*" or "*in connection with*" will similarly be given a broad interpretation by tribunals and the courts applying English law in the future. Some clauses augment the general words with additional words such as "*any question regarding the existence, validity or termination of the agreement*" to put the matter beyond doubt: others use their own specific language rather than a common form of words. If the parties want to exclude matters from the jurisdiction of the tribunal then they need to insert words to that effect in the arbitration clause.

The dispute does not have to be contractual.[5] Nonetheless, there are some matters which are not capable of being referred to arbitration, such as the enforcement of the criminal law, although civil fraud is often the subject matter of an arbitration. Section 82 of the 1996 Act defines a "*dispute*" as including "*any difference*". If the arbitration clause refers to disputes in the plural, then these can be arbitrated sequentially as they arise or simultaneously. A failure to make a payment admittedly due constitutes a dispute under

4. *Premium Nafta Products Limited and ors* v *Fili Shipping Company Limited and ors* [2007] UKHL 40. See also chapter 6 pages 44–45 and chapter 9 pages 63–64.
5. Section 6(1) of the 1996 Act.

English law: there is no difference between a refusal to admit a claim and a refusal to pay one.[6]

Finally, disputes arising after the commencement of the reference are not usually covered by the arbitration clause except where the clause itself permits, any rules to which it refers permit, or the parties so agree.

SET-OFFS AND COUNTERCLAIMS

A set-off or counterclaim may prove difficult to bring within an arbitration clause and accordingly give jurisdiction to the tribunal. Ultimately it is a question of construction of the arbitration clause according to the law of the clause, which may not necessarily be English law. It is advisable to check any institutional or other standard rules which apply, for while most refer to the ability to bring counterclaims, some such as the LCIA and ICC refer to "*any counterclaims*" and do not in terms refer to set-offs,[7] provided, of course, such counterclaims are within the scope of the arbitral agreement. Others, such as the UNCITRAL Rules, confine any counterclaim or set-off to those arising out of the same contract.[8] Where English law applies, a "*transaction*" set-off which provides a defence to the claim, is more likely to come within the jurisdiction of the tribunal than a set-off which is a cross-claim, but this is not always the case and it will ultimately depend on the construction of the arbitration clause.[9]

THE PARTIES TO THE ARBITRATION AGREEMENT

One of the most difficult issues facing a tribunal, and which likewise goes to the heart of its jurisdiction, is the identification of the parties to the arbitration clause. The tribunal only has jurisdiction over the parties to the agreement. This may involve just two parties or several parties. It needs to be stressed that the issue is who are the parties to the arbitration clause: not who are the parties

6. *Exfin Shipping (India) Ltd Mumbai* v *Tolani Shipping Co Ltd Mumbai* [2006] EWCA 1090 (Comm).

7. See e.g. Articles 2.1(b) and 15.3 of the LCIA Rules and 5.5 of the ICC Rules.

8. Rule 19.3.

9. A transaction set-off under English law is "*a cross-claim arising from the same transaction or one so closely related that it operates in law or in equity as a complete or partial defeasance of the plaintiff's claim*": *Aectra Refining and Manufacturing Inc.* v *Exmar NV* [1994] 1 W.L.R. 1634, 1649. See also e.g. *Metal Distributors (UK) Ltd* v *ZCCM Investment Holdings plc (a company incorporated in the Republic of Zambia)* [2005] EWHC 156 (Q.B.). A counterclaim arising in connection with a wholly unrelated agreement to which one of the parties to the arbitration agreement was not a party or in connection with alleged negligent misstatement concerning a wholly unrelated transaction or in connection with an alleged collateral contract concerning a wholly unrelated transaction was outside the jurisdiction of the tribunal. In *Econet Satellite Services Ltd* v *Vee Networks Ltd (formerly Econet Wireless Nigeria Ltd)* [2006] EWHC 1664 (Comm) arbitrators were held not to have jurisdiction in relation to a transaction set-off which arose out of a separate contract—UNCITRAL rules applied.

to the main agreement, as these may be different, although often there is some relationship between the two. The arbitration clause is an entirely separate agreement which survives the main agreement[10] and it may be governed by a different law from the main agreement. The issue of who are the parties to the arbitration agreement is one of substantive law and is determined by the applicable law of the arbitration agreement,[11] not procedural law.

NON-SIGNATORIES AND THIRD PARTIES

Frequently a claimant or counterclaimant desires to make a claim against a non-signatory to the arbitration clause on the basis that it is the real party to the dispute, or the party with the money, or because the party to the contract is insolvent or no longer exists. Alternatively a party may want to add a co-claimant, for example, if it is a holding company seeking to add claimants to recover losses through its subsidiaries. Such manoeuvres in turn usually lead to the non-signatory contesting the jurisdiction of the tribunal.

The absence of a signature to the main contract does not necessarily mean that a party is not bound by the arbitration clause. The 1996 Act does not require a signature: merely for the agreement to be in writing.[12] On the contrary, even a signature to the main agreement may not necessarily bind the party to arbitration. For example, a signature procured by fraud, or a signature which does not extend to the separate agreement to arbitrate, or a signature in a capacity other than as a party such as a guarantor or agent. The issues are ultimately ones of fact or mixed questions of fact and law.

The two most common ways of contending that a third party is the real party to any agreement is by alleging that the named party or signatory was either an agent or alter ego of the real party. These are not easy arguments to run. If the agent signs in a capacity as agent, the position is relatively straightforward. If, on the other hand, there is no such qualification, then the party seeking to enjoin the unnamed principal has to establish the agency relationship. Additionally, it has to show that the unnamed principal was the true party to the agreement and that the agent was authorised to enter into the agreement on his behalf. Otherwise the agent who signs without any qualification is presumed to contract personally. The reverse also applies in that a party which signs "*as agent only*" will deprive itself of the ability to be a party to the contract or arbitration clause.[13]

The alter ego argument involves the contention that the party to the arbitration agreement is effectively a nominee and not the true party. The use of a shell company to enter into an agreement may give rise to arguments that the

10. Section 7 of the 1996 Act and see also chapter 9 pages 63–64.
11. See chapter 3 pages 21–23.
12. See chapter 3 pages 16–17.
13. *Electrosteel Castings Ltd* v *Scan-Trans Shipping and Chartering SDN BHD* [2002] EWHC 1993 (Comm).

tribunal should lift the corporate veil, something which under English law will normally only be done where there is some form of iniquity or fraud. Similarly, in the context of states, a state-owned enterprise may in fact be no more than the cover for the state itself (see below).

Under English law, the Contracts (Rights of Third Parties) Act 1999 permits an identified third party to become a party to an arbitration agreement governed by the 1996 Act to enable it to enforce a term of the contract if the contract expressly provides that he may do so, or the contract as a matter of construction purports to confer an enforceable benefit on him.[14]

As the issue of who are the parties to the arbitration agreement is one of substantive law not procedural law, it may be possible where the applicable law is a foreign law to rely on other arguments not recognised under English law. In particular, international arbitrators do sometimes defer to the group of companies/single economic unit doctrine. This doctrine recognises that because a group of companies constitutes the same "*economic reality*", one company in the group can bind other companies in that group if this is what all the parties intended and it reflects international principles.[15] English law does not recognise the group of companies' doctrine.[16] Some national laws, such as French law, enable transnational law to be invoked to support arguments that a third party is in fact a party to the arbitration clause if justice demands. This would not be permitted under English law (see chapter 3 pages 21–23).

ASSIGNEES AND INSURERS

The 1996 Act applies to all persons acting "*under or through*" a party to the arbitration proceedings, even if not themselves parties as such.[17] Under English law, subrogated insurers are bound by the arbitration clause of their insured.[18] Similarly, if there is a valid assignment of a contract containing an arbitration clause this will bind the assignee. A written legal assignment which is absolute and not by way of charge only and of which notice is given to the other party, enables the assignee to bring or defend arbitration proceedings in its own name subject to the terms of the contract and the rights being capable

14. Sections 1 and 8 of the Contracts (Rights of Third Parties) Act 1999 and see *Nisshin Shipping Co. Ltd* v *Cleaves & Co. Ltd* [2003] EWHC 2602 (Comm).
15. *Dow Chemical* ICC 4131/1982 (Interim Award).
16. *Peterson Farms Inc.* v *C & M Farming Ltd* [2002] EWHC 121 (Comm).
17. Section 82(2) of the 1996 Act.
18. *Schiffahrtsgesellschaft Detlev Von Appen G.m.b.H* v *Voest Alpine Intertrading G.m.b.H. (The Jay Bola)* [1997] 2 Lloyd's Rep. 279; *West Tankers Inc* v *(1) Ras Riunione Adriatica Di Sicurta SpA (2) Generali Assicurazione Generali SpA sub nom the Front Comor* [2005] EWHC 454 (Comm) appealed to the House of Lords on a different point which has now been referred to the European Court.

of assignment.[19] Statutory assignments can also bind the assignee.[20] Assignment can also take place after the arbitration has commenced, provided both the other party and the arbitrator are notified and the latter consents.[21]

STATES

International commercial arbitrations involving states present a special problem in relation to determining the true parties to arbitration agreements in three respects. (Investment treaty arbitrations are dealt with in chapter 17.) First, governments often use or establish a specific state-owned entity to enter into international obligations. If such entities have no resources or become defunct, sometimes for purely political reasons, this can cause difficulties. It is for this reason that international tribunals try to invoke transnational law to buttress the substantive law, but this is not always available, for example, if the arbitration clause is governed by English law. Ultimately the facts will be determinative, but the use of transnational general principles of law also enable the tribunal to consider whether the result meets the fundamental requirements of justice in international trade.

The second problem relates to sovereign immunity. An express reservation or waiver of sovereign immunity in the agreement may well be relevant to the issue of construction of the arbitration clause and whether or not a state intended to be a party to it.[22] Sovereign immunity issues arise later in the process and are particularly relevant to issues of enforcement. The position under English law is governed by the State Immunity Act 1978. Section 9 provides that subject to any contrary provision in the arbitration agreement (not the main agreement): "*Where a State has agreed in writing to submit a dispute which has arisen, or may arise, to arbitration, the State is not immune as respects proceedings in the courts of the United Kingdom which relate to arbitration*". Consequently, the real question is frequently to determine whether or not the state is a party to the arbitration clause. It is thus sensible when there is an issue as to whether or not a state is a party, to assess carefully the extent to which any award could be defeated by arguments at the enforcement stage about sovereign immunity (see chapter 16 pages 128–130).

19. Section 136 Law of Property Act 1925. *Baytur S.A.* v *Finagro Holding S.A.* [1991] 4 All E.R. 129. An equitable assignee must give notice to the other party and submit to the jurisdiction of the arbitrator and join the assignor.

20. See e.g. Third Parties (Rights Against Insurers) Act 1930 which statutorily transfers claims by victims of insolvent wrongdoers to their insurers and the *Padre Island (No. 2)* [1990] 2 Lloyd's Rep. 191.

21. *Montedipe SpA* v *JTP-RO Jugotanker (The Jordan Nicolov)* [1990] 2 Lloyd's Rep. 11 and *Bayter (supra)*.

22. See e.g. *Svenska Petroleum Exploration AB* v *(1) Government of the Republic of Lithuania (2) AB Geonafta* [2006] EWCA Civ 1529.

Thirdly, under English law the Crown can enter into an arbitration agreement. However, not all foreign governments have the power to enter into arbitration agreements. This will depend on the state's constitution according to the relevant law.

CONSOLIDATION AND CONCURRENT HEARINGS

String and related contracts, each with individual arbitration clauses or some with an arbitration clause and others not, can give rise to multiple proceedings, extra cost and delay, and potentially inconsistent results. Absent (i) an issue estoppel between the parties, and even then a confidentiality agreement may prevent its use, (ii) an order of the court or (iii) consent of the parties, the award in one arbitration is not available to another because of the confidential nature of arbitration[23] (see chapter 14 pages 111–113). Where the parties are different, the solutions are even more limited. The 1996 Act permits consolidation and concurrent proceedings,[24] but this has to be by agreement and is not always given.

The LCIA Rules go some way towards permitting consolidation. They provide that unless the parties agree otherwise, the tribunal may permit a third party to become a party to the arbitral proceedings on the application of an existing party. This has to have the written consent of the third party and the applicant party, even if the other original party to the arbitration does not agree.[25] The tribunal is not obliged to agree to the application. It must balance the advantages of avoiding conflicting decisions and efficient justice with the possible delay or other proper reason which might militate against such a joinder.

The Swiss Rules of International Arbitration permit the institution to order consolidation of more than one arbitration, even if the parties are not identical, after consultation with all relevant parties and having taken account of all circumstances. They also enable the arbitral tribunal to allow a third party to participate in an existing arbitration at its request or at the request of a party to the arbitration, provided that the tribunal consults with all the parties and takes account of all circumstances which it deems relevant.[26] Sometimes parties seek to circumvent the problem by appointing a common arbitrator either as sole arbitrator or as one of the panel. However, at a practical level this can cause potential difficulties for the arbitrator, who might have to shut his or her eyes to evidence given in an earlier arbitration which contradicts that given in a later one.

23. *AEGIS* v *European Reinsurance Company of Zurich* [2003] UKPC 11.
24. Section 35 of the 1996 Act.
25. Article 22.1(h).
26. Article 4 of the Swiss Rules of International Arbitration.

OTHER ISSUES RELATING TO PARTIES

It is important to ascertain whether the party had the capacity to enter into the agreement and similarly to verify the identity of any corporate party. Issues as to capacity are likely to be determined by the law of the country in which the company is incorporated and searches may accordingly need to be made at the local registry. The 1996 Act provides that, subject to any law extinguishing the cause of action on death or agreement to the contrary, an arbitration agreement may be enforced by or against personal representatives.[27] Novation, where one of the parties is by agreement replaced by another, leads to the new party taking the place of the original party and being bound by the arbitration clause.[28] A novation may also arise where a party contracts on behalf of nominees as well as itself.[29] In the case of the compulsory winding up of an English company the trustee in bankruptcy may, with the court's sanction, bring or defend arbitration proceedings.

HOW THE PARTIES SHOULD APPROACH SUCH ISSUES

Issues as to the scope of an arbitration clause go directly to the jurisdiction of the tribunal. Under the 1996 Act, i.e. where the seat of the arbitration is London, the resisting party has a variety of options to deal with the issue of jurisdiction, but it must raise the issue no later than when it takes the first step in the proceedings to contest the merits, unless the delay is justified. The tribunal can either rule on its jurisdiction at the outset or deal with it in its award on the merits.[30] However, the court retains a residual jurisdiction during the process to deal with a tribunal's jurisdiction by way of determination of a preliminary point of jurisdiction, provided certain conditions are met.[31] It is also possible for a resisting party, who takes no part in the proceedings, to seek a declaration from the court.[32] After the award jurisdictional challenges can be made to the court automatically, again provided certain conditions are met.[33] Further challenges can be made at the time of enforcement of the award. These issues are dealt with more fully in other chapters of this book.[34]

Where there is doubt as to the ambit of the wording of the arbitration clause, whether relating to the nature or extent of the disputes covered or to the potential parties, a party will have to balance various factors in determining

27. Section 8 of the 1996 Act.
28. *Smith* v *Pearl Assurance Co. Ltd* [1939] 1 All E.R. 95.
29. *Charles M. Willie and Co. (Shipping) Ltd* v *Ocean Laser Shipping Ltd (The Smaro)* 1999 1 Lloyd's Rep. 225.
30. Sections 30–31 of the 1996 Act and subject to any contrary agreement by the parties.
31. Sections 32 and 73 of the 1996 Act.
32. Section 72 of the 1996 Act.
33. Sections 67, 70(2), (3) and 73 of the 1996 Act.
34. See chapters 9, 15 and 16.

what action to take. These include: the potential disadvantage of suing in the national courts of a possibly unfamiliar jurisdiction; where more than one claim or party is involved the additional risk of inconsistent decisions being made and at different times; the risks in terms of delay and costs of the arbitration award being rendered otiose; and any difficulties of enforcement arising from jurisdictional challenges in any enforcing jurisdiction. This leads to a strong incentive, particularly where there is doubt, to have the matter resolved early on. However, a decision on jurisdiction by a tribunal, while valuable, can occasionally be overturned at later stages in the process.

It is not a waiver of the right to contest jurisdiction before a tribunal that a party appoints an arbitrator, nor is the participation in the arbitration itself, provided that the jurisdictional issue is raised and it is without prejudice to it.[35]

Ultimately, the real consideration for a respondent where a tribunal finds that it has jurisdiction, is whether or not to participate in the arbitration under reservation and try to defeat the claim on the merits.

AVAILABILITY OF REMEDIES

Although the jurisdiction of a tribunal is wide, it is nonetheless advisable to ensure that the remedy sought is available and not, for example, excluded from the arbitration clause. The issue of remedies is dealt with in more detail in chapter 14 pages 107–109.

35. Section 31(1) of the 1996 Act.

CHAPTER 5

CHOOSING THE TRIBUNAL AND THE LEGAL TEAM

INTRODUCTION

Unlike court proceedings where the parties have no say in the selection of the judge, parties frequently have the ability to choose or provide input into the choice of the arbitral tribunal. The tribunal shapes the process. Choosing the right tribunal for the particular matter is therefore very important. It is a decision that has to be taken early on as it usually accompanies the initial request for arbitration (see chapter 7 pages 49–51). This chapter considers these issues under the following headings:

- choosing the tribunal;
- the ten criteria for nominating an arbitrator;
- finding out about English arbitrators; and
- choosing the legal team.

CHOOSING THE TRIBUNAL

The extent to which a party can choose its tribunal and the number of arbitrators is usually dictated by the arbitration agreement, either by express words in the clause itself or by reference to the rules of an arbitral institution or to the rules of an independent organisation such as UNCITRAL. Sometimes the arbitration agreement will specify the qualifications of the arbitrator, for example, that he or she is to be a Queen's Counsel or a commercial person or have some specific qualifications. If the agreement does not specify a number of arbitrators, then in default the tribunal consists of a sole arbitrator.[1] Reference has already been made in chapter 3 pages 19–20 to the unlimited number of permutations for the composition of a tribunal, the manner of their appointment and the pros and cons of a three-person tribunal compared with a sole arbitrator.

THE TEN CRITERIA FOR NOMINATING AN ARBITRATOR

Subject to any constraints in the arbitration agreement, the following ten considerations are relevant to nominating an arbitrator:

1. Section 15 of the 1996 Act.

i. Expertise

Does the arbitrator have the requisite expertise and experience not only of the subject-matter of the arbitration, but also of international arbitration? Is it an advantage to have someone with such expertise or would a fresh approach be preferable? In a weak case, parties sometimes think that the latter may be preferable. Do the parties want a lawyer or would an industry specialist be preferable?

ii. Reputation

Parties in substantial arbitrations are often concerned with an actual or perceived reputation of a particular arbitrator to find in a certain way in particular types of cases. On occasions, in very substantial matters, their lawyers can go to great lengths to try to ascertain this information at considerable cost. Some arbitrators are more legalistic than others who may be more commercially minded. Arbitrators are human. Yet whoever appoints them, once appointed they are bound to act independently and impartially.

iii. Civil lawyer versus common lawyer

Would a civil lawyer be preferable to a common lawyer? Although international arbitration has, to an extent, reached a consensus on procedure, there remain many variants and individual arbitrators approach arbitrations in different ways. Civil lawyers, for example, are more steeped in the written tradition than common lawyers and less inclined to order wide disclosure of documents, although the application of the IBA Rules on the Taking of Evidence in International Commercial Arbitration (the "IBA Rules of Evidence") or a variant thereof often joins the divide.

iv. The law of the contract

Where the agreement refers to a particular law, is it desirable to appoint an arbitrator whose practises the chosen law, for example, an English arbitrator if the law is English law? Alternatively, is the more important criterion the venue, so that an English lawyer would be preferable for a London arbitration, although the law is French? Would an English arbitrator, for example, be better able to handle English counsel appearing before him or her? If the tribunal is expert in the law of the contract, expert law may be unnecessary and some arbitrators decline to hear evidence of their own law and request submissions only. If the seat of the arbitration is London then there can be no appeal on issues of law other than English, Welsh or Northern Irish law. In such a case any appeal would be confined to a serious irregularity causing substantial injustice or a jurisdictional issue.[2] On the other hand, if the applicable law of the

2. Sections 67 and 68 of the 1996 Act and chapter 15.

contract is English law, then unless excluded by the parties, there is an appeal to the High Court with leave, provided certain criteria are met.[3]

v. Arbitral conduct

How does the arbitrator conduct hearings? How interventionist is the arbitrator? Will he or she interrupt submissions and evidence extensively or moderately? Has he or she got good interpersonal skills and will he or she put parties at their ease? Will the losing party feel it has had a fair hearing?

vi. Potential conflicts of interest

Does the arbitrator have any conflicts of interest with any of the parties? Arbitrators should at all times be independent and impartial. They have an on-going duty to disclose such conflicts of interest.

The IBA Rules on Conflicts of Interest in International Arbitration now provide useful guidelines on this topic. These guidelines provide what has become known as "*the traffic lights approach*" in three lists: the red list comprising non-waivable and waivable disclosure of situations which would disqualify an arbitrator; the orange list of disclosable situations which do not necessarily result in disqualification; and the green list of specific situations where no appearance of, and no actual conflict of interest exists, where there is no duty to disclose. The lists are non-exhaustive and are guidelines only. Thus, for example, a potential solicitor arbitrator has to make disclosure where his or her firm has within the past three years acted for one of the parties or an affiliate of one of the parties in an unrelated matter, even where it has been without the involvement of the potential arbitrator.[4] In the context of barristers, again under the orange list, it is said that a duty of disclosure arises where the arbitrator and another arbitrator or the counsel for one of the parties are members of the same barristers' chambers.[5]

The English courts have, however, taken a different view, and have confirmed that English barristers can appear in an arbitration under the 1996 Act before an arbitrator from the same set of chambers, as this fact on its own does not give rise to justifiable doubts as to an arbitrator's impartiality.[6] This attitude sometimes causes some concern on the part of foreign parties schooled in an undivided profession where all the lawyers in the firm, including trial lawyers, are partners. However, unlike solicitors or such trial lawyers, barristers are not partners and do not share profits and losses. As a result barristers from the same set of chambers are

3. Sections 69 and 82(1) of the 1996 Act and chapter 15.
4. Orange list 3.1.4.
5. Orange list 3.3.2 and see also section 4.5 of the Background Information issued by the Working Group available on the IBA website which acknowledges that "*there is a clear and obvious distinction to be drawn between barristers and law firms*", but nonetheless recommends disclosure.
6. *Laker Airways Inc.* v *(1) FLS Aerospace Ltd (2) Stanley Jeffrey Burnton* [2000] 1 W.L.R. 113.

permitted to appear against one another in cases and often do. Barristers can also appear for and against the same client at different times in respect of different matters, provided that in so doing they do not divulge confidential information or would find themselves professionally embarrassed.

vii. Availability

Does the arbitrator have reasonable availability to deal with the arbitration: any procedural and interim hearings; the main hearing and time for deliberations and drafting of the award? Will the arbitrator find it easy to travel to the location of the arbitration? One of the most important considerations for most businessmen and parties, unless they have a tactical reason to delay the process, is the speed with which a conclusion to the arbitration can be reached. Some arbitral rules lay down time limits for completion of the process subject to extensions[7]: others have more informal expectations.

viii. Efficiency

This is particularly important where parties are seeking jointly to nominate a sole arbitrator or a chairman. A good sole arbitrator or chair needs to keep on top of the arbitration, respond promptly, act fairly, but be decisive, laying down ground rules early on and working with the parties to set out a procedural framework. Some arbitrators are more interventionist than others, initiating steps along the way and monitoring compliance with orders and directions to avoid delay and unfairness to the other party.

ix. Language

Does the arbitrator speak the language in which the arbitration is to be held fluently?

x. Charges

What rates does the arbitrator charge? This is more relevant if the arbitration is ad hoc or no appointing or other institution is involved. It is not relevant if the institution provides for the arbitrators' fees to be part of an *ad valorem* charge such as the ICC. Most arbitral institutions permitting hourly or daily rates for arbitrators either have a specific range of charges, such as the LCIA, or allow the arbitrator to set out his or her charges on the website, for example, the ICDR.

FINDING OUT ABOUT ENGLISH ARBITRATORS

If the lawyer advising a nominating party considers that an English-based arbitrator would be suitable, but is from another jurisdiction, or is unfamiliar

7. See e.g. Articles 20(1) and 24 of the ICC Rules.

with the arbitral community, how does he or she find a suitable nominee? London-based arbitrators principally comprise: (i) specialist arbitrators (either retired solicitors or judges and foreign lawyers with a simultaneous base in London) with either English law expertise or other foreign common law expertise; (ii) Queen's Counsel, some of whom have a particular specialism also in international arbitration and regularly sit as arbitrators—others who are specialist in specific areas of the law; (iii) solicitors in law firms likewise specialising in international arbitration or a particular area of the law; and (iv) experts in particular industry fields. Some are well known by reputation or from their writings or lectures. Legal directories and websites are another source of information. If English counsel or solicitors are employed (see below) then they can, of course, assist with this task.

CHOOSING THE LEGAL TEAM

Unless the lawyer representing the party is familiar with arbitrating in London, it is advisable to get the legal team on board early on to give advice on tactics and presentation, the choice of arbitrator and the like. One regularly finds mixed teams in arbitration. Where the professional client is a foreign lawyer with no London base, he or she may wish to maintain an involvement with the client to avoid the risk of losing him to another law firm and to support the client. Nonetheless, such a foreign lawyer may want assistance with tactics, presentation and cross-examination.

One way this can be achieved is by the foreign lawyer instructing a barrister directly, as a barrister can be so instructed in relation to advocacy in international arbitration as well as for legal advice more generally. Barristers need to be instructed by solicitors for court work as there has to be an English solicitor on the court record. Alternatively, the foreign lawyer can advise the client to use an English solicitor or a foreign firm with a London base, who may or may not instruct an English barrister as well. An increasing number of solicitors, and foreign lawyers specialising in international arbitration who are based in London, undertake their own advocacy before international arbitral tribunals. Nonetheless, barristers still regularly form part of teams with solicitors and/or foreign lawyers (whether London based or not) in international arbitration. However, some foreign firms without a London base and in-house corporate counsel may feel more comfortable using English solicitors as well.

It is an individual choice and foreign lawyers familiar with the process, although not based in London, may consider that they are qualified to do the arbitration without assistance from English lawyers at all, save where there is a court application in which case, as explained above, an English solicitor has to be on the court record.

CHAPTER 6

ACTIVITY AND CONSIDERATIONS PRIOR TO COMMENCING AN ARBITRATION

INTRODUCTION

There are several matters which a prospective claimant may need to consider prior to the commencement of an arbitration. Apart from the nature of the arbitration clause itself[1] and deciding on a nominated arbitrator(s) if applicable,[2] these include whether:

- the matter is sufficiently urgent that if the rules permit, or by agreement, an expedited formation of the tribunal and hearing should be sought;
- any application should be made to the English court even before the request is sent, for example, for a restraining order to preserve assets;
- it is necessary to stay any pending or threatened litigation;
- the case is suitable for mediation or another form of dispute resolution;
- any time limits for commencing an arbitration have been complied with;
- the claim will be met by a counterclaim and whether this will be covered by the arbitration clause and, if not, the implications of potentially two different procedures and conclusions. Additionally, a small claim met by a large counterclaim can skew the advance on costs, particularly in ICC cases;
- the respondent is likely to participate and the impact particularly in ICC cases on the advance on costs if the sum at stake is large;
- adequate costs have been obtained from the client on account for the matter going forward;
- the remedies will be adequate, for example, an arbitrator cannot award an injunction backed by penal sanction;
- if successful, the claimant will be able to enforce the award, otherwise the result could be a pyrrhic victory—whether it should seek, for example, a freezing order; and

1. See chapters 3 and 4.
2. See chapter 5.

- there are any limitation problems relating to the cause of action which could affect the process and need to be catered for?

This chapter deals with the first four issues above: other matters are dealt with elsewhere in the book.

THE APPOINTMENT OF AN EMERGENCY ARBITRATOR OR EXPEDITED TRIBUNAL

While the English courts can and do provide interim relief in advance of the appointment of the tribunal (see below), there is a recognition that sometimes it is useful for urgent relief to be given by an arbitral tribunal, even if it is not the tribunal that hears the case. The ICDR have recently introduced a new rule, Article 37, to accommodate this, enabling a one-person tribunal to be constituted within one business day of the notice being received and for a very tight timetable. Under this provision the emergency arbitrator's power to act determines on the appointment of the tribunal hearing the arbitration which can then deal with the matter. The emergency arbitrator has the power to order or award any interim or conservatory measure that he or she deems necessary, including injunctive relief and measures for the protection or conservation of property by way of interim award or order. The order may be varied or modified. The emergency arbitrator must give reasons for his order. The appointment of an emergency arbitrator is not incompatible with an application to the courts. The rule is set out in full at Appendix B.3 pages 218–221.

The LCIA has a variant on the above under Article 9 of its rules by providing for the formation of an expedited tribunal in cases of urgency where the normal timescales are abridged. This rule is also set out in full at Appendix B.3 page 218.[3]

APPLICATIONS TO THE ENGLISH COURT BEFORE THE TRIBUNAL IS FULLY CONSTITUTED

The English court views its role as preserving the parties' rights and not as usurping the arbitral process. Section 44 of the 1996 Act gives the court certain discretionary powers in support of the process and in anticipation of an arbitration. Thus, it may, on the application of a proposed party to the arbitration and where the matter is urgent, make any of the following orders,

3. See also e.g. the Expedited Procedure in Article 42 of the Swiss Arbitration Procedure.

provided that it thinks that such orders are "*necessary for the purpose of preserving evidence or assets*":[4]

> "*(a) the taking of the evidence of witnesses;*
> *(b) the preservation of evidence;*
> *(c) making orders relating to property which is the subject of the proceedings or as to which any question arises in the proceedings:*
> *(i) for the inspection, photographing, preservation, custody or detention of the property, or*
> *(ii) ordering that samples be taken from, or any observation be made of or experiment conducted upon, the property; and for that purpose authorising any person to enter any premises in the possession or control of a party to the arbitration;*
> *(d) the sale of any goods the subject of the proceedings;*
> *(e) the granting of an interim injunction or the appointment of a receiver.*"

Unlike an arbitral tribunal, the court can direct its orders to third parties and can impose sanctions not available to a tribunal, such as the penal sanction of a committal order. Thus, the court can make, for example, restraining orders or freezing injunctions or search orders before a tribunal is constituted (see chapter 11 pages 84–85). However, the court will extract appropriate cross-undertakings, whether as to damages or otherwise, from the party seeking the relief so as not to prejudice the other party or the decision of the tribunal.

The court also has a useful power enabling it to direct that any order it makes by way of an interim order in advance of the constitution of the tribunal shall cease to have effect in whole or in part on the order of either the tribunal once formed, or of any such arbitral or other institution or person having power to act in relation to the subject-matter of the arbitration.[5]

Recent examples of the use of this power include the situation where a chose in action, namely a contractual right, was held to be an asset which the court could protect. In that case it granted a mandatory interim injunction to one of the parties in advance of the formation of a tribunal, as not to have done so would have rendered the process nugatory.[6] On another occasion the court confirmed that it had power to prevent disclosure of documents in breach of confidentiality of an arbitral process.[7] Where the intended seat of the arbitration is not England, such powers in anticipation of an arbitration will only be used exceptionally.[8]

4. Section 44(1), (2), (3), (6), 7(7) of the 1996 Act and *Cetelem SA* v *Roust Holdings Ltd* [2005] EWCA Civ 618, a case where the sale of one party's interest in a Russian bank under a sale and purchase agreement over which there was a dispute would have been frustrated and any arbitration rendered otiose if the condition precedent of the Russian Central Bank's approval had not been secured. This in turn required the selling party to submit various documents to the Central Bank.

5. Section 44(6) of the 1996 Act.

6. *Cetelem, supra.*

7. *Glidepath BV & ors* v *John Thompson & ors* [2005] EWHC 818 (Comm), Colman J.

8. *Econet Wireless Ltd* v *Vee Networks Ltd & Ors* [2006] EWHC 1568.

APPLICATIONS FOR A STAY OF COURT PROCEEDINGS

This section addresses the position where civil proceedings are brought in the English courts in breach of an arbitration agreement, whether the seat of the arbitration is England or outside the jurisdiction.[9] Such a situation is most likely to occur either before an arbitration has started or early in the process. Cross-border issues involving such remedies as anti-suit injunctions are dealt with in chapter 11 pages 87–88.

A party to an arbitration agreement against whom legal proceedings (whether by claim or counterclaim) are brought has a statutory entitlement to apply to the English court on notice to the other parties to the proceedings for a stay of those proceedings so far as they concern the matter to be arbitrated, whether or not the arbitration has commenced.[10] A party must first take the necessary procedural step, if any, to acknowledge the legal proceedings against it, usually by way of an acknowledgement of service, but it must not take any step in the action to answer the substantive claim or it will waive its right to a stay.[11] The court must grant a stay unless "*satisfied that the arbitration agreement is null and void, inoperative, or incapable of being performed*".[12] Attempts to litigate matters covered by the arbitration agreement will be stayed.

There is an important distinction between the issue of whether or not the arbitration agreement (as opposed to the main agreement) has come into existence at all or is otherwise directly impeached, when the court will refuse a stay, and issues concerning the scope or validity or effectiveness of the autonomous arbitration agreement, which are matters for the tribunal to determine (section 30 of the 1996 Act) and not for the court and a stay will be granted. The distinction is sometimes difficult to draw, although the recent decision of the House of Lords in *Premium Nafta*, formerly *Fiona Trust*,[13] has sought to clarify the position.

The case concerned eight charterparties which the owners alleged had been obtained by bribery. Each had an arbitration clause providing for arbitration in London. The owners sought a declaration under section 72 of the 1996 Act that the charterparties had been validly rescinded because of the bribery. The charterers sought a stay under section 9 of the Act. In explaining that section 7 of the 1996 Act means that the main agreement and the arbitration agreement have been separately concluded and are accordingly distinct agreements, Lord Hoffmann made it clear that "*the arbitration agreement can be invalidated only on a ground which relates to the arbitration agreement and is not merely a consequence of the invalidity of the main agreement.*"[14]

9. Section 2(2) of the 1996 Act.
10. Sections 9 and 82 of the 1996 Act.
11. Section 9(3) of the 1996 Act.
12. Section 9(4) of the 1996 Act.
13. *Premium Nafta Products Limited and ors* v *Fili Shipping Company Limited and ors* [2007] UKHL 40. The case also deals with construction issues: see chapter 4 page 26.
14. See also on the issue of separability and section 7 of the 1996 Act: chapter 9 pages 63–64.

Thus, in that case the issue of whether or not the arbitration agreement was procured by bribery was held to be a matter for the tribunal to determine. Allegations of illegality would likewise be for the tribunal to determine. On the other hand, the House of Lords suggested that an arbitration agreement entered into as a result of excess authority would be an example of direct impeachment of an arbitration clause. Similarly, where the issue was whether an arbitration agreement providing for an arbitration to be held in Malaysia had been concluded because the agreement was alleged to be a forgery, the English court declined to grant a permanent stay of the English proceedings and ordered an issue to be tried by the court.[15] The judge also decided that as section 9 of the 1996 Act gave the court jurisdiction only where an arbitration agreement had been concluded, the court retained a residual power under its inherent jurisdiction in exceptional circumstances to stay proceedings where the court cannot, on the available evidence, resolve whether or not the arbitration agreement was concluded. The court also retains a power under its inherent jurisdiction to grant a stay, for example, if the arbitration clause has not yet become effective.[16]

A court faced with a stay application, therefore, has four options, namely where:

i. it is clear that an arbitration clause does exist covering the disputes being litigated, it has a mandatory obligation to stay the proceedings;
ii. there is an issue going to the validity or effectiveness of the arbitration agreement which does not impeach the arbitration agreement itself, then the court will stay the proceedings for the arbitrators to resolve the jurisdictional issue;
iii. the issue is whether or not the arbitration agreement itself exists or is impeached, it will direct an issue to be tried by the court to determine the issue; and
iv. it is clear that no arbitration clause exists it will dismiss the stay application.

The opportunities for parties who are intent on undermining or delaying the arbitral process by use of stay applications have now been considerably reduced. Moreover, parties who begin proceedings in breach of an arbitration agreement, which proceedings are then stayed, are likely to have to pay costs on an indemnity basis where it can be established that the breach of the arbitration agreement has caused the innocent party reasonably to incur legal costs.[17]

15. *Nigel Peter Albon (trading as NA Carriage Co.)* v *Naza Motor Trading SDN BHD & another* [2007] EWHC 665 (Ch). But compare *AMR Amin Hamza El Nasharty* v *J. Sainsbury plc* [2007] EWHC 2618 (Comm) where the court granted a stay when the allegation was that a share sale agreement had been entered into under duress.

16. *Channel Tunnel Group Ltd and another* v *Balfour Beatty Construction Ltd and ors* [1993] 2 W.L.R. 262.

17. *A* v *B* [2007] EWHC 54 (Comm), but see also *C* v *D* [2007] EWCA Civ 1282.

MULTI-TIER CLAUSES AND ALTERNATIVE DISPUTE RESOLUTION

Occasionally one finds what are termed *Scott* v *Avery* clauses, the eponymous name given to such clauses following the case of that name in the nineteenth century.[18] As a result of such clauses parties agree that no action may be brought upon a contract until an arbitration award has been made. Such a provision is rendered ineffective if the court refuses a stay.[19]

Multi-tier clauses are a form of *Scott* v *Avery* clause. They can provide that the parties seek to resolve their dispute by mediation or some other form of consensual non-binding dispute resolution process prior to commencing an arbitration Although an agreement to agree or negotiate is not binding under English law the courts will recognise clear multi-tier clauses, if certain conditions exist. Thus, such a clause will be enforceable if: (a) the process is sufficiently certain that there is no need for an agreement at any stage before the alternative dispute resolution process can begin; (b) the administrative processes for selecting a party to resolve the dispute and to pay that person are defined; and (c) the process or at least a model of the process is set out so that its detail is sufficiently certain.[20]

Even where there is no multi-tier clause, whether enforceable or not, the parties may nonetheless still want to try to mediate their dispute to avoid an arbitration. Mediation, the most common form of alternative dispute resolution or ADR, can take place at any time, but before the process starts is certainly one time to be considered. There are several arbitral and other institutions which provide mediation schemes, but there are also many qualified mediators in London who can be approached directly without the need for the involvement of an institution (see also chapter 2 pages 13–14 and chapter 12 pages 98–99).

18. (1856) 25 L.J. Ex. 308.
19. Section 9(5) of the 1996 Act.
20. *(1) Neil Holloway (2) Samantha Holloway* v *Chancery Mead Ltd* [2007] EWHC 2495 (TCC).

CHAPTER 7

FIRST STEPS IN THE PROCESS

INTRODUCTION

Having considered the preliminary matters referred to in earlier chapters of this book, the process has to be initiated by the claimant, the respondent given an opportunity to respond and the tribunal appointed. This chapter, therefore, considers the early stages of the process and how to get the arbitration up and running. It discusses the following issues:

- starting the arbitration;
- the response and reply;
- appointing the tribunal;
- challenges to the arbitrator;
- arbitrators' tenure;
- matters for agreement between the parties; and
- advance costs and deposits.

STARTING THE ARBITRATION

The commencement of the arbitration is relevant not only to the initiation of the process, but also to any limitation issues. As to the latter this will cover any limitation period relating to the cause of action imposed by the foreign law of the contract if this is applicable.[1] The court's power to extend time for commencing an arbitration does not affect the operation of the Limitations Acts.[2] The parties can, however, agree when the arbitral proceedings are to be commenced for the purposes of the Limitations Acts.[3]

If the arbitration clause makes no provision for the commencement of the arbitral process, section 14 of the 1996 Act provides a default mechanism in three specific situations. First, where the arbitrator is named or designated in the agreement; secondly, where the arbitrator or arbitrators are to be appointed by the parties; and thirdly, where such appointment is to be by a person other than a party to the proceedings. In all cases the arbitration is commenced when the written notice is sent to the other party or parties

1. Sections 13(1), (4) and 14(1) of the 1996 Act.
2. Section 12(5) of the 1996 Act.
3. Section 14(1) of the 1996 Act and see e.g. Article 1.2 of the LCIA Rules. Under English law the limitation period in contract is six years from when the cause of action accrued (section 5 of the Limitation Act 1980). There are some limited instances in which the commencement of the period may be postponed e.g. in cases where there is justified delay in discovering fraud.

respectively requesting submission of the matter to the named or designated person; requiring them to appoint an arbitrator or agree to the appointment of an arbitrator; or by giving notice to the third party requesting the making of the appointment.

Sometimes there is an additional time bar relating to the time within which the arbitration or other pre-arbitral procedures have to be commenced. The English court has the discretion on the application of a party on notice to the other party to extend the time, provided that the claim has arisen and any available arbitral process for extending time has been exhausted. However, the party applying has to show that the circumstances are such as were outside the reasonable contemplation of the parties when they agreed the provision in question and it would be just to do so, or that the conduct of one party makes it unjust to hold the other party to the strict provisions of the agreement.[4]

An arbitration is commenced by filing or sending a request for or notice of arbitration.[5] This usually comprises a brief statement of the claim accompanied by key documents: a citation of the relevant arbitration clause; the choice of law clause, if any; other clauses relevant to the arbitration or appointment of the tribunal; the names and contact details of the parties if known; and of the claimant's lawyers and any nomination of an arbitrator[6] if relevant. Where the arbitration is to be conducted in accordance with specific rules the requirements vary slightly according the requisite rules. The requirements of the LCIA, ICC and ICDR and the UNCITRAL Rules can be seen at Appendix B.3 (see also the relevant indices at Appendices B.1 and B.2). The detail in which the claim is set out will also vary from claim to claim, but in most arbitrations, other than very straightforward ones, parties will serve more detailed written pleadings and/or submissions at a later stage (variously described as written briefs, submissions, pleadings and memorials). Where the tribunal is to be appointed by an arbitral institution it is advisable to include sufficient information to enable the institution to select an arbitrator or arbitrators with the requisite expertise and experience, although some institutions do consult with the parties before appointment in any event.

If an arbitral institution is involved, the request is served on the institution and copied to the other potential parties. The arbitration is normally deemed to have commenced upon receipt by the institution. Other rules not allied to a particular arbitral institution, such as the UNCITRAL Rules, provide for commencement of the arbitration upon receipt by the other party. If the parties agree to an ad hoc arbitration without the involvement of any arbitral institution, they will usually provide for the request to be sent directly to the tribunal with copies to the other parties. The arbitration will then be commenced at the time agreed, usually upon receipt by the other parties.

4. Section 12 of the 1996 Act.

5. The AAA/ICDR provides for on-line filing. Whether this facility will become more prevalent remains to be seen. The ICC uses NetCase.

6. See chapter 5.

THE RESPONSE AND REPLY

Upon receipt of the request for or notice of arbitration the respondent(s) should usually send a response or answer in writing to any arbitral institution involved and to all other parties. The response may include a counterclaim. Whether such counterclaim is covered by the arbitration clause is a separate question (see chapter 4 page 27). If there is a counterclaim, then a response to counterclaim may be needed. Further pleadings are normally considered later in the process (see chapter 10 pages 70–71). A reply or reply to defence to counterclaim may also be required. Arbitral rules, if applicable, set out time limits. Extensions of time can be given by the tribunal and are usually provided for in the relevant arbitral rules. The court also has a general power to extend all time limits once the arbitration has been commenced.[7] The comparative rules of the LCIA, ICC and ICDR are set out in Appendix B.3 (see also relevant indices at Appendices B.1 and B.2). These also contain the basic requirements of such a response or answer. UNCITRAL Rules, which are not allied to any arbitral institution, similarly set out in Appendices B.1–B.3, do not require a response prior to the appointment of the tribunal.

It not infrequently happens that a respondent fails to send a response either because it contests the jurisdiction of the tribunal or because it does not want to take any part in the process. This does not preclude the respondent from later denying the claim or advancing a counterclaim. However, deferring the response does preclude the respondent from having any input into the selection of the tribunal.

APPOINTING THE TRIBUNAL

As explained in chapter 3 pages 19–20, there are numerous permutations as to the make-up and manner of appointment of a tribunal. In the absence of any agreed timescale for the appointment of the tribunal, the 1996 Act provides a default timescale.[8] Where an arbitral institution is involved it will normally formally appoint any arbitrator, even if the arbitrator is to be party nominated. Arbitral rules will also contain default powers of appointment.[9] The court retains a residual power of appointment where there has been a default.[10] The failure to appoint a president of a tribunal in accordance with the agreed

7. Section 79 of the 1996 Act.

8. Sections 16 and 79 of the 1996 Act.

9. See e.g. Article 7.2 of the LCIA Rules and 8.4 of the ICC Rules. For multiple parties see e.g. Article 8.1–2 of the LCIA Rules and 10.1–2 of the ICC Rules. Although the UNCITRAL Rules are not allied to any specific appointing institution, they provide for the parties to allocate an appointing authority (and a mechanism for one to be allocated in default), particularly if the parties cannot agree on the appointment of the tribunal (Articles 6–8). The ICC has separate rules for appointing arbitrators where it is made the appointing authority in UNCITRAL or other ad hoc arbitration proceedings.

10. Sections 17, 18 and 19 of the 1996 Act.

procedure can render his or her participation in the arbitration unlawful and any consequent award a nullity.[11]

A party may have an opportunity to provide input into the selection of the tribunal. The principal situations where this happens are the following:

i. First, if a party is entitled to nominate one of the three arbitrators.
ii. Secondly, the arbitration clause may provide for a sole arbitrator to be appointed, chosen jointly by the parties, with a default provision in the event that agreement cannot be reached. How the parties go about achieving this varies. A common approach to initiate the process is for both parties to put forward a shortlist. If a name is on both lists that resolves the position, otherwise one party may agree to one of the other party's suggestions.
iii. Thirdly, arbitral institutions may ask the parties for their views, even though the ultimate decision is that of the institution. Rules of arbitral institutions often include criteria for appointment, for example, that a sole arbitrator or chair should not be the same nationality as the parties.[12]
iv. Fourthly, where the arbitration agreement provides for the two party appointed arbitrators to appoint a presiding arbitrator or chair, they will sometimes first seek views of the parties, although again the decision will remain theirs. It is advisable to confine this to views on the requirements rather than seeking a list of names, otherwise if a name is chosen which is only on one party's list, this can cause problems.

In selecting or nominating an arbitrator a party and its legal advisers should look for someone with as many of the ten criteria (as set out in chapter 5 pages 35–38) as are relevant. Parties sometimes like to interview prospective arbitrators to make a proper assessment, but they will not be able to talk about the actual arbitration. To avoid such interviews putting the potential arbitrator in a position where his or her independence and impartiality would be impugned, the Chartered Institute of Arbitrators has recently laid down guidelines concerning the interviewing of prospective arbitrators which some arbitrators may wish to follow.[13] In any event, it is normal practice for a party's lawyer to contact a potential arbitrator to ascertain whether or not the prospective arbitrator has any conflicts of interest which will preclude his or her accepting any appointment. The IBA Guidelines on Conflicts of Interest in International Arbitration with its "*traffic lights*" approach of red, orange and green representing degrees of actual or potential conflicts are a useful guide, although not binding (see chapter 5 pages 35–38).

11. *Sumakan Ltd* v *Commonwealth Secretariat* [2007] EWCA Civ 1148.
12. See e.g. Article 5.5 and 6.1–6.3 of the LCIA Rules and 9.1 and 9.5 of the ICC Rules.
13. Practice Guideline 16.

On appointment an arbitrator will be asked to confirm his or her independence and impartiality, which is an ongoing obligation of any arbitrator throughout the process. Most arbitral institutions require a declaration in writing from each arbitrator to the effect that there are no circumstances known to the arbitrator likely to give rise to any justifiable doubts as to the arbitrator's independence and impartiality.[14]

This is also the point at which agreement is reached as to an arbitrator's fees. Some arbitral institutions provide for hourly rates, for example, the LCIA. The current maximum hourly rate for an arbitrator under the LCIA Rules is £350, although in exceptional circumstances this can be higher. Arbitrators appointed under the LCIA Rules usually insert a cancellation provision to cover the situation where an arbitration is settled at short notice. Others have an *ad valorem* scale according to the amount at stake, for example, the ICC. In ad hoc arbitrations arbitrators fix their own fees. Subject to any contractual right of the arbitrator, parties are jointly and severally liable for arbitrators' fees and expenses.[15]

Some arbitrators, particularly chairs of tribunals, and, especially in substantial cases, may appoint administrative secretaries to the tribunal to assist them. Their role is limited to dealing with administrative work such as filing of papers. Their involvement is disclosed to the parties, who usually pay for their services. Secretaries have no adjudicative role, which role remains exclusively that of the tribunal.

CHALLENGES TO THE ARBITRATOR

Once appointed arbitrators are susceptible to challenges from the parties as to their impartiality and independence. This is usually confined to reasons of which the party became aware after appointment.[16] Frequently these challenges are on spurious grounds and represent a tactical manoeuvre to delay or derail the process. In the first instance the arbitral institution will, if involved, deal with a challenge, providing the challenge is made within the time provided in the rules.[17] The UNCITRAL Rules similarly include a procedure for challenging arbitrators.[18] An arbitrator may similarly be removed for other reasons, for instance, if he or she refuses or becomes unable to act or does not

14. See e.g. Article 5 of the LCIA Rules; Article 7 of the ICC Rules, Article 7 of the ICDR Rules and Article 9 of the UNCITRAL Rules.

15. Section 28(1) and (5) of the 1996 Act.

16. See e.g. Articles 10.3–4 and 11.1–2 of the LCIA Rules, Articles 7.4 and 11.1–3 of the ICC Rules, Articles 8.1–3 and 9 of the ICDR Rules and Articles 10.1–2, 11.1–3 and 12.1–2 of the UNCITRAL Rules.

17. See e.g. Article 10.4 of the LCIA Rules; Article 11.3 of the ICC Rules, and Article 9 of the ICDR Rules. In 2006 the LCIA decided to publish their decisions on challenges suitably redacted to preserve confidentiality.

18. Articles 10–12 of the UNCITRAL Rules which include a default designation of an appointing authority to deal with such issues.

act fairly as between the parties.[19] An application may in addition be made to the court at any time, but if there is an arbitral institution involved then the machinery for challenging under the institution's rules must first be exhausted.[20]

ARBITRATORS' TENURE

Once appointed, an arbitrator's authority continues until death, resignation,[21] agreement in writing of the parties including by way of settlement. An arbitrator can also be removed following a successful challenge to his independence by the parties or following a request from a co-arbitrator, or on the initiative of the arbitral institution or removal by the court.[22] The parties can agree what is to happen in the event of a vacancy, for instance, by reference to the rules of an arbitral institution or other set of rules such as the UNCITRAL Rules.[23] Some rules provide for the option of a truncated tribunal.[24] In the absence of agreement the 1996 Act provides a default mechanism for what is to happen if an arbitrator ceases to act for any of these reasons.[25]

MATTERS FOR AGREEMENT BETWEEN THE PARTIES

The 1996 Act gives supremacy to the parties' agreement, subject to certain mandatory provisions set out in Schedule 1. The provisions of the following sections of the 1996 Act are subject to the parties' agreement and are non-mandatory, namely: sections 3 (the seat of the arbitration); 4(3) (the application of institutional rules); 4(5) applicable law); 7 (separability of the arbitration clause in the case of invalidity etc.); 8 (the effect of death of a party on the arbitration agreement); 14–18 (various matters relating to the appointment of the tribunal); 20–23 (decision making powers of members of the tribunal); 24(2) (removal of an arbitrator where an institution is involved); 25 (resignation of an arbitrator); 26(2) (the effect of death of an arbitrator on the arbitration agreement); 27 (filling a vacancy in the tribunal); 30 (competence

19. See e.g. Article 10.1–2 of the LCIA Rules, Article 12.1–4 of the ICC Rules, Article 10 and 11.2 of the ICDR Rules and Articles 13.1–2 and 14 of the UNCITRAL Rules.

20. Section 24 of the 1996 Act and see also *(1) AT&T Corporation (2) Lucent Technologies Inc.* v *Saudi Cable Co.* [2000] 2 Lloyd's Rep. 127 where concerning an arbitration with a London seat, it was confirmed that the test was whether there was any real danger, viewed objectively, of unconscious or apparent bias on the part of the arbitrator.

21. Section 25 of the 1996 Act.

22. Sections 18(3), 23 and 24 of the 1996 Act. See also e.g. Article 12(2) of the ICC Rules which empowers the ICC Court to remove an arbitrator on its own initiative in certain circumstances.

23. See e.g. Article 11 of the LCIA Rules and Article 12.3–4 of the ICC Rules.

24. See e.g. Article 12.1–2 of the LCIA Rules, Article 12.5 of the ICC Rules and Article 11.1 of the ICDR Rules.

25. Section 27 of the 1996 Act.

of the tribunal to rule on its own jurisdiction); 34 (procedural and evidential matters); 35 (consolidation of proceedings and concurrent hearings); 36 (legal or other representation); 37(1) (power of the tribunal to appoint experts, legal advisers and assessors); 38 (general powers of the tribunal); 39 (power to make provisional awards); 41–42 (powers in relation to default and peremptory orders of the tribunal); 44 (court's powers exercisable in support of arbitral proceedings); 45 (court's power to determine a preliminary point of law); 46–55, 57 and 58 (various matters relating to awards and remedies); 61–65 (various matters relating to costs); 69 (appeal on a point of law); and 76–79 (miscellaneous matters relating to notices and time limits.

Chapter 3 considers some of the above in the context of what to include in an arbitration agreement. The same issues and additional ones may need consideration at the outset of the arbitration process, particularly if the arbitration agreement is not comprehensive or if there are no institutional or other arbitral rules which apply. Where possible, such matters should be agreed by the parties. This is preferable to relying on default provisions in sets of rules or resorting to the English court. The following are some examples:

i. there may, for instance, be deficiencies in the arbitration agreement which need to be filled, such as the failure to nominate a seat or to specify any rules under which the arbitration is to be conducted;
ii. the parties may want to exclude appeals on a point of law to the court (sections 45 and 69);
iii. the parties may want to change the arbitral institution under which the arbitration is to be administered or have no arbitral institution involved, yet adopt some or all of an arbitral institution's rules; or
iv. although arbitration proceedings are private and confidentiality attaches to the documents produced and evidence given, parties may nonetheless want to obtain an express confidentiality agreement, subject to certain provisos required by law, to avert any future attempt to seek disclosure from a court, which may not necessarily be an English court, or in a related arbitration. Some arbitral rules do provide this, for example, the LCIA Rules.[26] For more details on the English law of confidentiality as it affects arbitration see chapter 13 pages 104–105 and chapter 14 pages 111–113.

ADVANCE COSTS AND DEPOSITS

The rules of arbitral institutions provide[27] that parties have to pay the arbitrators' fees and any institution's administrative services up front and on an on-going basis throughout the arbitral process by way of deposit or advance.

26. Article 30.1 of the LCIA Rules.
27. See e.g. Articles 24.1–3 of the LCIA Rules; 30.3–5 of the ICC Rules; 33.1–4 of the ICDR Rules and 41.1–5 of the UNCITRAL Rules.

Payment is usually made in equal proportions by the parties, although adjustments can be made if, for example, a counterclaim is disproportionately large in comparison with the claim. Failure by a respondent or respondent to a counterclaim to pay the deposits in time or in any extended period will necessitate the claimant or counterclaimant paying both sides' costs if it wants to proceed with the arbitration.[28] Claimants and counterclaimants who fail to pay such advance costs when due are at risk of having their claims withdrawn. Subject to any contractual right of the arbitrator, parties are jointly and severally liable for arbitrators' fees and expenses.[29] In ad hoc arbitrations, parties are likely to be subjected to similar requirements imposed directly by the tribunal in respect of their fees.

28. Article 24.3 of the LCIA Rules entitles the party paying the substitute payment to recover the amount as a debt immediately due from the defaulting party.
29. Section 28(1) and (5) of the 1996 Act.

CHAPTER 8

ACTIVITY AND CONSIDERATIONS FOLLOWING THE FORMATION OF THE TRIBUNAL

INTRODUCTION

Once the tribunal is constituted, the control of the arbitral process rests with the arbitrators. Most arbitral institutions, such as the LCIA or the ICC, provide for the file to be sent to the tribunal at this point and for the tribunal in turn to notify the parties that henceforth all communications should be directly with the arbitrator(s), with copies to the arbitral institution. This chapter sets out the type of initial activity to which both the tribunal's and the parties' attention should be directed following the formation of the tribunal. Issues as to the tribunal's jurisdiction also have to be raised at the outset to avoid any waiver. Jurisdiction is dealt with separately in chapter 9. The following topics are addressed in this chapter:

- initial general communications and directions by the tribunal;
- non-participating parties;
- Terms of Reference;
- bifurcation and preliminary issues;
- security for costs;
- preservation and other interlocutory orders;
- an order limiting recoverable costs and other protective measures as to costs; and
- exclusion of recourse to the courts.

INITIAL GENERAL COMMUNICATIONS AND DIRECTIONS BY THE TRIBUNAL

Arbitrators approach matters in different ways. Some are more interventionist than others; some put more pressure on the parties to meet deadlines than others. Given the flexible nature of the process there is no absolute way of doing things, provided that the tribunal acts fairly and impartially, gives each party a reasonable opportunity of putting its case and dealing with that of its opponent, and adopts procedures suitable to the circumstances of the particular case.[1]

1. See e.g. Article 14.1(i) , (ii) of the LCIA Rules; Article 15.2 of the ICC Rules, Article 16.1–2 of the ICDR Rules and Article 15.1 of the UNCITRAL Rules and section 33 of the 1996 Act. Arbitrators are immune from suit save where they act in bad faith: section 29 of the 1996 Act.

However, once constituted a tribunal will as soon as practical communicate with the parties. In the absence of any intimated interim application, the tribunal will normally indicate what method of communication should be used and invite the parties to agree directions for the further progress of the arbitration.[2] Some arbitrators give the parties a steer at this point, such as reminding them that disclosure of documents is not wholesale in international arbitrations and inviting the parties to consider such issues as bifurcation (splitting the hearings) and procedural hearings. If there is a panel of three, then it is normal for the arbitrators to agree between themselves, and to notify the parties, that the chair or presiding arbitrator will deal with all routine procedural matters such as extensions of time, consulting with his co-arbitrators as appropriate.[3] Sometimes tribunals will ask lawyers to provide a power of attorney to act on behalf of their client, for instance, when signing Terms of Reference (see below).

NON-PARTICIPATING PARTIES

A particular and quite frequent problem arises for a tribunal when a respondent does not take part in the process and fails to file an answer or response. Arbitrators must always seek to produce an enforceable award[4] and hence ensure that a respondent is treated fairly and given a proper opportunity to be heard. The tribunal will normally first ensure that previous communications have reached the non-participating party. This can be by way of a further communication from the tribunal itself by post and courier, as companies, particularly in third world countries, may not have ready access to reliable e-mail or faxes.

The refusal of a respondent to participate, whether as a result of total silence or an indication that it contests the jurisdiction of the tribunal, can cause delay, as the tribunal will throughout want to ensure that the respondent has had every chance to participate (see also chapter 12 pages 92–93—peremptory orders). This can be frustrating for a claimant, particularly if it has to advance both sides' costs[5] which, for example, in a large claim under the ICC Rules, can be expensive. However, claimants have to recognise that it is in their interests to ensure that the award cannot be successfully challenged at the end of the day if they are successful in the arbitration. Arbitral rules usually provide for the arbitration to proceed despite the absence or non-compliance of a non-participating or defaulting party.[6]

2. Section 38(1) of the 1996 Act.
3. See e.g. Article 14.3 of the LCIA Rules; Article 26.2 of the ICDR Rules; Article 31.2 of the UNCITRAL Rules. Sections 20–22 of the 1996 Act provide default powers to deal with decision making.
4. See e.g. Article 32.2 of the LCIA Rules.
5. See e.g. Article 24.3 of the LCIA Rules and Article 30 of the ICC Rules.
6. See e.g. Article 15.8 of the LCIA Rules, Article 6.3 of the ICC Rules, Article 23 of the ICDR Rules and Article 28 of the UNCITRAL Rules.

TERMS OF REFERENCE

Terms of Reference are unique to the ICC.[7] The document sets out the respective contentions of the parties as set out in the request and response and any counterclaim or reply and summarises the issues. It also sets out other specific matters provided for in Article 18 of the ICC Rules, such as the arbitration clause, the names and addresses of the parties, the language and place of arbitration and additional provisions which may vary according to particular arbitrators' own practice. The Terms of Reference are drafted at the outset by the tribunal and sent in draft to the parties for their comments. The secretariat of the ICC court, to whom they are always copied in draft, considers them and will draw the tribunal's attention to any omissions or inaccuracies. They are then signed by the parties and provide the basis of the arbitration going forward. If a party refuses to sign them, they have to be submitted to the ICC court for approval. Once the Terms of Reference have been signed, the parties are not permitted to make any new claims or counterclaims not covered by the Terms of Reference without the permission of the tribunal.[8] Article 18 also provides for a provisional timetable. This is dealt with in chapter 10.

BIFURCATION AND PRELIMINARY ISSUES

An early consideration for both the parties and the tribunal is whether or not to segment the issues. The two most common methods of achieving this are bifurcation of liability and quantum and the hearing of preliminary issues. Several factors have to be balanced. The overriding consideration is usually whether or not such an order will lead to a saving of costs and time, either by disposing of the claim or part of it, or by narrowing the issues, which in turn can promote settlement.

Bifurcation is not always straightforward and the tribunal needs to have some information as to the nature of the damages claim, usually by way of pleadings or written submissions. Thus, the issue of bifurcation is often deferred until after the parties have pleaded their case and given at least some particulars of the damages claim, although the degree of detail will vary from case to case. It will sometimes be counterproductive to plead the damages claim in great detail. Nonetheless, the engagement of experts at the outset, at least on a preliminary basis, may be desirable.

Moreover, assessing damages is rarely just about quantification. Underlying any damages claim are factual issues. These are numerous, but may include one or more of the following: whether the business was a start up or had a trading history; what the future prospects were for the particular business;

7. Article 18 of the ICC Rules.
8. Article 19 of the ICC Rules.

whether or not the whole or only part of the loss was caused by the breach; whether the claimant had acted reasonably in mitigating its loss; and what the chances would have been of a profit being made in the future when that chance depends for instance on a third party. These factual issues may have to be addressed at the main liability hearing to avoid having to recall witnesses at any subsequent quantum hearing.

Thus, in deciding whether or not to bifurcate the liability and quantum stages, the tribunal has to consider various factors. These include: whether the damages claim is after all relatively straightforward not justifying any delay; whether there will be, and if so the extent of, any overlap of witnesses giving evidence on liability (assuming there is oral evidence), who would have to be recalled at a later date to deal with issues relevant to damages; what the costs and other implications of this are; the nature of any expert evidence; and how much delay would be caused by a deferral of the damages issues.

Sometimes, in the absence of agreement between the parties, the application for bifurcation can be a smokescreen by a claimant with a weak or inflated claim on damages who is seeking to delay pleading its case in detail, frequently in the unrealistic hope that its stronger claim on liability will lead to an inflated settlement. Conversely, a respondent with a weak or hopeless case can try to use the delays inherent in splitting the hearings to put off a final award. The tribunal will be alert to such tactical manoeuvres.

There is a growing willingness among international arbitrators in international commercial arbitrations to bifurcate hearings in complex cases, unless the parties jointly resist or the claimant's or counterclaimant's case is so obviously well founded and straightforward that no benefit would be gained by splitting the hearing. If a tribunal does split the hearings, it nonetheless retains the duty to manage the process of the overall arbitration.

Preliminary issues are also popular with parties, but once again care needs to be taken to see if they will actually achieve what they are designed to, namely eliminate issues, shorten the proceedings and save costs. Most arbitrators will carefully scrutinise the parties' formulation of preliminary issues to ensure that this is the case. Unless otherwise agreed by the parties,[9] if the issue is one of law, a party with the agreement of the other parties or the tribunal, can apply directly to the English court for a determination of a preliminary point of law if the court is satisfied that the question of law substantially affects the rights of one or more of the parties (see chapter 11 pages 86–87).[10] The court nonetheless retains a discretion as to whether or not to determine the question.[11] This will not hold up the arbitral process which can proceed in tandem.

9. Some arbitral rules preclude recourse to the national courts such as Articles 22.2, 23.4 and 26.9 of the LCIA Rules and Article 28.6 of the ICC Rules. The parties can independently make a similar agreement.

10. Section 45 of the 1996 Act.

11. *Taylor Woodrow Holdings Ltd & another* v *Barnes & Elliott Ltd* [2006] EWHC 1693 (TCC).

SECURITY FOR COSTS

The issue of security for costs for a claimant or counterclaimant is a matter exclusively for the tribunal. However, the power cannot be exercised on the ground that the claimant, if an individual, is ordinarily resident outside the United Kingdom or, if a corporation or association, was formed in a country outside the United Kingdom or whose central management and control is exercised outside the United Kingdom.[12] If a claimant fails to comply with an order of the tribunal to provide security for costs, the tribunal can make a preremptory order and if, in turn, a party fails to comply with such a preremptory order the tribunal then make an award dismissing the claim.[13]

PRESERVATION OF EVIDENCE AND OTHER INTERLOCUTORY APPLICATIONS

Parties will want to consider whether it is necessary to make any early application to the tribunal or even to an emergency tribunal if available for an order to preserve evidence or other assistance (see chapter 6 page 42). A party can seek directions from the tribunal:

> "*in relation to any property which is the subject of the proceedings or as to which any question arises in the proceedings and which is owned by or is in the possession of a party to the proceedings:*
>
> *a. for the inspection, photographing, preservation, custody or detention of the property by the tribunal, an expert or a party, or*
>
> *b. ordering that samples be taken from, or any observation be made of or experiment conducted upon, the property.*"[14]

The tribunal is also empowered to give directions to a party for the preservation for the purposes of the proceedings of any evidence in its custody or control.[15] The above powers are subject to any agreement of the parties.[16] The parties may confer on the tribunal the power to grant certain forms of relief by way of provisional award.[17] The rules of arbitral institutions and other rules, such as the UNCITRAL Rules, normally set out the powers of tribunals in relation to interim measures.[18]

Failure to comply with any order of the tribunal entitles it to seek enforcement by way of a peremptory order.[19] Failure to comply with a peremptory

12. Section 38(3) of the 1996 Act.
13. Section 41(5) and (6) of the 1996 Act.
14. Section 38(4) of the 1996 Act.
15. Section 38(6) of the 1996 Act.
16. Section 38(1) of the 1996 Act.
17. Section 39 of the 1996 Act. See also the discussion of provisional awards in chapter 12 page 94.
18. See e.g. Article 25 of the LCIA Rules, Article 23 of the ICC Rules, Article 21 of the ICDR Rules and Article 26 of the UNCITRAL Rules.
19. Section 41(5) of the 1996 Act.

order entitles the tribunal to impose certain sanctions.[20] Peremptory orders are considered in more detail in chapter 12 pages 92–93. In addition to these powers of a tribunal, unless otherwise agreed by the parties, the court can make an order requiring a party to comply with a peremptory order made by the tribunal. This has to be made on the application of the tribunal on notice to the parties or by a party on notice to the other parties and with the permission of the tribunal.[21] The court also has independent powers to make interim orders, which powers are dealt with in chapter 6 pages 42–43 and chapter 11.

A controversial issue in the context of interim applications to the tribunal is whether such applications can be made without notice to the other party or parties, as can be done in certain cases before the courts.[22] Problems with making such applications to the tribunal without notifying the other parties include: the possible impact on third parties who are not parties to the arbitration; the risk that it offends against the principle of equal treatment; and the risk that it threatens party confidence in the integrity of the arbitral process, which in turn can invite challenges at a later stage on the ground that the arbitral procedure was not in accordance with the parties' agreement. It is probably safer in such circumstances to seek an order from the court, as the situations where such an application can be made to the tribunal without causing potential difficulties are likely to be extremely rare and various safeguards would have to be imposed to protect other parties.

AN ORDER LIMITING RECOVERABLE COSTS AND OTHER PROTECTIVE MEASURES AS TO COSTS

In the absence of agreement by the parties a tribunal has the power to limit the recoverable costs to a specified amount. Such a direction may be made or varied at any stage, provided it is done sufficiently in advance of the incurring of costs to which it relates, or of the taking of any steps in the proceedings which may be affected by it.[23] It appears to be a little used provision, but is nonetheless a potentially useful one. There are other protective measures which a party can take in relation to costs, but these are more likely to become relevant as the process progresses than at the outset of proceedings when little is known about the respective cases of the parties and are accordingly dealt with in chapter 12 pages 97–98.

20. Section 41(6) of the 1996 Act.
21. Section 42 of the 1996 Act.
22. See the debate concerning the amendment to Article 17 of the UNCITRAL Model Law.
23. Section 65 of the 1996 Act.

EXCLUSION OF RECOURSE TO THE COURTS

As explained in chapter 7 pages 52–53 there are several non-mandatory provisions of the 1996 Act in respect of which the parties are permitted to agree to exclude a right of recourse to the courts. Procedural rules, whether of arbitral institutions or otherwise, normally give wide powers to the tribunal. The LCIA Rules and the ICC Rules, but not the ICDR or UNCITRAL Rules, exclude the right of appeal to state courts[24] (see chapter 15 pages 119–121 re section 69 of the 1996 Act). However, the LCIA Rules go further and provide that: "*the parties shall be treated as having agreed not to apply to any state court or other judicial authority for any order available from the Arbitral tribunal under Article 22.1, except with the agreement in writing of all parties.*"

It is, therefore, open to the parties to exclude court intervention at various stages or altogether, save where the provision is a mandatory one as set out in Schedule 1 to the 1996 Act. In the context of the position once the tribunal has been appointed and this chapter, the parties can agree to exclude the court's power to enforce peremptory orders (section 42 of the 1996 Act), to make various interlocutory orders (section 44 of the 1996 Act) and to determine a preliminary point of law (section 45 of the 1996 Act). Conversely, the parties can also limit the powers they give to the tribunal, for example, to decide procedural and evidential matters under section 34 of the 1996 Act or order security for costs under section 38 of the 1996 Act. Other matters which can be excluded, in particular an appeal on a point of law under section 69 of the 1996 Act, are dealt with elsewhere in this book.

24. See e.g. some arbitral rules preclude recourse to the national courts such as Articles 22.2, 23.4 and 26.9 of the LCIA Rules and Article 28.6 of the ICC Rules.

CHAPTER 9

JURISDICTION

INTRODUCTION

The determination of a tribunal's substantive jurisdiction is crucial. The question may involve considering such matters as whether or not there is a valid arbitration agreement, whether the tribunal is properly constituted, and what issues have been submitted to arbitration in accordance with the arbitration agreement.[1] Failure to raise the question of jurisdiction early may deprive a party of the opportunity of raising it later and can ultimately affect enforcement. Issues of substantive jurisdiction are principally for the tribunal to resolve. Its entitlement to do so is known as "*kompetenz-kompetenz*". Before any tribunal or court can consider the issue of jurisdiction arising out of the arbitration agreement, it will be necessary to determine the applicable law of the arbitration clause (see chapter 3 pages 21–23). Some arbitral institutions, such as the ICC, give themselves the option of considering the issues of the existence, validity or scope of the arbitration agreement or leaving it to the tribunal.[2]

This chapter focuses on the following issues:

- the autonomy of the arbitration agreement;
- the effect of delay in raising jurisdictional issues;
- the powers of the tribunal;
- the powers of the court prior to an award;
- applications to the court for determination of a preliminary point of jurisdiction;
- application to the court by a respondent for a declaration or injunction; and
- appeals and challenges to the award.

THE AUTONOMY OF THE ARBITRATION AGREEMENT

It is a fundamental principle of arbitration law enshrined in section 7 of the 1996 Act that the arbitration agreement is an autonomous agreement separate from the main agreement. Section 7 provides:

> "*Unless otherwise agreed by the parties, an arbitration agreement which forms or was intended to form part of another agreement [whether or not in writing] shall not be*

1. Sections 82(1) and 30 of the 1996 Act.
2. See e.g. Article 6.2 of the ICC Rules.

> *regarded as invalid, non-existent or ineffective because that other agreement is invalid, or did not come into existence or has become ineffective, and it shall for that purpose be treated as a distinct agreement.*"

In the recent *Premium Nafta* case[3] Lord Hoffmann stated that section 7 means that the main agreement and the arbitration agreement have been separately concluded and therefore:

> "*the arbitration agreement can be invalidated only on a ground which relates to the arbitration agreement and is not merely a consequence of the invalidity of the main agreement.*"

Lord Hope put it in these words:

> "*The doctrine of separability requires direct impeachment of the arbitration agreement before it can be set aside. This is an exacting test. The argument must be based on facts which are specific to the arbitration agreement. Allegations that are parasitical to a challenge to the validity of the main agreement will not do.*"

So the mere fact that the main agreement may have been vitiated by bribery, as was the allegation in that case, does not affect the validity of the entirely separate arbitration agreement. Thus, such issues should be resolved by the arbitrators. The corollary is that a decision of the tribunal that the main agreement is non-existent, invalid or ineffective shall not by itself render the arbitration agreement non-existent, invalid or ineffective.[4]

Therefore, there remain only very limited situations where the court will consider such issues. Examples would include where a signature was alleged to be forged[5] or made without authority, as that would also mean that the arbitration agreement was forged or made without authority, i.e. where the issue is whether there was ever a contract to arbitrate at all. On the other hand, an allegation that the main agreement was made under duress does not impeach the arbitration agreement.[6] Similarly, a mere excess of authority in entering into the main contract for improper reasons, as in *Premium Nafta*, does not necessarily mean that there was no authority to enter into the arbitration agreement. Ultimately it will be a factual issue or a question of mixed fact and law in the particular case. If there is no arbitration clause whether because it is void or voidable, then an arbitrator's award on the merits can have no effect.

THE EFFECT OF DELAY IN RAISING JURISDICTIONAL ISSUES

A party must raise its objection to jurisdiction of the tribunal no later than at the time it takes the first step in the proceedings to contest the merits of any

3. *Premium Nafta Products Limited and ors* v *Fili Shipping Company Limited and ors* [2007] UKHL 40. See also chapter 4 pages 26–27 and chapter 6 pages 44–45.
4. See e.g. Article 6.4 of the ICC Rules.
5. *Nigel Peter Albon (trading as NA Carriage Co.) and Naza Motor Trading SDN BHD & another* [2007] EWHC 665 (Ch).
6. *AMR Amin Hamza El Nasharty* v *J Sainsbury plc* [2007] EWHC 2618 (Comm).

matter in relation to which it challenges the tribunal's jurisdiction. Arbitral rules, or the arbitration agreement itself, may lay down specific times.[7] This does not preclude a party from appointing or participating in the appointment of an arbitrator. Similarly, any objection during the course of the arbitral proceedings that the tribunal is exceeding its jurisdiction must be made as soon as possible after the matter alleged to be beyond jurisdiction is raised. The tribunal does have power to extend the time if it considers that the delay is justified.[8]

A party who fails to raise the issue of jurisdiction before a tribunal in the time allowed is precluded from raising that issue later before the tribunal or the court "*unless he shows that, at the time he took part or continued to take part in the proceedings, he did not know and could not with reasonable diligence have discovered the grounds for the objection*".[9] Similarly, where the tribunal rules it has jurisdiction, and a party could have questioned that ruling fails either (a) to utilise any available arbitral process of appeal or review or (b) to challenge the award in time or at all, it is prevented from objecting later to the tribunal's substantive jurisdiction on any ground which was the subject of such ruling.[10] Arbitral rules have waiver provisions to like effect.[11]

THE POWERS OF THE TRIBUNAL

Subject to the agreement of the parties, the tribunal can either rule on the issue of jurisdiction separately and make an award to that effect, or reserve the issue and deal with it in the award on the merits. The tendency is for tribunals to deal with the issue at the outset, often at a separate oral hearing, unless the issue is a short one in which case it can be dealt with by way of written submissions. Arbitral rules empower tribunals to resolve their own jurisdiction.[12]

Parties have to make a difficult choice when they contest jurisdiction between participating on the issue of jurisdiction and/or the merits without prejudice to their contention that the tribunal does not have jurisdiction or not participating at all. If the arbitration involves a state, additional issues of sovereign immunity can complicate the jurisdictional question (see in the context of enforcement, chapter 16 pages 128–130). The costs of the hearing, the chances of success on the merits and the impact on ultimate enforcement will in most cases be the main considerations. Failure to participate in the merits hearing can carry the risk of an award against a party which otherwise

7. See e.g. Article 23.2 of the LCIA Rules.
8. Section 31(1)–(3) of the 1996 Act.
9. Section 73(1) of the 1996 Act.
10. Section 73(2) of the 1996 Act.
11. See e.g. Article 32.1 of the LCIA Rules, Article 33 of the ICC Rules, Article 25 of the ICDR Rules and Article 30 of the UNCITRAL Rules.
12. See e.g. Article 23 of the LCIA Rules, Article 6.2 of the ICC Rules, Article 15 of the ICDR Rules and Article 21 of the UNCITRAL Rules.

might have succeeded. Even if a party does not participate, the tribunal will nonetheless continue to communicate with it and invite it to participate at the various stages of the hearing. It will simultaneously remind such party of the tribunal's powers under any applicable arbitral rules or under the 1996 Act to continue, despite the party's non-appearance (see also chapter 12 pages 92–93—peremptory orders).

THE POWERS OF THE COURT PRIOR TO AN AWARD

The restrictive judicial approach referred to above does not prevent parties nonetheless trying to bring such issues before the courts, although the courts are alert to unmeritorious applications made for tactical reasons or to delay the process. There are five principal routes to the court:

i. A party may apply for a stay of legal proceedings in the English courts under section 9 of the 1996 Act (see chapter 6 pages 44–45).
ii. A respondent who has taken no part in the arbitration may seek a declaration or injunction from the court as to the validity of the arbitration agreement or as to what matters have been submitted to arbitration under section 72 of the 1996 Act (see below).
iii. The court has power under section 32 of the 1996 Act, provided certain pre-conditions are complied with, to determine any question as to the substantive jurisdiction of the tribunal. Unless the parties agree otherwise, the arbitration can continue meanwhile (see below).
iv. After an award, a party can on appeal under section 67 of the 1996 Act raise the issue of jurisdiction, but a party can lose that right by prior waiver, for example, by participating in the arbitration without reservation (see chapter 15, in particular pages 115–117).
v Finally, jurisdiction can arise on enforcement both under section 66 of the 1996 Act and in relation to the New York Convention, sections 100–104 of the 1966 Act, but there are limitations (see chapter 16).

In this chapter two of the above options are discussed, namely sections 32 (decisions on a preliminary point of jurisdiction) and section 72 of the 1996 Act (application for a declaration or injunction).

APPLICATIONS TO THE COURT FOR DETERMINATION OF A PRELIMINARY POINT OF JURISDICTION

A party may apply to the court under section 32 of the 1996 Act (subject to not having waived its right to do so—see above), to determine the issue of a tribunal's jurisdiction on notice to the other parties, but the circumstances in which such an application can be made are limited. Section 32 is a mandatory provision which cannot be excluded. A decision of the court under section 32 is a judgment of the court with all the benefits that that carries with it. An application under section 32 cannot be made unilaterally. It can be made only with the written agreement of all the parties to the proceedings or with the permission of the tribunal.[13] In the latter case the grounds of the application must be set out. In addition the court has to be satisfied that the determination of the question is likely to produce substantial savings in costs, that there has been no delay and that there is a good reason why the matter should be decided by the court. An application to the court under this section does not prevent the tribunal from continuing the arbitration up to and including the making of an award.

APPLICATION TO THE COURT BY A RESPONDENT FOR A DECLARATION OR INJUNCTION

From the perspective of the respondent, section 72 of the 1996 Act enables a party, who takes no part in the arbitration, to seek a declaration or injunction or other appropriate relief to resolve the position at an early stage. Where English proceedings are started and an application is made for a stay under section 9 of the 1996 Act to restrain such proceedings, section 72 should not be used.[14] This does not appear to preclude a respondent from setting out its objections to jurisdiction, provided that it does not seek a ruling from the arbitral institution or the tribunal. The ICC, for example, provides for an initial consideration of jurisdiction by the court of the ICC.[15] Any attempt to circumvent the statutory provisions by seeking a declaration in advance of the commencement of arbitral proceedings under other provisions of English law and procedure will not succeed.[16]

APPEALS AND CHALLENGES TO THE AWARD

Any decision of the court on the issue of jurisdiction is treated as a judgment of the court from which an appeal can be made only with leave of the court. Such leave will be granted only if the question involves a point of law which is one of general importance or is one which for some other special reason

13. See Articles 23.4 of the LCIA Rules and 6.3 of the ICC Rules.
14. *Fiona Trust & Holding Corporation & ors* v *Yuri Primalov & ors* [2007] EWCA Civ 20 affirmed on other points in *Premium Nafta Products Limited and ors* v *Fili Shipping Company Limited and ors* [2007] UKHL 40.
15. Rule 6(2) of the ICC Rules.
16. *Vale do Rio Doce Navegacao S.A. & anor* v *Shanghai Bao Steel Ocean Shipping Co. Ltd (t/a Baosteel Ocean Shipping Co.) and anor* [2000] 2 Lloyd's Rep. 1.

should be considered by the Court of Appeal.[17] There is no appeal without leave from the decision of the court as to whether the conditions of the application have been met.[18]

17. Section 32(6) of the 1996 Act.
18. Section 32(5) of the 1996 Act.

CHAPTER 10

DIRECTIONS AND TIMETABLE

INTRODUCTION

In order to ensure that the arbitration runs smoothly a procedural order, provisional timetable (ICC),[1] or similar method of communicating the directions of the tribunal as to the future progress of the arbitration is an early requirement. This chapter considers the directions which need to be considered by a tribunal and the parties and the way this is done.

The consensual nature of the process enables the parties to agree as much as possible and they are encouraged to do so. Nonetheless, an experienced tribunal will ensure that the process runs smoothly and expeditiously, aim to avoid unnecessary costs, and provide for any omissions to the agreed directions consistent with the general principles set out in the 1996 Act. A tribunal which, at the outset, exerts its authority to manage the process, is more likely to achieve this.[2]

In more complex cases in particular, an early procedural hearing is recommended. Directions can thus be made following such a hearing. The procedural hearing can be in person or by way of video conference or telephone conference. It is a useful way for the tribunal to impose its authority on the parties, face to face in some cases, and for all issues to be discussed fully and ironed out, often more satisfactorily than by way of written communication alone. Some complex arbitrations call for more than one such hearing (see also below).

This chapter discusses the menu of most of the usual possible directions, many of which would be given by an international tribunal sitting anywhere in the world. The degree of detail in which the directions are given varies from tribunal to tribunal and arbitration to arbitration.[3] Some international arbitrators have their own particular style. Similarly, some of the directions will not be appropriate in a particular case. Attention is also drawn to the various arbitral rules which may circumscribe what can be done, although most leave the matter to the tribunal, subject to the agreement of the parties. Tribunals take account of costs and delay including issues of relevance and proportionality when making directions.[4]

1. Article 18(4) of the ICC Rules.
2. See section 34(1) of the 1996 Act.
3. See also the UNCITRAL Notes on Organizing Arbitral Proceedings.
4. See the recent Report of the ICC Commission on Arbitration "Techniques for Controlling Time and Costs in Arbitration", where it was stated that 82% of the costs of an institution-managed arbitration was represented by lawyers' fees.

The tribunal and the parties will also want to consider the extent to which, if at all, the IBA Rules of Evidence or the CIArb Protocol should be incorporated in relation to all or any of the following: disclosure; party-appointed experts; tribunal-appointed experts; on-site inspections; the taking of samples and analyses; evidentiary hearings; admissibility; and assessment of evidence.

The time when a tribunal gives directions varies. Some tribunals prefer to wait until after the first round of written statements has been exchanged so that such directions can be made in the light of all the issues: others prefer to make directions at an earlier stage. If the arbitration is under the ICC Rules then a provisional timetable will follow the Terms of Reference. Some of these directions may be revisited and updated, or deferred altogether, until nearer the main hearing (see chapter 12). If the proceedings are bifurcated or otherwise split into separate hearings, for example on jurisdiction or for the purpose of determining preliminary issues, the timing, frequency and nature of the directions will need to be adjusted to ensure that the tribunal manages the overall process and that costs are not wasted.

The following topics are discussed in this chapter:

- further written statements or submissions;
- disclosure issues between the parties;
- disclosure from third parties;
- expert evidence;
- witnesses of fact;
- other common directions;
  - fixing hearing dates;
  - communications between the parties and between the parties and the tribunal;
  - inter-lawyer correspondence;
  - further procedural hearings;
  - oral hearings;
  - the venue for the hearing;
  - documentation for the hearing;
  - pre-hearing written material;
  - directions for the main hearing;
  - post-hearing briefs and closing submissions;
  - a timetable; and
- ensuring compliance.

FURTHER WRITTEN STATEMENTS OR SUBMISSIONS

Unless the case is relatively straightforward the parties often expand upon their initial pleadings by way of further written statements, variously described as pleadings, written statements, submissions, briefs or memorials. Some sets of arbitral rules provide a default timescale which can be extended, others leave it entirely to the tribunal and the parties. These written statements should contain all issues of fact and law and have attached to them all the documents on which the party relies, but it is open to tribunals to limit their length, if appropriate. They need not be in the form of a court pleading.

DISCLOSURE ISSUES BETWEEN THE PARTIES

Disclosure of documents is probably the most contentious issue in the early stages of any arbitration with varying demands, from US-style full blown discovery to civil law narrow disclosure. It is a matter exclusively for the arbitral tribunal and not the courts.[5] Nor will the English courts order disclosure in aid of an international arbitration.[6] Tricky issues can still arise given the increasing scope for disclosure with e-mail, Blackberries, PIN messaging, SKYPE records and SMS text messaging. Electronic disclosure can be disproportionately expensive.

There is now a consensus in international arbitration that disclosure[7] has to be limited. The IBA Rules of Evidence[8] have proved a useful blueprint for the ambit of disclosure and these rules are frequently used and adjusted to meet the particular arbitration. They are only guidelines and are not mandatory. On other occasions the parties or arbitrators fashion their own directions, but wholesale discovery or disclosure will not be permitted in international arbitration.

The IBA Rules of Evidence provide a mid-way solution with disclosure in waves. Initially a party has to produce "*all documents available to it on which it relies*". Often a number of these documents will already have been appended to the written statements. A party may then submit a request to produce within a specific time ordered by the tribunal. The receiving party can then comply or object, whether on legal professional privilege grounds, relevance or otherwise. A party may also want to redact parts of a document in order to protect trade secrets or commercially sensitive material.[9] If there is an objection to production which cannot be resolved between the parties, the matter is resolved by the tribunal.

As a practical way of dealing with such objections, a schedule will frequently be ordered with the parties listing the documents required in one column, the reasons therefore and references to any relevant paragraph in the written statements in the second column, those documents to which no objection is made in the third column, the reasons for the objection of the remaining

5. Section 34(2)(d) of the 1996 Act.
6. *BNP Paribas & ors* v *Deloitte & Touche LLP* [2003] EWHC 2874 (Comm).
7. In national courts sometimes known as discovery.
8. Articles 3 and 9 and see Appendix F.
9. See e.g. Article 20(7) of the ICC Rules.

documents in the fourth column, and a fifth column left blank for the tribunal's comments.[10]

Parties should also address such issues as authenticity, as copies of documents will be presumed to be authentic unless challenged.

DISCLOSURE FROM THIRD PARTIES

Disclosure from third parties cannot be ordered by a tribunal, because an arbitral tribunal has no jurisdiction over third parties. A tribunal is limited to encouraging or urging a third party to assist voluntarily. An application therefore has to be made to the English court, which will permit a targeted request to a witness to produce specific documents, provided these are identified with sufficient certainty.[11] This is not the same as the court ordering disclosure. The procedure is by way of a witness summons to a United Kingdom witness to bring the documents to the tribunal. If the documents are too widely drawn the application will be refused because it will be regarded as tantamount to disclosure. Moreover, because a failure to comply carries with it a potential penal sanction for contempt, in contrast to non-compliance with disclosure obligations, the court will carefully scrutinise any such request. The application is made under section 43 of the 1996 Act and requires the permission of the tribunal or the agreement of the other parties.[12]

In rare cases section 44 of the 1996 Act, which is the section dealing with interim measures, may be used to obtain documents from third parties, provided the requirements of the section are complied with.[13] The court will order production of such documents in order to preserve the evidence and, in exceptional cases, will do so even before the commencement of the arbitration, but not as part of a disclosure order.[14] Section 44 can be excluded by agreement of the parties in writing, whereas section 43 is a mandatory provision.

The court may also have an inherent jurisdiction to order third parties who have become involved in or "mixed up" in wrongdoing to provide information and documents, particularly where no arbitrator has been appointed, no arbitration proceedings commenced and there is evidence of fraud.[15]

10. This has come to be known as a Redfern schedule after the leading international arbitrator Alan Redfern who first started using such schedules.

11. See e.g. *BNP Paribas, supra*; *Tajik Aluminium Plant* v *Hydro Aluminium and another* [2005] EWCA Civ 1218.

12. Part 34 CPR.

13. *Assimina Maritime Ltd* v *Pakistan Shipping Corporation and HR Wallingford Limited* [2004] EWHC 3005 (Comm).

14. *Cetelem SA* v *Roust Holdings* [2005] EWCA Civ 618.

15. *Glidepath Holding BV & ors* v *Thompson & ors* [2004] EWHC 2234 (Q.B.), but *quaere* the impact of subsequent case law such as *Starlight Shipping Co. & anor* v *Tai Ping Insurance Co. Ltd, Hubei Branch and ors* [2007] EWHC 1893 (Comm).

EXPERT EVIDENCE

Expert evidence is another "hot" topic in international arbitration. Like disclosure, it is viewed as one of the main contributors to delay and extra cost if not properly managed. Expert evidence is relevant both to issues of liability, for instance, in relation to a particular technology or industry or foreign law, and in relation to damages, but the considerations may be different. In order to rationalise the expert evidence a tribunal needs to have some understanding of the issues which such experts will address. Where the quantum is bifurcated, parties may nonetheless need to engage their accountancy experts early on, albeit not in the depth that might be necessary for the full quantum hearing. This is because expert evidence on damages is only as good as the facts on which the expert opinion is based. These facts, which may be contentious, have to be established from the evidence. This task may have to be accomplished at the liability stage of the arbitration to avoid witnesses returning at a later stage. It will vary from case to case.

The parties or tribunal may want to adopt in part or in whole the relatively new "Protocol for the Use of Party-Appointed Expert Witnesses in International Arbitration" produced by the Chartered Institute of Arbitrators (the "CIArb Protocol") or the IBA Rules of Evidence, each of which deals specifically with some of the points set out below. Both are guidelines only.

Any directions of the tribunal are, of course, subject to the agreement of the parties, who are well advised to consider such directions even if they cannot agree upon them. The following are some of the considerations relating to directions concerning expert of evidence which a tribunal is likely to take into account when making directions[16]:

i. Where the arbitration is bifurcated, the determination of what precisely is to be deferred. For example, should some of the factual evidence be heard and/or resolved at the liability hearing to save costs, thus deferring only the expert evidence relating to calculation or should everything relating to damages be postponed?
ii. Defining the issues. Ensuring that the nature of the specific expertise is identified and the scope of any expert's report, or of any tests or analyses that have to be carried out, is clear. This in turn involves determining the best way to define such issues and whether or not they are relevant. For example, the recommendation in the CIArb Protocol that experts alone should define the issues at the outset may not be suitable for accountants dealing with damages issues when such issues are intermingled with factual issues. Instead, in the early stages it may be more effective for the lawyers to assist in

16. In the context of experts and other issues relating to damages see: "Assessing Damages in International Arbitration", Hilary Heilbron Q.C. in the second edition of "The Leading Arbitrators' Guide to International Arbitration" from which the above list is quoted with some adjustments.

defining the issues on which expert evidence is needed. The tribunal may also wish to indicate to the parties and the experts which areas it considers expert evidence is relevant and those areas where it is not.

iii. General timing issues. Matters for consideration will include: should reports be exchanged early even though a hearing is bifurcated; should reports follow the exchange of witness statements; should experts' reports be exchanged contemporaneously or served sequentially; and should there be reply reports?

iv. Questions relating to the number of experts. These will include considering whether the parties are relying unnecessarily on too many experts and whether so many experts can be justified, or the reverse situation, whether all the technical issues which require expert evidence have been covered.

v. Tribunal experts. Consideration of whether the tribunal should appoint its own expert or experts instead of or in addition to the parties' experts.[17]

vi. The presentation of the written evidence. Many major accounting and consulting firms now have specialist forensic departments which are used to present material in a user-friendly way. Nonetheless, consideration should be given to the need for schedules, graphs, slides, glossaries and the like, where appropriate, to assist tribunals. Sometimes there may be force in trying to get the parties to address the issues under the same headings and in the same order.

vii. Meetings of experts. Even where it may not be appropriate for the experts to meet at the outset for the purpose of defining the issues, nonetheless the tribunal will usually direct the experts to meet as the process evolves to try to narrow and refine what remains at issue. There are differing views as to whether it is beneficial for the experts to meet early or whether such meeting should be deferred until after the exchange of their reports. It may well depend on the nature of expertise involved and the facts of the case.

viii. Presentation of the oral evidence. Should the experts give evidence in the traditional way, with each side's counsel asking questions by way of cross-examination, or would witness conferencing, where the tribunal is the principal interrogator and both sides' experts are questioned simultaneously, or a variant thereof, be more appropriate?[18] Alternatively, should the tribunal in advance of the hearing give the experts a list of questions to which to respond?

17. See e.g. Article 21 of the LCIA Rules, Article 20(4) of the ICC Rules and section 37 of the 1996 Act.

18. "Witness Conferencing", by Wolfgang Peter, *LCIA Arbitration International*, Volume 18 Number 1, 2002.

ix. Ensuring a level playing field between experts in relation to the duties they owe concerning the presentation of their evidence and the extent of disclosure as to their instructions etc.[19]

x. Translations. Considering whether these are needed in relation to the expert's evidence or supporting documents, for example, in the case of foreign law.

WITNESSES OF FACT

Directions relating to factual witnesses tend to be more straightforward. The principal considerations are the identification of the witnesses who will give evidence, the timing for service of any witness statements which will usually follow the completion of disclosure, and whether these should be exchanged or sequential. It is a frequent misconception that the more witnesses who are available to support a case, the better.[20] On the other hand, omitting an obvious witness can lead to comment from one's opponent as to his or her absence and possible consequent adverse inferences from the tribunal. Choosing the right witnesses to support a case is very important. If the witness cannot speak the language of the arbitration then translations of the witness statements, certified if required, will need to be provided. Directions may also be given at an early stage that the witness statements should stand as direct evidence. Parties are asked to indicate within a certain time period before the hearing which witnesses they wish to cross-examine. Tribunals will also want to ensure that before any hearing the references to any documents in the witness statements are to the pages in the hearing bundles and not some earlier pagination.

OTHER COMMON DIRECTIONS

Depending on the arbitration, the tribunal will give directions only up to a certain point in time, such as after exchange of experts' reports, or up to and including the main hearing, possibly making the later directions provisional only. The rules of the various arbitral institutions or the UNCITRAL Rules give the tribunal wide powers to conduct the arbitration, but these rules should be consulted as they do vary as to precisely what is allowed. The following is a list of some of the other directions that may need consideration by both the parties and the tribunal either at the outset and/or at a later procedural hearing (see also chapter 12 where some of these issues are re-visited).

19. See e.g. Articles 4, 5, 7.4 and 8 of the CIArb Protocol.

20. The tendency to produce too many witnesses to prove the same facts or issues should be avoided: they add an extra layer of risk of internal contradiction, lengthen the proceedings and increase the costs. Tribunals may question the necessity of duplication.

i. Fixing hearing dates

One of the constraints to a speedy arbitration is securing the time of the tribunal, particularly if it is a panel of three busy arbitrators from different jurisdictions. Some arbitrators, therefore, like to secure a provisional time in their diaries for the main hearing as early as possible. This focuses the parties' attention on an ultimate deadline, provides a framework for the timetable, and ensures the availability of the tribunal. It is also a good idea to make provision in the timetable to allow for slippage along the way and for time for the tribunal's deliberations on the award following the hearing. Provisional dates for further procedural hearings should similarly be set at this stage.

ii. Communications between the parties and between the parties and tribunal

E-mail, although convenient, is not always appropriate without some other form of additional communication such as fax, courier or post, as there is no means of knowing if an e-mail has been received or not. Exclusive e-mail exchange can therefore be problematic, particularly where one party does not participate in the arbitral process or is behaving in a recalcitrant manner. In some countries, electronic systems break down and thus post and/or the use of a courier is essential as a back-up to enable the tribunal to know that a party has received all relevant communications. Other ways of dealing with the problem where the parties are participating willingly is to request notification of receipt of an e-mail. Sending bulky documents by e-mail or fax is not satisfactory either. There are many permutations, but the issue of communication has to be resolved at the outset.

Most arbitral institutions require to be copied on all exchanges with the tribunal.

iii. Inter-lawyer correspondence

Tribunals can be bombarded with wholesale correspondence between lawyers, often increasingly acrimonious, only copied to them in the mistaken belief that it will impress the tribunal. It is little understood that this usually has the reverse effect. While it is appreciated this tends to be done to explain to the client that the tribunal has been informed of what is happening, at the end of the day such correspondence increases costs, is largely irrelevant to what the tribunal has to determine, and often irritates the tribunal. Such correspondence is only relevant if an issue flowing from it has to be resolved by the tribunal, for example, as to disclosure or costs or delay. Often the respective contentions can be better explained by way of a schedule or written submissions, if necessary by reference to some letters to show dates and the like. Tribunals, therefore, sometimes order the parties only to copy inter-lawyer correspondence to the tribunal when specific intervention is sought from the tribunal, such as an order or direction, or where it is necessary to inform the tribunal of an agreed change to the procedure or timetable.

iv. Further procedural hearings

Tribunals frequently order a procedural hearing a few weeks before the main hearing to ensure that everyone is ready and that all issues have been dealt with. This can always be dispensed with at a later date if it becomes unnecessary. Additional interim hearings may be necessary. These may be either planned in advance or may arise during the course of the arbitration, such as a hearing to resolve emerging disclosure issues or as a result of a separate hearing of preliminary issues. Agendas and skeleton or outline written submissions before such procedural hearings are frequently ordered. All procedural hearings are held in private unless otherwise agreed by the parties and/or the tribunal.

v. Oral hearings

Consideration needs to be given to the need for an oral hearing as opposed to a determination based on written submissions and documents alone. Sometimes the issues are relatively straightforward or require no oral evidence, in which case the parties may agree that an oral hearing is unnecessary or the tribunal may suggest such a course, but a party has a right to request an oral hearing.[21]

vi. The venue for the hearing

Even if the seat is London, the parties and the tribunal may agree to hear the proceedings elsewhere, for example in Paris. However, the mere fact that an arbitration, whose seat is outside the jurisdiction, is heard for convenience in London will not invoke the provisions of the 1996 Act and only those limited provisions relating to foreign arbitrations will apply.[22]

vii. Documentation for the hearing

Many arbitrators now prefer the majority of the documents to be provided electronically and, where appropriate, with software for storage and retrieval. If counsel or the witnesses are to use electronic documentation, then facilities will need to be provided at the hearing. Other arbitrators request documents to be copied on to both sides of A5 paper rather than A4 paper to reduce bulk, not least because many foreign arbitrators may have to travel abroad with the documents. Some arbitrators, experienced at the frustration incorrectly produced documentation can cause, may even specify the types of binders, pagination, distribution of the documentation, etc. It is a rare arbitration when far too many documents are not provided. Most arbitrations turn on a limited number of documents. Core bundles are useful, but inevitably are seldom comprehensive. Inter-lawyer correspondence rarely turns out to be relevant save on discrete issues.

21. See e.g. Article 19.1 of the LCIA Rules and Article 20.6 of the ICC Rules.
22. See chapter 3 pages 21–23 and chapter 11 pages 88–89.

viii. Pre-hearing written material

A list of live issues in dispute, agreed if possible, is frequently required in advance of the hearing and sometimes at significant stages of the process. This is always helpful, as by the time of the hearing some of the issues have fallen by the wayside and others have taken on more importance than previously thought. The practice of tribunals varies as to whether or not additional skeleton or outline written arguments or more detailed written submissions or pre-hearing briefs should be ordered in addition to the parties' earlier written statements or briefs to cater for the developments since the arbitration started. Directions will also need to be given as to whether these are to be exchanged or sequential.

Another consideration may be which party is to open the case. The party with the burden of proving the main allegations is usually the party which begins and opens the case. For example, a claim for money due may be met by a detailed counterclaim alleging defective work around which the issues of the hearing will revolve. In such cases the respondent may have the real burden of the hearing. A list of persons involved in the dispute, a reading list and a chronology are also useful directions to make.

ix. Directions for the main hearing

The following are some of the directions concerning the main hearing which may be made early on in the process or left until later:

a. An estimate of time for the hearing. Tribunals may query long estimates in order to save costs. The tribunal's availability may also require the hearing to span a shorter period, possibly with longer hours or weekend hearings.
b. The need to reserve a hearing room and break-out rooms and facilities for lunch and coffees and teas.[23]
c. The need for interpreters, which party should in the first instance pay for them, and whether interpretation should be simultaneous, which is costly, or not. The latter can slow down the hearing.
d. The need for a daily transcript and how and by whom this is to be paid for.
e. Other orders relating to the evidence of witnesses in addition to those referred to above, for example, that each party shall have the responsibility of ensuring the attendance of those witnesses on whose evidence it relies and for their costs of their attendance at the hearing, subject to any later costs order.
f. Time allocation. Some arbitrators will distribute the available time for the hearing equally leaving the parties to work out how they wish to

23. There are a variety of meeting rooms available for arbitral hearings, such as the ICDR and the Chartered Institute of Arbitrators. In addition some barristers' chambers and solicitors' offices provide meeting rooms for arbitrations.

use the time[24]: others will segment the hearing using specific time periods. This does not always work out fairly as it often happens that one party has a greater burden than the other. Arbitrators devise different approaches to ensure that all parties have a fair hearing.

g. Opening statements. If detailed written statements, memorials or briefs have been provided, oral opening statements can be relatively brief and often are.
h. The language of the hearing.
i. Whether to apply strict rules of evidence (or any other rules) as to the admissibility, relevance or weight of any oral or written material.
j. Whether, and the extent to which, the tribunal should take the initiative in ascertaining the facts and the law and asking for evidence to be provided, a matter which the various arbitral rules often specifically empower them to do.[25]

x. Post-hearing briefs and closing submissions

Sometimes it is necessary to resolve the issue of post-hearing submissions early on so that the parties and the tribunal can make the necessary time available. On other occasions this is left until the hearing itself. There is no uniform practice as to closing submissions, whether oral or in writing or both. The various options are referred to in chapter 13 page 104.

xi. A timetable

Keeping track of compliance with deadlines is not always easy for busy lawyers and arbitrators. It is therefore the author's practice to set out at the end of any procedural order a table with three columns: the first with the date for compliance; the second showing any revised date for compliance; and the third describing the nature of the order, such as service of the claimant's witness statement. Sometimes a fourth column with a reference to the paragraph in the relevant procedural order can also be useful. Thus, the parties can see at a glance what has to be done and by when.

ENSURING COMPLIANCE

While many parties respect the tribunal's authority and abide by its directions or seek extensions of time for compliance,[26] there has to be some sanction for those that do not. The issue of default is discussed in more detail in chapter 12 pages 92–93—peremptory orders. The tribunal has the power to issue peremptory orders, non-compliance with which entitles the tribunal to make various consequential orders. The court can also, in certain circumstances,

24. This is sometimes referred to as the "chest clock" approach.
25. See e.g. Article 22.1(c) of the LCIA Rules.
26. See e.g. Articles 4.7 and 22.1(b) of the LCIA Rules and 32 of the ICC Rules and section 79 of the 1996 Act.

issue appropriate sanctions following a peremptory order made by the tribunal.[27] Both these provisions can be excluded by agreement. However, where parties are proceeding with the arbitration, a tribunal can often ensure compliance using the ordinary tools available to it. For example, under the LCIA Rules there is a provision which enables the arbitral tribunal "*in advance of any hearing [to] submit to the parties a list of questions which it wishes them to answer with special attention*".[28] This can be used to elucidate or clarify reasons for non-compliance.

27. Section 42 of the 1996 Act.
28. Article 19.3 of the LCIA Rules.

CHAPTER 11

APPLICATIONS TO THE COURT PRIOR TO THE HEARING

INTRODUCTION

A tribunal's powers, although broad, are nonetheless limited. For instance, a tribunal cannot direct an order against a third party or grant injunctions.[1] Moreover, sometimes parties need relief before the tribunal is constituted. The court, therefore, has a role in protecting the process and ensuring that it is not rendered otiose for want of some form of interim relief. This chapter, therefore, considers the court's role in the early stages of an arbitration. Other areas of court intervention are dealt with elsewhere in this book. The following topics are addressed:

- procedure;
- injunctions, including freezing orders, relating to London arbitration;
- other provisional measures;
- section 44(6) of the 1996 Act;
- preliminary points of law;
- anti-suit injunctions to restrain foreign proceedings and anti-arbitration injunctions; and
- aiding foreign arbitrations.

PROCEDURE

The procedure in relation to arbitration claims is governed by Part 62 of the Civil Procedure Rules (the "CPR") together with the Part 62 Practice Direction as supplemented by such other Parts of the CPR and their respective Practice Directions as may be relevant in the particular circumstances. Most such rules have both Parts and Practice Directions, both of which should be consulted, and many have pre-action protocols and standard forms which also have to be used where applicable. The summary below can only be brief. Potential litigants are, therefore, advised to look carefully at the relevant Parts of the CPR and the corresponding Practice Directions together with the

1. Section 39 of the 1996 Act entitles the tribunal to grant certain forms of relief on a provisional basis, but only if the parties confer such a power on the tribunal. Provisional awards are considered further in chapter 12 page 94.

Admiralty and Commercial Courts Guide,[2] in particular sections F and O, or, as appropriate, the Guide to the Technology and Construction Court Guide, to ensure compliance. These set out comprehensive procedures and include details of the contents of and documents to be appended to any court applications. Non-compliance with the rules can cause delay or have costs implications or even lead to the application being dismissed. Part 62 together with its accompanying Practice Direction is set out in Appendices C.1 and C.2 and Parts F and O of the Admiralty and Commercial Courts Guide at Appendix D.

CPR Part 62 extends not only to any application to the court under the 1996 Act, but also to other related claims concerning arbitration as specified in CPR Part 62.2(1). It is a wide and all-embracing definition. All applications relating to arbitration claims as defined in CPR Part 62.2(1) (an "*arbitration claim*") are started by the issue of an arbitration claim form which has to contain certain information.[3] The application has to be served on the other parties to the arbitration within one month (unless extended) from the date of issue in accordance with Part 6 of the CPR, unless an order for alternative service is obtained. In some circumstances it must also be served on the arbitrator(s).[4]

As is usually the case in international arbitration held in London, the party to whom an interim order is directed—or for that matter any arbitration claim—will usually be domiciled out of the jurisdiction. There is a procedure under CPR Part 62.5 for serving an arbitration claim form out of the jurisdiction on parties to the arbitration.[5] This allows for service out of the jurisdiction where the claim is for an order under section 44 of the 1996 Act (the court's powers in support of arbitral proceedings),[6] or where the claimant seeks some other remedy or requires a question to be decided by the court affecting an arbitration, an arbitration agreement or an arbitration award, provided that the seat of the arbitration is within the jurisdiction. As arbitration is excluded from the EC Regulation,[7] permission needs to be obtained for an arbitration claim to be served out of the jurisdiction even if the defendant to the application is domiciled in a Member State of the European Union. If a party is represented by English solicitors or foreign lawyers within the jurisdiction they may have been instructed to accept service on their client's behalf which will avoid the need to obtain such permission. The normal period within which a

2. The CPR including the court guides is available at: http://www.justice.gov.uk/civil/procrules_fin/index.htm.
3. CPR Part 62.3–4.
4. CPR Part 62.4(2) and 62.6.
5. This procedure does not extend to someone who is not a party to an arbitration agreement, even if the question raised relates to an arbitration or an arbitration agreement. See: *Vale do Rio Doce Navagavao S.A. & Ors* v *Shanghai BAO Steel Co. Ltd* [2000] 2 Lloyd's Rep. 1 and *Starlight Shipping Co. & anor* v *Tai Ping Insurance Co., Hubei Branch & anor* [2007] EWHC 1893 (Comm).
6. CPR Part 62.5(1)b.
7. Council Regulation (EC) No. 44/2001.

respondent has to serve an acknowledgement of service is 14 days, although this will be longer where there has been permission to serve the application out of the jurisdiction.[8]

The court has power to order that an arbitration claim be heard in public or in private, although most of the early applications dealt with in this chapter are likely to be heard in private.[9] No oral evidence, expert evidence or cross-examination is allowed on any such application without the permission of the court. Any evidence of the parties must be filed respectively with the arbitration claim form or the acknowledgement of service. Skeleton arguments need to be provided to the court by counsel for the parties in advance of any hearing. High Court arbitration claims are heard either in the Commercial Court or, if it is a construction or similar matter, in the Technology and Construction Court. Appeals to the Court of Appeal, if allowed by the 1996 Act, are rare and are only with the permission of the original court. It is worth noting that the 1996 Act refers to the "*leave*" of the court, whereas the CPR refers to "*permission*". The latter has become the accepted terminology in court, but in this book the word "*leave*" is used in the context of the 1996 Act.

A few arbitration-related applications attract different procedures. Special rules, for instance, apply in relation to applications to enforce awards which are discussed in chapter 16 pages 123–126. Where the application is to stay legal proceedings, the application will instead be made on notice in those proceedings.[10] This may not necessarily be in the Commercial Court. In the case of an application for an anti-suit or other injunction under section 37 of the Supreme Court Act 1982 relating to proceedings where the seat of the arbitration is outside the jurisdiction, permission to serve any claim form and application notice out of the jurisdiction will need to be obtained (unless service is accepted or the party is otherwise within the jurisdiction) pursuant to one of the gateways in CPR Part 6.20(5), for example, where "*a claim is made in respect of a contract*" which is governed by English law.[11]

These applications will normally be made by English counsel or, depending on the complexity, by Leading Counsel. Solicitor-advocates, i.e. those with higher rights of audience, also appear in the High Court on such applications. An English solicitor needs to be on the court record in order to conduct litigation and to instruct a barrister to appear in an English court (which is not the case for appearance in an arbitration). In order to ensure a seamless transition, foreign lawyers with no London base who wish to remain involved in the arbitration, can make whatever arrangements they want with an English solicitor to deal with their respective input in relation to any such application to the courts (see chapter 1 pages 2–3).

8. CPR Parts 62.5(4) and 8.2–8.3.
9. CPR Part 62.10.
10. CPR Part 62.8.
11. See e.g. *Nigel Peter Albon* v *Naza Motor Trading SDN BHD & ors* [2007] EWHC 1879.

INJUNCTIONS, INCLUDING FREEZING ORDERS, RELATING TO LONDON ARBITRATION

Tribunals have no power to order injunctions. A tribunal has defined powers in relation to the preservation of evidence and similar protective measures under section 38 of the 1996 Act (see chapter 8 pages 59–60). Parties can also confer on a tribunal the power to give certain relief on a provisional basis and to make such other orders as the tribunal deems appropriate.[12] Arbitral rules frequently confer such powers (see chapter 12 page 94 in relation to provisional awards). Thus, although a tribunal can order parties to do or not to do things, its powers are constrained. Its sanctions are limited to those set out in section 41(7) of the 1996 Act, namely: depriving a party from relying on an allegation or evidence; drawing adverse inferences; proceeding to an award in the absence of further materials; or making costs orders. It can make a peremptory order under section 41(5) of the 1996 Act which in turn can be enforced by the court under section 42 of the 1996 Act, but this is a lengthy process and does not always meet the urgency of the case (see chapter 12 pages 92–93—peremptory orders). Moreover, tribunals cannot make orders against third parties.

The court has power under section 44(1) and 44(2)(e) of the 1996 Act to grant an interim injunction "*for the purposes of and in relation to arbitral proceedings*". However, the court's powers to intervene by injunction before an award is made by arbitrators are very limited. In particular:

i. the powers are subject to any agreement of the parties to the contrary;
ii. the court will only act on the application of a party on notice to the other party and with the permission of the tribunal or by agreement of the parties; and
iii. the court will only act if the tribunal does not have the power or is unable to act for the time being effectively.

The court also has power to grant injunctions (both interlocutory and final) under section 37(1) of the Supreme Court Act 1981 "*in all cases in which it appears to the court to be just and convenient to do so*". However, where the seat of the arbitration is London, it is unlikely to be used in a way which would undermine the principles of the 1996 Act and the limited role of the courts in relation to injunctions in matters concerning arbitration.[13]

Applications for injunctions can also be made to the court in cases of urgency before the tribunal is constituted "*for the purpose of preserving evidence*

12. Section 38(1) and section 39 of the 1996 Act.
13. See in the context of anti-suit injunctions: *Elektrim S.A.* v *Vivendi Universal and ors* [2007] EWHC 571 (Comm) and *Starlight Shipping Co. & anor* v *Tai Ping Insurance Co. Ltd, Hubei Branch & anor* [2007] EWHC 1893 (Comm).

or assets". Injunctions are discretionary remedies.[14] The most common such application is for a freezing injunction (previously known as a Mareva injunction after one of the parties in which it was first granted) to prevent an intended respondent from dissipating its assets and removing them from the jurisdiction with the purpose of defeating the enforcement of an award. The court has jurisdiction to order a worldwide freezing order in an appropriate case.[15] The court can also make mandatory orders.[16]

In order to obtain a freezing order the applicant has to show that it has a good arguable case on the merits and that there is a real risk of dissipation of assets. The order will apply only to assets of a value equal to a specified sum of money. Freezing injunctions are frequently accompanied by disclosure orders relating to the presence of assets. Permission of the court is needed to enforce a worldwide freezing order in any country outside its jurisdiction. Guidelines have recently been laid down as to when a court will give such permission in the case of a worldwide freezing order and the procedure for making such an application.[17]

In applying for an injunction the various rules and practice directions have to be carefully followed.[18] Applications can, if the circumstances require, be made without notice to the other party. The applicant has to make full and frank disclosure and be in a position to give a cross-undertaking as to damages, which can, if necessary, be by way of bank guarantee. Wherever possible it is better to make any application for an injunction on notice. Applications, made on the appropriate form, should be accompanied by an affidavit, a draft order, a skeleton argument and a copy of the claim, save in cases of extreme urgency. To enable subsequent committal proceedings to be made for contempt, any order should be stamped on the front with a penal notice or notices as applicable. In all applications for an injunction, the court will consider first whether or not damages are an adequate remedy and only then balance the competing arguments, the balance of convenience, as to whether it will grant an injunction.[19]

OTHER PROVISIONAL MEASURES

Section 44 of the 1996 Act also enables the court to make other provisional orders in support of the arbitral process, such intervention being limited in the

14. An injunction cannot be granted against a state unless there is specific written consent. Nor can a penalty by way of committal or fine be exacted against a state in respect of failure or refusal to disclose or produce any document or other information for the purpose of proceedings to which it is a party: section 13(1)–(3) of the State Immunity Act 1978.

15. See: *Babanaft International Co. S.A.* v *Bassatne* [1990] Ch. 13; *Derby & Co. Ltd* v *Weldon* [1990] Ch. 65.

16. *Cetelem S.A.* v *Roust Holdings Ltd* [2005] EWCA Civ 618.

17. *Dadourian Group Int. Inc.* v *Simms & ors* [2006] EWCA Civ 399.

18. See in particular Parts 62, 23 and 25 of the CPR as applicable and the accompanying Practice Directions and the Commercial Courts Guide.

19. *American Cyanamide Co.* v *Ethicon Ltd* [1975] A.C. 396.

same way as in relation to injunctions (see above). The court can make orders relating to:

> "*(a) the taking of evidence of witnesses;*
> *(b) the preservation of evidence;*
> *(c) making orders relating to property which is the subject of the proceedings or as to which any question arises in the proceedings:*
> *i. for the inspection, photographing, preservation, custody or detention of the property, or*
> *ii. ordering that samples be taken from, or any observation be made of or experiment conducted upon, the property; and for that purpose authorising any person to enter any premises in the possession or control of a party to the arbitration;*
> *(d) the sale of any goods the subject of the proceedings.*"

Thus, for example, the powers have been used to obtain documents, provided the requirements of the section are complied with,[20] and even, in exceptional cases, before the commencement of the arbitration, but not as part of a disclosure order.[21]

SECTION 44(6) OF THE 1996 ACT

Section 44(6) of the 1996 Act enables the court to provide that any order it makes shall cease to have effect in whole or in part on the order of the tribunal, or of any such arbitral or other institution or person having power to act in relation to the subject-matter of the order. This can be a very useful provision.

PRELIMINARY POINTS OF LAW

The court has a limited power to determine points of law substantially affecting one or more of the parties early in the proceedings.[22] The power does not extend to issues of foreign law which are not questions of law for this purpose. This provision can be excluded by agreement of the parties. Either all the parties to the arbitration can apply to the court or an application can be made by one party with the permission of the tribunal. In the latter case the court has to be satisfied that the determination of the question is likely to produce substantial savings in costs and that the application is made promptly. It is a discretionary remedy.[23] Unless otherwise agreed this will not prevent the arbitral proceedings continuing. No appeal lies from the determination of

20. *Assimina Maritime Ltd* v *Pakistan Shipping Corporation and HR Wallingford Limited* [2004] EWHC 3005 (Comm).
21. *Cetelem S.A.* v *Roust Holdings* [2005] EWCA Civ 618.
22. Sections 45 and 82(1) of the 1996 Act.
23. *(1) Taylor Woodrow Holdings Ltd (2) George Wimpey Southern Counties Ltd* v *Barnes & Elliott Ltd* [2006] EWHC 1693 (TCC).

whether or not the pre-conditions are satisfied, but an appeal does lie to the Court of Appeal with leave on the question of law, provided that the court considers that the question is one of general importance or is one which for some other special reason should be considered by the Court of Appeal.

ANTI-SUIT INJUNCTIONS TO RESTRAIN FOREIGN PROCEEDINGS AND ANTI-ARBITRATION INJUNCTIONS

Parties frequently seek to circumvent the arbitral process where the seat of the arbitration is London by commencing proceedings or threatening to commence proceedings in a foreign jurisdiction. The English courts will readily grant an anti-suit injunction, whether or not an arbitration has been commenced, to a party who, in breach of contract, seeks to bring a claim in the courts in breach of an English arbitration clause.[24] If a party commences an action in England in breach of an arbitration clause then, of course, an application to stay those proceedings can be brought (see chapter 6 pages 44–45).

The English court's powers to grant anti-suit injunctions in support of an English arbitration derive from the same legislative provisions as in relation to other injunctions (see above),[25] although the use of permanent injunctions in this context is rare. There is jurisdiction to obtain an anti-suit injunction to protect a party's right to arbitrate under section 44(4) in the case of urgency, at least until such time as the tribunal can itself make a final award, if the conditions of section 44 are complied with, although such applications are more frequently made under section 37(1) of the Supreme Court Act 1981.[26]

The 1996 Act defines parties as including "*any person claiming under or through a party to the agreement*".[27] Thus, parties, including insurers and assignees, or those who have novated the contract, are also bound by the arbitration clause and are liable to be prevented from bringing a claim in the courts in breach of the arbitration clause.[28] While English courts will in their discretion usually grant such injunctions, the current legal position in England

24. *The Angelic Grace* [1995] 1 Lloyd's Rep. 87.

25. *West Tankers Inc. (respondents)* v *RAS Riunione Adriatica di Sicurta SpA and ors (appellants)* [2007] UKHL 4. See also chapter 1 page 5 and chapter 2 page 11.

26. *Elektrim S.A.* v *Vivendi Universal and ors* [2007] EWHC 571 (Comm) and *Starlight Shipping Co. & anor* v *Tai Ping Insurance Co. Ltd, Hubei Branch & anor* [2007] EWHC 1893 (Comm).

27. Section 82(2) of the 1996 Act. Costs will be awarded on an indemnity basis: *A* v *B* [2007] EWHC 54 (Comm), but see also *C* v *D* [2007] EWCA Civ 1282.

28. See the recent trilogy of cases where the jurisprudential reasoning differed: *Through Transport Mutual Insurance Association (Eurasia) Limited* v *New India Assurance Association Company Limited* [2004] EWCA (Civ) 1598; *Schiffahrtsgesellschaft Detlev Von Appen GmbH* v *Voest Alpine Intertrading GmbH* v *Wiener Allianz Versicherung A.G. and Voest Alpine Intertrading GmbH (The Jay Bola)* [1997] 2 Lloyd's Rep. 279; and *West Tankers Inc.* v. *(1) Ras Riunione Adriatica Di Sicurta SpA (2) Generali Assicurazione Generali SpA (The Front Comor)* [2005] EWHC 454 (Comm) (first instance) and [2007] UKHL 4 (House of Lords). See also chapter 4 pages 29–30.

in the context of Member States remains uncertain. This is because, although arbitration is excluded from the EC Regulation, recent European Case law[29] has raised the issue of whether or not the English courts can make an order to restrain a person from commencing or continuing proceedings in another Member State on the ground that such proceedings are in breach of an arbitration agreement. The House of Lords have now referred this question to the European Court.[30]

The remedy for an anti-suit injunction is a discretionary one. The court's jurisdiction to grant an anti-suit injunction may be invoked in two possible situations. First, where the action is brought in breach of contract and, secondly where the prosecution of the action is oppressive or vexatious or unconscionable. Each case will turn on its own particular facts. The court may provide a substitute remedy, for example, where an award had been given and the proceedings in the US were advanced, the court substituted a temporary injunction with a declaration as to the scope and validity of the arbitration clause.[31] An English court does not have jurisdiction to grant anti-suit injunctions against a defendant who is not a party to the arbitration clause.

Although the court has jurisdiction to grant an anti-arbitration injunction, it will be a rare case where it does. Thus, for example, the court refused an anti-arbitration injunction to prevent the continuation of an arbitration in England where the party seeking the injunction delayed too long and the court proceedings related to fraud issues.[32]

AIDING FOREIGN ARBITRATIONS

Section 43 of the 1996 Act (securing the attendance of witnesses) and section 44 of the 1996 Act (court's powers exercisable in support of arbitral proceedings) can be used even where the seat of the arbitration is, or is likely to be when designated, outside the jurisdiction of England and Wales and Northern Ireland. However, there is an additional requirement to the exercise of the discretion, namely that it is appropriate to do so.

Thus, if a party wishes to obtain evidence from a third party in support of a foreign arbitration the method is to use the discretionary power under

29. *Gasser GmbH* v *MISAT Srl (Case G116/02)* [2003] ECR I-14693 (an exclusive jurisdiction case) and *Turner* v *Grovit (Case G159/02)* [2004] ECR I-3565 (a case of proceedings commenced in bad faith), but see also *Marc Rich & Co.* v. *Societa Italiana Impianti PA (The Atlantic Emperor)* [1991] ECR I-3855.

30. *West Tankers, supra.*

31. *(1) Noble Assurance Co. (2) Shell Petroleum Inc.* v *Gerling-Kinzern General Insurance Co.* [2007] EWHC 253 (Comm).

32. *Intermet FZCO (a company incorporated in Dubai) & Ors* v *Ansol Ltd (a company incorporated in Guernsey) & Ors* [2007] EWHC 226, but see also the reasoning in *Elektrim S.A.* v *Vivendi Universal S.A. and ors* [2007] EWHC 571 (Comm). Contrast *Nigel Peter Albon* v. *Naza Motor Trading SDN BHD & ors* [2007] EWCA Civ 1124 where an injunction was granted to restrain Malaysian arbitration proceedings.

section 44. Considerations will include the specificity with which the application was made, how burdensome the request is and the similarity of the procedures to English law. It has been held that a letter of request pursuant to the Evidence (Proceedings in Other Jurisdictions) Act 1975, section 1(a) of which permits an application to be made "*in pursuance of a request issued by or on behalf of a court or tribunal*" does not extend to a private arbitral tribunal for the purpose of depositions.[33] It would seem that this would apply equally in the context of document disclosure even if the application was made by a court on behalf of such a tribunal.

If the arbitration in question does not have its seat in London, then exceptionally the English court does have jurisdiction, absent a submission to the jurisdiction, but only in relation to injunctions under section 37(1) of the Supreme Court Act 1981, if the applicant can obtain leave to serve its claim and application out of the jurisdiction pursuant to CPR Part 6.20.[34]

33. *Viking Insurance Co.* v *Edward George Rossdale and ors*, unreported, 1 August 2001. New York arbitration being conducted in New York.

34. *Nigel Peter Albon* v *Naza Motor Trading SDN BHD & ors* [2007] EWHC 1879 (Ch) and [2007] EWCA Civ 1124.

CHAPTER 12

ONGOING ISSUES AND PREPARING FOR THE HEARING

INTRODUCTION

There are a host of issues and problems which can arise as the arbitral process moves forward towards a hearing. Many of these will necessitate the intervention of the tribunal. The tribunal retains a monitoring role, but usually this is pre-empted by one or other of the parties drawing the matter to the tribunal's attention. This chapter therefore considers the following:

- common issues and problems:
  - delays,
  - inordinate and inexcusable delay by claimants,
  - non-compliance with the tribunal's orders,
  - peremptory orders,
  - amendments,
  - disclosure,
  - failure to participate;
- procedural orders and hearings;
- provisional awards;
- costs and charges;
- court applications;
- hearing preparation;
- initiatives from the tribunal;
- protection as to costs; and
- mediation.

COMMON ISSUES AND PROBLEMS

The variety of problems and issues that can arise during an arbitration is huge, but undoubtedly some occur more regularly than others.

i. Delays

One of the most frequent issues to arise is for a party or its legal advisers to seek extra time for compliance with a direction of the tribunal. It is for this reason that experienced tribunals allow a little slippage time when initially setting out a timetable, unless the matter is very urgent. In most arbitrations parties can agree such extensions, but sometimes the tribunal has to make an order. The matter tends to become contentious when repeated extensions are sought, or when one party appears to be flouting the authority of the tribunal, or relying on spurious excuses. The tribunal and the arbitral institution, if involved, must be informed of any changes to the timetable, even if agreed by the parties.

ii. Inordinate and inexcusable delay by claimants

Where it is the claimant who is at fault, and there has been inordinate and inexcusable delay in pursuing the claim, section 41(2) and (3) of the 1996 Act permits the tribunal (subject to agreement of the parties to the contrary) to dismiss a claim, provided that the delay (a) gives rise, or is likely to give rise, to a substantial risk that it is not possible to have a fair resolution of the issues in the claim or (b) has caused, or is likely to cause, serious prejudice to the respondent.

iii. Non-compliance with the tribunal's orders

If the delay or other non-compliance is unjustified or continuous then either an application is made to the tribunal or the tribunal of its own motion will try to ensure compliance. In practice the tribunal's sanctions are limited, short of issuing peremptory orders and exercising the powers under section 41(7) of the 1996 Act, or seeking the assistance of the court under section 42 (see below). Tribunals prefer to find alternative means to issuing peremptory orders in order to ensure compliance with their orders, if possible, but this is not always the case (see chapter 10 pages 79–80).

iv. Peremptory orders

Peremptory orders provide a useful way of dealing with recalcitrant parties or absent respondents. The threat of their imposition is often as effective as their actual use. If peremptory orders are imposed, it is usually after more than one opportunity has been given to comply with the tribunal's order and following the non-compliant party having been warned of the consequences of further non-compliance. Tribunals, therefore, often give an early warning that they will make such a peremptory order under section 41(5) and (7) of the 1996 Act if there is non-compliance. Upon expiry of a peremptory order the tribunal has the following powers, depending on the context. It can either:

a. direct that the party in default shall not be entitled to rely upon any allegation or material which is the subject-matter of the order;
b. draw such adverse inferences from the act of non-compliance as the circumstances justify;
c. proceed to an award on the basis of such materials as have been properly provided to it; or
d. make such order as it thinks fit as to the payment of costs of the arbitration incurred in consequence of the non-compliance.

Section 42 of the 1996 Act gives the court a residual power to enforce a peremptory order made by a tribunal where it is satisfied that the applicant has exhausted any available arbitral process in respect of non-compliance with a tribunal's order. An application for such an order has to be made either by the tribunal upon notice to the parties, or by a party to the arbitral proceedings with the permission of the tribunal and upon notice to the other parties, or by agreement. The court has to be satisfied of the failure to comply within the prescribed time or, if no time is prescribed, within a reasonable time. The procedure is not widely used by tribunals, but a court, unlike a tribunal, has a wider range of ways in which it can enforce its orders, such as by way of committal.

The powers of a tribunal in the case of a party's default can be agreed by the parties and both sections 41 and 42 of the 1996 Act can, therefore, be excluded by their agreement.

v. Amendments

As the arbitration develops parties may seek to amend their claim or defence and, in the absence of agreement between the parties, the tribunal will frequently be asked to allow amendments. If it does so the tribunal can impose conditions as to costs and otherwise as it deems appropriate.[1]

vi. Disclosure

This invariably raises problematic issues. It is rare that disclosure of documents proceeds without a hiccup. This usually necessitates the tribunal making an order, either following written submissions or at a hearing. Schedules are now routinely sought to assist the tribunal in resolving these issues (for more details see chapter 10 pages 71–72).

vii. Failure to participate

Another problem is the non-participation of one of the parties. Tribunals anxious to ensure that their award cannot be challenged will probably give more leeway to such a party to enable it to participate than would be the case if the party was present, particularly if it is not legally represented, and this can cause delay.[2] (For more details see chapter 8 page 56.)

PROCEDURAL ORDERS AND HEARINGS

Tribunals will normally give their directions by way of procedural order, numbered sequentially. Sometimes a more informal approach is adopted, for example, where an extension of time is agreed between the parties. Most

1. See e.g. Article 22.1(a) of the LCIA Rules and Article 19 of the ICC Rules.
2. See section 33 of the 1996 Act.

on-going procedural matters are dealt with in writing. If there is a panel of three, this is normally undertaken by the chair or presiding arbitrator consulting the other two arbitrators as appropriate, following a prior agreement to resolve such issues in this way. However, there are occasions where the matter is more complex or where more than two parties are involved, in which case the tribunal will convene an additional procedural hearing, which can either be face to face or by way of video link or conference call as suits (see also chapter 10 page 77).

PROVISIONAL AWARDS

The parties may by agreement specifically confer certain powers in relation to provisional relief (as opposed to making a partial award) upon the tribunal. Thus, by agreement the tribunal may be empowered to order provisional relief, such as for the payment of money, or the disposition of property as between the parties, or an interim payment on account of costs. Any such order must, however, be subject to the tribunal's final adjudication. Any award on the merits or as to costs needs to take account of any such order.[3]

COSTS AND CHARGES

International arbitration can be a costly process. It is a contentious issue as to whether or not it is becoming as expensive as litigation. Lawyers' costs represent the bulk of the expense.[4] In addition payment has to be reserved for the arbitrators and administrative costs and the hiring of rooms and interpreters. If an arbitral institution is involved it will regularly seek payment from both parties on account to cover the ongoing costs of the arbitral institution and the arbitrators. If a respondent defaults the claimant will usually have to advance both parties' costs. In ad hoc arbitrations different arrangements will be made. Costs are likely to escalate as the matter progresses. No award will be given to the parties unless full payment has been made to the institution to cover its administrative charges and the arbitrators' fees or, in the case of an ad hoc arbitration, payment has been made directly to the arbitrators concerned. At a practical level, therefore, money will need to be obtained from the clients on account at the outset and/or at regular intervals.

3. Section 39 of the 1996 Act.

4. The recent Report from the ICC Commission on Arbitration, "Techniques for Controlling Time and Costs in Arbitration" found, based on ICC cases that went to a final award in 2003 and 2004, that 82% of the overall cost of arbitrations were lawyers' costs, 16% arbitrators' fees and expenses and 2% the administrative expense of the ICC.

COURT APPLICATIONS

Reference has been made in chapter 11 to interim court applications. Some will necessarily be more relevant to the later stages of the process, such as subpoenas for witness attendance which can, of course, apply only to witnesses from England and Wales or Northern Ireland.[5]

HEARING PREPARATION

As with any dispute resolution process the preparation is key. The burden of proving issues is on the party alleging them.[6] The following are some of the matters which require attention. Many have already been referred to in the context of directions (see chapter 10), but need to be re-visited as the arbitration progresses. Some may be obvious, but it is surprising how frequently they are neglected:

i. Witness statements

a. These should set out certain basic information such as the deponent's full name, address and past and present relationship to any of the parties and be signed by the witness. The witness should confirm that the contents of the statement are true.[7]
b. Witness statements are now regularly drafted by lawyers which can be counter-productive. The more that is in the witness's own words the better and the less likely he or she is to contradict it in cross-examination.
c. Witnesses should explain their knowledge of the events to avoid purporting to give evidence on matters of which they have no direct knowledge. If the knowledge is indirect, the source of such knowledge should also be given. Frequently witnesses of fact are tendered who give evidence largely based on assumption or by way of a vague notion of what they heard from someone.
d. Witnesses often depose to the same issue using exactly the same words. This only serves to indicate that the statement has been drafted by lawyers and is therefore ripe for the cross-examiner to query. A better practice, when the same issue arises for testimony from various witnesses, is for the second and subsequent witnesses to confirm the accuracy of the information by reference to the earlier witness statement and to state that he or she agrees with it.

5. Section 43 of the 1996 Act.
6. Article 24(1) of UNCITRAL specifically sets this out.
7. See e.g. Article 4(5) of the IBA Rules.

e. The witness statements should preferably deal with the issues in either chronological order or each in the same sequence of topics to make for easier understanding.
f. Document references should be to pages in the hearing bundles and not to earlier pagination. This may necessitate amending the references nearer the hearing.
g. Witnesses should be shown all the documents and witness statements to avoid them being taken by surprise at the hearing.
h. Attendance at witness training programmes within certain parameters is permitted in civil cases in the English courts.[8]
i. English lawyers are not permitted to coach witnesses.[9]
j. The availability of witnesses for the hearing should be checked.
k. Translations should be provided if relevant.

ii. Expert witnesses

An expert's report should similarly contain certain basic information and an acknowledgement of the expert's independence.[10] Where a meeting of experts has been ordered, confirmation that it has taken place and that the experts have produced any agreed report or statement should be sought. Additionally, the experts' availability to give evidence and be present when the other side's expert is giving evidence should be confirmed.

iii. Documents

Missing pages, illegible documents, broken lever arch files—there is nothing more conducive to irritation than such easily avoidable problems which can arise in the course of preparation for a hearing. The tribunal, with the assistance of the parties, will at some point during the process make directions as to how the documents should be presented (see chapter 10 page 77).

iv. Facilities

Consideration should be given as to whether the following, where applicable, have been arranged:

a. Transcripts, including the means of getting them speedily delivered to the tribunal and other parties after the hearing.
b. A suitable meeting room with sufficient break-out rooms and refreshments.
c. Interpreters, if needed.
d. Any overhead projectors or similar machinery if necessary.

8. For further explanation of what is and what is not permitted see: *(1) Northern Star Systems (2) Seaquest Systems Ltd (3) Ultraframe (UK) Ltd* v *Fielding & ors* [2005] EWHC (Ch) 1638 paras 22–31.

9. See e.g. para. 705 of the Code of Conduct of the Bar of England and Wales at www.barstandardsboard.org.uk.

10. See Article 5 of the IBA Rules and Article 8 of the CIArb Protocol.

v. Other matters directed by the tribunal

Normally a tribunal will arrange a further procedural hearing a few weeks before the main hearing to ensure that everything is ready for the hearing. At such a hearing final issues and problems can be resolved. Additional matters to be considered will include: the provision of an up-to-date list of issues; the timing, length and content of any further pre-hearing briefs or outline arguments; a list of people involved in the arbitration; a list of witnesses; a reading list for the arbitrator(s); and a chronology. The tribunal will also indicate how the time of the hearing should be allocated and may also indicate when any post-hearing oral or written submissions should be made or defer this decision until after the hearing.

INITIATIVES FROM THE TRIBUNAL

Mention has been made earlier in this book about the powers of a tribunal to appoint its own expert.[11] Sometimes tribunals take the initiative in other ways too. For example, the LCIA Rules provide for the tribunal in advance of any hearing to submit to the parties a list of questions which it wishes them to answer with special attention.[12] These rules also enable a tribunal, absent any agreement of the parties to the contrary, to conduct such enquiries "*as may appear necessary or expedient including whether and to what extent the Arbitral tribunal should itself take the initiative in identifying the issues and ascertaining the relevant facts and the law(s) or rules of law applicable to the arbitration, the merits of the parties' dispute and the Arbitration Agreement.*"[13]

Tribunals, for instance, can query the relevance of evidence, determine whether or not the strict rules of evidence should apply, and can also ask for evidence or supporting legal cases if the parties have failed to address issues which the tribunal considers relevant.[14]

PROTECTION AS TO COSTS

If they have not already done so (see chapter 8 page 60), parties may want to protect themselves as to costs. There are six options available. They all require difficult judgments as to how much should be offered. The party which seeks such protection can make one of the following:

i. An open offer, i.e. one which is made known to the tribunal by the parties, which may be accepted and may be taken into account by

11. See chapter 10 pages 73–75.
12. Article 19.3 of the LCIA Rules.
13. Article 22.1(c) of the LCIA Rules.
14. Section 34 of the 1996 Act. See also Article 22(1)(c) and (f) of the LCIA Rules and Article 20.5 of the ICC Rules.

the tribunal at the costs stage, although the tribunal still retains a discretion.

ii. A "without prejudice" offer, which will not be known to the tribunal, covering the substantive claim and costs, which similarly may be accepted, but will not be taken into account by the tribunal at the costs stage.

iii. A "without prejudice" offer save as to costs which will only be disclosed to the tribunal at the time of consideration of costs. This is usually accomplished by the provision of a letter from one party to the other proposing settlement terms to be accepted within a specific time frame, possibly including terms as to costs, and a specific reference to the fact that the letter will be referred to on the question of costs. In English proceedings, such letters are referred to as "Calderbank letters" after the name of the parties to the case where this mechanism was first used.[15] This will enable the tribunal to consider the offer at the costs stage of the proceedings as part of its overall exercise of discretion on the issue.

iv. A sealed offer which is handed to the tribunal, but not opened until after the award is given. Unless agreement is made with the other party, the tribunal will become aware that an offer has been made, but not its terms. If the successful party has been awarded less than the sum offered, then the tribunal will normally award the party which has tendered the offer its costs from the date of the sealed offer, although the tribunal still retains a discretion. If the award is more, then the sealed offer is unlikely to give any protection.

v. A request to the tribunal to direct that the recoverable costs of the arbitration, or any part of the arbitral proceedings, shall be limited to a specified amount by putting a cap on damages where such a provision is available, but this should really be done at the outset of the proceedings.[16]

vi. An agreement with the other party or parties as to the allocation of costs in advance. There is, however, an important proviso to this, namely that if such an agreement allocates costs to a party in any event it is only valid if entered into after the dispute in question has arisen. This is the result of section 60 of the 1996 Act, which is a mandatory provision.

MEDIATION

Mediation, or other forms of alternative dispute resolution, should always be addressed as an ongoing consideration. Mediations, even if not wholly successful, can narrow the issues. The best time to achieve this will vary from case

15. *Calderbank* v *Calderbank* [1976] Fam. 93.
16. Section 65 of the 1996 Act.

to case. Sometimes it is better at the outset, on other occasions it is preferable to wait until more is known about the respective cases of the parties, and in some arbitrations mediation is more successful nearer the hearing. The downside of the last option is that by delaying a mediation the costs are likely to have increased considerably and can in themselves become an obstacle to settlement (see also chapter 2 pages 13–14 and chapter 6 page 46).

There are considerable difficulties in an arbitrator acting as the mediator in the dispute in which he or she is the arbitrator. Many arbitrators are reluctant to undertake this even if all parties agree. The risk is that the process of mediation may preclude the arbitrator from continuing with the arbitration if the mediation fails, because of the confidential information made available to him or her during the mediation. It is better, usually, to involve an independent mediator. London has a large number of very experienced mediators available if required. Mediators can be approached directly or via an institution. Many of the arbitral institutions have their own mediation rules and can give guidance as to mediators.[17] Mediations, even if not wholly successful, can often narrow the issues.

The extent to which an arbitrator can nonetheless encourage settlement is the subject of different views. However, most arbitrators will encourage the parties to resolve issues and will always be willing to adjourn hearings in progress if there is a genuine attempt to settle the dispute.

17. Other bodies which provide mediation services include CEDR and the Chartered Institute of Arbitrators.

CHAPTER 13

HEARINGS

INTRODUCTION

Arbitration has not yet advanced to the stage where hearings are conducted and awards are made by robot, so the human element in the make-up of the tribunal is immensely important. Most arbitrators have their own style and idiosyncrasies built upon their experience and depending on whether or not they are common lawyers or steeped in the civil law. Thus, every hearing is conducted slightly differently, but there are some common themes which can be deduced. Procedures may need to be adjusted, depending on whether there is going to be a preliminary hearing, for example on jurisdiction, or a split hearing between liability and quantum, or a hearing in which all issues are resolved together. The following matters are relevant to most full hearings and some are relevant in varying degrees to split or preliminary hearings and are discussed in this chapter:

- miscellaneous matters;
- written submissions;
- opening statements;
- oral evidence;
- experts;
- applicable law;
- final submissions; and
- privacy and confidentiality.

MISCELLANEOUS MATTERS

Parties can appear in person or be represented. There are frequently issues that arise unexpectedly during a hearing, such as a request for disclosure of a new document from one of the parties, or an application to put in new evidence or to run a new point. On occasions, without showing sufficient cause, a party fails to attend or be represented at a hearing or fails to respond to written submissions where an oral hearing is dispensed with. In such instances, subject to any agreement of the parties to the contrary, the tribunal can proceed with a hearing if appropriate, usually after a prior warning of the consequences of failing to participate or attend.[1] The tribunal also has to be alert to money laundering issues and act appropriately in accordance with

1. Section 41(4) of the 1996 Act and see also e.g. Article 21.2 of the ICC Rules.

English legislation.[2] Tribunals resolve issues on the principle that the burden of proof in civil cases is the balance of probabilities.

WRITTEN SUBMISSIONS

Detailed written submissions are usually provided to the tribunal in advance of any hearing. Sometimes these need only supplement existing earlier written pleadings. Drafting such submissions can be challenging. In most international arbitrations these are drafted by the parties' legal advisers. Tribunals will inevitably be less familiar with the issues than counsel presenting them. The skill of the advocate is to encapsulate complex issues in a way which is simple to understand and persuasive. This skill applies no less to written advocacy than it does to oral advocacy. Repetition and unnecessarily lengthy submissions do not necessarily improve the points to be made. Clear structures, indices and summaries are all helpful aids in complex cases. A good practice is for the drafter to have an eye to making their submissions the basis of any award. Thus, the summary of the evidence and the arguments have the appeal of not only being integrally justifiable on the material available, but also, if the party is successful, they can be used as a model for the award. The balance in arbitration is towards the written rather than the oral in the context of submissions, certainly at the outset of the hearing.

OPENING STATEMENTS

If the parties have provided detailed written statements or briefs, then oral opening statements are usually relatively short. They present an opportunity for the parties to draw the tribunal's attention to the key points and at the same time enable the tribunal to clarify any issues from their pre-hearing reading.

ORAL EVIDENCE

Apart from identifying his or her witness statement, confirming its truth and perhaps clarifying some points, the witness does not give direct evidence, but is instead then immediately tendered for cross-examination. The witness statement thus stands as the evidence-in-chief or direct evidence of the witness concerned. Cross-examination in arbitrations can be rather different from cross-examination in court, particularly if the tribunal comes from a jurisdiction where the process is not familiar. A good cross-examiner will adjust the technique to the witness. It is better to elicit agreement from some witnesses

2. The Proceeds of Crime Act 2002 and the Money Laundering Regulations 2003.

such as experts: other witnesses require a more persistent approach. Bullying and aggressive cross-examination does not usually go down well: the points can be made without the need for flamboyant cross-examination. However, there may be occasions when a stronger approach is necessary, for instance, a deliberately lying witness who will not answer the question. A honed cross-examination, confined to the matters upon which the witness can give evidence as opposed to comment, is in the end far more effective before international arbitral tribunals than lengthy questions on all the documents. Asking questions of witnesses on matters or documents of which they have no direct knowledge should be avoided. If the tribunal divides the time equally or otherwise between the parties then any questioning has to factor this in.

It is extremely rare for witnesses giving evidence before arbitral tribunals to take an oath, although the tribunal does have power to administer an oath unless the parties agree otherwise.[3] However, as explained earlier, witness statements should have statements of truth and be signed by the witness. Nonetheless, the tribunal will explain to the witness the importance of telling the truth. Similarly, unless a party requests, such as where there is a fundamental issue as to credibility or the truth of something, future witnesses can be present during the hearing of evidence of other witnesses. The practice varies. Tribunals are accommodating and if there is a genuine problem with the availability of a witness they will normally permit changes to the running order or sit longer hours, if feasible. On occasions oral evidence is taken by way of video.

Every witness who has provided a witness statement is obliged to appear at the hearing to be cross-examined unless the parties have agreed to the contrary. Such agreement dispensing with cross-examination does not necessarily mean that that witness's evidence is accepted as being true. Where, on the other hand, a party who has provided a witness statement does not appear without a valid reason, the tribunal is entitled to attach such weight as it deems appropriate to it, including wholly disregarding it.[4] The tribunal may be empowered to request evidence.[5] Sometimes witnesses only appear following a subpoena.[6]

Some arbitrators like to ask questions of the witnesses, whereas others only interrupt to try to bring the questioner back on track or to assist the witness if he or she does not understand the question. Most arbitrators tend to wait at least until the end of the particular topic, if not until the end of the cross-examination, to ask their questions so as to avoid interrupting the flow of the questions. Arbitrators will, however, intervene if the witness does not understand the question.

3. Section 38(1) and (5) of the 1996 Act.
4. See e.g. Article 20.4 of the LCIA Rules and Article 4(8) of the IBA Rules.
5. See e.g. Article 22.1(c) of the LCIA Rules, Article 20.5 of the ICC Rules and Article 4(11) of the IBA Rules.
6. Section 43 of the 1996 Act.

EXPERTS

It is usually better to hear the expert evidence after the factual witnesses. The traditional way of dealing with experts is for one party's counsel to cross-examine the other party's witness. However, the flexibility of the process enables the tribunal to request that other methods be adopted, such as witness conferencing where the questions are posed by the tribunal to the expert witnesses simultaneously.[7] Sometimes the tribunal will appoint its own expert instead of or in addition to the parties' experts (see chapter 10 pages 73–75 for more details re expert evidence).

APPLICABLE LAW

In the English courts establishing a foreign law is a question of fact. This is not necessarily how it is viewed in international arbitration. Common lawyers would address the issue of foreign law by using expert witnesses. The position can be different if the arbitral panel includes civil lawyers. Where, for example, an arbitration is conducted in England relating to a contract governed by French law and the tribunal is a French lawyer, it may be an uphill struggle to persuade the tribunal to have expert evidence on the subject and the issues would be dealt with by way of submissions.[8]

FINAL SUBMISSIONS

At the conclusion of the hearing the parties' lawyers will make submissions. The normal practice is for a combination of oral and written submissions or post-hearing briefs. The order in which this is done varies according to the preference of the tribunal and the nature of the arbitration, as does the time in which these are to be accomplished. Another practice which is emerging is for the tribunal to deliberate and then ask its own questions of the parties in relation to matters upon which it needs help.[9] In any event guidance from the tribunal as to the areas to which to direct submissions is always helpful to counsel.

PRIVACY AND CONFIDENTIALITY

All hearings are held in private with only the parties and those involved in the proceedings entitled to be present, unless the parties and/or the tribunal agree

7. "Witness Conferencing", Wolfgang Peter, *LCIA Arbitration International*, Vol. 18, No. 1, 2002.

8. See chapter 15 pages 119–121: "appeals on points of law", if not excluded by the parties, are restricted to matters of English law.

9. See *Global Arbitration Review*, January 2008: "The Sachs-Wälde-Reichert method".

otherwise. The arbitral rules may provide in terms for this.[10] All documents disclosed in the arbitration or produced for the purpose of the arbitration are likewise confidential and cannot be disclosed to third parties without agreement or a court order. Confidentiality is discussed in chapter 14 pages 111–113. Some arbitral rules spell this out, such as the LCIA Rules, whereas others do not, such as the ICC and UNCITRAL Rules.[11] It is often advisable for the parties either in the arbitration agreement or at the commencement of the hearing to enter into a written confidentiality agreement.

10. See e.g. Article 19.4 of the LCIA Rules and Article 21.3 of the ICC Rules. Some ICC awards are published, suitably redacted to preserve confidentiality. The LCIA does not publish awards even in redacted form.
11. See e.g. Article 30.1 of the LCIA Rules.

CHAPTER 14

AWARDS

INTRODUCTION

Following the conclusion of the hearing the tribunal adjourns to deliberate. How long after the conclusion of hearing the tribunal will take to provide an award is not predictable. It depends upon the diligence and availability of the tribunal and the complexity of the case. It is a rule of thumb that an award from a three-person tribunal will take a little longer than one from a sole arbitrator, because of the need for communication between the three arbitrators. Some arbitration agreements provide for a strict time[1] within which the award is to be delivered. The English court has a residual discretion to extend any such deadline if necessary.[2]

The following aspects of the tribunal's deliberations and writing of an award are discussed in this chapter:

- remedies;
- assessing damages;
- form and contents of awards;
- partial awards;
- costs;
- settlements;
- communicating the award to the parties; and
- confidentiality.

REMEDIES

Unless otherwise agreed by the parties or precluded by the applicable law, an arbitral tribunal has the following powers: it can order the payment of a sum of money in any currency; make a declaration as to any matter to be determined in the proceedings; order a party to refrain from doing anything; order specific performance of a contract (other than one relating to land) or order rectification[3]; or set aside or cancel a deed or document.[4] It has a complete discretion in relation to the award of interest to meet the justice of the case,

1. Article 24.1–2 of the ICC Rules stipulates that the final award should be made within six months, but in practice in major arbitrations this is rarely achieved and extensions are given.
2. Section 50 of the 1996 Act.
3. See e.g. Article 22.1(g) of the LCIA Rules.
4. Section 48 of the 1996 Act.

including whether it should be simple or compound, the amount, the start date and the rests.[5] It also retains some discretion, subject to the applicable law, as to the currency in which to award damages so as to reflect the true loss.[6]

ASSESSING DAMAGES

Assessment of damages can often be as complex as resolving liability.[7] Any award of damages has to take account of the applicable law and be based on the factual evidence. Resolution of conflicting factual evidence is, therefore, necessary before any quantification can be made. Various issues usually need to be considered in the context of an assessment of damages. These include: the standard or measure of loss; issues of causation and remoteness of damage according to the applicable law; mitigation of loss; whether the contract makes any provision for damages which over-rides an assessment at large, for example, a cap or formula or algorithm or a liquidated damages provision; the time at which the loss should be calculated, for example, at breach or at award[8]; and whether the loss is truly the loss of a chance requiring an assessment of the chance of that lost opportunity.

The method of calculation used will depend upon a large number of factors including: the nature of the claim and the type of business; whether the business is a start-up or well established; the amount of information available; the contractual provisions; whether it is a construction claim for delay and disruption; or whether the claim is principally a debt claim, i.e. recovery of a specific sum of money due with an add-on claim for damages.

The most common method adopted by international tribunals to assess future or hypothetical past loss is the discounted cash flow method (the "DCF method"). Such calculations are produced by the expert accountants. Actual past loss will not need to be accelerated or discounted. The DCF method puts a present value on future loss, for example, at breach or award. It does this by crystallising future cash flow at a certain date, the terminal value and incorporating discounts for accelerated payment, i.e. the time value of money (the effect of future inflation) and future operational and other risks such as sector

5. Section 49 of the 1996 Act. See also *Sempra Metals Ltd (formerly Metallgesellschaft Limited)* v *Her Majesty's Commissioners of Inland Revenue and another* [2007] UKHL 34 where it was held by a majority that the court had jurisdiction at common law to award compound interest where the claimant sought a restitutionary remedy for the time value of money paid under a mistake. The majority also held that the English court had a common law jurisdiction to award compound interest as damages on claims for non-payment of debts as well as on claims for breach of contract and tort.

6. *Lesotho Highlands Development Authority* v *Impregilo SpA & ors* [2005] UKHL 43.

7. See: "Assessing damages in International Arbitration", Hilary Heilbron QC in the second edition of *The Leading Arbitrators' Guide to International Arbitration* excerpts from which are included above with adjustments.

8. *Golden Strait Corporation* v *Nippon Yusen Kibishka Kaisha* [2007] UKHL 12, a recent majority decision of the House of Lords.

and country-specific issues. Cash flows are not the same thing as profits. They take account of capital expenditure, operating costs, taxes and working capital, but exclude depreciation and amortisation and make allowances for timing differences in debtors and creditors. Determining the discount rate can make a huge difference to the result.

While most claims for future loss can be calculated by the DCF method, some, particularly where they are start-ups, fall into the category of being almost impossible to calculate. Here, the loss is really one of lost opportunity and chance: the opportunity for profits has a value in itself. So where, for example, the loss relates to a business where a licence is given to excavate for minerals, the tribunal may have to assess the chance of there ever being mineral deposits found and in what quantity and assess the damages on the basis of such chance.

Sometimes parties seek to prove their loss by reference to the net asset value or book value, i.e. the replacement cost of the asset. This is the historic cost of the original investment adjusted to take account of inflation, depreciation and development expenditure. It is useful, for example, where there is a limited trading history on which to calculate future profits. In other words, it represents the wasted cost of the investment, but it tends to produce a lower result than using the DCF method.

FORM AND CONTENTS OF AWARDS

The form of an award is a matter of individual style, but there are certain basic requirements.[9] Where there is a panel of three, the award is usually written by the chair or presiding arbitrator, with contributions from the co-arbitrators. The allocation of written drafting by the co-arbitrators will depend on the case and its complexity and the ability to compartmentalise it. Arbitral institutions have their own, sometimes formal, requirements. However, awards will normally recite at varying length the earlier history of the process, certain mandatory provisions such as the seat and date of the award and, unless the parties agree otherwise, will give reasons by way of a detailed award akin to a judgment, although probably less legalistic. The parties need to understand why the tribunal ruled as it did, as the opportunity to challenge or appeal any award where the seat is London is now very limited (see chapter 15). The award will normally be signed by all members of the tribunal. An award can be by way of a majority and very rarely an arbitrator will write a dissenting award, in which case it is sufficient if the award is signed by the majority.

Awards in ICC arbitrations must be sent in draft to the ICC Court for scrutiny and approval.[10] This formal scrutiny is unique to the ICC, although other arbitral institutions will informally draw a tribunal's attention to any

9. Section 52 of the 1996 Act, but this is subject to the agreement of the parties to the contrary.
10. Article 27 of the ICC Rules.

obvious errors or formal omissions (not relating to their reasoning or decision) on the face of the award. Clerical and similar errors in the award can be corrected within certain time limits. The tribunal may also be asked to interpret or make an additional award in relation to matters presented, but which have not been determined by it.[11] Subject to any agreement to the contrary, or any right to challenge or appeal the award, once made an award is final and binding.[12]

PARTIAL AWARDS

Partial or interim awards are relatively common,[13] for instance, because either there has been a hearing relating to jurisdiction or to preliminary issues, or the hearing on quantum has been bifurcated, or the issue of costs has been deferred until after the result of the main hearing. Awards have advantages over orders in that they can be enforced as a judgment (see chapter 16). Once the tribunal makes a final award it is *functus*, i.e. it no longer has jurisdiction over the matter.

COSTS

The legal and other costs of reaching an award can be substantial. Opportunities for losing parties to protect themselves against an award of costs are dealt with in chapter 12 pages 97–98. While some individual arbitrators, in particular those used to litigation in the United States, are not used to awarding winning parties their costs, nonetheless in international commercial arbitration it is usual for the winning party to be awarded its costs. This power is sometimes embedded in the arbitral rules while simultaneously leaving open a wide discretion to the tribunal. Other arbitral rules simply give the tribunal a wide discretion.[14] An agreement which has the effect that a party is to pay the whole or part of the costs of the arbitration in any event is only valid if made after the dispute in question has arisen.[15] Similarly, these arbitral rules may describe what costs are recoverable.[16] In the absence of agreement it is for the tribunal to determine what costs are recoverable and the amount. The English court retains default powers in relation to costs.[17]

11. See e.g. Article 27 of the LCIA Rules; Article 29 of the ICC Rules and also section 57 of the 1996 Act.
12. Section 58 of the 1996 Act.
13. Section 47 of the 1996 Act and see e.g. Article 26(7) of the LCIA Rules; Article 2(iii) of the ICC Rules, and Article 32.1 of the UNCITRAL Rules.
14. See e.g. Article 28.3 of the LCIA Rules, Article 31(3) of the ICC Rules and see also section 61 of the 1996 Act.
15. Section 60 of the 1996 Act. This is a mandatory provision.
16. See e.g. Article 28 of the LCIA Rules, Article 31 of the ICC Rules, Article 31 of the ICDR Rules and Articles 38 and 40 of the UNCITRAL Rules.
17. Sections 63–64 of the 1996 Act.

However, the position in relation to "other costs" is less clear. These principally comprise: time spent by in-house counsel; costs of other executives' management time in preparing the case; and travel and subsistence time attending the hearing even if not giving evidence as a witness. There is a growing tendency to award such costs if and to the extent that they are justified and clearly set out. This view is justified on the basis that such costs should be regarded as part of the compensation to which a winning party is entitled to enable it to recoup its loss. Other arbitrators are more reluctant to award such costs, or at least those which do not involve legal counsel.

The practice as to when the issue of costs is determined varies. Frequently the tribunal will make a partial award save as to costs. Sometimes it will hear submissions as to costs in advance of the awards: on other occasions these submissions follow the award.[18]

SETTLEMENTS

Unless the parties otherwise agree, where the arbitration has settled the tribunal will terminate the proceedings. If the parties so request, unless the tribunal otherwise objects, the tribunal will incorporate the settlement into the form of an agreed award. Such an award will have the same status as any other award on the merits.[19] The arbitral rules similarly empower the tribunal to make a consent award without any reasons if so requested.[20]

COMMUNICATING THE AWARD TO THE PARTIES

Parties are not usually entitled to receive the award until payment has been made in full to the arbitrator(s).[21] Where an arbitral institution is involved the tribunal will send the requisite number of copies of the award to the institution. The institution will then have the carriage of the mechanics of ensuring that payment is made for the institution's fees as well as for those of the tribunal. It will also be responsible for sending the award to the parties concerned.[22]

CONFIDENTIALITY

Arbitral proceedings are held in private and the evidence, documentation and awards are confidential. Although some jurisdictions have made inroads into

18. See for a model procedure—Vol.1, Issue 2, *Global Arbitration Review* (April 2006): "The Sting in the Tail", by Klaus Reichert and James Hope.
19. Section 51 of the 1996 Act.
20. Article 26.8 of the LCIA Rules, Article 26 of the ICC Rules, Article 29 of the ICDR Rules and Article 34 of the UNCITRAL Rules.
21. Section 56(1) of the 1996 Act.
22. See e.g. Article 26.5 of the LCIA Rules, 28.1–2 of the ICC Rules.

this principle, notably in Australia,[23] English law maintains the confidentiality of the process.[24] Nonetheless, an express confidentiality clause makes the position much clearer. Not all arbitral rules provide expressly for confidentiality of the process. The LCIA does, however, provide by Article 30.1 as follows:

> "*Unless the parties expressly agree in writing to the contrary, the parties undertake as a general principle to keep confidential all awards in their arbitration, together with all materials in the proceedings created for the purpose of the arbitration and all other documents produced by another party in the proceedings not otherwise in the public domain—save and to the extent that disclosure may be required of a party by legal duty, to protect or pursue a legal right or to enforce or challenge an award in bona fide legal proceedings before a state court or other judicial authority.*"

The deliberations of the members of the tribunal are also confidential. If there is an appeal to the court, then the court will take account of the confidentiality of the arbitral process, although the parties are normally named and a summary of the dispute is given.[25] However, if the matter is particularly sensitive and confidential a judgment on an appeal will not be published.[26]

Problems arise where a party wants to rely on an award for some purpose other than enforcement or to use materials from one arbitration in another arbitration. Under English law there is a duty of confidentiality in relation to all material (oral and written) concerning an arbitration, implied as a matter of law.[27] An express confidentiality agreement made between the parties and clearly defined will normally put the issue beyond doubt. This implied duty is not an immunity and is subject to certain limited and specific exceptions, namely:

a. consent of the parties to the earlier arbitration;
b. an order of the court; or
c. leave of the court. Leave will be given only:
   (i) where the disclosure falls within the test of reasonable necessity;
   (ii) in the interests of justice, for example, inconsistent testimony from a witness.

23. *Esso Australia Resources Ltd* v *The Honourable Sidney James Plowman* (1995) 183 C.L.R. 10.

24. However, confidentiality does have its limitations in that it is not always possible to ensure that witnesses maintain confidentiality unless they are required to sign a confidentiality agreement prior to giving evidence.

25. But see *C* v *D* [2007] EWCA Civ 1282.

26. *Department of Economics, Policy & Development of the City of Moscow* v *Bankers Trust Co. & ors* [2004] EWCA Civ 314.

27. *Ali Shipping Corporation* v *Shipyard Trogir* [1999] 1 W.L.R. 314. The basis of such confidentiality has been doubted, *obiter*, by the Privy Council as failing to differentiate between different types of confidentiality which attach to different documents or documents obtained in different ways and for eliding privacy and confidentiality: *AEGIS Ltd* v *European Re* [2003] 1 W.L.R. 1041.

Parties who wish to obtain material from an earlier hearing for use in a subsequent hearing or for some other reason must, absent consent, obtain the leave of the court or risk being on the receiving end of an injunction. The exception as to reasonable necessity covers both the award and its reasons, as well as pleadings, written submissions, proofs of witnesses, transcripts and notes of evidence given in arbitrations.

Such leave would be granted where it is reasonably necessary for the establishment or protection of the legal rights of a party to an earlier arbitration against a third party, in order to found a cause of action against a third party, or to defend a claim or counterclaim brought by a third party. Thus, a reassured was entitled to refer to an award and its reasons in its subsequent claim in court against brokers.[28] But a claimant in arbitration proceedings was not able to refer to a previous award to raise a case of issue estoppel which was bound to fail because the parties were different.[29] An award and its reasons may also be used for certain accountancy purposes, for example, if it is reasonably necessary for an agent to run off the reinsurance contracts.[30]

In the case of pleadings, written submissions, proofs of witnesses as well as transcripts and notes of evidence given in arbitrations, the "raw data", it may well be more difficult to establish the gateway of reasonable necessity. Such disclosure will also have to be justified as both relevant and reasonably necessary in the context of the subsequent arbitration or proceedings in which the disclosure is sought. Moreover, documents disclosed in any previous arbitration, carry an implied obligation that they are to be used only for the purpose of that original dispute.[31] The test of reasonable necessity has thus to be dealt with on a case by case basis and may vary according to the material in issue.

28. *Hassneh Insurance Co. of Israel and ors* v *Steuart J. Mew* [1993] 2 Lloyd's Rep. 243.

29. *Ali Shipping*, *supra* and *(1) Sun Life Assurance Co of Canada & ors* v *The Lincoln National Life Insurance Co.* [2004] EWCA Civ 1660 where confidentiality had been waived, but the relevant finding was in any event also collateral to the early tribunal's decision and hence could not be relied upon as founding an issue estoppel even had the parties been the same.

30. *Hassneh*, *supra* and *AEGIS* v *European Reinsurance Company of Zurich* [2003] UKPC 11.

31. *Dolling-Baker* v *Merrett* [1990] 1 W.L.R. 1205 (C.A.).

CHAPTER 15

CHALLENGES TO AN AWARD AND APPEALS GENERALLY

INTRODUCTION

London has become an increasingly more attractive venue for arbitrations since the 1996 Act, which together with its sensible interpretation by the English courts, has made challenges to and appeals from an arbitration award relatively rare.[1] Thus, extra costs and delay are avoided in the vast majority of cases, yet there remains the safety net for the rare case when the arbitral process goes radically wrong for some unforeseen reason.

Three sections of the 1996 Act are of particular relevance, namely: section 67 (challenging substantive jurisdiction of the tribunal); section 68 (serious irregularity in the arbitral process); and section 69 (appeal on a point of law). Sections 67 and 68 do not require any leave of the court before such a challenge can be made. In contrast, an appeal under section 69 requires the leave of the court or agreement of all the parties, but appeals under section 69 can be excluded by the agreement of the parties. It is not uncommon for applications under the various sections to be combined in various permutations and for there to be joint hearings of procedural challenges and for leave or permission to appeal under section 69.

This chapter shall address the following:

- section 67 of the 1996 Act;
- section 68 of the 1996 Act;
- section 69 of the 1996 Act;
- challenges and appeals generally; and
- appeals to the Court of Appeal.

SECTION 67 OF THE 1996 ACT (JURISDICTION)

Section 67 of the 1996 Act entitles a party to challenge any award as to the substantive jurisdiction of the arbitral tribunal or to seek an order declaring an

1. Informal statistics from the Commercial Court indicate that in the period between 1 October 1996 and 30 September 2007 out of the arbitration claims that were issued, there were five section 67 applications; ten section 68 applications; and forty-six section 69 applications together with seven further claims involving a combination of one or more of these. Leave was only granted in approximately one quarter of the section 69 applications, so the number of section 69 cases which reached a hearing is quite small. The statistics do not indicate which, if any, of these appeals, assuming they have reached a hearing, succeeded.

award on the merits to be of no effect, in whole or in part, because the tribunal did not have substantive jurisdiction.[2] Thus, an application can be made whether a tribunal has made a partial award on the issue or has decided to deal with jurisdiction in its award on the merits.[3] In either case the arbitral process may continue pending a decision of the court. The court has the power to ask the tribunal to set out its reasoning in more detail.[4] This right to challenge the jurisdiction of the tribunal must be considered with the other provisions as to jurisdiction set out in chapter 9.

Although no leave is required to make such an application, there are certain prerequisites to such an application:

i. the application has to be on notice to the other parties and to the tribunal[5];
ii. the party challenging jurisdiction must not have waived its right to do so by: (a) failing to raise the issue within the time allowed by the arbitration agreement; or (b) by raising the issue after the time the party takes the first step in the action to contest the merits of any matter in relation to which jurisdiction is challenged; or (c) not doing so as soon as possible after it acquired knowledge of the jurisdictional issue. The tribunal may itself have allowed a longer period for initial challenge[6];
iii. the applicant must first have exhausted any available arbitral process of appeal or review and any available recourse for the correction of an award or additional award, such powers of correction being available either by agreement of the parties or under section 57 of the 1996 Act[7];
iv. any application must be made within 28 days of the date of the award or, if there has been any arbitral process of appeal or review, of the date when the applicant or appellant was notified of the result of that process. The court does have power to extend this time, subject to any agreement of the parties to the contrary[8]; and
v. the court may impose conditions, including conditions as to security for costs or bringing the money payable under the award into court, as applicable.[9]

A person alleged to be a party to arbitral proceedings, but who has taken no part in them, may also challenge the award on the ground of lack of substantive jurisdiction by an application under section 67 of the 1996 Act

2. Section 67(1) of the 1996 Act. Substantive jurisdiction is defined in section 82(1) of the 1996 Act by reference to section 30(1).
3. Section 30(2) of the 1996 Act.
4. Section 70(4)–(5) of the 1996 Act.
5. Section 67(1) of the 1996 Act.
6. Sections 67(1), 72, 31(1)–(3) of the 1996 Act.
7. Sections 67(1) and 70(2) of the 1996 Act.
8. Sections 67(1), 70(3), 78(3), 79(1) of the 1996 Act.
9. Section 70(6)–(7) of the 1996 Act.

without having exhausted all arbitral procedures.[10] An appeal under section 67 is by way of re-hearing, although the court may be reluctant to hear fresh evidence.[11] On an application under section 67 the court may either confirm, vary or set aside in whole or in part the award.[12] No appeal can be made to the Court of Appeal without the leave of the court and the court may impose conditions of such leave.[13] This restricted right of appeal, which is the same as in relation to section 68, has been held not to be incompatible with Article 6 of the European Convention on Human Rights 1950.[14]

SECTION 68 OF THE 1996 ACT (SERIOUS IRREGULARITY)

A party may apply to the court challenging the award on the ground of serious irregularity affecting the tribunal, the proceedings, or the award. No leave is required. The court has the power to ask the tribunal to set out its reasoning in more detail.[15] Serious irregularity is defined in the 1996 Act[16] as meaning:

> "*An irregularity of one or more of the following kinds which the court considers has caused or will cause substantial injustice to the applicant—*
> - *(a) failure by the tribunal to comply with section 33 (general duty of tribunal);*
> - *(b) the tribunal exceeding its powers (otherwise than by exceeding its substantive jurisdiction: see section 67);*
> - *(c) failure by the tribunal to conduct the proceedings in accordance with the procedure agreed by the parties;*
> - *(d) failure by the tribunal to deal with all the issues that were put to it;*
> - *(e) any arbitral or other institution or person vested by the parties with powers in relation to the proceedings or the award exceeding its powers;*
> - *(f) uncertainty or ambiguity as to the effect of the award;*
> - *(g) the award being obtained by fraud or the award or the way in which it was procured being contrary to public policy;*
> - *(h) failure to comply with the requirements as to the form of the award; or*
> - *(i) any irregularity in the conduct of the proceedings or in the award which is admitted by the tribunal or by any arbitral or other institution or person vested by the parties with powers in relation to the proceedings or the award.*"

There are some prerequisites to such an application in common with section 67 applications:

10. Section 72(2) of the 1996 Act.
11. *Republic of Ecuador* v *Occidental Exploration & Production (No. 2)* [2006] EWHC 345 (Comm) and *Czech Republic* v *European Media Ventures S.A.* [2007] EWHC 2851 (Comm).
12. Section 67(3) of the 1996 Act.
13. Sections 67(4) and 70(8) of the 1996 Act.
14. *Kazakhstan* v *ISTIL Group Inc* [2007] EWCA Civ 471.
15. Section 70(4)–(5) of the 1996 Act.
16. Section 68(2) of the 1996 Act.

i. the application has to be on notice to the other parties and to the tribunal[17];
ii. the applicant must first have exhausted any available arbitral process of appeal or review and any available recourse for the correction of an award or additional award, such powers of correction being available either by agreement of the parties or under section 57 of the 1996 Act[18];
iii. any application must be made within 28 days of the date of the award or, if there has been any arbitral process of appeal or review, of the date when the applicant or appellant was notified of the result of that process. The court does have power to extend this time, subject to any agreement of the parties to the contrary[19];
iv. the court may impose conditions, including conditions as to security for costs or bringing the money payable under the award into court as applicable.[20]

A person alleged to be a party to arbitral proceedings, but who has taken no part in them, may also challenge the award on the ground of serious irregularity by an application under section 68 of the 1996 Act without having exhausted all arbitral procedures.[21] Section 68 is by way of review. On an application under section 68, if the court finds there has been a serious irregularity, it may either remit the award to the tribunal in whole or in part for reconsideration, set aside the award in whole or in part or declare the award to be of no effect in whole or in part.[22] No appeal can be made to the Court of Appeal without the leave of the court.[23]

Informal statistics from the Commercial Court referred to at footnote 1 in this chapter indicate that sections 67 and 68 are now little used. Applications under section 68 are likely to have reduced as a result of the impact of a recent House of Lords' decision.[24] The House of Lords, by a majority, held that an error of law, in that case relating to the nature of the currency in which the award was made and the payment of pre-award interest, did not amount to an excess of power under section 68(2)(b). An appeal on a point of law had been excluded because it was an ICC case and the attempt to dress the issues up as a serious irregularity therefore failed.

The courts are attuned to section 68 being used as a device to delay enforcement of an award. They will regularly dismiss frivolous applications. The allegation has to be serious, such as bias or failing to give a party an

17. Section 68(1) of the 1996 Act.
18. Sections 68(1) and 70(2) of the 1996 Act. See e.g. *Torch Offshore LLC & Anor* v *Cable Shipping Inc.* [2004] EWHC 787.
19. Sections 68(1), 70(3), 78(3), 79(1) of the 1996 Act.
20. Section 70(6)–(7) of the 1996 Act.
21. Section 72(2) of the 1996 Act.
22. Section 68(3) of the 1996 Act.
23. Sections 68(4) and 70(8) of the 1996 Act.
24. *Lesotho Highlands Development Authority* v *Impregilo SPA & ors* [2005] UKHL 43.

opportunity to be heard. It is not sufficient that the court hearing the application considered that it might have done things differently or expressed its conclusions on essential issues at greater length.[25]

SECTION 69 OF THE 1996 ACT (APPEAL ON POINT OF LAW)

The ability to apply to the courts under section 69 differs from sections 67 and 68 in two material respects.

First, the parties can agree to exclude the right to make such appeals. Thus, for example, application of the LCIA or ICC Rules will exclude such an appeal, but the UNCITRAL Rules will not.[26] Clear words are necessary to exclude an appeal.[27] Such an exclusion is not contrary to Article 6 of the European Convention on Human Rights.[28] Parties who enter into ad hoc agreements will want to consider very carefully whether or not to exclude such an appeal. Similarly, an agreement to dispense with reasons for the tribunal's award will be considered to be an agreement to exclude the court's jurisdiction to consider an appeal on a point of law,[29] as will an agreement to determine an arbitration "*ex aequo et bono*". Law for the purpose of the appeal means English, Welsh or Northern Irish law.[30] Thus, no application can be made under this section if the governing law is a foreign law and the parties can in such circumstances only rely upon sections 67 and 68 of the 1996 Act.

Secondly, the appeal is not automatic: leave or the agreement of all parties to the proceedings is required.[31] The application must identify the question of law to be determined and state the grounds on which it is alleged that leave to appeal should be granted.[32] Such leave is usually applied for on paper, although sometimes an oral application is made.[33] The submissions for any application for leave to appeal should be short, focussed, and capable of being read and digested by the judge in half an hour.[34] Hopeless cases are discouraged and parties cannot obtain leave by dressing up questions of fact as issues of law.[35] Leave will only be given if the court is satisfied:

25. *ABB AG* v *Hochtief Airport GmbH & anor* [2006] EWHC 388 and note also para. 87 of the judgment.
26. See e.g. Articles 26.9 and 29.2 of the LCIA Rules and Article 28.6 of the ICC Rules.
27. *Essex County Council* v *Premier Recycling Ltd* [2006] EWHC 3594 (TCC).
28. *Sumukan Ltd* v *Commonwealth Secretariat* [2007] EWCA Civ 243.
29. Section 69(1) of the 1996 Act.
30. Section 82(1) of the 1996 Act; *Reliance Industries Ltd* v *Enron Oil and Gas India* [2002] 1 Lloyd's Rep. 645.
31. Section 69(2) of the 1996 Act.
32. Section 69(4) of the 1996 Act.
33. See section O 8.5 of the Commercial Courts Guide.
34. *CMA CGM SA* v *Beteiligungs-Kommanditgesellschaft Ms Northern Pioneer Schiffahrtgesellschaft MBH & Co. & ors* [2002] EWCA Civ 1878.
35. See e.g. *Surefire Systems* v *Guardian ECL Ltd* [2005] EWHC 1860 (TCC) and *Penwith District Council* v *VP Developments Ltd (in company voluntary arrangement)* [2007] EWHC 2544 (TCC).

"*(a) that the determination of the question will substantially affect the rights of one or more of the parties,*
(b) that the question is one which the tribunal was asked to determine,
(c) that, on the basis of the findings of fact in the award—
(i) the decision of the tribunal on the question is obviously wrong, or
(ii) the question is one of general public importance and the decision of the tribunal is at least open to serious doubt, and
(d) that, despite the agreement of the parties to resolve the matter by arbitration, it is just and proper in all the circumstances for the court to determine the question."[36]

The following pre-conditions to the grant of leave also apply:

1. the application has to be on notice to the other parties and to the tribunal[37];
2. the applicant must first have exhausted any available arbitral process of appeal or review and any available recourse for the correction of an award or additional award as agreed by the parties or under section 57 of the 1996 Act[38];
3. any application must be made within 28 days of the date of the award or, if there has been any arbitral process of appeal or review, of the date when the applicant or appellant was notified of the result of that process. The court does have power to extend this time, subject to any agreement of the parties to the contrary[39];
4. the court may impose conditions, including conditions as to security for costs or bringing the money payable under the award into court as applicable.[40]

There is no appeal to the Court of Appeal from the preliminary issue as to whether or not there is an exclusion agreement, but see below in respect of residual jurisdiction.[41] Leave of the court is required to appeal against a decision of the court to grant or refuse leave to appeal.[42]

On an appeal under this section the court may either confirm or vary the award, or remit the award to the tribunal, in whole or in part, for reconsideration in the light of the court's determination. Alternatively it may set aside the award in whole or in part, but will not do so unless it is satisfied that it would be inappropriate to remit the matters in question to the tribunal for reconsideration.[43] In considering an appeal on a question of law the court will look principally at the award, together with any document referred to in the award that needs to be read to determine that question of law, but will not reopen the facts.[44] An erroneous finding of fact or a finding against the weight of the

36. Section 69(3) of the 1996 Act and see e.g. *CMA, supra.*
37. Section 69(2) of the 1996 Act.
38. Sections 69(2) and 70(2) of the 1996 Act.
39. Sections 69(2), 70(3), 78(3), 79(1) of the 1996 Act.
40. Section 70(6)–(7) of the 1996 Act.
41. See *Sumukan, supra.*
42. Section 69(6) of the 1996 Act.
43. Section 69(7) of the 1996 Act.
44. *Kershaw Mechanical Services Ltd* v *Kendrick Construction Ltd* [2006] EWHC 727.

evidence is not a question of law for the purposes of section 69 of the 1996 Act.[45] The decision of the court on an appeal under section 69, following leave to appeal having been granted, is treated as a judgment of the court for the purposes of a further appeal. Leave of the court is necessary for an appeal to the Court of Appeal which will only be given where the court considers that the question is one of general importance or is one which for some other special reason should be considered by the Court of Appeal.[46]

CHALLENGES AND APPEALS GENERALLY

In respect of all three types of application, where the award is varied, the variation has effect as part of the tribunal's award. Where the award is remitted to the tribunal, in whole or in part, for reconsideration, the tribunal is obliged to make a fresh award in respect of the matters remitted within three months of the date of the order for remission or such longer or shorter period as the court may direct. Where the award is set aside or declared to be of no effect, in whole or in part, the court may also order that any provision that an award is a condition precedent to the bringing of legal proceedings in respect of a matter to which the arbitration agreement applies, is of no effect as regards the subject matter of the award or, as the case may be, the relevant part of the award.[47]

The procedure is for an application to be made by way of arbitration claim (see chapter 11 pages 81–83 for details of the procedure). Reference should also be made to the tribunal's right to determine its own jurisdiction (chapter 9).

Parties may also need to consider whether or not to apply for security for costs in relation to any of these applications, provided that the party against whom such an order is sought is not a member of the European Union, or for an order that a sum of money representing the award is paid into court or for a freezing order.[48]

Although a larger number of section 69 claims are lodged than under the other two sections, informal statistics from the Commercial Court indicate that only approximately a quarter reach a hearing as leave to appeal is refused. Section 69 applications can be avoided if the parties exclude this right of appeal on points of law. The number of section 67 and 68 applications which are brought is relatively small (see foonote 1 to this chapter).

45. *Demco Investments & Commercial SA & ors* v *SE Banken Foesakring Holding Aktiebolag* [2005] EWHC 1398.

46. Section 69(8) of the 1996 Act.

47. Section 71 of the 1996 Act. See chapter 6 page 46 and *Scott* v *Avery* clauses.

48. Section 70(6) and (7) of the 1996 Act, section 37 of the Supreme Court Act and CPR 25.12 and 13.

APPEALS TO THE COURT OF APPEAL

Where the statute provides, as it does in several sections, that the leave of "the court" is required for a further appeal to the Court of Appeal, this means the first instance court and no further attempt to obtain the leave of the Court of Appeal is permitted.[49] In some sections the conditions for appeal are spelt out, as in section 69 above, section 32 (determination of preliminary point of jurisdiction—see chapter 9 pages 66–67) and section 45 (determination of preliminary point of law—see chapter 11 pages 86–87). In other cases the discretion is wide, for instance, section 44 (the court's powers in support of arbitral proceedings—see chapter 11 pages 84–88) and section 50 (extension of time for making an award—see chapter 14 page 107).

Nonetheless, the Court of Appeal does have a residual jurisdiction to hear an appeal from a first instance decision where there is an issue as to whether the first instance judge had jurisdiction to make the order in the first place,[50] or as to whether or not there has been an exclusion agreement for the purposes of section 69.[51] The Court of Appeal has also accepted a residual jurisdiction against a refusal of the judge of first instance to grant leave to appeal, either to the High Court from the award under section 69 of the 1996 Act, or to the Court of Appeal against its decision, but only where there has been unfairness in the process contrary to Article 6. However, there has to be a realistic argument that the judge's decision contravened Article 6.[52] These instances are rare and exceptional, hardly ever acceded to, and should not be regarded as a way round the strict limitations on appeal provided by the 1996 Act.

49. See e.g. *Henry Boot Construction (UK) Ltd* v *Malmaison Hotel (Manchester) Ltd* [2001] 1 Q.B. 388 (section 69); *Athletic Union Constantinople* v *National Basketball Association (No. 2)* [2002] EWCA Civ 830 (section 67); *Davinder Singh Virdee* v *Amritpal Singh Virdi* [2003] EWCA Civ 41 (section 18(5)); and *Cetelem S.A.* v *Roust Holding Ltd* [2005] 1 W.L.R. 618 (section 44(7)).

50. *Cetelem, supra.*

51. *Sumukan, supra.*

52. *North Range Shipping Ltd* v *Seatrans Shipping Co.* [2002] EWCA Civ 405 (section 69(6)); *BLCT (13096) Ltd* v *J. Sainsbury plc* [2003] EWCA Civ 884 (section 69(6)); *CGU International Insurance plc and others* v *AstraZeneca Insurance Co.* [2006] EWCA Civ 1340 (section 69(8)); and *ASM Shipping Ltd of India* v *TTMI Ltd of England* [2006] EWCA Civ 1341 (section 68(4)).

CHAPTER 16

ENFORCEMENT OF AN ENGLISH OR FOREIGN AWARD

INTRODUCTION

Voluntary compliance or successful enforcement of an award is the ultimate goal of a claimant. The knowledge that the latter is available as the ultimate sanction can assist in the former. Some parties do, however, seek to resist enforcement. There are two principal ways of enforcing awards under the 1996 Act:

1. First, under section 66 of the 1996 Act. Arbitral awards made both in the United Kingdom, i.e. domestic awards, and those made where the seat is outside the jurisdiction can be enforced under this section.[1] No prior recognition is necessary. Enforcement is discretionary, but will rarely be refused.
2. Secondly, under sections 100–103 of the 1996 Act. These provisions mirror the New York Convention. They do not apply to an award made in the United Kingdom. Most countries involved in international commercial activities have now signed the New York Convention.[2] If an award is to be enforced against assets in England it must first be recognised. Recognition and enforcement is mandatory unless the party against whom enforcement is sought can bring itself within one of the narrow exceptions.

These sections are not mutually exclusive. The 1996 Act preserves other means of enforcing awards such as at common law.[3] This chapter considers how to enforce both an English and a foreign award. It deals with the following:

- enforcement of awards under section 66 of the 1996 Act;
- recognition and enforcement of New York Convention awards;
- procedure;
- ancillary measures:
  - security for costs;
  - freezing orders;
  - stay of execution;
  - third party debt orders;

1. Section 2(2) of the 1996 Act.
2. There are currently 142 signatories.
3. Sections 66(4), 81(1) and 104 of the 1996 Act.

- charging orders; and
- states.

ENFORCEMENT UNDER SECTION 66 OF THE 1996 ACT

This section entitles a successful party to enforce an award summarily wherever the seat of the arbitration (and also if it is a New York Convention award) in the same manner as a judgment or order of the court to the same effect. The leave of the court is required. Leave will not be given where, and to the extent that, the party against whom it is sought to enforce the award shows that the tribunal lacked jurisdiction. However, the court will not accede to such a defence to enforcement where the right to raise this plea has been lost by delay, or where there has been a failure to raise the issue earlier before the tribunal, or the court by way of a preliminary point of jurisdiction before the courts, or by way of appeal under section 67[4] (see also chapter 9 pages 66–67 and chapter 15 pages 115–117. Enforcement under section 66 of the 1996 Act is a discretionary remedy. Once leave is obtained the award can be enforced in the same way as any other judgment of the court or judgment may be entered in the terms of the award. Once judgment is entered the award merges with the judgment and has, therefore, to be enforced as a judgment. Even if leave is granted, the party against whom enforcement is sought may challenge the decision and/or seek a stay on enforcement.

RECOGNITION AND ENFORCEMENT OF NEW YORK CONVENTION AWARDS

Sections 101–104 of the 1996 Act apply to awards made in pursuance of agreements in writing where the seat of the arbitration is a party to the New York Convention 1958. Recognition and enforcement under these provisions is mandatory unless the party against whom enforcement is sought can establish one of the limited number of exceptions. This means of enforcement is to be contrasted with section 66 which permits an unlimited discretion, although in practice enforcement under that provision will only rarely be refused.

A New York Convention award will, therefore, be recognised as binding on the persons as between whom it was made. It can accordingly be relied upon by way of defence, set-off, or otherwise in any legal proceedings in England and Wales or Northern Ireland. Such an award may, by leave of the court, be enforced in the same manner as a judgment or order of the court to the same effect and where leave is so given, judgment may be entered in terms of the

4. Section 73 of the 1996 Act. See also sections 30–32 and 67.

award.[5] A party seeking the recognition or enforcement of a New York Convention award must produce:

(a) the duly authenticated original award or a duly certified copy of it (with a certified translation if appropriate); and
(b) the original arbitration agreement or a duly certified copy of it (with a certified translation if appropriate).[6]

Section 103 of the 1996 Act provides that the court may only refuse recognition or enforcement of a New York Convention award if the person against whom it is invoked proves one or more of the following:

"(a) that a party to the arbitration agreement was (under the law applicable to him) under some incapacity;
(b) that the arbitration agreement was not valid under the law to which the parties subjected it or, failing any indication thereon, under the law of the country where the award was made;
(c) that he was not given proper notice of the appointment of the arbitrator or of the arbitration proceedings or was otherwise unable to present his case[7]*;*
(d) that the award deals with a difference not contemplated by or not falling within the terms of the submission to arbitration or contains decisions on matters beyond the scope of the submission to arbitration (but see subsection (4));
(e) that the composition of the arbitral tribunal or the arbitral procedure was not in accordance with the agreement of the parties or, failing such agreement, with the law of the country in which the arbitration took place;
(f) that the award has not yet become binding on the parties, or has been set aside or suspended by a competent authority of the country in which, or under the law of which, it was made."[8]

In relation to *(f)* above, the English court may, if it considers it proper, adjourn the decision on the recognition or enforcement of the award.[9]

Recognition or enforcement of the award may also be refused if the award is in respect of a matter which is not capable of settlement by arbitration, or if it would be contrary to public policy to recognise or enforce the award. The courts will approach attempts to resist enforcement on public policy grounds with extreme caution. Public policy in this context is confined to the public policy of England (as the country in which enforcement is sought) in maintaining the fair and orderly administration of justice.[10] These are also New York Convention grounds. Even when a ground for refusing enforcement is established, the court retains a discretion whether or not to enforce the

5. Section 101 of the 1996 Act.
6. Section 102 of the 1996 Act.
7. See e.g. *Minmetals Germany GmbH* v *Ferco Steel Ltd* [1999] CLC 647; *Kanoria & ors* v *Guinness & Anor* [2006] EWCA Civ 222.
8. Section 103(1)–(2) of the 1996 Act.
9. Section 103(5) of the 1996 Act.
10. Section 103(3) of the 1996 Act and see e.g. *DST* v *Rakoil* [1987] 2 Lloyd's Rep. 246, 254; *Ipco (Nigeria) Ltd* v *Nigerian National Petroleum Corporation* [2005] EWHC 726. See also e.g. *Minmetals, supra*, a case of alleged procedural injustice.

award.[11] An award which contains decisions on matters not submitted to arbitration may be recognised or enforced to the extent that it contains decisions on matters submitted to arbitration, which can be separated from those on matters not so submitted.[12]

PROCEDURE

An application for leave to enforce an award as a judgment under either section 66 or 101 of the 1996 Act is made in an arbitration claim form in the first instance. Notice does not have to be given to the party against whom enforcement is sought at this stage. The application is made to the judge with the appropriate evidence in support, as specified by the CPR and the 1996 Act. The documents needed include the original award and arbitration agreement or duly authenticated copies thereof, translated if necessary.[13] Further details of the procedure in relation to arbitration applications are set out in chapter 11 pages 81–83.

If the court gives leave this must then be served on the defendant to the proceedings. If the defendant is domiciled out of the jurisdiction then the leave of the court must be obtained to serve the order and any further application on the defendant. The defendant is then given an opportunity to resist enforcement. The judgment cannot be enforced until either after such hearing or, where no application is made to set aside the leave, after the expiry of such period as ordered by the court. Costs orders relating to the application usually follow the event, but remain in the discretion of the court. Appeals to the Court of Appeal are permissible with the leave of the first instance court, or on refusal, by permission of the Court of Appeal.[14]

ANCILLARY MEASURES

The following are the main ancillary or supportive orders that may be relevant at the time of or in anticipation of enforcement of an award.

i. Security for costs

The court is unlikely, save in an exceptional case, to order security for costs against an award creditor where a party challenges leave to enforce an award, whether it be a domestic award under section 66 of the 1996 Act or a New York Convention award under section 101 of the 1996 Act even if, which is

11. *Ipco, supra.* However, this is not an open discretion: *Dardana Ltd* v *Youkos Oil Co.* [2002] EWCA Civ 543; *Kanoria & Ors* v *Guinness & Anor* [2006] EWCA Civ 222.
12. Section 103(4) of the 1996 Act.
13. Section 102 of the 1996 Act and Part 62.18 and Practice Direction 62 of the CPR.
14. Part 52.3 of the CPR.

doubted, jurisdiction exists to do so.[15] The court also has jurisdiction to adjourn a New York Convention award under section 103(2)(f) on terms that the sum indisputably due is paid to the claimant together with appropriate security.[16]

ii. Freezing injunctions

The English courts have jurisdiction to grant freezing orders in support of arbitration awards or judgments following upon arbitration awards. This is a discretionary remedy and the pre-requisites for obtaining such an order need to be complied with (see chapter 11 pages 84–85). However, where a foreign award is to be enforced against assets within the jurisdiction, the English courts will only grant worldwide orders, as opposed to orders directed to assets within the jurisdiction, in exceptional cases.[17] Worldwide freezing orders will be granted if the appropriate conditions prevail in relation to English arbitration awards. However, there is jurisdiction to enable a party, in appropriate circumstances, to obtain an order for disclosure extended to foreign assets in aid of execution once an award has been made, either before or after its conversion into a judgment.[18]

iii. Stay of execution

A court has power under its inherent jurisdiction, following the granting of leave to enforce an award granted under section 66 of the 1996 Act, to stay enforcement of an English arbitration award pending determination of an application to set it aside, upon condition that the amount of the award be paid into court or otherwise secured. The position where the seat of the award is outside the jurisdiction is dealt with under section 103(5) of the 1996 Act.

iv. Third party debt order

Where a debt is "*due or accruing due*", from a third party to the judgment debtor, the court may make an order for the third party to pay the whole or such part of that debt as is sufficient to satisfy the judgment debt and the judgment creditor's costs of the application to the judgment creditor.[19]

v. Charging orders

Upon judgment or court order requiring payment of a sum of money to a judgment creditor, the court may make a charging order in accordance with

15. *Gater Assets Ltd* v *Nak Naftogaz Ukrainiy* [2007] EWCA Civ 988.
16. *Ipco, supra.*
17. *Rosseel N.V.* v *Oriental Commercial Shipping (U.K.) Ltd & ors* [1990] 1 W.L.R. 1387.
18. *Gidrxslme Shipping Co. Ltd* v *Tantomar-Transportes Maritimos LDA* [1995] 1 W.L.R. 299.
19. The procedure for obtaining such an order is set out in Part 72 and Practice Direction 72 of the CPR.

the Charging Orders Act 1979 charging such property of the debtor as may be specified in the order to secure the payment of any money due or to become due under the judgment or order. This is also a discretionary remedy.[20]

STATES

States and state-owned entities frequently present an additional hurdle to enforcement by reason of claims of sovereign immunity. Proceedings in England are governed by the State Immunity Act 1978. Where the seat of the arbitration is London it is likely that these issues will have been raised at an earlier stage before the tribunal and/or in the English courts, principally in relation to jurisdiction. Nonetheless, a non-participating respondent state may emerge to contest its amenability to the English courts only at the enforcement stage. Where a party seeks to enforce a foreign award in England, the issue may similarly arise for the first time at the recognition and enforcement stage.

States retain a presumption of immunity from legal proceedings in the English courts, but subject to several exceptions, not all of which are set out below, and in relation to which the State Immunity Act 1978 should be consulted. In the context of arbitral enforcement the following are likely to be most relevant:

i. Immunity is lost by a state "*as respects proceedings of which it has submitted to the jurisdiction*".[21] A state may submit to the jurisdiction either after the dispute has arisen or by a prior written agreement.[22]

ii. Unless the parties to the dispute have agreed otherwise in writing, a state is not immune "*as respects proceedings relating to a commercial transaction entered into by a State*".[23]

   A commercial transaction is defined[24] as:

   "*(a) any contract for the supply of goods or services;*
   (b) any loan or other transaction for the provision of finance and any guarantee or indemnity in respect of any such transaction or of any other financial obligations; and
   (c) any other transaction or activity (whether of a commercial, industrial, financial, professional or other similar character) into which a State enters or in which it engages otherwise than in the exercise of sovereign authority."

iii. Unless the parties to the dispute have agreed otherwise in writing, a state is not immune "*as respects proceedings relating to the obligation of*

20. See in particular sections 1 and 2 of the Charging Orders Act 1979 which sets out the court's jurisdiction, powers and the property against which such an order can be made and Part 73 and Practice Direction 73 of the CPR for the procedure.
21. Section 2(1) of the State Immunity Act 1978.
22. Section 2(2) and (7) of the State Immunity Act 1978.
23. Section 3(1)(a) and (2) of the State Immunity Act 1978.
24. Section 3(3) of the State Immunity Act 1978.

the State" where a contractual obligation is to be performed partly or wholly in the United Kingdom, whether it is a commercial contract or not, with limited exceptions.[25]

iv. Where a state "*has agreed in writing to submit a dispute which has arisen, or may arise, to arbitration*" it loses its immunity "*as respects proceedings in the courts of the United Kingdom which relate to the arbitration*". However the parties may agree in writing to the contrary and the provision does not apply to arbitration between states.[26]

v. Where the proceedings relate to either an interest of the state in, or its possession or use of, immovable property in the United Kingdom or an obligation of the state arising therefrom, the state is not immune.[27]

vi. A separate state entity is not immune from the jurisdiction of the courts unless the proceedings relate to anything done by it in the exercise of sovereign authority, in which case it shares the same immunities as a state.[28]

Whether or not a state is a party to an arbitration agreement can raise difficult questions according to the applicable law of the arbitration agreement, absent express agreement. The clearest way, therefore, to avoid immunity issues arising at the enforcement stage is to ensure that the state is made a party to the independent arbitration agreement (section 9 of the State Immunity Act 1978). An unqualified signature to the main agreement is likely to be sufficient. However, because of the separability of the arbitration agreement and the need to construe it according to its applicable law, it does not necessarily follow. An alternative, but less conclusive way of excluding immunity at the enforcement stage, is for the state to waive immunity to enforcement in terms in the agreement. However if, such waiver is not sufficiently explicit it can give rise to issues of construction according to the applicable law of the contract (sections 1 and 13 of the State Immunity Act 1978). A general waiver will not suffice. Enforcement proceedings are not proceedings relating to a commercial transaction within section 3 of the State Immunity Act 1978.[29]

Difficult issues can also arise as to whether a state entity is the real party to the agreement or merely the alter ego or agent of the state, or whether a qualified signature by, for instance, a minister, binds the state. A failure to challenge a tribunal's finding on jurisdiction in the relevant national supervisory courts such that it becomes final and binding does not necessarily preclude reliance on section 103(2) of the 1996 Act. However, a failure to

25. Section 3(1)(b) and (2) of the State Immunity Act 1978.

26. Section 9 of the State Immunity Act 1978. This provision applies to both foreign and domestic awards: *Svenska Petroleum Exploration AB* v *(1) Government of the Republic of Lithuania (2) AB Geonafta* [2006] EWCA Civ 1529, para. 121.

27. Section 6 of the State Immunity Act 1978.

28. Section 14(2) of the State Immunity Act 1978.

29. *Svenska, supra.*

challenge a tribunal's decision on who are the parties to a written arbitration agreement (usually raised in the context of the jurisdiction of the tribunal), may amount to an issue estoppel on the issue of sovereign immunity for the purposes of section 9 of the State Immunity Act 1978. If such a finding is not challenged in the national courts of the seat of the arbitration the state may be prevented from later raising the issue at the enforcement stage before the English courts.[30]

Even if the state is not immune from recognition and enforcement procedures, there remains the potential further issue as to whether there are non-sovereign assets available against which to attach an award. This is not necessarily a straightforward question and will depend on the facts of each case. Again the State Immunity Act 1978 provides a regime. Essentially the position is that:

i. An award or judgment cannot be enforced against the property of a state nor can an injunction be granted against a state save in limited circumstances,[31] namely:
   a. where the state gives consent. This may be by way of prior written agreement and may be limited or general. However, a provision submitting to the jurisdiction of the courts, i.e. for its adjudicative process, does not amount to consent for the purposes of enforcement;
   b. aside from specific provisions relating to the European Convention on State Immunity, where the property is for the time being "*in use or intended for use for commercial purposes*".
ii. A separate entity (other than a state's central bank or other monetary authority), which having sovereign immunity waives it, is subject to enforcement against property for the time being "*in use or intended for use for commercial purposes*" in the same way as a state.
iii. Property of a state's central bank or other monetary authority is in a special position.[32] This extends to any asset in which the central bank has some kind of "property" interest, which asset is allocated to or held in the name of the central bank, irrespective of the capacity in which the central bank holds it or the purpose for which the property is held.[33]

Property for the purposes of sections 13 and 14 of the State Immunity Act 1978 has been defined as including "*all real and personal property*" and embracing "*any right or interest, legal, equitable, or contractual in assets that might be held by a State or any 'emanation of the State' or central bank or other monetary authority*" and probably therefore includes a chose in action.[34]

30. *Svenska, supra.*
31. Section 13 of the State Immunity Act 1978. See section 14(1)–(3) in relation to the position of a state entity.
32. Section 14(3) and (4) of the State Immunity Act 1978.
33. *AIG Capital Partners Inc. & anor* v *Kazakhstan & ors* [2005] EWHC 2239 (Comm).
34. *AIG Capital Partners Inc., supra.*

CHAPTER 17

INVESTMENT TREATY ARBITRATION

INTRODUCTION

The brevity of this chapter is no reflection of the growing importance of international investment treaty arbitration. However, many such arbitrations are heard under the ICSID Convention Regulations and Rules. These do not specify a seat, as the rules of law pursuant to which the arbitration is conducted derive from the ICSID Convention as interpreted under principles of public international law. Accordingly the 1996 Act does not apply to ICSID arbitrations. It is thus beyond the scope of this book. It is only if the seat is expressed or chosen to be London, for example, if the UNCITRAL Rules apply, that such arbitrations are held in London.

In these cases, to a large extent, the arbitration itself will be conducted in a similar manner to international commercial arbitration, save that the issues will be those of public international law rather than private international and national law. To date there has been limited experience of such arbitrations in London, although this trend may well change in the future, particularly given the robust attitude of the English courts. Parties can apply for a stay in relation to a breach of such agreements.

This chapter will, therefore, be confined to dealing with two specific issues, namely:

- justiciability; and
- enforcement.

JUSTICIABILITY

Although no recourse is currently available to the English courts in relation to ICSID arbitrations save in relation to execution of assets, other investment treaty arbitrations, where the seat of the arbitration is London, are not affected. Even though the arbitration agreement may be governed by international law, the English court has held that such arbitrations are justiciable and are subject, for instance, to the challenge procedure as to jurisdiction under section 67 of the 1996 Act.[1]

1. *Occidental Exploration & Production Co.* v *Republic of Ecuador* [2005] EWCA Civ 1116—a BIT claim under UNCITRAL Rules held in London. Following the finding of justiciability the court proceeded to hear a section 67 challenge. See also *Czech Republic* v *European Media Ventures* [2007] EWHC 2851 (Comm).

ENFORCEMENT

The United Kingdom, as a party to the ICSID Convention[2] has a mandatory obligation to recognise an arbitration award made pursuant to the ICSID Convention. Contracting states will:

> "*enforce the pecuniary obligations imposed by that award within its territories as if it were a final judgment of a court of that State.*"[3]

The Convention further provides for execution of the award to be governed by the laws concerning the execution of judgments in force in the state in whose territories such execution is sought.[4] However, sovereign immunity is specifically reserved, but only in relation to execution.[5] Article 55 of the ICSID Convention states expressly that:

> "*Nothing in Article 54 shall be construed as derogating from the law in force in any Contracting State relating to immunity of that State or any foreign State from execution*".

A person seeking recognition or enforcement of an ICSID Award is "*entitled to have the award registered in the High Court*".[6] Finally, section 2 of the Arbitration (International Investment Disputes) Act 1966 provides that, subject to the provisions of the Act, an award registered under the Act:

> " . . . *shall, as respects the pecuniary obligations which it imposes, be of the same force and effect for the purposes of execution as if it had been a judgment of the High Court given when the award was rendered pursuant to the Convention and entered on the date or registration under this Act, and, so far as relates to such pecuniary obligations—*
> *(a) proceedings may be taken on the award,*
> *(b) the sum for which the award is registered shall carry interest,*
> *(c) the High Court shall have the same control over the execution of the award,*
> *as if the award had been such a judgment of the High Court.*"

Thus, in contrast to a New York Convention Award, which would apply if the arbitration was conducted according to UNCITRAL Rules for example, the procedure following an ICSID award is slightly different.[7] The ICSID scheme has its own enforcement mechanism. There are basically two grounds of resistance to enforcement. First, if either an application has been made for annulment under the ICSID procedure, which if granted might result in a stay of enforcement of the award, or the enforcement has in fact been stayed (provisionally or otherwise) under the Convention.[8] Secondly, in relation to execution when sovereign immunity issues can be raised as to the assets against which execution is sought.[9]

2. The Arbitration (International Investment Disputes) Act 1966.
3. ICSID Convention Art 54(1).
4. ICSID Convention Article 54(3).
5. See the previous chapter and *AIG Capital, supra*.
6. Section 1(2) of the Arbitration (International Investment Disputes) Act 1966 and subject to various other matters set out in this Act. See also Part 62.21 and Practice Direction 62 of the CPR.
7. Parts 62.21, 74 and 8 plus the respective practice directions of the CPR.
8. ICSID Article 53; Part 62.21(5) of the CPR.
9. See e.g. *AIG Capital, supra*.

APPENDIX A

ARBITRATION ACT 1996

CONTENTS

Part I—Arbitration Pursuant to an Arbitration Agreement
Introductory
1. General principles
2. Scope of application provisions
3. The seat of the arbitration
4. Mandatory and non-mandatory provision
5. Agreements to be in writing

The Arbitration Agreement
6. Definition of arbitration agreement
7. Separability of arbitration agreement
8. Whether agreement discharged by death of a party

Stay of Legal Proceedings
9. Stay of legal proceedings
10. Reference of interpleader issue to arbitration
11. Retention of security where Admiralty proceedings stayed

Commencement of Arbitral Proceedings
12. Power of court to extend time for beginning arbitral proceedings, &c
13. Application of Limitation Acts
14. Commencement of arbitral proceedings

The Arbitral Tribunal
15. The arbitral tribunal
16. Procedure for appointment of arbitrators
17. Power in case of default to appoint sole arbitrator
18. Failure of appointment procedure
19. Court to have regard to agreed qualifications
20. Chairman
21. Umpire
22. Decision-making where no chairman or umpire
23. Revocation of arbitrator's authority
24. Power of court to remove arbitrator
25. Resignation of arbitrator
26. Death of arbitrator or person appointing him
27. Filling of vacancy, &c
28. Joint and several liability of parties to arbitrators for fees and expenses
29. Immunity of arbitrator

Jurisdiction of the Arbitral Tribunal
30. Competence of tribunal to rule on its own jurisdiction
31. Objection to substantive jurisdiction of tribunal
32. Determination of preliminary point of jurisdiction

The Arbitral Proceedings
33. General duty of the tribunal
34. Procedural and evidential matters
35. Consolidation of proceedings and concurrent hearings

36. Legal or other representation
37. Power to appoint experts, legal advisers or assessors
38. General powers exercisable by the tribunal
39. Power to make provisional awards
40. General duty of parties
41. Powers of tribunal in case of party's default

Powers of Court in Relation to Arbitral Proceedings

42. Enforcement of peremptory orders of tribunal
43. Securing the attendance of witnesses
44. Court powers exercisable in support of arbitral proceedings
45. Determination of preliminary point of law

The Award

46. Rules applicable to substance of dispute
47. Awards on different issues, &c
48. Remedies
49. Interest
50. Extension of time for making award
51. Settlement
52. Form of award
53. Place where award treated as made
54. Date of award
55. Notification of award
56. Power to withhold award in case of non-payment
57. Correction of award or additional award
58. Effect of award

Costs of the Arbitration

59. Costs of the arbitration
60. Agreement to pay costs in any event
61. Award of costs
62. Effect of agreement or award about costs
63. The recoverable costs of the arbitration
64. Recoverable fees and expenses of arbitrators
65. Power to limit recoverable costs

Powers of the Court in Relation to Award

66. Enforcement of the award
67. Challenging the award: substantive jurisdiction
68. Challenging the award: serious irregularity
69. Appeal on point of law
70. Challenge or appeal: supplementary provisions
71. Challenge or appeal: effect of order of court

Miscellaneous

72. Saving for rights of person who takes no part in proceedings
73. Loss of right to object
74. Immunity of arbitral institutions, &c
75. Charge to secure payment of solicitors' costs

Supplementary

76. Service of notices, &c
77. Powers of court in relation to service of documents
78. Reckoning periods of time
79. Power of court to extend time limits relating to arbitral proceedings
80. Notice and other requirements in connection with legal proceedings
81. Saving for certain matters governed by common law
82. Minor definitions

83. Index of defined expressions: Part I
84. Transitional provisions

Part II—Other Provisions relating to Arbitration

Domestic Arbitration Agreements

85. Modification of Part I in relation to domestic arbitration agreement
86. Staying of legal proceedings
87. Effectiveness of agreement to exclude court's jurisdiction
88. Power to repeal or amend sections 85 to 87

Consumer Arbitration Agreements

89. Application of unfair terms regulations to consumer arbitration agreements
90. Regulations apply where consumer is a legal person
91. Arbitration agreement unfair where modest amount sought

Small Claims Arbitration in the County Court

92. Exclusion of Part I in relation to small claims arbitration in the county court

Appointment of Judges as Arbitrators

93. Appointment of judges as arbitrators

Statutory Arbitration

94. Application of Part I to statutory arbitrations
95. General adaptation of provisions in relation to statutory arbitrations
96. Specific adaptations of provisions in relation to statutory arbitrations
97. Provisions excluded from applying to statutory arbitrations
98. Power to make further provision by regulations

Part III—Recognition and Enforcement of Certain Foreign Awards

Enforcement of Geneva Convention Awards

99. Continuation of Part II of the Arbitration Act 1950

Recognition and Enforcement of New York Convention Awards

100. New York Convention awards
101. Recognition and enforcement of awards
102. Evidence to be produced by party seeking recognition or enforcement
103. Refusal of recognition or enforcement
104. Saving for other bases of recognition or enforcement

Part IV—General Provisions

105. Meaning of "the court": jurisdiction of High Court and county court
106. Crown application
107. Consequential amendments and repeals
108. Extent
109. Commencement
110. Short title

Schedules

Schedule 1—Mandatory provisions of Part I

Schedule 2—Modification of Part I in relation to judge-arbitrators

Schedule 3—Consequential amendments

Schedule 4—Repeals

PART I ARBITRATION PURSUANT TO AN ARBITRATION AGREEMENT

Introductory

General principles

1. The provisions of this Part are founded on the following principles, and shall be construed accordingly—

(a) the object of arbitration is to obtain the fair resolution of disputes by an impartial tribunal without unnecessary delay or expense;
(b) the parties should be free to agree how their disputes are resolved, subject only to such safeguards as are necessary in the public interest;
(c) in matters governed by this Part the court should not intervene except as provided by this Part.

Scope of application of provisions

2.—(1) The provisions of this Part apply where the seat of the arbitration is in England and Wales or Northern Ireland.

(2) The following sections apply even if the seat of the arbitration is outside England and Wales or Northern Ireland or no seat has been designated or determined

(a) sections 9 to 11 (stay of legal proceedings, &c.), and
(b) section 66 (enforcement of arbitral awards).

(3) The powers conferred by the following sections apply even if the seat of the arbitration is outside England and Wales or Northern Ireland or no seat has been designated or determined

(a) section 43 (securing the attendance of witnesses), and
(b) section 44 (court powers exercisable in support of arbitral proceedings);

but the court may refuse to exercise any such power if in the opinion of the court, the fact that the seat of the arbitration is outside England and Wales or Northern Ireland, or that when designated or determined the seat is likely to be outside England and Wales or Northern Ireland, makes it inappropriate to do so.

(4) The court may exercise a power conferred by any provision of this Part not mentioned in subsection (2) or (3) for the purpose of supporting the arbitral process where—

(a) no seat of the arbitration has been designated or determined, and
(b) by reason of a connection with England and Wales or Northern Ireland the court is satisfied that it is appropriate to do so.

(5) Section 7 (separability of arbitration agreement) and section 8 (death of a party) apply where the law applicable to the arbitration agreement is the law of England and Wales or Northern Ireland even if the seat of the arbitration is outside England and Wales or Northern Ireland or has not been designated or determined.

The seat of the arbitration

3. In this Part "the seat of the arbitration" means the juridical seat of the arbitration designated—

(a) by the parties to the arbitration agreement, or
(b) by any arbitral or other institution or person vested by the parties with powers in that regard, or
(c) by the arbitral tribunal if so authorised by the parties,

or determined, in the absence of any such designation, having regard to the parties' agreement and all the relevant circumstances.

Mandatory and non-mandatory provisions

4.—(1) The mandatory provisions of this Part are listed in Schedule 1 and have effect notwithstanding any agreement to the contrary.

(2) The other provisions of this Part (the "non-mandatory provisions") allow the parties to make their own arrangements by agreement but provide rules which apply in the absence of such agreement.

(3) The parties may make such arrangements by agreeing to the application of institutional rules or providing any other means by which a matter may be decided.

(4) It is immaterial whether or not the law applicable to the parties' agreement is the law of England and Wales or, as the case may be, Northern Ireland.

(5) The choice of a law other than the law of England and Wales or Northern Ireland as the applicable law in respect of a matter provided for by a non-mandatory provision of this Part is equivalent to an agreement making provision about that matter.

For this purpose an applicable law determined in accordance with the parties' agreement, or which is objectively determined in the absence of any express or implied choice, shall be treated as chosen by the parties.

Agreements to be in writing

5.—(1) The provisions of this Part apply only where the arbitration agreement is in writing, and any other agreement between the parties as to any matter is effective for the purposes of this Part only if in writing.

The expressions "agreement", "agree" and "agreed" shall be construed accordingly.

(2) There is an agreement in writing—

(a) if the agreement is made in writing (whether or not it is signed by the parties),

(b) the agreement is made by exchange of communications in writing, or

(c) if the agreement is evidenced in writing.

(3) Where parties agree otherwise than in writing by reference to terms which are in writing, they make an agreement in writing.

(4) An agreement is evidenced in writing if an agreement made otherwise than in writing is recorded by one of the parties, or by a third party with the authority of the parties to the agreement.

(5) An exchange of written submissions in arbitral or legal proceedings in which the existence of an agreement otherwise than in writing is alleged by one party against another party and not denied by the other party in his response constitutes as between those parties an agreement in writing to the effect alleged.

(6) References in this Part to anything being written or in writing include its being recorded by any means.

The Arbitration Agreement

Definition of arbitration agreement

6.—(1) In this Part an "arbitration agreement" means an agreement to submit to arbitration present or future disputes (whether they are contractual or not).

(2) The reference in an agreement to a written form of arbitration clause or to a document containing an arbitration clause constitutes an arbitration agreement if the reference is such as to make that clause part of the agreement.

Separability of arbitration agreement

7. Unless otherwise agreed by the parties, an arbitration agreement which forms or was intended to form part of another agreement (whether or not in writing) shall not be regarded as invalid, non-existent or ineffective because that other agreement is invalid, or did not come into existence or has become ineffective, and it shall for that purpose be treated as a distinct agreement.

Whether agreement discharged by death of a party

8.—(1) Unless otherwise agreed by the parties, an arbitration agreement is not discharged by the death of a party and may be enforced by or against the personal representatives of that party.

(2) Subsection (1) does not affect the operation of any enactment or rule of law by virtue of which a substantive right or obligation is extinguished by death.

Stay of Legal Proceedings

Stay of legal proceedings

9.—(1) A party to an arbitration agreement against whom legal proceedings are brought (whether by way of claim or counterclaim) in respect of a matter which under the agreement is to be referred to arbitration may (upon notice to the other parties to the proceedings) apply to the court in which the proceedings have been brought to stay the proceedings so far as they concern that matter.

(2) An application may be made notwithstanding that the matter is to be referred to arbitration only after the exhaustion of other dispute resolution procedures.

(3) An application may not be made by a person before taking the appropriate procedural step (if any) to acknowledge the legal proceedings against him or after he has taken any step in those proceedings to answer the substantive claim.

(4) On an application under this section the court shall grant a stay unless satisfied that the arbitration agreement is null and void, inoperative, or incapable of being performed.

(5) If the court refuses to stay the legal proceedings, any provision that an award is a condition precedent to the bringing of legal proceedings in respect of any matter is of no effect in relation to those proceedings.

Reference of interpleader issue in arbitration

10.—(1) Where in legal proceedings relief by way of interpleader is granted and any issue between the claimants is one in respect of which there is an arbitration agreement between them, the court granting the relief shall direct that the issue be determined in accordance with the agreement unless the circumstances are such that proceedings brought by a claimant in respect of the matter would not be stayed.

(2) Where subsection (1) applies but the court does not direct that the issue be determined in accordance with the arbitration agreement, any provision that an award is a condition precedent to the bringing of legal proceedings in respect of any matter shall not affect the determination of that issue by the court.

Retention of security where Admiralty proceedings stayed

11.—(1) Where Admiralty proceedings are stayed on the ground that the dispute in question should be submitted to arbitration, the court granting the stay may, if in those proceedings property has been arrested or bail or other security has been given to prevent or obtain release from arrest—

(a) order that the property arrested be retained as security for the satisfaction of any award given in the arbitration in respect of that dispute, or

(b) order that the stay of these proceedings be conditional on the provision of equivalent security for the satisfaction of any such award.

(2) Subject to any provision made by rules of court and to any necessary modification, the same law and practice shall apply in relation to property retained in pursuance of an order as would apply if it were held for the purposes of proceedings in the court making the order.

Commencement of Arbitral Proceedings

Power of court to extend time for beginning arbitral proceedings, &c

12.—(1) Where an arbitration agreement to refer future disputes to arbitration provides that a claim shall be barred, or the claimant's right extinguished, unless the claimant takes within a time fixed by the agreement some step—

(a) to begin arbitral proceedings, or

(b) to begin other dispute resolution procedures which must be exhausted before arbitral proceedings can be begun,

the court may by order extend the time for taking that step.

(2) Any party to the arbitration agreement may apply for such an order (upon notice to the other parties), but only after a claim has arisen and after exhausting any available arbitral process for obtaining an extension of time.

(3) The court shall make an order only if satisfied—

(a) that the circumstances are such as were outside the reasonable contemplation of the parties when they agreed the provision in question, and that it would be just to extend the time, or

(b) that the conduct of one party makes it unjust to hold the other party to the strict terms of the provision in question.

(4) The court may extend the time for such period and on such terms as it thinks fit, and may do so whether or not the time previously fixed by agreement or by a previous order has expired.

(5) An order under this section does not affect the operation of the Limitation Acts (see section 13).

(6) The leave of the court is required for any appeal from a decision of the court under this section.

Application of Limitation Acts

13.—(1) The Limitation Acts apply to arbitral proceedings as they apply to legal proceedings.

(2) The court may order that in computing the time prescribed by the Limitation Acts for the commencement of proceedings (including arbitral proceedings) in respect of a dispute which was the subject matter—

(a) of an award which the court orders to be set aside or declares to be of no effect, or

(b) of the affected part of an award which the court orders to be set aside in part, or declares to be in part of no effect, the period between the commencement of the arbitration and the date of the order referred to in paragraph (a) or (b) shall be excluded.

(3) In determining for the purposes of the Limitation Acts when a cause of action accrued, any provision that an award is a condition precedent to the bringing of legal proceedings in respect of a matter to which an arbitration agreement applies shall be disregarded.

(4) In this Part "the Limitation Acts" means

(a) in England and Wales, the Limitation Act 1980, the Foreign Limitation Periods Act 1984 and any other enactment (whenever passed) relating to the limitation of actions;

(b) in Northern Ireland, the Limitation (Northern Ireland) Order 1989, the Foreign Limitation Periods (Northern Ireland) Order 1985 and any other enactment (whenever passed) relating to the limitation of actions.

Commencement of arbitral proceedings

14.—(1) The parties are free to agree when arbitral proceedings are to be regarded as commenced for the purposes of this Part and for the purposes of the Limitation Acts.

(2) If there is no such agreement the following provisions apply.

(3) Where the arbitrator is named or designated in the arbitration agreement, arbitral proceedings are commenced in respect of a matter when one party serves on the other party or parties a notice in writing requiring him or them to submit that matter to the person so named or designated.

(4) Where the arbitrator or arbitrators are to be appointed by the parties, arbitral proceedings are commenced in respect of a matter when one party serves on the other party or parties notice in writing requiring him or them to appoint an arbitrator or to agree to the appointment of an arbitrator in respect of that matter.

(5) Where the arbitrator or arbitrators are to be appointed by a person other than a party to the proceedings, arbitral proceedings are commenced in respect of a matter when one party gives notice in writing to that person requesting him to make the appointment in respect of that matter.

The Arbitral Tribunal

The arbitral tribunal

15.—(1) The parties are free to agree on the number of arbitrators to form the tribunal and whether there is to be a chairman or umpire.

(2) Unless otherwise agreed by the parties, an agreement that the number of arbitrators shall be two or any other even number shall be understood as requiring the appointment of an additional arbitrator as chairman of the tribunal.

(3) If there is no agreement as to the number of arbitrators, the tribunal shall consist of a sole arbitrator.

Procedure for appointment of arbitrators

16.—(1) The parties are free to agree on the procedure for appointing the arbitrator or arbitrators, including the procedure for appointing any chairman or umpire.

(2) If or to the extent that there is no such agreement, the following provisions apply.

(3) If the tribunal is to consist of a sole arbitrator, the parties shall jointly appoint the arbitrator not later than 28 days after service of a request in writing by either party to do so.

(4) If the tribunal is to consist of two arbitrators, each party shall appoint one arbitrator not later than 14 days after service of a request in writing by either party to do so.

(5) If the tribunal is to consist of three arbitrators—

(a) each party shall appoint one arbitrator not later than 14 days after service of a request in writing by either party to do so, and

(b) the two so appointed shall forthwith appoint a third arbitrator as the chairman of the tribunal.

(6) If the tribunal is to consist of two arbitrators and an umpire—

(a) each party shall appoint one arbitrator not later than 14 days after service of a request in writing by either party to do so, and

(b) the two so appointed may appoint an umpire at any time after they themselves are appointed and shall do so before any substantive hearing or forthwith if they cannot agree on a matter relating to the arbitration.

(7) In any other case (in particular, if there are more than two parties) section 18 applies as in the case of a failure of the agreed appointment procedure.

Power in case of default to appoint sole arbitrator

17.—(1) Unless the parties otherwise agree, where each of two parties to an arbitration agreement is to appoint an arbitrator and one party ("the party in default") refuses to do so, or fails to do so within the time specified, the other party, having duly appointed his arbitrator, may give notice in writing to the party in default that he proposes to appoint his arbitrator to act as sole arbitrator.

(2) If the party in default does not within 7 clear days of that notice being given—

(a) make the required appointment, and

(b) notify the other party that he has done so,

the other party may appoint his arbitrator as sole arbitrator whose award shall be binding on both parties as if he had been so appointed by agreement.

(3) Where a sole arbitrator has been appointed under subsection (2), the party in default may (upon notice to the appointing party) apply to the court which may set aside the appointment.

(4) The leave of the court is required for any appeal from a decision of the court under this section.

Failure of appointment procedure

18.—(1) The parties are free to agree what is to happen in the event of a failure of the procedure for the appointment of the arbitral tribunal.

There is no failure if an appointment is duly made under section 17 (power in case of default to appoint sole arbitrator), unless that appointment is set aside.

(2) If or to the extent that there is no such agreement any party to the arbitration agreement may (upon notice to the other parties) apply to the court to exercise its powers under this section.

(3) Those powers are—

(a) to give directions as to the making of any necessary appointments;

(b) to direct that the tribunal shall be constituted by such appointments (or any one or more of them) as have been made;

(c) to revoke any appointments already made;
(d) to make any necessary appointment itself.

(4) An appointment made by the court under this section has effect as if made with the agreement of the parties.

(5) The leave of the court is required for any appeal from a decision of the court under this section.

Court to have regard to agreed qualifications

19. In deciding whether to exercise, and in considering how to exercise, any of its powers under section 16 (procedure for appointment of arbitrators) or section 18 (failure of appointment procedure), the court shall have due regard to any agreement of the parties as to the qualifications required of the arbitrators.

Chairman

20.—(1) Where the parties have agreed that there is to be a chairman, they are free to agree what the functions of the chairman are to be in relation to the making of decisions, orders and awards.

(2) If or to the extent that there is no such agreement, the following provisions apply.

(3) Decisions, orders and awards shall be made by all or a majority of the arbitrators (including the chairman).

(4) The view of the chairman shall prevail in relation to a decision, order or award in respect of which there is neither unanimity nor a majority under subsection (3).

Umpire

21.—(1) Where the parties have agreed that there is to be an umpire, they are free to agree what the functions of the umpire are to be, and in particular—

(a) whether he is to attend the proceedings, and
(b) when he is to replace the other arbitrators as the tribunal with power to make decisions, orders and awards.

(2) If or to the extent that there is no such agreement, the following provisions apply.

(3) The umpire shall attend the proceedings and be supplied with the same documents and other materials as are supplied to the other arbitrators.

(4) Decisions, orders and awards shall be made by the other arbitrators unless and until they cannot agree on a matter relating to the arbitration.

In that event they shall forthwith give notice in writing to the parties and the umpire, whereupon the umpire shall replace them as the tribunal with power to make decisions, orders and awards as if he were sole arbitrator.

(5) If the arbitrators cannot agree but fail to give notice of that fact, or if any of them fails to join in the giving of notice, any party to the arbitral proceedings may (upon notice to the other parties and to the tribunal) apply to the court which may order that the umpire shall replace the other arbitration as the tribunal with power to make decisions, orders and awards as if he were sole arbitrator.

(6) The leave of the court is required for any appeal from a decision of the court under this section.

Decision-making where no chairman or umpire

22.—(1) Where the parties agree that there shall be two or more arbitrators with no chairman or umpire, the parties are free to agree how the tribunal is to make decisions, orders and awards.

(2) If there is no such agreement, decisions, orders and awards shall be made by all or a majority of the arbitrators.

Revocation of arbitrator's authority

23.—(1) The parties are free to agree in what circumstances the authority of an arbitrator may be revoked.

(2) If or to the extent that there is no such agreement the following provisions apply.

(3) The authority of an arbitrator may not be revoked except—

- (a) by the parties acting jointly, or
- (b) by an arbitral or other institution or person vested by the parties with powers in that regard.

(4) Revocation of the authority of an arbitrator by the parties acting jointly must be agreed in writing unless the parties also agree (whether or not in writing) to terminate the arbitration agreement.

(5) Nothing in this section affects the power of the court—

- (a) to revoke an appointment under section 18 (powers exercisable in case of failure of appointment procedure), or
- (b) to remove an arbitrator on the grounds specified in section 24.

Power of court to remove arbitrator

24.—(1) A party to arbitral proceedings may (upon notice to the other parties, to the arbitrator concerned and to any other arbitrator) apply to the court to remove an arbitrator on any of the following grounds—

- (a) that circumstances exist that give rise to justifiable doubts as to his impartiality;
- (b) that he does not possess the qualifications required by the arbitration agreement;
- (c) that he is physically or mentally incapable of conducting the proceedings or there are justifiable doubts as to his capacity to do so;
- (d) that he has refused or failed—
  - (i) properly to conduct the proceedings, or
  - (ii) to use all reasonable despatch in conducting the proceedings or making an award, and that substantial injustice has been or will be caused to the applicant.

(2) If there is an arbitral or other institution or person vested by the parties with power to remove an arbitrator, the court shall not exercise its power of removal unless satisfied that the applicant has first exhausted any available recourse to that institution or person.

(3) The arbitral tribunal may continue the arbitral proceedings and make an award while an application to the court under this section is pending.

(4) Where the court removes an arbitrator, it may make such order as it thinks fit with respect to his entitlement (if any) to fees or expenses, or the repayment of any fees or expenses already paid.

(5) The arbitrator concerned is entitled to appear and be heard by the court before it makes any order under this section.

(6) The leave of the court is required for any appeal from a decision of the court under this section.

Resignation of arbitrator

25.—(1) The parties are free to agree with an arbitrator as to the consequences of his resignation as regards—

(a) his entitlement (if any) to fees or expenses, and

(b) any liability thereby incurred by him.

(2) If or to the extent that there is no such agreement the following provisions apply.

(3) An arbitrator who resigns his appointment may (upon notice to the parties) apply to the court—

(a) to grant him relief from any liability thereby incurred by him, and

(b) to make such order as it thinks fit with respect to his entitlement (if any) to fees or expenses or the repayment of any fees or expenses already paid.

(4) If the court is satisfied that in all the circumstances it was reasonable for the arbitrator to resign, it may grant such relief as is mentioned in subsection (3)(a) on such terms as it thinks fit.

(5) The leave of the court is required for any appeal from a decision of the court under this section.

Death of arbitrator or person appointing him

26.—(1) The authority of an arbitrator is personal and ceases on his death.

(2) Unless otherwise agreed by the parties, the death of the person by whom an arbitrator was appointed does not revoke the arbitrator's authority.

Filling of vacancy, &c

27.—(1) Where an arbitrator ceases to hold office, the parties are free to agree—

(a) whether and if so how the vacancy is to be filled,

(b) whether and if so to what extent the previous proceedings should stand, and

(c) what effect (if any) his ceasing to hold office has on any appointment made by him (alone or jointly).

(2) If or to the extent that there is no such agreement, the following provisions apply.

(3) The provisions of sections 16 (procedure for appointment of arbitrators) and 18 (failure of appointment procedure) apply in relation to the filling of the vacancy as in relation to an original appointment.

(4) The tribunal (when reconstituted) shall determine whether and if so to what extent the previous proceedings should stand.

This does not affect any right of a party to challenge those proceedings on any ground which had arisen before the arbitrator ceased to hold office.

(5) His ceasing to hold office does not affect any appointment by him (alone or jointly) of another arbitrator, in particular any appointment of a chairman or umpire.

Joint and several liability of parties to arbitrators for fees and expenses

28.—(1) The parties are jointly and severally liable to pay to the arbitrators such reasonable fees and expenses (if any) as are appropriate in the circumstances.

(2) Any party may apply to the court (upon notice to the other parties and to the arbitrators) which may order that the amount of the arbitrators' fees and expenses shall be considered and adjusted by such means and upon such terms as it may direct.

(3) If the application is made after any amount has been paid to the arbitrators by way of fees or expenses, the court may order the repayment of such amount (if any) as is shown to be excessive but shall not do so unless it is shown that it is reasonable in the circumstances to order repayment.

(4) The above provisions have effect subject to any order of the court under section 24(4) or 25(3)(b) (order as to entitlement to fees or expenses in case of removal or resignation of arbitrator).

(5) Nothing in this section affects any liability of a party to any other party to pay all or any of the costs of the arbitration (see sections 59 to 65) or any contractual right of an arbitrator to payment of his fees and expenses.

(6) In this section references to arbitrators include an arbitrator who has ceased to act and an umpire who has not replaced the other arbitrators.

Immunity of arbitrator

29.—(1) An arbitrator is not liable for anything done or omitted in the discharge or purported discharge of his functions as arbitrator unless the act or omission is shown to have been in bad faith.

(2) Subsection (1) applies to an employee or agent of an arbitrator as it applies to the arbitrator himself.

(3) This section does not affect any liability incurred by an arbitrator by reason of his resigning (but see section 25).

Jurisdiction of the Arbitral Tribunal

Competence of tribunal to rule on its own jurisdiction

30.—(1) Unless otherwise agreed by the parties, the arbitral tribunal may rule on its own substantive jurisdiction, that is, as to—

(a) whether there is a valid arbitration agreement,
(b) whether the tribunal is properly constituted, and
(c) what matters have been submitted to arbitration in accordance with the arbitration agreement.

(2) Any such ruling may be challenged by any available arbitral process of appeal or review or in accordance with the provisions of this Part.

Objection to substantive jurisdiction of tribunal

31.—(1) An objection that the arbitral tribunal lacks substantive jurisdiction at the outset of the proceedings must be raised by a party not later than the time he takes the first step in the proceedings to contest the merits of any matter in relation to which he challenges the tribunal's jurisdiction.

A party is not precluded from raising such an objection by the fact that he has appointed or participated in the appointment of an arbitrator.

(2) Any objection during the course of the arbitral proceedings that the arbitral tribunal is exceeding its substantive jurisdiction must be made as soon as possible after the matter alleged to be beyond its jurisdiction is raised.

(3) The arbitral tribunal may admit an objection later than the time specified in subsection (1) or (2) if it considers the delay justified.

(4) Where an objection is duly taken to the tribunal's substantive jurisdiction and the tribunal has power to rule on its own jurisdiction, it may—

(a) rule on the matter in an award as to jurisdiction, or
(b) deal with the objection in its award on the merits.

If the parties agree which of these courses the tribunal should take, the tribunal shall proceed accordingly.

(5) The tribunal may in any case, and shall if the parties so agree, stay proceedings whilst an application is made to the court under section 32 (determination of preliminary point of jurisdiction).

Determination of preliminary point of jurisdiction

32.—(1) The court may, on the application of a party to arbitral proceedings (upon notice to the other parties), determine any question as to the substantive jurisdiction of the tribunal.

A party may lose the right to object (see section 73).

(2) An application under this section shall not be considered unless—

(a) it is made with the agreement in writing of all the other parties to the proceedings, or
(b) it is made with the permission of the tribunal and the court is satisfied—
 (i) that the determination of the question is likely to produce substantial savings in costs,
 (ii) that the application was made without delay, and
 (iii) that there is good reason why the matter should be decided by the court.

(3) An application under this section, unless made with the agreement of all the other parties to the proceedings, shall state the grounds on which it is said that the matter should be decided by the court.

(4) Unless otherwise agreed by the parties, the arbitral tribunal may continue the arbitral proceedings and make an award while an application to the court under this section is pending.

(5) Unless the court gives leave, no appeal lies from a decision of the court whether the conditions specified in subsection (2) are met.

(6) The decision of the court on the question of jurisdiction shall be treated as a judgment of the court for the purposes of an appeal.

But no appeal lies without the leave of the court which shall not be given unless the court considers that the question involves a point of law which is one of general importance or is one which for some other special reason should be considered by the Court of Appeal.

The Arbitral Proceedings

General duty of the tribunal

33.—(1) The tribunal shall—

(a) act fairly and impartially as between the parties, giving each party a reasonable opportunity of putting his case and dealing with that of his opponent, and

(b) adopt procedures suitable to the circumstances of the particular case, avoiding unnecessary delay or expense, so as to provide a fair means for the resolution of the matters falling to be determined.

(2) The tribunal shall comply with that general duty in conducting the arbitral proceedings, in its decisions on matters of procedure and evidence and in the exercise of all other powers conferred on it.

Procedural and evidential matters

34.—(1) It shall be for the tribunal to decide all procedural and evidential matters, subject to the right of the parties to agree any matter.

(2) Procedural and evidential matters include—

(a) when and where any part of the proceedings is to be held;

(b) the language or languages to be used in the proceedings and whether translation of any relevant documents are to be supplied;

(c) whether any and if so what form of written statements of claim and defence are to be used, when these should be supplied and the extent to which such statements can be later amended;

(d) whether any and if so which documents or classes of documents should be disclosed between and produced by the parties and at what stage;

(e) whether any and if so what questions should be put to and answered by the respective parties and when and in what form this should be done;

(f) whether to apply strict rules of evidence (or any other rules) as to the admissibility, relevance or weight of any material (oral, written or other) sought to be tendered on any matters of fact or opinion, and the time, manner and form in which such material should be exchanged and presented;

(g) whether and to what extent the tribunal should itself take the initiative in ascertaining the facts and the law;

(h) whether and to what extent there should be oral or written evidence or submissions.

(3) The tribunal may fix the time within which any directions given by it are to be complied with, and may if it thinks fit extend the time so fixed (whether or not it has expired).

Consolidation of proceedings and concurrent hearings

35.—(1) The parties are free to agree—

(a) that the arbitral proceedings shall be consolidated with other arbitral proceedings, or

(b) that concurrent hearings shall be held, on such terms as may be agreed.

(2) Unless the parties agree to confer such power on the tribunal, the tribunal has no power to order consolidation of proceedings or concurrent hearings.

Legal or other representation

36. Unless otherwise agreed by the parties, a party to arbitral proceedings may be represented in the proceedings by a lawyer or other person chosen by him.

Power to appoint experts, legal advisers or assessors

37.—(1) Unless otherwise agreed by the parties—

(a) the tribunal may—

(i) appoint experts or legal advisers to report to it and the parties, or
(ii) appoint assessors to assist it on technical matters,

and may allow any such expert, legal adviser or assessor to attend the proceedings; and

(b) the parties shall be given a reasonable opportunity to comment on any information, opinion or advice offered by any such person.

(2) The fees and expenses of an expert, legal adviser or assessor appointed by the tribunal for which the arbitrators are liable are expenses of the arbitrators for the purposes of this Part.

General powers exercisable by the tribunal

38.—(1) The parties are free to agree on the powers exercisable by the arbitral tribunal for the purposes of and in relation to the proceedings.

(2) Unless otherwise agreed by the parties the tribunal has the following powers.

(3) The tribunal may order a claimant to provide security for the costs of the arbitration.

This power shall not be exercised on the ground that the claimant is—

(a) an individual ordinarily resident outside the United Kingdom, or
(b) a corporation or association incorporated or formed under the law of a country outside the United Kingdom, or whose central management and control is exercised outside the United Kingdom.

(4) The tribunal may give directions in relation to any property which is the subject of the proceedings or as to which any question arises in the proceedings, and which is owned by or is in the possession of a party to the proceedings—

(a) for the inspection, photographing, preservation, custody or detention of the property by the tribunal, an expert or a party, or
(b) ordering that samples be taken from, or any observation be made of or experiment conducted upon, the property.

(5) The tribunal may direct that a party or witness shall be examined on oath or affirmation, and may for that purpose administer any necessary oath or take any necessary affirmation.

(6) The tribunal may give directions to a party for the preservation for the purposes of the proceedings of any evidence in his custody or control.

Power to make provisional awards

39.—(1) The parties are free to agree that the tribunal shall have power to order on a provisional basis any relief which it would have power to grant in a final award.

(2) This includes, for instance, making—

(a) a provisional order for the payment of money or the disposition of property as between the parties, or
(b) an order to make an interim payment on account of the costs of the arbitration.

(3) Any such order shall be subject to the tribunal's final adjudication; and the tribunal's final award, on the merits or as to costs, shall take account of any such order.

(4) Unless the parties agree to confer such power on the tribunal, the tribunal has no such power.

This does not affect its powers under section 47 (awards on different issues, &c).

General duty of parties

40.—(1) The parties shall do all things necessary for the proper and expeditious conduct of the arbitral proceedings.

(2) This includes—

(a) complying without delay with any determination of the tribunal as to procedural or evidential matters, or with any order or directions of the tribunal, and

(b) where appropriate, taking without delay any necessary steps to obtain a decision of the court on a preliminary question of jurisdiction or law (see sections 32 and 45).

Powers of tribunal in case of party's default

41.—(1) The parties are free to agree on the powers of the tribunal in case of a party's failure to do something necessary for the proper and expeditious conduct of the arbitration.

(2) Unless otherwise agreed by the parties, the following provisions apply.

(3) If the tribunal is satisfied that there has been inordinate and inexcusable delay on the part of the claimant in pursuing his claim and that the delay—

(a) gives rise, or is likely to give rise, to a substantial risk that it is not possible to have a fair resolution of the issues in that claim, or

(b) has caused, or is likely to cause, serious prejudice to the respondent, the tribunal may make an award dismissing the claim.

(4) If without showing sufficient cause a party—

(a) fails to attend or be represented at an oral hearing of which due notice was given, or

(b) where matters are to be dealt with in writing, fails after due notice to submit written evidence or make written submissions,

the tribunal may continue the proceedings in the absence of that party or, as the case may be, without any written evidence or submissions on his behalf, and may make an award on the basis of the evidence before it.

(5) If without showing sufficient cause a party fails to comply with any order or directions of the tribunal, the tribunal may make a peremptory order to the same effect, prescribing such time for compliance with it as the tribunal considers appropriate.

(6) If a claimant fails to comply with a peremptory order of the tribunal to provide security for costs, the tribunal may make an award dismissing his claim.

(7) If a party fails to comply with any other kind of peremptory order, then, without prejudice to section 42 (enforcement by court of tribunal's peremptory orders), the tribunal may do any of the following—

(a) direct that the party in default shall not be entitled to rely upon any allegation or material which was the subject matter of the order;

(b) draw such adverse inferences from the act of non-compliance as the circumstances justify;

(c) proceed to an award on the basis of such materials as have been properly provided to it;

(d) make such order as it thinks fit as to the payment of costs of the arbitration incurred in consequence of the non-compliance.

Powers of Court in Relation to Arbitral Proceedings

Enforcement of peremptory orders of tribunal

42.—(1) Unless otherwise agreed by the parties, the court may make an order requiring a party to comply with a peremptory order made by the tribunal.

(2) An application for an order under this section may be made—

(a) by the tribunal (upon notice to the parties),
(b) by a party to the arbitral proceedings with the permission of the tribunal (and upon notice to the other parties), or
(c) where the parties have agreed that the powers of the court under this section shall be available.

(3) The court shall not act unless it is satisfied that the applicant has exhausted any available arbitral process in respect of failure to comply with the tribunal's order.

(4) No order shall be made under this section unless the court is satisfied that the person to whom the tribunal's order was directed has failed to comply with it within the time prescribed in the order or, if no time was prescribed, within a reasonable time.

(5) The leave of the court is required for any appeal from a decision of the court under this section.

Securing the attendance of witnesses

43.—(1) A party to arbitral proceedings may use the same court procedures as are available in relation to legal proceedings to secure the attendance before the tribunal of a witness in order to give oral testimony or to produce documents or other material evidence.

(2) This may only be done with the permission of the tribunal or the agreement of the other parties.

(3) The court procedures may only be used if—

(a) the witness is in the United Kingdom, and
(b) the arbitral proceedings are being conducted in England and Wales or, as the case may be, Northern Ireland.

(4) A person shall not be compelled by virtue of this section to produce any document or other material evidence which he could not be compelled to produce in legal proceedings.

Court powers exercisable in support of arbitral proceedings

44.—(1) Unless otherwise agreed by the parties, the court has for the purposes of and in relation to arbitral proceedings the same power of making orders about the matters listed below as it has for the purposes of and in relation to legal proceedings.

(2) Those matters are—

(a) the taking of the evidence of witnesses;
(b) the preservation of evidence;
(c) making orders relating to property which is the subject of the proceedings or as to which any question arises in the proceedings—
  (i) for the inspection, photographing, preservation, custody or detention of the property or
  (ii) ordering that samples be taken from, or any observation be made of or experiment conducted upon, the property;

  and for that purpose authorising any person to enter any premises in the possession or control of a party to the arbitration;
(d) the sale of any goods the subject of the proceedings;
(e) the granting of an interim injunction or the appointment of a receiver.

(3) If the case is one of urgency, the court may, on the application of a party or proposed party to the arbitral proceedings, make such orders as it thinks necessary for the purpose of preserving evidence or assets.

(4) If the case is not one of urgency, the court shall act only on the application of a party to the arbitral proceedings (upon notice to the other parties and to the tribunal) made with the permission of the tribunal or the agreement in writing of the other parties.

(5) In any case the court shall act only if or to the extent that the arbitral tribunal, and any arbitral or other institution or person vested by the parties with power in that regard, has no power or is unable for the time being to act effectively.

(6) If the court so orders, an order made by it under this section shall cease to have effect in whole or in part on the order of the tribunal or of any such arbitral or other institution or person having power to act in relation to the subject-matter of the order.

(7) The leave of the court is required for any appeal from a decision of the court under this section.

Determination of preliminary point of law

45.—(1) Unless otherwise agreed by the parties, the court may on the application of a party to arbitral proceedings (upon notice to the other parties) determine any question of law arising in the course of the proceedings which the court is satisfied substantially affects the rights of one or more of the parties.

An agreement to dispense with reasons for the tribunal's award shall be considered an agreement to exclude the court's jurisdiction under this section.

(2) An application under this section shall not be considered unless—

(a) it is made with the agreement of all the other parties to the proceedings, or

(b) it is made with the permission of the tribunal and the court is satisfied—

(i) that the determination of the question is likely to produce substantial savings in costs, and

(ii) that the application was made without delay.

(3) The application shall identify the question of law to be determined and unless made with the agreement of all the other parties to the proceedings, shall state the grounds on which it is said that the question should be decided by the court.

(4) Unless otherwise agreed by the parties, the arbitral tribunal may continue the arbitral proceedings and make an award while an application to the court under this section is pending.

(5) Unless the court gives leave, no appeal lies for a decision of the court whether the conditions specified in subsection (2) are met.

(6) The decision of the court on the question of law shall be treated as a judgment of the court for the purposes of an appeal.

But no appeal lies without the leave of the court which shall not be given unless the court considers that the question is one of general importance, or is one which for some other special reason should be considered by the Court of Appeal.

The Award

Rules applicable to substance of dispute

46.—(1) The arbitral tribunal shall decide the dispute—

(a) in accordance with the law chosen by the parties as applicable to the substance of the dispute, or

(b) if the parties so agree, in accordance with such other considerations as are agreed by them or determined by the tribunal.

(2) For this purpose the choice of the laws of a country shall be understood to refer to the substantive laws of that country and not its conflict of laws rules.

(3) If or to the extent that there is no such choice or agreement, the tribunal shall apply the law determined by the conflict of laws rules which it considers applicable.

Awards on different issues, &c

47.—(1) Unless otherwise agreed by the parties, the tribunal may make more than one award at different times on different aspects of the matters to be determined.

(2) The tribunal may, in particular make an award relating—

(a) to an issue affecting the whole claim, or

(b) to a part only of the claims or cross-claims submitted to it for decision.

(3) If the tribunal does so, it shall specify in its award the issue, or the claim or part of a claim, which is the subject matter of the award.

Remedies

48.—(1) The parties are free to agree on the powers exercisable by the arbitral tribunal as regards remedies.

(2) Unless otherwise agreed by the parties, the tribunal has the following powers.

(3) The tribunal may make a declaration as to any matter to be determined in the proceedings.

(4) The tribunal may order the payment of a sum of money, in any currency.

(5) The tribunal has the same powers as the court

(a) to order a party to do or refrain from doing anything;

(b) to order specific performance of a contract (other than a contract relating to land);

(c) to order the rectification, setting aside or cancellation of a deed or other document.

Interest

49.—(1) The parties are free to agree on the powers of the tribunal as regards the award of interest.

(2) Unless otherwise agreed by the parties the following provisions apply.

(3) The tribunal may award simple or compound interest from such dates, at such rates and with such rests as it considers meets the justice of the case—

(a) on the whole or part of any amount awarded by the tribunal, in respect of any period up to the date of the award;

(b) on the whole or part of any amount claimed in the arbitration and outstanding at the commencement of the arbitral proceedings but paid before the award was made, in respect of any period up to the date of payment.

(4) The tribunal may award simple or compound interest from the date of the award (or any later date) until payment, at such rates and with such rests as it considers meets the justice of the case, on the outstanding amount of any award (including any award of interest under subsection (3) and any award as to costs).

(5) References in this section to an amount awarded by the tribunal include an amount payable in consequence of a declaratory award by the tribunal.

(6) The above provisions do not affect any other power of the tribunal to award interest.

Extension of time for making award

50.—(1) Where the time for making an award is limited by or in pursuance of the arbitration agreement, then, unless otherwise agreed by the parties, the court may in accordance with the following provisions by order extend that time.

(2) An application for an order under this section may be made—

(a) by the tribunal (upon notice to the parties), or

(b) by any party to the proceedings (upon notice to the tribunal and the other parties),

but only after exhausting any available arbitral process for obtaining an extension of time.

(3) The court shall only make an order if satisfied that a substantial injustice would otherwise be done.

(4) The court may extend the time for such period and on such terms as it thinks fit, and may do so whether or not the time previously fixed (by or under the agreement or by a previous order) has expired.

(5) The leave of the court is required for any appeal from a decision of the court under this section.

Settlement

51.—(1) If during arbitral proceedings the parties settle the dispute, the following provisions apply unless otherwise agreed by the parties.

(2) The tribunal shall terminate the substantive proceedings and, if so requested by the parties and not objected to by the tribunal, shall record the settlement in the form of an agreed award.

(3) An agreed award shall state that it is an award of the tribunal and shall have the same status and effect as any other award on the merits of the case.

(4) The following provisions of this Part relating to awards (sections 52 to 58) apply to an agreed award.

(5) Unless the parties have also settled the matter of the payment of the costs of the arbitration, the provisions of this Part relating to costs (sections 59 to 65) continue to apply.

Form of award

52.—(1) The parties are free to agree on the form of an award.

(2) If or to the extent that there is no such agreement, the following provisions apply.

(3) The award shall be in writing signed by all the arbitrators or all those assenting to the award.

(4) The award shall contain the reasons for the award unless it is an agreed award or the parties have agreed to dispense with reasons.

(5) The award shall state the seat of the arbitration and the date when the award is made.

Place where award treated as made

53. Unless otherwise agreed by the parties, where the seat of the arbitration is in England and Wales or Northern Ireland, any award in the proceedings shall be treated

as made there, regardless of where it was signed, despatched or delivered to any of the parties.

Date of award

54.—(1) Unless otherwise agreed by the parties, the tribunal may decide what is to be taken to be the date on which the award was made.

(2) In the absence of any such decision, the date of the award shall be taken to be the date on which it is signed by the arbitrator or, where more than one arbitrator signs the award, by the last of them.

Notification of award

55.—(1) The parties are free to agree on the requirements as to notification of the award to the parties.

(2) If there is no such agreement, the award shall be notified to the parties by service on them of copies of the award, which shall be done without delay after the award is made.

(3) Nothing in this section affects section 56 (power to withhold award in case of non-payment).

Power to withhold award in case of non-payment

56.—(1) The tribunal may refuse to deliver an award to the parties except upon full payment of the fees and expenses of the arbitrators.

(2) If the tribunal refuses on that ground to deliver an award, a party to the arbitral proceedings may (upon notice to the other parties and the tribunal) apply to the court, which may order that—

(a) the tribunal shall deliver the award on the payment into court by the applicant of the fees and expenses demanded, or such lesser amount as the court may specify,

(b) the amount of the fees and expenses properly payable shall be determined by such means and upon such terms as the court may direct, and

(c) out of the money paid into court there shall be paid out such fees and expenses as may be found to be properly payable and the balance of the money (if any) shall be paid out to the applicant.

(3) For this purpose the amount of fees and expenses properly payable is the amount the applicant is liable to pay under section 28 or any agreement relating to the payment of the arbitrators.

(4) No application to the court may be made where there is any available arbitral process for appeal or review of the amount of the fees or expenses demanded.

(5) References in this section to arbitration include an arbitrator who has ceased to act and an umpire who has not replaced the other arbitrators.

(6) The above provisions of this section also apply in relation to any arbitral or other institution or person vested by the parties with powers in relation to the delivery of the tribunal's award.

As they so apply, the references to the fees and expenses of the arbitrators shall be construed as including the fees and expenses of that institution or person.

(7) The leave of the court is required for any appeal from a decision of the court under this section.

(8) Nothing in this section shall be construed as excluding an application under section 28 where payment has been made to the arbitrators in order to obtain the award.

Correction of award or additional award

57.—(1) The parties are free to agree on the powers of the tribunal to correct an award or make an additional award.

(2) If or to the extent there is no such agreement, the following provisions apply.

(3) The tribunal may on its own initiative or on the application of a party—

(a) correct an award so as to remove any clerical mistake or error arising from an accidental slip or omission or clarify or remove any ambiguity in the award, or

(b) make an additional award in respect of any claim (including a claim for interest or costs) which was presented to the tribunal but was not dealt with in the award.

These powers shall not be exercised without first affording to the other parties a reasonable opportunity to make representations to the tribunal.

(4) Any application for the exercise of those powers must be made within 28 days of the date of the award or such longer period as the parties may agree.

(5) Any correction of an award shall be made within 28 days of the date the application was received by the tribunal or, where the correction is made by the tribunal on its own initiative, within 28 days of the date of the award or, in either case, such longer period as the parties may agree.

(6) Any additional award shall be made within 56 days of the date of the original award or such longer period as the parties may agree.

(7) Any correction of an award shall form part of the award.

Effect of award

58.—(1) Unless otherwise agreed by the parties, an award made by the tribunal pursuant to an arbitration agreement is final and binding both on the parties and on any persons claiming through or under them.

(2) This does not affect the right of a person to challenge the award by any available arbitral process of appeal or review or in accordance with the provisions of this Part.

Costs of the Arbitration

Costs of the arbitration

59.—(1) References in this Part to the costs of the arbitration are to—

(a) the arbitrators' fees and expenses,

(b) the fees and expenses of any arbitral institution concerned, and

(c) the legal or other costs of the parties.

(2) Any such reference includes the costs of or incidental to any proceedings to determine the amount of the recoverable costs of the arbitration (see section 63).

Agreement to pay costs in any event

60. An agreement which has the effect that a party is to pay the whole or part of the costs of the arbitration in any event is only valid if made after the dispute in question has arisen.

Award of costs

61.—(1) The tribunal may make an award allocating the costs of the arbitration as between the parties, subject to any agreement of the parties.

(2) Unless the parties otherwise agree, the tribunal shall award costs on the general principle that costs should follow the event except where it appears to the tribunal that in the circumstances this is not appropriate in relation to the whole or part of the costs.

Effect of agreement or award about costs

62. Unless the parties otherwise agree, any obligation under an agreement between them as to how the costs of the arbitration are to be borne, or under an award allocating the costs of the arbitration, extends only to such costs as are recoverable.

The recoverable costs of the arbitration

63.—(1) The parties are free to agree what costs of the arbitration are recoverable.

(2) If or to the extent there is no such agreement, the following provisions apply.

(3) The tribunal may determine by award the recoverable costs of the arbitration on such basis as it thinks fit. If it does so, it shall specify—

(a) the basis on which it has acted, and

(b) the items of recoverable costs and the amount referable to each.

(4) If the tribunal does not determine the recoverable costs of the arbitration, any party to the arbitral proceedings may apply to the court (upon notice to the other parties) which may—

(a) determine the recoverable costs of the arbitration on such basis as it thinks fit, or

(b) order that they shall be determined by such means and upon such terms as it may specify.

(5) Unless the tribunal or the court determines otherwise—

(a) the recoverable costs of the arbitration shall be determined on the basis that there shall be allowed a reasonable amount in respect of all costs reasonably incurred, and

(b) any doubt as to whether costs were reasonably incurred or were reasonable in amount shall be resolved in favour of the paying party.

(6) The above provisions have effect subject to section 64 (recoverable fees and expenses of arbitrators).

(7) Nothing in this section affects any right of the arbitrators, any expert, legal adviser or assessor appointed by the tribunal, or any arbitral institution, to payment of their fees and expenses.

Recoverable fees and expenses of arbitrators

64.—(1) Unless otherwise agreed by the parties, the recoverable costs of the arbitration shall include in respect of the fees and expenses of the arbitrators only such reasonable fees and expenses as are appropriate in the circumstances.

(2) If there is any question as to what reasonable fees and expenses are appropriate in the circumstances, and the matter is not already before the court on an application under section 63(4), the court may on the application of any party (upon notice to the other parties)

(a) determine the matter, or

(b) order that it be determined by such means and upon such terms as the court may specify.

(3) Subsection (1) has effect subject to any order of the court under section 24(4) or 25(3)(b) (order as to entitlement to fees or expenses in case of removal or resignation of arbitrator).

(4) Nothing in this section affects any right of the arbitrator to payment of his fees and expenses.

Power to limit recoverable costs

65.—(1) Unless otherwise agreed by the parties, the tribunal may direct the recoverable costs of the arbitration, or of any part of the arbitral proceedings, shall be limited to a specified amount.

(2) Any direction may be made or varied at any stage, but this must be done sufficiently in advance of the incurring of costs to which it relates, or the taking of any steps in the proceedings which may be affected by it, for the limit to be taken into account.

Powers of the Court in Relation to Award

Enforcement of the award

66.—(1) An award made by the tribunal pursuant to an arbitration agreement may, by leave of the court, be enforced in the same manner as a judgment or order of the court to the same effect.

(2) Where leave is so given, judgment may be entered in terms of the award.

(3) Leave to enforce an award shall not be given where, or to the extent that, the person against whom it is sought to be enforced shows that the tribunal lacked substantive jurisdiction to make the award.

The right to raise such an objection may have been lost (see section 73).

(4) Nothing in this section affects the recognition or enforcement of an award under any other enactment or rule of law, in particular under Part II of the Arbitration Act 1950 (enforcement of awards under Geneva Convention) or the provisions of Part III of this Act relating to the recognition and enforcement of awards under the New York Convention or by an action on the award.

Challenging the award: substantive jurisdiction

67.—(1) A party to arbitral proceedings may (upon notice to the other parties and to the tribunal) apply to the court—

(a) challenging any award of the arbitral tribunal as to its substantive jurisdiction; or

(b) for an order declaring an award made by the tribunal on the merits to be of no effect, in whole or in part, because the tribunal did not have substantive jurisdiction.

A party may lose the right to object (see section 73) and the right to apply is subject to the restrictions in section 70(2) and (3).

(2) The arbitral tribunal may continue the arbitral proceedings and make a further award while an application to the court under this section is pending in relation to an award as to jurisdiction.

(3) On an application under this section challenging an award of the arbitral tribunal as to its substantive jurisdiction, the court may by order—

(a) confirm the award,

(b) vary the award, or
(c) set aside the award in whole or in part.

(4) The leave of the court is required for any appeal from a decision of the court under this section.

Challenging the award: serious irregularity

68.—(1) A party to arbitral proceedings may (upon notice to the other parties and to the tribunal) apply to the court challenging an award in the proceedings on the ground of serious irregularity affecting the tribunal, the proceedings or the award.

A party may lose the right to object (see section 73) and the right to apply is subject to the restrictions in section 70(2) and (3).

(2) Serious irregularity means an irregularity of one or more of the following kinds which the court considers has caused or will cause substantial injustice to the applicant—

(a) failure by the tribunal to comply with section 33 (general duty of tribunal);
(b) the tribunal exceeding its powers (otherwise than by exceeding its substantive jurisdiction: see section 67);
(c) failure by the tribunal to conduct the proceedings in accordance with the procedure agreed by the parties;
(d) failure by the tribunal to deal with all the issues that were put to it;
(e) any arbitral or other institution or person vested by the parties with powers in relation to the proceedings or the award exceeding its powers;
(f) uncertainty or ambiguity as to the effect of the award;
(g) the award being obtained by fraud or the award or the way in which it was procured being contrary to public policy;
(h) failure to comply with the requirements as to the form of the award; or
(i) any irregularity in the conduct of the proceedings or in the award which is admitted by the tribunal or by any arbitral or other institution or person vested by the parties with powers in relation to the proceedings or the award.

(3) If there is shown to be serious irregularity affecting the tribunal, the proceedings or the award, the court may—

(a) remit the award to the tribunal, in whole or in part, for reconsideration,
(b) set the award aside in whole or in part, or
(c) declare the award to be of no effect, in whole or in part.

The court shall not exercise its power to set aside or to declare an award to be of no effect, in whole or in part, unless it is satisfied that it would be inappropriate to remit the matters in question to the tribunal for reconsideration.

Appeal on point of law

69.—(1) Unless otherwise agreed by the parties, a party to arbitral proceedings may (upon notice to the other parties and to the tribunal) appeal to the court on a question of law arising out of an award made in the proceedings.

An agreement to dispense with reasons for the tribunal's award shall be considered an agreement to exclude the court's jurisdiction under this section.

(2) An appeal shall not be brought under this section except—

(a) with the agreement of all the other parties to the proceedings, or
(b) with the leave of the court.

The right to appeal is also subject to the restrictions in section 70(2) and (3).

(3) Leave to appeal shall be given only if the court is satisfied—

(a) that the determination of the question will substantially affect the rights of one or more of the parties,
(b) that the question is one which the tribunal was asked to determine,
(c) that, on the basis of the findings of fact in the award—
(i) the decision of the tribunal on the question is obviously wrong, or
(ii) the question is one of general public importance and the decision of the tribunal is at least open to serious doubt, and
(d) that, despite the agreement of the parties to resolve the matter by arbitration, it is just and proper in all the circumstances for the court to determine the question.

(4) An application for leave to appeal under this section shall identify the question of law to be determined and state the grounds on which it is alleged that leave to appeal should be granted.

(5) The court shall determine an application for leave to appeal under the section without a hearing unless it appears to the court that a hearing is required.

(6) The leave of the court is required for any appeal from a decision of the court under this section to grant or refuse leave to appeal.

(7) On an appeal under this section the court may by order—
(a) confirm the award,
(b) vary the award,
(c) remit the award to the tribunal, in whole or in part, for reconsideration in the light of the court's determination, or
(d) set aside the award in whole or in part.

The court shall not exercise its power to set aside an award, in whole or in part, unless it is satisfied that it would be inappropriate to remit the matters in question to the tribunal for reconsideration.

(8) The decision of the court on an appeal under this section shall be treated as a judgment of the court for the purposes of a further appeal.

But no such appeal lies without the leave of the court which shall not be given unless the court considers that the question is one of general importance or is one which for some other special reason should be considered by the Court of Appeal.

Challenge or appeal: supplementary provisions

70.—(1) The following provisions apply to an application or appeal under section 67, 68 or 69.

(2) An application or appeal may not be brought if the applicant or appellant has not first exhausted—
(a) any available arbitral process of appeal or review, and
(b) any available recourse under section 57 (correction of award or additional award).

(3) Any application or appeal must be brought within 28 days of the date of the award or, if there has been any arbitral process of appeal or review, of the date when the applicant or appellant was notified of the result of that process.

(4) If on an application or appeal it appears to the court that the award—
(a) does not contain the tribunal's reasons, or
(b) does not set out the tribunal's reasons in sufficient detail to enable the court properly to consider the application or appeal,

the court may order the tribunal to state the reasons for its award in sufficient detail for that purpose.

(5) Where the court makes an order under subsection (4), it may make such further order as it thinks fit with respect to any additional costs of the arbitration resulting from its order.

(6) The court may order the applicant or appellant to provide security for the costs of the application or appeal, and may direct that the application or appeal be dismissed if the order is not complied with.

The power to order security for costs shall not be exercised on the ground that the applicant or appellant is—

(a) an individual ordinarily resident outside the United Kingdom, or
(b) a corporation or association incorporated or formed under the law of a country outside the United Kingdom, or whose central management and control is exercised outside the United Kingdom.

(7) The court may order that any money payable under the award shall be brought into court or otherwise secured pending the determination of the application or appeal, and may direct that the application or appeal be dismissed if the order is not complied with.

(8) The court may grant leave to appeal subject to conditions to the same or similar effect as an order under subsection (6) or (7).

This does not affect the general discretion of the court to grant leave subject to conditions.

Challenge or appeal: effect of order of court

71.—(1) The following provisions have effect where the court makes an order under section 67, 68 or 69 with respect to an award.

(2) Where the award is varied, the variation has effect as part of the tribunal's award.

(3) Where the award is remitted to the tribunal, in whole or in part, for reconsideration, the tribunal shall make a fresh award in respect of the matters remitted within three months of the date of the order for remission or such longer or shorter period as the court may direct.

(4) Where the award is set aside or declared to be of no effect, in whole or in part, the court may also order that any provision that an award is a condition precedent to the bringing of legal proceedings in respect of a matter to which the arbitration agreement applies, is of no effect as regards the subject matter of the award or, as the case may be, the relevant part of the award.

Miscellaneous

Saving for rights of person who takes no part in proceedings

72.—(1) A person alleged to be a party to arbitral proceedings but who takes no part in the proceedings may question—

(a) whether there is a valid arbitration agreement,
(b) whether the tribunal is properly constituted, or
(c) what matters have been submitted to arbitration in accordance with the arbitration agreement,

by proceedings in the court for a declaration or injunction or other appropriate relief.

(2) He also has the same right as a party to the arbitral proceedings to challenge an award—

(a) by an application under section 67 on the ground of lack of substantive jurisdiction in relation to him, or
(b) by an application under section 68 on the ground of serious irregularity (within the meaning of that section) affecting him;

and section 70(2) (duty to exhaust arbitral procedures) does not apply in his case.

Loss of right to object

73.—(1) If a party to arbitral proceedings takes part, or continues to take part, in the proceedings without making, either forthwith or within such time as is allowed by the arbitration agreement or the tribunal or by any provision of this Part, any objection—

(a) that the tribunal lacks substantive jurisdiction,
(b) that the proceedings have been improperly conducted,
(c) that there has been a failure to comply with the arbitration agreement or with any provision of this Part, or
(d) that there has been any other irregularity affecting the tribunal or the proceedings,

he may not raise that objection later, before the tribunal or the court, unless he shows that, at the time he took part or continued to take part in the proceedings, he did not know and could not with reasonable diligence have discovered the grounds for the objection.

(2) Where the arbitral tribunal rules that it has substantive jurisdiction and a party to arbitral proceedings who could have questioned that ruling—

(a) by any available arbitral process of appeal or review; or
(b) by challenging the award

does not do so, or does not do so within the time allowed by the arbitration agreement or any provisions of this Part, he may not object later to the tribunal's substantive jurisdiction on any ground which was the subject of that ruling.

Immunity of arbitral institutions, &c

74.—(1) An arbitral or other institution or person designated or requested by the parties to appoint or nominate an arbitrator is not liable for anything done or omitted in the discharge or purported discharge of that function unless the act or omission is shown to have been in bad faith.

(2) An arbitral or other institution or person by whom an arbitrator is appointed or nominated is not liable, by reason of having appointed or nominated him, for anything done or omitted by the arbitrator (or his employees or agents) in the discharge or purported discharge of his functions as arbitrator.

(3) The above provisions apply to an employee or agent of an arbitral or other institution or person as they apply to the institution or person himself.

Charge to secure payment of solicitors' costs

75. The powers of the court to make declarations and orders under section 73 of the Solicitors Act 1974 or Article 71H of the Solicitors (Northern Ireland) Order 1976 (power to charge property recovered in the proceedings with the payment of solicitors' costs) may be exercised in relation to arbitral proceedings as if those proceedings were proceedings in the court.

Supplementary

Service of notices, &c

76.—(1) The parties are free to agree on the manner of service of any notice or other document required or authorised to be given or served in pursuance of the arbitration agreement or for the purposes of the arbitral proceedings.

(2) If or to the extent that there is no such agreement the following provisions apply.

(3) A notice or other document may be served on a person by any effective means.

(4) If a notice or other document is addressed, pre-paid and delivered by post

(a) to the addressee's last known principal residence or, if he is or has been carrying on a trade, profession or business, his last known principal business address, or

(b) where the addressee is a body corporate, to the body's registered or principal office,

it shall be treated as effectively served.

(5) This section does not apply to the service of documents for the purposes of legal proceedings, for which provision is made by rules of court.

(6) References in this Part to a notice or other document include any form of communication in writing and references to giving or serving a notice or other document shall be construed accordingly.

Powers of court in relation to service of documents

77.—(1) This section applies where service of a document on a person in the manner agreed by the parties, or in accordance with provisions of section 76 having effect in default of agreement, is not reasonably practicable.

(2) Unless otherwise agreed by the parties, the court may make such order as it thinks fit—

(a) for service in such manner as the court may direct, or

(b) dispensing with service of the document.

(3) Any party to the arbitration agreement may apply for an order, but only after exhausting any available arbitral process for resolving the matter.

(4) The leave of the court is required for any appeal from a decision of the court under this section.

Reckoning periods of time

78.—(1) The parties are free to agree on the method of reckoning periods of time for the purposes of any provision agreed by them or any provision of this Part having effect in default of such agreement.

(2) If or to the extent there is no such agreement, periods of time shall be reckoned in accordance with the following provisions.

(3) Where the act is required to be done within a specified period after or from a specified date, the period begins immediately after that date.

(4) Where the act is required to be done a specified number of clear days after a specified date, at least that number of days must intervene between the day on which the act is done and that date.

(5) Where the period is a period of seven days or less which would include a Saturday, Sunday or a public holiday in the place where anything which has to be done within the period falls to be done, that day shall be excluded.

In relation to England and Wales or Northern Ireland, a "public holiday" means Christmas Day, Good Friday or a day which under the Banking and Financial Dealings Act 1971 is a bank holiday.

Power of court to extend time limits relating to arbitral proceedings

79.—(1) Unless the parties otherwise agree, the court may by order extend any time limit agreed by them in relation to any matter relating to the arbitral proceedings or specified in any provision of this Part having effect in default of such agreement.

This section does not apply to a time limit to which section 12 applies (power of court to extend time for beginning arbitral proceedings, &c.).

(2) An application for an order may be made—

(a) by any party to the arbitral proceedings (upon notice to the other parties and to the tribunal), or

(b) by the arbitral tribunal (upon notice to the parties).

(3) The court shall not exercise its power to extend a time limit unless it is satisfied—

(a) that any available recourse to the tribunal, or to any arbitral or other institution or person vested by the parties with power in that regard, has first been exhausted, and

(b) that a substantial injustice would otherwise be done.

(4) The court's power under this section may be exercised whether or not the time has already expired.

(5) An order under this section may be made on such terms as the court thinks fit.

(6) The leave of the court is required for any appeal from a decision of the court under this section.

Notice and other requirements in connection with legal proceedings

80.—(1) References in this Part to an application, appeal or other step in relation to legal proceedings being taken "upon notice" to the other parties to the arbitral proceedings, or to the tribunal, are to such notice of the originating process as is required by rules of court and do not impose any separate requirement.

(2) Rules of court shall be made—

(a) requiring such notice to be given as indicated by any provision of this Part, and

(b) as to the manner, form and content of any such notice.

(3) Subject to any provision made by rules of court, a requirement to give notice to the tribunal of legal proceedings shall be construed—

(a) if there is more than one arbitrator, as a requirement to give notice to each of them; and

(b) if the tribunal is not fully constituted, as a requirement to give notice to any arbitrator who has been appointed.

(4) References in this Part to making an application or appeal to the court within a specified period are to the issue within that period of the appropriate originating process in accordance with rules of court.

(5) Where any provision of this Part requires an application or appeal to be made to the court within a specified time, the rules of court relating to the reckoning of periods, the extending or abridging of periods, and the consequences of not taking a step within the period prescribed by the rules, apply in relation to that requirement.

(6) Provision may be made by rules of court amending the provisions of this Part—

(a) with respect to the time within which any application or appeal to the court must be made,

(b) so as to keep any provision made by this Part in relation to arbitral proceedings in step with the corresponding provision of rules of court applying in relation to proceedings in the court, or

(c) so as to keep any provision made by this Part in relation to legal proceedings in step with the corresponding provision of rules of court applying generally in relation to proceedings in this court.

(7) Nothing in this section affects the generality of the power to make rules of court.

Saving for certain matters governed by common law

81.—(1) Nothing in this Part shall be construed as excluding the operation of any rule of law consistent with the provisions of this Part, in particular, any rule of law as to—

(a) matters which are not capable of settlement by arbitration;
(b) the effect of an oral arbitration agreement; or
(c) the refusal of recognition or enforcement of an arbitral award on grounds of public policy.

(2) Nothing in this Act shall be construed as reviving any jurisdiction of the court to set aside or remit an award on the ground of errors of fact or law on the face of the award.

Minor definitions

82.—(1) In this Part—

"arbitrator", unless the context otherwise requires, includes an umpire;
"available arbitral process", in relation to any matter, includes any process of appeal to or review by an arbitral or other institution or person vested by the parties with powers in relation to that matter;
"claimant", unless the context otherwise requires, includes a counterclaimant, and related expressions shall be construed accordingly;
"dispute" includes any difference;
"enactment" includes an enactment contained in Northern Ireland legislation;
"legal proceedings" means civil proceedings in the High Court or a county court;
"peremptory order" means an order made under section 41(5) or made in exercise of any corresponding power conferred by the parties;
"premises" includes land, building, moveable structures, vehicles, vessels, aircraft and hovercraft;
"question of law" means—

(a) for a court in England and Wales, a question of the law of England and Wales, and
(b) for a court in Northern Ireland, a question of the law of Northern Ireland;

"substantive jurisdiction", in relation to an arbitral tribunal, refers to the matters specified in section 30(1)(a) to (c), and references to the tribunal exceeding its substantive jurisdiction shall be construed accordingly.

(2) References in this Part to a party to an arbitration agreement include any person claiming under or through a party to the agreement.

Index of defined expressions: Part I

83. In this Part the expressions listed below are defined or otherwise explained by the provisions indicated—

agreement, agree and agreed	section 5(1)
agreement in writing	section 5(2) to (5)

arbitration agreement	sections 6 and 5(1)
arbitrator	section 82(1)
available arbitral process	section 82(1)
claimant	section 82(1)
commencement (in relation to arbitral proceedings)	section 14
costs of the arbitration	section 59
the court	section 105
dispute	section 82(1)
enactment	section 82(1)
legal proceedings	section 82(1)
Limitation Acts	section 13(4)
notice (or other document)	section 76(6)
party—	
—in relation to an arbitration agreement	section 82(2)
—where section 106(2) or (3) applies	section 106(4)
peremptory order	section 82(1) (and see section 41(5))
premises	section 82(1)
question of law	section 82(1)
recoverable costs	sections 63 and 64
seat of the arbitration	section 3
serve and service (of notice or other document)	section 76(6)
substantive jurisdiction (in relation to an arbitral tribunal)	section 82(1) (and see section 30(1)(a) to (c))
upon notice (to the parties or the tribunal)	section 80
written and in writing	section 5(6)

Transitional provisions

84.—(1) The provisions of this Part do not apply to arbitral proceedings commenced before the date on which this Part comes into force.

(2) They apply to arbitral proceedings commenced on or after that date under an arbitration agreement whenever made.

(3) The above provisions have effect subject to any transitional provision made by an order under section 109(2) (power to include transitional provisions in commencement order).

PART II OTHER PROVISIONS RELATING TO ARBITRATION

Domestic Arbitration Agreements

Modification of Part I in relation to domestic arbitration agreement

85.—(1) In the case of a domestic arbitration agreement the provisions of Part I are modified in accordance with the following sections.

(2) For this purpose a "domestic arbitration agreement" means an arbitration agreement to which none of the parties is—

(a) an individual who is a national of or habitually resident in, a state other than the United Kingdom, or

(b) a body corporate which is incorporated in, or whose central control and management is exercised in, a state other than the United Kingdom, and under which the seat of the arbitration (if the seat has been designated or determined) is in the United Kingdom.

(3) In subsection (2) "arbitration agreement" and "seat of the arbitration" have the same meaning as in Part I (see sections 3, 5(1) and 6).

Staying of legal proceedings

86.—(1) In section 9 (stay of legal proceedings), subsection (4) (stay unless the arbitration agreement is null and void, inoperative, or incapable of being performed) does not apply to a domestic arbitration agreement.

(2) On an application under that section in relation to a domestic arbitration agreement the court shall grant a stay unless satisfied—

- (a) that the arbitration agreement is null and void, inoperative, or incapable of being performed, or
- (b) that there are other sufficient grounds for not requiring the parties to abide by the arbitration agreement.

(3) The court may treat as a sufficient ground under subsection (2)(b) the fact that the applicant is or was at any material time not ready and willing to do all things necessary for the proper conduct of the arbitration or of any other dispute resolution procedures required to be exhausted before resorting to arbitration.

(4) For the purposes of this section the question whether an arbitration agreement is a domestic arbitration agreement shall be determined by reference to the facts at the time the legal proceedings are concerned.

Effectiveness of agreement to exclude court's jurisdiction

87.—(1) In the case of a domestic arbitration agreement any agreement to exclude the jurisdiction of the court under

- (a) section 45 (determination of preliminary point of law), or
- (b) section 69 (challenging the award: appeal on point of law),

is not effective unless entered into after the commencement of the arbitral proceedings in which the question arises or the award is made.

(2) For this purpose the commencement of the arbitral proceedings has the same meaning as in Part I (see section 14).

(3) For the purposes of this section the question whether an arbitration agreement is a domestic arbitration agreement shall be determined by reference to the facts at the time the agreement is entered into.

Power to repeal or amend sections 85 to 87

88.—(1) The Secretary of State may by order repeal or amend the provisions of sections 85 to 87.

(2) An order under this section may contain such supplementary, incidental and transitional provisions as appear to the Secretary of State to be appropriate.

(3) An order under this section shall be made by statutory instrument and no such order shall be made unless a draft of it has been laid before and approved by a resolution of each House of Parliament.

Consumer Arbitration Agreements

Application of unfair terms regulations to consumer arbitration agreements

89.—(1) The following sections extend the application of the Unfair Terms in

Consumer Contracts Regulations 199[9] in relation to a term which constitutes an arbitration agreement.

For this purpose "arbitration agreement" means an agreement to submit to arbitration present or future disputes or differences (whether or not contractual).

(2) In those sections "the Regulations" mean those regulations and includes any regulations amending or replacing those regulations.

(3) Those sections apply whatever the law applicable to the arbitration agreement.

Regulations apply where consumer is a legal person

90. The Regulations apply where the consumer is a legal person as they apply where the consumer is a natural person.

Arbitration agreement unfair where modest amount sought

91.—(1) A term which constitutes an arbitration agreement is unfair for the purposes of the Regulations so far as it relates to a claim for a pecuniary remedy which does not exceed the amount specified by order for the purposes of this section.

(2) Orders under this section may make different provision for different cases and for different purposes.

(3) The power to make orders under this section is exercisable—

(a) for England and Wales, by the Secretary of State with the concurrence of the Lord Chancellor,

(b) for Scotland, by the Secretary of State with the concurrence of the Lord Advocate, and

(c) for Northern Ireland, by the Department of Economic Development for Northern Ireland with the concurrence of the Lord Chancellor.

(4) Any such order for England and Wales or Scotland shall be made by statutory instrument which shall be subject to annulment in pursuance of a resolution of either House of Parliament.

(5) Any such order for Northern Ireland shall be a statutory rule for the purposes of the Statutory Rules (Northern Ireland) Order 1979 and shall be subject to negative resolution, within the meaning of section 41(6) of the Interpretation Act (Northern Ireland) Order 1954.

Small Claims Arbitration in the County Court

Exclusion of Part I in relation to small claims arbitration in the county court

92. Nothing in Part I of this Act applies to arbitration under section 64 of the County Courts Act 1984.

Appointment of Judges as Arbitrators

Appointment of judges as arbitrators

93.—(1) A judge of the Commercial Court or an official referee may, if in all the circumstances he thinks fit, accept appointment as a sole arbitrator or as umpire by or by virtue of an arbitration agreement.

(2) A judge of the Commercial Court shall not do so unless the Lord Chief Justice has informed him that, having regard to the state of business in the High Court and the Crown Court, he can be made available.

(3) An official referee shall not do so unless the Lord Chief Justice has informed him that, having regard to the state of official referees' business, he can be made available.

(4) The fees payable for the services of a judge of the Commercial Court or official referee as arbitrator or umpire shall be taken in the High Court.

(5) In this section—

"arbitration agreement has the same meaning as in Part I; and

"official referee" means a person nominated under section 68(1)(a) of the Supreme Court Act 1981 to deal with official referees' business.

(6) The provisions of Part I of this Act apply to arbitration before a person appointed under this section with the modifications specified in Schedule 2.

Statutory Arbitrations

Application of Part I to statutory arbitrations

94.—(1) The provisions of Part I apply to every arbitration under an enactment (a "statutory arbitration"), whether the enactment was passed or made before or after the commencement of this Act subject to the adaptations and exclusions specified in sections 95 to 98.

(2) The provisions of Part I do not apply to a statutory arbitration if or to the extent that their application—

(a) is inconsistent with the provisions of the enactment concerned, with any rules or procedure authorised or recognised by it, or

(b) is excluded by any other enactment.

(3) In this section and the following provisions of this Part "enactment"

(a) in England and Wales, includes an enactment contained in subordinate legislation within the meaning of the Interpretation Act 1978;

(b) in Northern Ireland, means a statutory provision within the meaning of section 1(f) of the Interpretation Act (Northern Ireland) 1954.

General adaptation of provisions in relation to statutory arbitrations

95.—(1) The provisions of Part I apply to a statutory arbitration—

(a) as if the arbitration were pursuant to an arbitration agreement and as if the enactment were that agreement, and

(b) as if the persons by and against whom a claim subject to arbitration in pursuance of the enactment may be or has been made were parties to that agreement.

(2) Every statutory arbitration shall be taken to have its seat in England and Wales or, as the case may be, in Northern Ireland.

Specific adaptations of provisions in relation to statutory arbitrations

96.—(1) The following provisions of Part I apply to a statutory arbitration with the following adaptations.

(2) In section 30(1) (competence of tribunal to rule on its own jurisdiction), the reference to paragraph (a) to whether there is a valid arbitration agreement shall be construed as a reference to whether the enactment applies to the dispute or difference in question.

(3) Section 35 (consolidation of proceedings and concurrent hearings) applies only so as to authorise the consolidation of proceedings, or concurrent hearings in proceedings, under the same enactment.

(4) Section 46 (rules applicable to substance of dispute) applies with the omission of subsection (1)(b) (determination in accordance with considerations agreed by parties).

Provisions excluded from applying to statutory arbitrations

97. The following provisions of Part I do not apply in relation to a statutory arbitration—

(a) section 8 (whether agreement discharged by death of a party);
(b) section 12 (power of court to extend agreed time limits);
(c) sections 9(5), 10(2) and 71(4) (restrictions on effect of provision that award condition precedent to right to bring legal proceedings).

Power to make further provisions by regulations

98.—(1) The Secretary of State may make provision by regulations for adapting or excluding any provision of Part I in relation to statutory arbitration in general or statutory arbitrations of any particular description.

(2) The power is exercisable whether the enactment concerned is passed or made before or after the commencement of this Act.

(3) Regulations under this section shall be made by statutory instrument which shall be subject to annulment in pursuance of a resolution of either House of Parliament.

PART III RECOGNITION AND ENFORCEMENT OF CERTAIN FOREIGN AWARDS

Enforcement of Geneva Convention Awards

Continuation of Part II of the Arbitration Act 1950

99. Part II of the Arbitration Act 1950 (enforcement of certain foreign awards) continues to apply in relation to foreign awards within the meaning of that Part which are not also New York Convention awards.

Recognition and Enforcement of New York Convention Awards

New York Convention awards

100.—(1) In this Part a "New York Convention award" means an award made, in pursuance of an arbitration agreement, in the territory of a state (other than the United Kingdom) which is a party to the New York Convention.

(2) For the purposes of subsection (1) and of the provisions of this Part relating to such awards—

(a) "arbitration agreement" means an arbitration agreement in writing, and
(b) an award shall be treated as made at the seat of the arbitration, regardless of where it was signed, despatched or delivered to any of the parties.

In this subsection "agreement in writing" and "seat of the arbitration" have the same meaning as in Part I.

(3) If Her Majesty by Order in Council declares that a state specified in the Order is a party to the New York Convention, or is a party in respect of any territory so specified, the Order shall, while in force, be conclusive evidence of that fact.

(4) In this section "the New York Convention" means the Convention on the Recognition and Enforcement of Foreign Arbitral Awards adopted by the United Nations Conference on International Commercial Arbitration on 10 June 1958.

Recognition and enforcement of awards

101.—(1) A New York Convention award shall be recognised as binding on the persons as between whom it was made, and may accordingly be relied on by those persons by way of defence, set-off or otherwise in any legal proceedings in England and Wales or Northern Ireland.

(2) A New York Convention award may, by leave of the court, be enforced in the same manner as a judgment or order of the court to the same effect.

As to the meaning of "the court" see section 105.

(3) Where leave is so given, judgment may be entered in terms of the award.

Evidence to be produced by party seeking recognition or enforcement

102.—(1) A party seeking the recognition or enforcement of a New York Convention award must produce—

(a) the duly authenticated original award or a duly certified copy of it, and

(b) the original arbitration agreement or a duly certified copy of it.

(2) If the award or agreement is in a foreign language, the party must also produce a translation of it certified by an official or sworn translator or by a diplomatic or consular agent.

Refusal of recognition or enforcement

103.—(1) Recognition or enforcement of a New York Convention award shall not be refused except in the following cases.

(2) Recognition or enforcement of the award may be refused if the person against whom it is invoked proves—

(a) that a party to the arbitration agreement was (under the law applicable to him) under some incapacity;

(b) that the arbitration agreement was not valid under the law to which the parties subjected it or, failing any indication thereon, under the law of the country where the award was made;

(c) that he was not given proper notice of the appointment of the arbitrator or of the arbitration proceedings or was otherwise unable to present his case;

(d) that the award deals with a difference not contemplated by or not falling within the terms of the submission to arbitration or contains decisions on matters beyond the scope of the submission to arbitration (but see subsection (4));

(e) that the composition of the arbitral tribunal or the arbitral procedure was not in accordance with the agreement of the parties or, failing such agreement, with the law of the country in which the arbitration took place;

(f) that the award has not yet become binding on the parties, or has been set aside or suspended by a competent authority of the country in which, or under the law of which it was made.

(3) Recognition or enforcement of the award may also be refused if the award is in respect of a matter which is not capable of settlement by arbitration, or if it would be contrary to public policy to recognise or enforce the award.

(4) An award which contains decisions on matters not submitted to arbitration may be recognised or enforced to the extent that it contains decisions on matters submitted to arbitration which can be separated from those on matters not so submitted.

(5) Where an application for the setting aside or suspension of the award has been made to such a competent authority as is mentioned in subsection (2)(f), the court before which the award is sought to be relied upon may, if it considers it proper, adjourn the decision on the recognition or enforcement of the award.

It may also on the application of the party claiming recognition or enforcement of the award order the other party to give suitable security.

Saving for other bases of recognition or enforcement

104. Nothing in the preceding provisions of this Part affects any right to rely upon or enforce a New York Convention award at common law or under section 66.

PART IV GENERAL PROVISIONS

Meaning of "the court": jurisdiction of High Court and county court

105.—(1) In this Act "the court" means the High Court or a county court, subject to the following provisions.

(2) The Lord Chancellor may by order make provision—

(a) allocating proceedings under this Act to the High Court or to county courts; or

(b) specifying proceedings under this Act which may be commenced or taken only in the High Court or in a county court.

(3) The Lord Chancellor may by order make provision requiring proceedings of any specified description under this Act in relation to which a county court has jurisdiction to be commenced or taken in one or more specified county courts.

Any jurisdiction so exercisable by a specified county court is exercisable throughout England and Wales or, as the case may be, Northern Ireland.

(4) An order under this section

(a) may differentiate between categories of proceedings by reference to such criteria as the Lord Chancellor sees fit to specify, and

(b) may make such incidental or transitional provision as the Lord Chancellor considers necessary or expedient.

(5) An order under this section for England and Wales shall be made by statutory instrument which shall be subject to annulment in pursuance of a resolution of either House of Parliament.

(6) An order under this section for Northern Ireland shall be a statutory rule for the purposes of the Statutory Rules (Northern Ireland) Order 1979 which shall be subject to annulment in pursuance of a resolution of either House of Parliament in like manner

as a statutory instrument and section 5 of the Statutory Instruments Act 1946 shall apply accordingly.

Crown application

106.—(1) Part I of this Act applies to any arbitration agreement to which Her Majesty either in right of the Crown or of the Duchy of Lancaster or otherwise, or the Duke of Cornwall, is a party.

(2) Where Her Majesty is party to an arbitration agreement otherwise than in right of the Crown, Her Majesty shall be represented for the purpose of any arbitral proceedings—

(a) where the agreement was entered into by Her Majesty in right of the Duchy of Lancaster, by the Chancellor of the Duchy or such person as he may appoint, and

(b) in any other case, by such person as Her Majesty may appoint in writing under the Royal Sign Manual.

(3) Where the Duke of Cornwall is party to an arbitration agreement, he shall be represented for the purposes of any arbitral proceedings by such person as he may appoint.

(4) References in Part I to a party or the parties to the arbitration agreement or to arbitral proceedings shall be construed, where subsection (2) or (3) applies, as references to the person representing Her Majesty or the Duke of Cornwall.

Consequential amendments and repeals

107.—(1) The enactments specified in Schedule 3 are amended in accordance with that Schedule, the amendments being consequential on the provisions of this Act.

(2) The enactments specified in Schedule 4 are repealed to the extent specified.

Extent

108.—(1) The provisions of this Act extend to England and Wales and, except as mentioned below, to Northern Ireland.

(2) The following provisions of Part II do not extend to Northern Ireland—

section 92 (exclusion of Part I in relation to small claims arbitration in the county court), and

section 93 and Schedule 2 (appointment of judges as arbitrators).

(3) Sections 89, 90 and 91 (consumer arbitration agreements), extend to Scotland and the provisions of Schedules 3 and 4 (consequential amendments and repeals) extend to Scotland as far as they relate to enactments which so extend subject as follows.

(4) The repeal of the Arbitration Act 1975 extends only to England and Wales and Northern Ireland.

Commencement

109.—(1) The provisions of this Act come into force on such a day as the Secretary of State may appoint by order made by statutory instrument, and different days may be appointed for different purposes.

(2) An order under subsection (1) may contain such transitional provisions as appear to the Secretary of State to be appropriate.

Short title

110. This Act may be cited as the Arbitration Act 1996.

SCHEDULES

SCHEDULE 1 MANDATORY PROVISIONS OF PART I (SECTION 4(1))

sections 9 to 11 (stay of legal proceedings);
section 12 (power of court to extend agreed time limits);
section 13 (application of Limitation Acts);
section 24 (power of court to remove arbitrator);
section 26(1) (effect of death of arbitrator);
section 28 (liability of parties for fees and expenses of arbitrators);
section 29 (immunity of arbitrator);
section 31 (objection to substantive jurisdiction of tribunal);
section 32 (determination of preliminary point of jurisdiction);
section 33 (general duty of tribunal);
section 37(2) (items to be treated as expenses of arbitrators);
section 40 (general duty of parties);
section 43 (securing the attendance of witnesses);
section 56 (power to withhold award in case of non-payment);
section 60 (effectiveness of agreement for payment of costs in any event);
section 66 (enforcement of award);
sections 67 and 68 (challenging the award: substantive jurisdiction and serious irregularity), and sections 70 and 71 (supplementary provisions; effect of order of court) so far as relating to those sections;
section 72 (saving for rights of person who takes no part in proceedings);
section 73 (loss of right to object);
section 74 (immunity of arbitral institutions, &c.);
section 75 (charge to secure payment of solicitors' costs).

The provisions listed in this Schedule are mandatory and cannot be ousted by the agreement of the parties. The Schedule refers back to section 4 of the Act.

SCHEDULE 2 MODIFICATIONS OF PART I IN RELATION TO JUDGE-ARBITRATORS (SECTION 93(6))

Introductory

1. In this Schedule "judge-arbitrator" means a judge of the Commercial Court or official referee appointed as arbitrator or umpire under section 93.

General

2.—(1) Subject to the following provisions of this Schedule, references in Part I to the court shall be construed in relation to a judge-arbitrator, or in relation to the appointment of a judge-arbitrator, as references to the Court of Appeal.

(2) The references in sections 32(6), 45(6) and 69(8) to the Court of Appeal shall in such a case be construed as references to the House of Lords.

Arbitrator's Fees

3.—(1) The power of the court in section 28(2) or other consideration and adjustment of the liability of a party for the fees of an arbitrator may be exercised by a judge-arbitrator.

(2) Any such exercise of the power is subject to the powers of the Court of Appeal under sections 24(4) and 25(3)(b) (directions as to entitlement to fees or expenses in case of removal or resignation).

Exercise of Court Powers in Support of Arbitration

4.—(1) Where the arbitral tribunal consists of or includes a judge-arbitrator the powers of the court under sections 42 to 44 (enforcement of peremptory orders, summoning witnesses, and other court powers) are exercisable by the High Court and also by the judge-arbitrator himself.

(2) Anything done by a judge-arbitrator in the exercise of those powers shall be regarded as done by him in his capacity as judge of the High Court and have effect as if done by that court.

Nothing in this sub-paragraph prejudices any power vested in him as arbitrator or umpire.

Extension of Time for Making Award

5.—(1) The power conferred by section 50 (extension of time for making award) is exercisable by the judge-arbitrator himself.

(2) Any appeal from a decision of a judge-arbitrator under that section lies to the Court of Appeal with the leave of that court.

Withholding Award in Case of Non-payment

6.—(1) The provisions of paragraph 7 apply in place of the provisions of section 56 (power to withhold award in the case of non-payment) in relation to the withholding of an award for non-payment of the fees and expenses of a judge-arbitrator.

(2) This does not affect the application of section 56 in relation to the delivery of such an award by an arbitral or other institution or person vested by the parties with powers in relation to the delivery of the award.

7.—(1) A judge-arbitrator may refuse to deliver an award except upon payment of the fees and expenses mentioned in section 56(1).

(2) The judge-arbitrator may, on an application by a party to the arbitral proceedings, order that if he pays into the High Court the fees and expenses demanded, or such lesser amount as the judge-arbitrator may specify—

(a) the award shall be delivered,
(b) the amount of the fees and expenses properly payable shall be determined by such means and upon such terms as he may direct, and
(c) out of the money paid into court there shall be paid out such fees and expenses as may be found to be properly payable and the balance of the money (if any) shall be paid out to the applicant.

(3) For this purpose the amount of fees and expenses properly payable is the amount the applicant is liable to pay under section 28 or any agreement relating to the payment of the arbitrator.

(4) No application to the judge-arbitrator under this paragraph may be made where there is any available arbitral process for appeal or review of the amount of the fees or expenses demanded.

(5) Any appeal from a decision of a judge-arbitrator under this paragraph lies to the Court of Appeal with the leave of that court.

(6) Where a party to arbitral proceedings appeals under sub-paragraph (5), an arbitrator is entitled to appear and be heard.

Correction of Award or Additional Award

8. Subsections (4) to (6) of section 57 (correction of award or additional award: time limit for application or exercise of power) do not apply to a judge-arbitrator.

Costs

9. Where the arbitral tribunal consists of or includes a judge-arbitrator the powers of the court under section 63(4) (determination of recoverable costs) shall be exercised by the High Court.

10.—(1) The power of the court under section 64 to determine an arbitrator's reasonable fees and expenses may be exercised by a judge-arbitrator.

(2) Any such exercise of the power is subject to the powers of the Court of Appeal under sections 24(4) and 25(3)(b) (directions as to entitlement to fees or expenses in case of removal or resignation).

Enforcement of Award

11. The leave of the court required by section 66 (enforcement of award) may in the case of an award of a judge-arbitrator be given by the judge-arbitrator himself.

Solicitor's Costs

12. The powers of the court to make declarations and orders under the provisions applied by section 75 (power to charge property recovered in arbitral proceedings with the payment of solicitors' costs) may be exercised by the judge-arbitrator.

Powers of Court in Relation to Service of Documents

13.—(1) The power of the court under section 77(2) (powers of court in relation to service of documents) is exercisable by the judge-arbitrator.

(2) Any appeal from a decision of a judge-arbitrator under that section lies to the Court of Appeal with the leave of that court.

Powers of Court to Extend Time Limits Relating to Arbitral Proceedings

14.—(1) The power conferred by section 79 (power of court to extend time limits relating to arbitral proceedings) is exercisable by the judge-arbitrator himself.

(2) Any appeal from a decision of a judge-arbitrator under that section lies to the Court of Appeal with the leave of that court.

SCHEDULE 3 CONSEQUENTIAL AMENDMENTS (SECTION 107(1))

Merchant Shipping Act 1894 (c.60)

1. In section 496 of the Merchant Shipping Act 1894 (provisions as to deposits by owners of goods), after subsection (4) insert—

"(5) In subsection (3) the expression 'legal proceedings' includes arbitral proceedings and as respects England and Wales and Northern Ireland the provisions of section 14 of the Arbitration Act 1996 apply to determine when such proceedings are commenced.".

Stannaries Court (Abolition) Act 1896 (c.45)

2. In section 4(1) of the Stannaries Court (Abolition) Act 1896 (references of certain disputes to arbitration), for the words from "tried before" to "any such reference" substitute "referred to arbitration before himself or before an arbitrator agreed on by the parties or an officer of the court".

Tithe Act 1936 (c.43)

3. In section 39(1) of the Tithe Act 1936 (proceedings of Tithe Redemption Commission)—

(a) for "Arbitration Acts 1889 to 1934" substitute "Part I of the Arbitration Act 1996";

(b) for paragraph (e) substitute—

"(e) the making of an application to the court to determine a preliminary point of law and the bringing of an appeal to the court on a point of law;";

(c) for "the said Acts" substitute "Part I of the Arbitration Act 1996".

. . .

Commonwealth Telegraphs Act 1949 (c.39)

5. Section 8(2) of the Commonwealth Telegraphs Act 1949 (proceedings of referees under the Act) for "the Arbitration Acts 1889 to 1934, or the Arbitration Act (Northern Ireland) 1937," substitute "Part I of the Arbitration Act 1996".

Lands Tribunal Act 1949 (c.42)

6. In section 3 of the Lands Tribunal Act 1949 (proceedings before the Lands Tribunal)—

(a) in subsection (6)(c) (procedural rules: power to apply Arbitration Acts), and

(b) in subsection (8) (exclusion of Arbitration Acts except as applied by rules),

for "the Arbitration Acts 1889 to 1934" substitute "Part I of the Arbitration Act 1996".

Wireless Telegraphy Act 1949 (c.54)

7. In the Wireless Telegraphy Act 1949, Schedule 2 (procedure of appeals tribunal), in paragraph 3(1)—
(a) for the words "the Arbitration Acts 1889 to 1934" substitute "Part I of the Arbitration Act 1996";
(b) after the word "Wales" insert "or Northern Ireland"; and
(c) for "the said Acts" substitute "Part I of that Act".

Patents Act 1949 (c.87)

8. In section 67 of the Patents Act 1949 (proceedings as to infringement of pre-1978 patents referred to comptroller), for "The Arbitration Acts 1889 to 1934" substitute "Part I of the Arbitration Act 1996".

National Health Service (Amendment) Act 1949 (c.93)

9. In section 7(8) of the National Health Service (Amendment) Act 1949 (arbitration in relation to hardship arising from the National Health Service Act 1946 or the Act), for "the Arbitration Acts 1889 to 1934" substitute "Part I of the Arbitration Act 1996" and for "the said Acts" substitute "Part I of that Act".

Arbitration Act 1950 (c.27)

10. In section 36(1) of the Arbitration Act 1950 (effect of foreign awards enforceable under Part II of that Act) for "section 26 of this Act" substitute "section 66 of the Arbitration Act 1996".

Interpretation Act (Northern Ireland) 1954 (c.33 (N.I.))

11. In section 46(2) of the Interpretation Act (Northern Ireland) 1954 (miscellaneous definitions), for the definition of "arbitrator" substitute—
" 'arbitrator' has the same meaning as in Part I of the Arbitration Act 1996;".

Agricultural Marketing Act 1958 (c.47)

12. In section 12(1) of the Agricultural Marketing Act 1958 (application of provisions of Arbitration Act 1950)—
(a) for the words from the beginning to "shall apply" substitute "Sections 45 and 69 of the Arbitration Act 1996 (which relate to the determination by the court of questions of law) and section 66 of that Act (enforcement of awards) apply"; and
(b) for "an arbitration" substitute "arbitral proceedings".

Carriage by Air Act 1961 (c.27)

13.—(1) The Carriage by Air Act 1961 is amended as follows.
(2) In section 5(3) (time for bringing proceedings)—
(a) for "an arbitration" in the first place where it occurs substitute "arbitral proceedings"; and

(b) for the words from “and subsections (3) and (4)” to the end substitute “and the provisions of section 14 of the Arbitration Act 1996 apply to determine when such proceedings are commenced.”.

(3) In section 11(c) (application of section 5 to Scotland)—

(a) for “subsections (3) and (4)” substitute “the provisions of section 14 of the Arbitration Act 1996”; and

(b) for “an arbitration” substitute “arbitral proceedings”.

Factories Act 1961 (c.34)

14. In the Factories Act 1961, for section 171 (application of Arbitration Act 1950), substitute—

“**Application of the Arbitration Act 1996**

171. Part I of the Arbitration Act 1996 does not apply to proceedings under this Act except in so far as it may be applied by regulations made under this Act.”.

Clergy Pensions Measure 1961 (No. 3)

15. In the Clergy Pensions Measure 1961, section 38(4) (determination of questions), for the words “The Arbitration Act 1950” substitute “Part I of the Arbitration Act 1996”.

Transport Act 1962 (c.46)

16.—(1) The Transport Act 1962 is amended as follows.

(2) In section 74(6)(f) (proceedings before referees in pension disputes), for the words “the Arbitration Act 1950” substitute “Part I of the Arbitration Act 1996”.

(3) In section 81(7) (proceedings before referees in compensation disputes), for the words “the Arbitration Act 1950” substitute “Part I of the Arbitration Act 1996”.

(4) In Schedule 7, Part IV (pensions), in paragraph 17(5) for the words “the Arbitration Act 1950” substitute “Part I of the Arbitration Act 1996”.

Corn Rents Act 1963 (c.14)

17. In the Corn Rents Act 1963, section 1(5) (schemes for apportioning corn rents, &c.), for the words “the Arbitration Act 1950” substitute “Part I of the Arbitration Act 1996”.

. . .

Lands Tribunal and Compensation Act (Northern Ireland) 1964 (c.29 (N.I.))

19. In section 9 of the Lands Tribunal and Compensation Act (Northern Ireland) 1964 (proceedings of Lands Tribunal), in subsection (3) (where Tribunal acts as arbitrator) for “the Arbitration Act (Northern Ireland) 1937” substitute “Part I of the Arbitration Act 1996”.

Industrial and Provident Societies Act 1965 (c.12)

20.—(1) Section 60 of the Industrial and Provident Societies Act 1965 is amended as follows.

(2) In subsection (8) (procedure for hearing disputes between society and member, &c.)—

(a) in paragraph (a) for "the Arbitration Act 1950" substitute "Part I of the Arbitration Act 1996"; and

(b) in paragraph (b) omit "by virtue of section 12 of the said Act of 1950".

(3) For subsection (9) substitute—

"(9) the court or registrar to whom any dispute is referred under subsections (2) to (7) may at the request of either party state a case on any question of law arising in the dispute for the opinion of the High Court or, as the case may be, the Court of Session".

Carriage of Goods by Road Act 1965 (c.37)

21. In section 7(2) of the Carriage of Goods by Road Act 1965 (arbitrations: time at which deemed to commence), for paragraphs (a) and (b) substitute—

"(a) as respects England and Wales and Northern Ireland, the provisions of section 14(3) to (5) of the Arbitration Act 1996 (which determine the time at which an arbitration is commenced) apply;".

Factories Act (Northern Ireland) 1965 (c.20 (N.I.))

22. In section 171 of the Factories Act (Northern Ireland) 1965 (application of Arbitration Act), for "The Arbitration Act (Northern Ireland) 1937" substitute "Part I of the Arbitration Act 1996".

Commonwealth Secretariat Act 1966 (c.10)

23. In section 1(3) of the Commonwealth Secretariat Act 1966 (contracts with Commonwealth Secretariat to be deemed to contain provision for arbitration), for "the Arbitration Act 1950 and the Arbitration Act (Northern Ireland) 1937" substitute "Part I of the Arbitration Act 1996".

Arbitration (International Investment Disputes) Act 1966 (c.41)

24. In the Arbitration (International Investment Disputes) Act 1966, for section 3 (application of Arbitration Act 1950 and other enactments) substitute—

"**Application of provisions of Arbitration Act 1996**

3.—(1) The Lord Chancellor may by order direct that any of the provisions contained in sections 36 and 38 to 44 of the Arbitration Act 1996 (provisions concerning the conduct of arbitral proceedings, &c.) shall apply to such proceedings pursuant to the Convention as are specified in the order with or without any modifications or exceptions specified in the order.

(2) Subject to subsection (1), the Arbitration Act 1996 shall not apply to proceedings pursuant to the Convention, but this subsection shall not be taken as affecting section 9 of that Act (stay of legal proceedings in respect of matter subject to arbitration).

(3) An order made under this section—

(a) may be varied or revoked by a subsequent order so made, and

(b) shall be contained in a statutory instrument.".

Poultry Improvement Act (Northern Ireland) 1968 (c.12 (N.I.))

25. In paragraph 10(4) of the Schedule to the Poultry Improvement Act (Northern Ireland) 1968 (reference of disputes), for "The Arbitration Act (Northern Ireland) 1937" substitute "Part I of the Arbitration Act 1996".

Industrial and Provident Societies Act (Northern Ireland) 1969 (c.24 (N.I.))

26.—(1) Section 69 of the Industrial and Provident Societies Act (Northern Ireland) 1969 (decision of disputes) is amended as follows.

(2) In subsection (7) (decision of disputes)—

(a) in the opening words, omit the words from "and without prejudice" to "1937";

(b) at the beginning of paragraph (a) insert "without prejudice to any powers exercisable by virtue of Part I of the Arbitration Act 1996,"; and

(c) in paragraph (b) omit "the registrar or" and "registrar or" and for the words from "as might have been granted by the High Court" to the end substitute "as might be granted by the registrar".

(3) For subsection (8) substitute—

"(8) The court or registrar to whom any dispute is referred under subsections (2) to (6) may at the request of either party state a case on any question of law arising in the dispute for the opinion of the High Court.".

Health and Personal Social Services (Northern Ireland) Order 1972 (N.I. 14)

27. In Article 105(6) of the Health and Personal Social Services (Northern Ireland) Order 1972 (arbitrations under the Order), for "the Arbitration Act (Northern Ireland) 1937" substitute "Part I of the Arbitration Act 1996".

Consumer Credit Act 1974 (c.39)

28.—(1) Section 146 of the Consumer Credit Act 1974 is amended as follows.

(2) In subsection (2) (solicitor engaged in contentious business), for "section 86(1) of the Solicitors Act 1957" substitute "section 87(1) of the Solicitors Act 1974".

(3) In subsection (4) (solicitor in Northern Ireland engaged in contentious business), for the words from "business done" to "Administration of Estates (Northern Ireland) Order 1979" substitute "contentious business (as defined in Article 3(2) of the Solicitors (Northern Ireland) Order 1976.".

Friendly Societies Act 1974 (c.46)

29.—(1) The Friendly Societies Act 1974 is amended as follows.

(2) For section 78(1) (statement of case) substitute—

"(1) any arbitrator, arbiter or umpire to whom a dispute falling within section 76 above is referred under the rules of a registered society or branch may at the request of either party state a case on any question of law arising in the dispute for the opinion of the High Court or, as the case may be, the Court of Session.".

(3) In section 83(3) (procedure on objections to amalgamations &c. of friendly

societies), for "the Arbitration Act 1950 or, in Northern Ireland, the Arbitration Act (Northern Ireland) 1937" substitute "Part I of the Arbitration Act 1996".

Industry Act 1975 (c.68)

30. In Schedule 3 to the Industry Act (arbitration of disputes relating to vesting and compensation orders), in paragraph 14 (application of certain provisions of Arbitration Acts)—

(a) for "the Arbitration Act 1950 or, in Northern Ireland, the Arbitration Act (Northern Ireland) 1937" substitute "Part I of the Arbitration Act 1996", and

(b) for "that Act" substitute "that Part".

. . .

Aircraft and Shipbuilding Industries Act 1977 (c.3)

32. In Schedule 7 to the Aircraft and Shipbuilding Industries Act 1977 (procedure of Arbitration Tribunal), in paragraph 2—

(a) for "the Arbitration Act 1950 or, in Northern Ireland, the Arbitration Act (Northern Ireland) 1937" substitute "Part I of the Arbitration Act 1996", and

(b) for "that Act" substitute "that Part".

Patents Act 1977 (c.37)

33. In section 130 of the Patents Act 1977 (interpretation), in subsection (8) (exclusion of Arbitration Act) for "The Arbitration Act 1950" substitute "Part I of the Arbitration Act 1996".

Judicature (Northern Ireland) Act 1978 (c.23)

34.—(1) The Judicature (Northern Ireland) Act 1978 is amended as follows.

(2) In section 35(2) (restrictions on appeals to the Court of Appeal), after paragraph (f) insert—

"(fa) except as provided by Part I of the Arbitration Act 1996, from any decision of the High Court under that Part;".

(3) In section 55(2) (rules of court), after paragraph (c) insert—

"(cc) providing for any prescribed part of the jurisdiction of the High Court in relation to the trial of any action involving matters of account to be exercised in the prescribed manner by a person agreed by the parties and for the remuneration of any such person;".

Health and Safety at Work (Northern Ireland) Order 1978 (N.I. 9)

35. In Schedule 4 to the Health and Safety at Work (Northern Ireland) Order 1978 (licensing provisions), in paragraph 3, for "the Arbitration Act (Northern Ireland) 1937" substitute "Part I of the Arbitration Act 1996".

County Courts (Northern Ireland) Order 1980 (N.I. 3)

36.—(1) The County Courts (Northern Ireland) Order 1980 is amended as follows.

(2) In Article 30 (civil jurisdiction exercisable by district judge)—

(a) for paragraph (2) substitute—

"(2) Any order, decision or determination made by a district judge under this Article (other than one made in dealing with a claim by way of arbitration under paragraph (3)) shall be embodied in a decree which for all purposes (including the right of appeal under Part VI) shall have the like effect as a decree pronounced by a county court judge.";

(b) for paragraphs (4) and (5) substitute—

"(4) Where in any action to which paragraph (1) applies the claim is dealt with by way of arbitration under paragraph (3)—

(a) any award made by the district judge in dealing with the claim shall be embodied in a decree which for all purposes (except the right of appeal under Part VI) shall have the like effect as a decree pronounced by a county court judge;

(b) the district judge may, and shall if so required by the High Court, state for the determination of the High Court any question of law arising out of an award so made;

(c) except as provided by sub-paragraph (b), any award so made shall be final; and

(d) except as otherwise provided by county court rules, no costs shall be awarded in connection with the action.

(5) Subject to paragraph (4), county court rules may—

(a) apply any of the provisions of Part I of the Arbitration Act 1996 to arbitrations under paragraph (3) with such modifications as may be prescribed;

(b) prescribe the rules of evidence to be followed on any arbitration under paragraph (3) and, in particular, make provision with respect to the manner of taking and questioning evidence.

(5A) Except as provided by virtue of paragraph (5)(a), Part I of the Arbitration Act 1996 shall not apply to an arbitration under paragraph (3).".

(3) After Article 61 insert—

"**Appeals from decisions under Part I of Arbitration Act 1996**

61A.—(1) Article 61 does not apply to a decision of a county court judge made in the exercise of the jurisdiction conferred by Part I of the Arbitration Act 1996.

(2) Any party dissatisfied with a decision of the county court made in the exercise of the jurisdiction conferred by any of the following provisions of Part I of the Arbitration Act 1996, namely—

(a) section 32 (question as to substantive jurisdiction of arbitral tribunal);

(b) section 45 (question of law arising in course of arbitral proceedings);

(c) section 67 (challenging award of arbitral tribunal; substantive jurisdiction);

(d) section 68 (challenging award of arbitral tribunal; serious irregularity);

(e) section 69 (appeal on point of law),

may, subject to the provisions of that Part, appeal from that decision to the Court of Appeal.

(3) Any party dissatisfied with any decision of a county court made in the exercise of the jurisdiction conferred by any other provision of Part I of the Arbitration Act 1996 may, subject to the provisions of that Part, appeal from that decision to the High Court.

(4) The decision of the Court of Appeal on an appeal under paragraph (2) shall be final.".

Supreme Court Act 1981 (c.54)

37.—(1) The Supreme Court Act 1981 is amended as follows.

(2) In section 18(1) (restrictions on appeals to the Court of Appeal), for paragraph (g) substitute—

"(g) except as provided by Part I of the Arbitration Act 1996, from any decision of the High Court under that Part;".

(3) In section 151 (interpretation, &c.), in the definition of "arbitration agreement", for "the Arbitration Act 1950 by virtue of section 32 of that Act;" substitute "Part I of the Arbitration Act 1996;".

Merchant Shipping (Liner Conferences) Act 1982 (c.37)

38. In section 7(5) of the Merchant Shipping (Liner Conferences) Act 1982 (stay of legal proceedings), for the words from "section 4(1)" to the end substitute "section 9 of the Arbitration Act 1996 (which also provides for the staying of legal proceedings).".

Agricultural Marketing (Northern Ireland) Order 1982 (N.I. 12)

39. In Article 14 of the Agricultural Marketing (Northern Ireland) Order 1982 (application of provisions of Arbitration Act (Northern Ireland) 1937)—

(a) for the words from the beginning to "shall apply" substitute "Section 45 and 69 of the Arbitration Act 1996 (which relate to the determination by the court of questions of law) and section 66 of that Act (enforcement of awards)" apply; and

(b) for "an arbitration" substitute "arbitral proceedings".

Mental Health Act 1983 (c.20)

40. In section 78 of the Mental Health Act 1983 (procedure of Mental Health Review Tribunals), in subsection (9) for "The Arbitration Act 1950" substitute "Part I of the Arbitration Act 1996".

Registered Homes Act 1984 (c.23)

41. In section 43 of the Registered Homes Act 1984 (procedure of Registered Homes Tribunals), in subsection (3) for "The Arbitration Act 1950" substitute "Part I of the Arbitration Act 1996".

Housing Act 1985 (c.68)

42. In section 47(3) of the Housing Act 1985 (agreement as to determination of

matters relating to service charges) for "section 32 of the Arbitration Act 1950" substitute "Part I of the Arbitration Act 1996".

. . .

Credit Unions (Northern Ireland) Order 1985 (N.I. 12)

44.—(1) Article 72 of the Credit Unions (Northern Ireland) Order 1985 (decision of disputes) is amended as follows.

(2) In paragraph (7)—

(a) in the opening words, omit the words from "and without prejudice" to "1937";

(b) at the beginning of sub-paragraph (a) insert "without prejudice to any powers exercisable by virtue of Part I of the Arbitration Act 1996,"; and

(c) in sub-paragraph (b) omit "the registrar or" and "registrar or" and for the words from "as might have been granted by the High Court" to the end substitute "as might be granted by the registrar".

(3) For paragraph (8) substitute—

"(8) The court or registrar to whom any dispute is referred under paragraphs (2) to (6) may at the request of either party state a case on any question of law arising in the dispute for the opinion of the High Court.".

Agricultural Holdings Act 1986 (c.5)

45. In section 84(1) of the Agricultural Holdings Act 1986 (provisions relating to arbitration), for "the Arbitration Act 1950" substitute "Part I of the Arbitration Act 1996".

Insolvency Act 1986 (c.45)

46. In the Insolvency Act 1986, after section 349 insert—

"**Arbitration agreements to which bankrupt is party**

349A.—(1) This section applies where a bankrupt had become party to a contract containing an arbitration agreement before the commencement of his bankruptcy.

(2) If the trustee in bankruptcy adopts the contract, the arbitration agreement is enforceable by or against the trustee in relation to matters arising from or connected with the contract.

(3) If the trustee in bankruptcy does not adopt the contract and a matter to which the arbitration agreement applies requires to be determined in connection with or for the purposes of the bankruptcy proceedings—

(a) the trustee with the consent of the creditors' committee, or

(b) any other party to the agreement,

may apply to the court which may, if it thinks fit in all the circumstances of the case, order that the matter be referred to arbitration in accordance with the arbitration agreement.

(4) In this section—

'arbitration agreement' has the same meaning as in Part I of the Arbitration Act 1996; and

'the court' means the court which has jurisdiction in the bankruptcy proceedings.".

Building Societies Act 1986 (c.53)

47. In Part II of Schedule 14 to the Building Societies Act 1986 (settlement of disputes: arbitration), in paragraph 5(6) for "the Arbitration Act 1950 and the Arbitration Act 1979 or, in Northern Ireland, the Arbitration Act (Northern Ireland) 1937" substitute "Part I of the Arbitration Act 1996".

Mental Health (Northern Ireland) Order 1986 (N.I. 4)

48. In Article 83 of the Mental Health (Northern Ireland) Order 1986 (procedure of Mental Health Review Tribunal), in paragraph (8) for "The Arbitration Act (Northern Ireland) 1937" substitute "Part I of the Arbitration Act 1996".

Multilateral Investment Guarantee Agency Act 1988 (c.8)

49. For section 6 of the Multilateral Investment Guarantee Agency Act 1988 (application of Arbitration Act) substitute—

"**Application of Arbitration Act**

6.—(1) The Lord Chancellor may by order made by statutory instrument direct that any of the provisions of sections 36 and 38 to 44 of the Arbitration Act 1996 (provisions in relation to the conduct of the arbitral proceedings, &c.) apply, with such modifications or exceptions as are specified in the order, to such arbitration proceedings pursuant to Annex II to the Convention as are specified in the order.

(2) Except as provided by an order under subsection (1) above, no provision of Part I of the Arbitration Act 1996 other than section 9 (stay of legal proceedings) applies to any such proceedings.".

Copyright, Designs and Patents Act 1988 (c.48)

50. In section 150 of the Copyright, Designs and Patents Act 1988 (Lord Chancellor's power to make rules for Copyright Tribunal), for subsection (2) substitute—

"(2) The rules may apply in relation to the Tribunal, as respects proceedings in England and Wales or Northern Ireland, any of the provisions of Part I of the Arbitration Act 1996.".

Fair Employment (Northern Ireland) Act 1989 (c.32)

51. In the Fair Employment (Northern Ireland) Act 1989 section 5(7) (procedure of Fair Employment Tribunal), for "The Arbitration Act (Northern Ireland) 1937" substitute "Part I of the Arbitration Act 1996".

Limitation (Northern Ireland) Order 1989 (N.I. 11)

52. In Article 2(2) of the Limitation (Northern Ireland) Order 1989 (interpretation), in the definition of "arbitration agreement", for "the Arbitration Act (Northern Ireland) 1937" substitute "Part I of the Arbitration Act 1996".

Insolvency (Northern Ireland) Order 1989 (N.I. 19)

53. In the Insolvency (Northern Ireland) Order 1989, after Article 320 insert—

"Arbitration agreements to which bankrupt is party

320A.—(1) This Article applies where a bankrupt had become party to a contract containing an arbitration agreement before the commencement of his bankruptcy.

(2) If the trustee in bankruptcy adopts the contract, the arbitration agreement is enforceable by or against the trustee in relation to matters arising from or connected with the contract.

(3) If the trustee in bankruptcy does not adopt the contract and a matter to which the arbitration agreement applies requires to be determined in connection with or for the purposes of the bankruptcy proceedings—

(a) the trustee with the consent of the creditors' committee, or

(b) any other party to the agreement,

may apply to the court which may, if it thinks fit in all the circumstances of the case, order that the matter be referred to arbitration in accordance with the arbitration agreement.

(4) In this Article—

'arbitration agreement' has the same meaning as in Part I of the Arbitration Act 1996; and

'the court' means the court which has jurisdiction in the bankruptcy proceedings.".

. . .

Social Security Administration (Northern Ireland) Act 1992 (c.8)

55. In section 57 of the Social Security Administration (Northern Ireland) Act 1992 (procedure for inquiries, &c.), in subsection (6) for "the Arbitration Act (Northern Ireland) 1937" substitute "Part I of the Arbitration Act 1996".

Trade Union and Labour Relations (Consolidation) Act 1992 (c.52)

56. In sections 212(5) and 263(6) of the Trade Union and Labour Relations (Consolidation) Act 1992 (application of Arbitration Act) for "the Arbitration Act 1950" substitute "Part I of the Arbitration Act 1996".

Industrial Relations (Northern Ireland) Order 1992 (N.I. 5)

57. In Articles 84(9) and 92(5) of the Industrial Relations (Northern Ireland) Order 1992 (application of Arbitration Act) for "The Arbitration Act (Northern Ireland) 1937" substitute "Part I of the Arbitration Act 1996".

Registered Homes (Northern Ireland) Order 1992 (N.I. 20)

58. In Article 33(3) of the Registered Homes (Northern Ireland) Order 1992 (procedure of Registered Homes Tribunal) for "The Arbitration Act (Northern Ireland) 1937" substitute "Part I of the Arbitration Act 1996".

. . .

Roads (Northern Ireland) Order 1993 (N.I. 15)

60.—(1) The Roads (Northern Ireland) Order 1993 is amended as follows.

(2) In Article 131 (application of Arbitration Act) for "the Arbitration Act (Northern Ireland) 1937" substitute "Part I of the Arbitration Act 1996".
(3) In Schedule 4 (disputes), in paragraph 3(2) for "the Arbitration Act (Northern Ireland) 1937" substitute "Part I of the Arbitration Act 1996".

Merchant Shipping 1995 (c.21)

61. In Part II of Schedule 6 to the Merchant Shipping Act 1995 (provisions having effect in connection with Convention Relating to the Carriage of Passengers and Their Luggage by Sea), for paragraph 7 substitute—

"7. Article 16 shall apply to arbitral proceedings as it applies to an action; and, as respects England and Wales and Northern Ireland, the provisions of section 14 of the Arbitration Act 1996 apply to determine for the purposes of that Article when an arbitration is commenced.".

Industrial Tribunals Act 1996 (c.17)

62. In section 6(2) of the Industrial Tribunals Act 1996 (procedure of industrial tribunals), for "The Arbitration Act 1950" substitute "Part of the Arbitration Act 1996".

SCHEDULE 4 REPEALS (SECTION 107(2))

Chapter	Short title	Extent of repeal
1892 c. 43.	Military Lands Act 1892.	In section 21(b), the words "under the Arbitration Act 1889".
1922 c. 51.	Allotments Act 1922.	In section 21(3), the words "under the Arbitration Act 1889".
1937 c. 8 (N.I.).	Arbitration Act (Northern Ireland) 1937.	The whole Act.
1949 c. 54.	Wireless Telegraphy Act 1949.	In Schedule 2, paragraph 3(3).
1949 c. 97.	National Parks and Access to the Countryside Act 1949.	In section 18(4), the words from "Without prejudice" to "England or Wales".
1950 c. 27.	Arbitration Act 1950.	Part I. Section 42(3).
1958 c. 47.	Agricultural Marketing Act 1958.	Section 53(8).
1962 c. 46.	Transport Act 1962.	In Schedule 11, Part II, paragraph 7.
1964 c. 14.	Plant Varieties and Seeds Act 1964.	In section 10(4) the words from "or in section 9" to "three arbitrators)". Section 39(3)(b)(i).
1964 c. 29 (N.I.).	Lands Tribunal and Compensation Act (Northern Ireland) 1964.	In section 9(3) the words from "so, however, that" to the end.
1965 c. 12.	Industrial and Provident Societies Act 1965.	In section 60(8)(b), the words "by virtue of section 12 of the said Act of 1950".
1965 c. 37.	Carriage of Goods by Road Act 1965.	Section 7(2)(b).

Chapter	Short title	Extent of repeal
1965 c. 13 (N.I.).	New Towns Act (Northern Ireland) 1965.	In section 27(2), the words from "under and in accordance with" to the end.
1969 c. 24 (N.I.).	Industrial and Provident Societies Act (Northern Ireland) 1969.	In section 69(7)— (a) in the opening words, the words from "and without prejudice" to "1937"; (b) in paragraph (b), the words "the registrar or" and "registrar or".
1970 c. 31.	Administration of Justice Act 1970.	Section 4. Schedule 3.
1973 c. 41.	Fair Trading Act 1973.	Section 33(2)(d).
1973 N.I. 1.	Drainage (Northern Ireland) Order 1973.	In Article 15(4), the words from "under and in accordance" to the end. Article 40(4). In Schedule 7, in paragraph 9(2), the words from "under and in accordance" to the end.
1974 c. 47.	Solicitors Act 1974.	In section 87(1), in the definition of "contentious business", the words "appointed under the Arbitration Act 1950".
1975 c. 3.	Arbitration Act 1975.	The whole Act.
1975 c. 74.	Petroleum and Submarine Pipelines Act 1975.	In Part II of Schedule 2— (a) in model clause 40(2), the words "in accordance with the Arbitration Act 1950"; (b) in model clause 40(2B), the words "in accordance with the Arbitration Act (Northern Ireland) 1937". In Part II of Schedule 3, in model clause 38(2), the words "in accordance with the Arbitration Act 1950".
1976 N.I. 12.	Solicitors (Northern Ireland) Order 1976.	In Article 3(2), in the entry "contentious business", the words "appointed under the Arbitration Act (Northern Ireland) 1937". Article 71H(3).
1977 c. 37.	Patents Act 1977.	In section 52(4) the words "section 21 of the Arbitration Act 1950 or, as the case may be, section 22 of the Arbitration Act (Northern Ireland) 1937 (statement of cases by arbitrators); but". Section 131(e).
1977 c. 38.	Administration of Justice Act 1977.	Section 17(2).
1978 c. 23.	Judicature (Northern Ireland) Act 1978.	In section 35(2), paragraph (g)(v). In Schedule 5, the amendment to the Arbitration Act 1950.
1979 c. 42.	Arbitration Act 1979.	The whole Act.
1980 c. 58.	Limitation Act 1980.	Section 34.

Chapter	Short title	Extent of repeal
1980 N.I. 3.	County Courts (Northern Ireland) Order 1980.	Article 31(3).
1981 c. 54.	Supreme Court Act 1981.	Section 148.
1982 c. 27.	Civil Jurisdiction and Judgments Act 1982.	Section 25(3)(c) and (5). In section 26— (a) in subsection (1), the words "to arbitration or"; (b) in subsection (1)(a)(i), the words "arbitration or"; (c) in subsection (2), the words "arbitration or".
1982 c. 53.	Administration of Justice Act 1982.	Section 15(6). In Schedule 1, Part IV.
1984 c. 5.	Merchant Shipping Act 1984.	Section 4(8).
1984 c. 12.	Telecommunications Act 1984.	Schedule 2, paragraph 13(8).
1984 c. 16.	Foreign Limitation Periods Act 1984.	Section 5.
1984 c. 28.	County Courts Act 1984.	In Schedule 2, paragraph 70.
1985 c. 61.	Administration of Justice Act 1985.	Section 58. In Schedule 9, paragraph 15.
1985 c. 68.	Housing Act 1985.	In Schedule 18, in paragraph 6(2) the words from "and the Arbitration Act 1950" to the end.
1985 N.I. 12.	Credit Unions (Northern Ireland) Order 1985.	In Article 72(7)— (a) in the opening words, the words from "and without prejudice" to "1937"; (b) in sub-paragraph (b), the words "the registrar of" and "registrar or".
1986 c. 45.	Insolvency Act 1986.	In Schedule 14, the entry relating to the Arbitration Act 1950.
1988 c. 8.	Multilateral Investment Guarantee Agency Act 1988.	Section 8(3).
1988 c. 21.	Consumer Arbitration Agreements Act 1988.	The whole Act.
1989 N.I. 11.	Limitation (Northern Ireland) Order 1989.	Article 72. In Schedule 3, paragraph 1.
1989 N.I. 19.	Insolvency (Northern Ireland) Order 1989.	In Part II of Schedule 8, paragraph 66.
1990 c. 41.	Courts and Legal Services Act 1990.	Sections 99 and 101 to 103.
1991 N.I. 7.	Food Safety (Northern Ireland) Order 1991.	In Articles 8(8) and 11(10), the words from "and the provisions" to the end.
1992 c. 40.	Friendly Societies Act 1992.	In Schedule 16, paragraph 30(1).
1995 c. 8.	Agricultural Tenancies Act 1995.	Section 28(4).
1995 c. 21.	Merchant Shipping Act 1995.	Section 96(10). Section 264(9).
1995 c. 42.	Private International Law (Miscellaneous Provisions) Act 1995.	Section 3.

APPENDIX B.1

INDEX TO COMPARISON OF THE RULES OF THE LCIA, ICC, ICDR AND UNCITRAL[1]

Note: The way that the various rules are formulated makes it extremely difficult to categorise the rules precisely. The table must therefore be viewed with this in mind and regarded as a guide only. Additional consideration and checking of the relevant rules is advisable.

This index is prepared to reflect the chronological progress through the arbital process rather than alphabetically. A numerical index is at Appendix B.2.

Page

The Institution and its role:
Articles 3.1–3 and 29.1 of the LCIA Rules; Articles 1.1–5 of the ICC Rules; and Article 1.3 of the ICDR Rules. 200

Definitions and interpretation:
Articles 5.1 and 32.2 of the LCIA Rules; and Articles 2(i)–(iii) and 35 of the ICC Rules; and Article 36 of the ICDR Rules. 201

Effect of the arbitration agreement:
Introduction to the LCIA Rules; Article 6.1 of the ICC Rules; Article 1.1–2 of the ICDR Rules; and Article 1.1–2 of the UNCITRAL Rules. 202

Commencing the arbitration:
Article 1.1–2 of the LCIA Rules; Article 4.1–5 of the ICC Rules; Article 2.1–4 of the ICDR Rules; and Article 3.1–4 of the UNCITRAL Rules. 203

The Response/Answer, Counterclaim and Reply:
Article 2.1–3 of the LCIA Rules; Article 5.1–6 of the ICC Rules; and Article 3.1–4 of the ICDR Rules. 205

Calculation of time, notices and other communications:
Article 4.1–6 of the LCIA Rules; Article 3.1–4 of the ICC Rules; Article 18.1–2 of the ICDR Rules; and Article 2.1–2 of the UNCITRAL Rules. 206

Extension of time:
Articles 4.7 and 22.1(b) of the LCIA Rules; Article 32.1–2 of the ICC Rules; Article 17.2 of the ICDR Rules; and Article 23 of the UNCITRAL Rules. 208

1. The LCIA Arbitration Rules; the International Court of the ICC Rules of Arbitration; the International Rules of the ICDR; and the UNCITRAL Arbitration Rules.

Page

Variation provisions relating to the formation of the arbitral tribunal:

Independence and impartiality:
Article 5.2–3 of the LCIA Rules; Articles 7.1–3 and 7.5 of the ICC Rules; Article 7.1–2 of the ICDR Rules; and Article 9 of the UNCITRAL Rules. 209

Institutional appointment of arbitrators and procedure:
Articles 5.4–6 and 7.1 of the LCIA Rules; Articles 7.4, 7.6 and 9.2–4 of the ICC Rules; and Article 8.1–2 of the UNCITRAL Rules. 210

Criteria for appointment:
Articles 5.5 and 6.1–3 of the LCIA Rules; Articles 9.1 and 9.5 of the ICC Rules; Article 6.4 of the ICDR Rules; and Article 6.4 of the UNCITRAL Rules. 212

Number of arbitrators, party appointments and default appointment by the institution:
Articles 2.3, 5.4 and 7.1–2 of the LCIA Rules; Articles 8.1–4 and 9.6 of the ICC Rules; Articles 5 and 6.1–3 of the ICDR Rules; and Articles 5, 6.1–3 and 7.1–3 of the UNCITRAL Rules. 213

Multiple parties:
Article 8.1–2 of the LCIA Rules; and Article 10.1–2 of the ICC Rules and Article 6.5 of the ICDR Rules. 217

Expedited formation:
Article 9.1–3 of the LCIA Rules; and Article 37.1–9 of the ICDR Rules. 218

Fees for arbitrators:
Article 5.3 of the LCIA Rules; Article 31.2 and App.III Article 2(1) of the ICC Rules; Article 32 of the ICDR Rules; and Article 39.1–4 of the UNCITRAL Rules. 221

Replacement of arbitrators:
Articles 10.1–2 and 11.1–2 of the LCIA Rules; Article 12.1–4 of the ICC Rules; Articles 10 and 11.1–2 of the ICDR Rules; and Articles 13.1–2 and 14 of the UNCITRAL Rules. 223

Truncated tribunals:
Article 12.1–3 of the LCIA Rules; Article 12.5 of the ICC Rules; and Article 11.1 of the ICDR Rules. 224

Party challenges and procedure:
Article 10.3–4 of the LCIA Rules; Article 11.1–3 of the ICC Rules; Articles 8.1–3 and 9 of the ICDR Rules; and Articles 10.1–2, 11.1–3 and 12.1–2 of the UNCITRAL Rules. 225

Communications between parties and the arbitral tribunal:
Article 13.1–3 of the LCIA Rules; Article 13 of the ICC Rules; Article 12 of the ICDR Rules and Article 4 of the UNCITRAL Rules. 228

Terms of Reference and provisional timetable:
Article 18.1–4 of the ICC Rules. 229

Page

Conduct of the arbitration:
Article 14.1–2 of the LCIA Rules; Articles 15.1–2 and 20.1 of the ICC Rules; Article 16.1–4 of the ICDR Rules; and Article 15.1 and 15.3 of the UNCITRAL Rules. 231

Further written statements or pleadings:
Article 15.1–7 of the LCIA Rules; Article 17.1–2 of the ICDR Rules; Articles 18.1–2, 19.1–4, 22 and 23 of the UNCITRAL Rules. 232

Amendments and new claims including counterclaims and set-offs:
Article 22.1(a) of the LCIA Rules; Articles 4.6 and 19 of the ICC Rules; Article 4 of the ICDR Rules; and Article 20 of the UNCITRAL Rules. 235

Language of the arbitration:
Article 17.1–4 of the LCIA Rules; Article 16 of the ICC Rules; Article 14 of the ICDR Rules; and Article 17.1–2 of the UNCITRAL Rules. 236

Seat and place of arbitration:
Article 16.1–2 of the LCIA Rules; Article 14.1–3 of the ICC Rules; Article 13.1–2 of the ICDR Rules; and Article 16.1–4 of the UNCITRAL Rules. 237

Various other provisions relating to hearings:

Party representation:
Article 18.1–2 of the LCIA Rules; Article 21.4 of the ICC Rules; Article 12 of the ICDR Rules; and Article 4 of the UNCITRAL Rules. 238

Oral hearings versus decisions on documents alone:
Article 19.1–2 and 19.5 of the LCIA Rules; Articles 20.2–3, 20.6 and 21.1 of the ICC Rules; Article 20.1–3 of the ICDR Rules; and Articles 15.2 and 25.1–3 of the UNCITRAL Rules. 238

Burden of proof:
Article 19.1 of the ICDR Rules and Article 24.1 of the UNCITRAL Rules. 240

Privacy and confidentiality and admission of witnesses:
Articles 19.4 and 30.1–3 of the LCIA Rules; Article 21.3 of the ICC Rules; Articles 20.4, 27.4, 27.8 and 34 of the ICDR Rules; and Articles 25.4 and 32.5 of the UNCITRAL Rules. 240

Evidence: documents, witnesses and other evidence:
Articles 20.1–7 and 22.1(e) and (f) of the LCIA Rules; Article 20.5 of the ICC Rules; Articles 19.2–3 and 20.4–6 of the ICDR Rules; and Articles 24.2–3 and 25.4–6 of the UNCITRAL Rules. 241

Experts:
Article 21.1–3 of the LCIA Rules; Article 20.4 of the ICC Rules; Article 22.1–4 of the ICDR Rules; and Article 27.1–4 of the UNCITRAL Rules. 244

Applicable rules of law:
Articles 16.3 and 22.3–4 of the LCIA Rules; Article 17.1–3 of the ICC Rules; Article 28.1–3 of the ICDR Rules; and Article 33.1–3 of the UNCITRAL Rules. 245

Page

Consolidation and additional parties:
Article 22.1(h) of the LCIA Rules. 246

Additional powers of the tribunal:
Articles 19.3 and 22.1(c), (d) and (g) of the LCIA Rules; and Article 20.7 of the ICC Rules. 247

Procedural issues:
Article 14.3 of the LCIA Rules; Article 26.2 of the ICDR Rules; and Article 31.2 of the UNCITRAL Rules. 248

Default by parties:
Article 15.8 of the LCIA Rules; Articles 6.3 and 21.2 of the ICC Rules; Article 23.1–3 of the ICDR Rules; and Article 28.1–3 of the UNCITRAL Rules. 248

Closure of proceedings:
Article 22.1–2 of the ICC Rules; Article 24.1–3 of the ICDR Rules; and Article 29.1–2 of the UNCITRAL Rules. 249

Conservatory and interim measures and security for costs:
Article 25.1(a)–(c) and 25.2–3 of the LCIA Rules; Article 23.1–2 of the ICC Rules; Article 21.1–4 of the ICDR Rules; and Article 26.1–3 of the UNCITRAL Rules. 250

Jursidiction:
Article 23.1–4 of the LCIA Rules; Article 6.2 and 6.4 of the ICC Rules; Article 15.1–3 of the ICDR Rules; and Article 21.1–4 of the UNCITRAL Rules. 253

The award:

Form and effect of the award:
Article 26.1 and 26.9 of the LCIA Rules; Articles 25.2–3 and 28.6 of the ICC Rules; Article 27.1–3 of the ICDR Rules; and Article 32.2–4 of the UNCITRAL Rules. 254

Arbitrator's duties re awards:
Articles 26.2 and 26.4–5 of the LCIA Rules. 255

Majority decisions:
Article 26.3 of the LCIA Rules; Article 25.1 of the ICC Rules; Article 26.1 of the ICDR Rules; and Article 31.1 of the UNCITRAL Rules. 256

Separate and interim awards:
Article 26.7 of the LCIA Rules; Article 27.7 of the ICDR Rules; and Article 32.1 of the UNCITRAL Rules. 256

Currency and interest:
Article 26.6 of the LCIA Rules; and Article 28.4 of the ICDR Rules. 256

Settlement or other reasons for termination:
Article 26.8 of the LCIA Rules; Article 26 of the ICC Rules; Article 29.1–2 of the ICDR Rules; and Article 34.1–3 of the UNCITRAL Rules. 257

Page

Time limits for awards:
Article 24.1–2 of the ICC Rules. 258

Correction and interpretation of awards and additional awards:
Article 27.1–3 of the LCIA Rules; Article 29.1–3 of the ICC Rules; Article 30.1–2 of the ICDR Rules; and Articles 35.1–2, 36.1–2 and 37.1–3 of the UNCITRAL Rules. 258

Scrutiny of awards:
Article 27 of the ICC Rules. 260

Notification of the award:
Article 26.5 of the LCIA Rules; Article 28.1–5 of the ICC Rules; Article 27.5–6 of the ICDR Rules; and Article 32.6–7 of the UNCITRAL Rules. 261

Deposits and advance costs:
Article 24.1–4 of the LCIA Rules; Article 30.1–5 of the ICC Rules; Article 33.1–4 of the ICDR Rules; and Article 41.1–5 of the UNCITRAL Rules. 261

Arbitration and legal costs:
Article 28.1–5 of the LCIA Rules; Article 31.1–3 of the ICC Rules; Article 31.1(a)–(e) of the ICDR Rules; and Articles 38(a)–(f) and 40.1–4 of the UNCITRAL Rules. 263

Exclusion of recourse to the courts:
Articles 22.2, 23.4, 26.9 and 29.2 of the LCIA Rules; and Articles 6.2 and 28.6 of the ICC Rules. 266

Waiver of rules:
Article 32.1 of the LCIA Rules; Article 33 of the ICC Rules; Article 25 of the ICDR Rules; and Article 30 of the UNCITRAL Rules. 267

Exclusion of liability:
Article 31.1–2 of the LCIA Rules; Article 34 of the ICC Rules; and Article 35 of the ICDR Rules. 267

Punitive and exemplary damage:
Article 28.5 of the ICDR Rules. 268

APPENDIX B.2

INDEX OF THE LCIA, ICC, ICDR AND UNCITRAL RULES IN NUMERICAL ORDER

Note: Page references are to the page numbers in the Comparative Index.

LCIA Rules

Article No.		*Page*
1.	The Request for Arbitration	203
2.	The Response	205, 213
3.	The LCIA Court and Registrar	200
4.	Notices and Periods of Time	206, 208
5.	Formation of the Arbitral Tribunal	201, 209, 210, 212, 213
6.	Nationality of Arbitrators	212, 221
7.	Party and Other Nominations	210, 213
8.	Three or More Parties	217
9.	Expedited Formation	218
10.	Revocation of Arbitrator's Appointment	223, 225
11.	Nomination and Replacement of Arbitrators	223
12.	Majority Power to Continue Proceedings	224
13.	Communications	228
14.	Conduct of the Proceedings	231, 248
15.	Submission of Written Statements and Documents	232, 248
16.	Seat of Arbitration and Place of Hearings	237, 245
17.	Language of Arbitration	236
18.	Party Representation	238
19.	Hearings	238, 240, 247
20.	Witnesses	241
21.	Experts to the Arbitral Tribunal	244
22.	Additional Powers of the Arbitral Tribunal	208, 235, 241, 245, 246, 247, 266
23.	Jurisdiction of the Arbitral Tribunal	253, 266
24.	Deposits	261
25.	Interim and Conservatory Measures	250
26.	The Award	254, 255, 256, 257, 261, 266
27.	Correction of Awards and Additional Awards	258
28.	Arbitration and Legal Costs	263
29.	Decisions by the LCIA Court	200, 266
30.	Confidentiality	240
31.	Exclusion of Liability	267
32.	General Rules	201, 267

ICC Rules[1]

Article No.		Page
1.	International Court of Arbitration	200
2.	Definitions	201
3.	Written Notification and Communications; Time Limits	206
4.	Request for Arbitration	203, 235
5.	Answer to the Request; Counterclaims	205
6.	Effect of the Arbitration Agreement	202, 248, 253, 266
7.	General Provisions	209, 210
8.	Number of Arbitrators	213
9.	Appointment and Confirmation of the Arbitrators	210, 212, 213
10.	Multiple Parties	217
11.	Challenge of Arbitrators	225
12.	Replacement of Arbitrators	223, 224
13.	Transmission of the File to the Arbitral Tribunal	228
14.	Place of the Arbitration	237
15.	Rules Governing the Proceedings	231
16.	Language of the Arbitration	236
17.	Applicable Rules of Law	245
18.	Terms of Reference; Procedural Timetable	229
19.	New Claims	235
20.	Establishing the Facts of the Case	231, 238, 244, 247
21.	Hearings	238, 240, 241, 248
22.	Closing of the Proceedings	249
23.	Conservatory and Interim Measures	250
24.	Time Limit for the Award	258
25.	Making of the Award	254, 256
26.	Award by Consent	257
27.	Scrutiny of the Award by the Court	260
28.	Notification, Deposit and Enforceability of the Award	254, 261, 266
29.	Correction and Interpretation of the Award	258
30.	Advance to Cover the Costs of the Arbitration	261
31.	Decision as to the Costs of the Arbitration	221, 263
32.	Modified Time Limts	208
33.	Waiver	267
34.	Exclusion of Liability	267
35.	General Rule	201

ICDR International Arbitration Rules

Article No.		Page
1.	Commencing the Arbitration	200, 202
2.	Notice of Arbitration and Statement of Claim	203
3.	Statement of Defense and Counterclaim	205
4.	Amendments to Claims	235
5.	The Tribunal	213

1. The International Chamber of Commerce (ICC) is the publisher and copyright holder of the ICC Rules. Please see www.iccarbitration.org for further information on ICC arbitration and for the complete text of the Rules. The Rules are also available in full in ICC Publication 838, which can be obtained from ICC, International Court of Arbitration, 38 Cours Albert 1er, 75008 Paris, France.

6.	Number of Arbitrators	213, 213, 217
7.	Appointment of Arbitrators	209
8.	Impartiality and Independence of Arbitrators	225
9.	Challenge of Arbitrators	225
10.	Replacement of an Arbitrator	223
11.	General Conditions	223, 224
12.	Representation	228, 238
13.	Place of Arbitration	237
14.	Language	236
15.	Pleas as to Jurisdiction	253
16.	Conduct of the Arbitration	231
17.	Further Written Statements	208, 232
18.	Notices	206
19.	Evidence	240, 241
20.	Hearings	238, 240, 241
21.	Interim Measures of Protection	250
22.	Experts	244
23.	Default	248
24.	Closure of Hearing	249
25.	Waiver of Rules	267
26.	Awards, Decisions and Rulings	248, 256
27.	Form and Effect of the Award	240, 254, 256, 261
28.	Applicable Laws and Remedies	245, 256, 268
29.	Settlement or Other Reasons for Termination	257
30.	Interpretation or Correction of the Award	258
31.	Costs	263
32.	Compensation of Arbitrators	221
33.	Deposit of Costs	261
34.	Confidentiality	240
35.	Exclusion of Liability	267
36.	Interpretation of Rules	201
37.	Emergency Measures of Protection	218

UNCITRAL Rules[2]

Article No.		*Page*
1.	Scope of Application	202
2.	Notice, Calculation of Periods of Time	206
3.	Notice of Arbitration	203
4.	Representation and Assistance	228, 238
5.	Number of Arbitrators	213
6–8.	Appointment of Arbitrators	210, 212, 213
9–12.	Challenge of Arbitrators	209, 225
13.	Replacement of an Arbitrator	223
14.	Repetition of Hearings in the Event of the Replacement of an Arbitrator	223
15.	General Provisions	231, 238
16.	Place of Arbitration	237

2. The UNCITRAL Rules can be found at www.uncitral.org.

17.	Language	236
18.	Statement of Claim	232
19.	Statement of Defence	232
20.	Amendment to the Claim or Defence	235
21.	Pleas as to the Jurisdiction of the Arbitral Tribunal	253
22.	Further Written Statements	232
23.	Periods of Time	208, 232
24–25.	Evidence and Hearings	238, 240, 241
26.	Interim Measures of Protection	250
27.	Experts	244
28.	Default	248
29.	Closure of Hearings	249
30.	Waiver of Rules	267
31.	Decisions	248, 256
32.	Form and Effect of the Award	240, 254, 256, 261
33.	Applicable Law, *Amiable Compositeur*	245
34.	Settlement or other Grounds for Termination	257
35.	Interpretation of the Award	258
36.	Correction of the Award	258
37.	Additional Award	258
38–40.	Costs	221, 263
41.	Deposit of Costs	261

APPENDIX B.3

COMPARISON OF THE RULES OF THE LCIA, ICC, ICDR AND UNCITRAL

LCIA	ICC	ICDR	UNCITRAL	1996 ACT
THE INSTITUTION AND ITS ROLE				
The LCIA Court and Registrar	**The International Court of Arbitration**	**The ICDR**	**Not applicable**	
3.1 The functions of the LCIA Court under these Rules shall be performed in its name by the President or a Vice President of the LCIA Court or by a division of three or five members of the LCIA Court appointed by the President or a Vice President of the LCIA Court, as determined by the President. 3.2 The functions of the Registrar under these Rules shall be performed by the Registrar or any deputy Registrar of the LCIA Court under the supervision of the LCIA Court. 3.3 All communications from any party or arbitrator to the LCIA Court shall be addressed to the Registrar. 29.1 The decisions of the LCIA Court with respect to all matters relating to the arbitration shall be conclusive and binding upon the parties and the Arbitral Tribunal. Such decisions are to be treated as	1.1 The International Court of Arbitration (the "Court") of the International Chamber of Commerce (the "ICC") is the arbitration body attached to the ICC. The statutes of the Court are set forth in Appendix I. Members of the Court are appointed by the World Council of the ICC. The function of the Court is to provide for the settlement by arbitration of business disputes of an international character in accordance with the Rules of Arbitration of the International Chamber of Commerce (the "Rules"). If so empowered by an arbitration agreement, the Court shall also provide for the settlement by arbitration in accordance with these Rules of business disputes not of an international character. 1.2 The Court does not itself settle disputes. It has the function of ensuring the application of these Rules. It draws up its own Internal Rules (Appendix II).	1.3 These rules specify the duties and responsibilities of the administrator, the International Centre for Dispute Resolution, a division of the American Arbitration Association. The administrator may provide services through its Centre, located in New York, or through the facilities of arbitral institutions with which it has agreements of cooperation.		

administrative in nature and the LCIA Court shall not be required to give any reasons.	1.3 The Chairman of the Court or, in the Chairman's absence or otherwise at his request, one of its Vice-Chairmen shall have the power to take urgent decisions on behalf of the Court, provided that any such decision is reported to the Court at its next session. 1.4 As provided for in its Internal Rules, the Court may delegate to one or more committees composed of its members the power to take certain decisions, provided that any such decision is reported to the Court at its next session. 1.5 The Secretariat of the Court (the "Secretariat") under the direction of its Secretary General (the "Secretary General") shall have its seat at the headquarters of the ICC.			
DEFINITIONS AND INTERPRETATION 5.1 The expression "the Arbitral Tribunal" in these Rules includes a sole arbitrator or all of the arbitrators where more than one. All references to an arbitrator shall include the masculine and feminine. (References to the President, Vice President and members of the LCIA Court, the	In these Rules 2(i) "Arbitral Tribunal" includes one or more arbitrators. 2(ii) "Claimant" includes one or more claimants and "Respondent" includes one or more respondents. 2(iii) "Award" includes, *inter alia*, an interim, partial or final Award	36. The tribunal shall interpret and apply these rules insofar as they relate to its powers and duties. The administrator shall interpret and apply all other rules.		

LCIA	ICC	ICDR	UNCITRAL	1996 ACT
Registrar or deputy Registrar, expert, witness, party and legal representative shall be similarly understood.) 32.2 In all matters not expressly provided for in these Rules, the LCIA Court, the Arbitral Tribunal and the parties shall act in the spirit of these Rules and shall make every reasonable effort to ensure that an award is legally enforceable.	35. In all matters not expressly provided for in these Rules, the Court and the Arbitral Tribunal shall act in the spirit of these Rules and shall make every effort to make sure that the Award is enforceable at law.			
EFFECT OF THE ARBITRATION AGREEMENT				
Recital: Where any agreement, submission or reference provides in writing and in whatsoever manner for arbitration under the rules of the LCIA or by the Court of the LCIA ("the LCIA Court"), the parties shall be taken to have agreed in writing that the arbitration shall be conducted in accordance with the following rules ("the Rules") or such amended rules as the LCIA may have adopted hereafter to take effect before the commencement of the arbitration. The Rules include the Schedule of Costs in effect at the commencement of the arbitration, as separately amended from time to time by the LCIA Court.	6.1. Where the parties have agreed to submit to arbitration under the Rules, they shall be deemed to have submitted *ipso facto* to the Rules in effect on the date of commencement of the arbitration proceedings, unless they have agreed to submit to the Rules in effect on the date of their arbitration agreement.	1.1. Where parties have agreed in writing to arbitrate disputes under these International Arbitration Rules or have provided for arbitration of an international dispute by the International Centre for Dispute Resolution or the American Arbitration Association without designating particular rules, the arbitration shall take place in accordance with these rules, as in effect at the date of commencement of the arbitration, subject to whatever modifications the parties may adopt in writing. 1.2. These rules govern the arbitration, except that, where any such rule is in conflict with any provision of the law applicable to the arbitration from which the parties cannot derogate, that provision shall prevail.	1.1. Where the parties to a contract have agreed in writing that disputes in relation to that contract shall be referred to arbitration under the UNCITRAL Arbitration Rules, then such disputes shall be settled in accordance with these Rules subject to such modification as the parties may agree in writing. 1.2. These Rules shall govern the arbitration except that where any of these Rules is in conflict with a provision of the law applicable to the arbitration from which the parties cannot derogate, that provision shall prevail.	S.5: Arbitration agreements must be in writing. S.6: Definition of arbitration agreements. S.81(1)(b): Saving provision

COMMENCING THE ARBITRATION				
1.1 Any party wishing to commence an arbitration under these Rules ("the Claimant") shall send to the Registrar of the LCIA Court ("the Registrar") a written request for arbitration ("the Request"), containing or accompanied by: (a) the names, addresses, telephone, facsimile, telex and e-mail numbers (if known) of the parties to the arbitration and of their legal representatives; (b) a copy of the written arbitration clause or separate written arbitration agreement invoked by the claimant ("the Arbitration Agreement"), together with a copy of the contractual documentation in which the arbitration clause is contained or in respect of which the arbitration arises; (c) a brief statement describing the nature and circumstances of the dispute, and specifying the claims advanced by the Claimant against another party to the arbitration ("the Respondent"); (d) a statement of any matters (such as the seat or language(s) of the arbitration, or the number of arbitrators, or their qualifications or identities) on which the parties have already agreed in writing for the arbitration or in respect of which the Claimant wishes to make a proposal;	4.1. A party wishing to have recourse to arbitration under these Rules shall submit its Request for Arbitration (the "Request") to the Secretariat, which shall notify the Claimant and Respondent of the receipt of the Request and the date of such receipt. 4.2. The date on which the Request is received by the Secretariat shall, for all purposes, be deemed to be the date of the commencement of the arbitral proceedings. 4.3. The Request shall, *inter alia*, contain the following information: (a) the name in full, description and address of each of the parties; (b) a description of the nature and circumstances of the dispute giving rise to the claim(s) (c) a statement of the relief sought, including, to the extent possible, an indication of any amount(s) claimed; (d) the relevant agreements and, in particular, the arbitration agreement; (e) all relevant particulars concerning the number of arbitrators and their choice in accordance with the provisions of Articles 8, 9 and 10, and any nomination of an arbitrator required thereby; and (f) any comments as to the place of arbitration, the applicable rules of law and the language of the arbitration.	2.1. The party initiating arbitration ("claimant") shall give written notice of arbitration to the administrator and at the same time to the party against whom a claim is being made ("respondent"). 2.2 Arbitral proceedings shall be deemed to commence on the date on which the administrator receives the notice of arbitration. 2.3. The notice of arbitration shall contain a statement of claim including the following: (a) a demand that the dispute be referred to arbitration; (b) the names, addresses and telephone numbers of the parties; (c) a reference to the arbitration clause or agreement that is invoked; (d) a reference to any contract out of or in relation to which the dispute arises; (e) a description of the claim and an indication of the facts supporting it; (f) the relief or remedy sought and the amount claimed; and (g) may include proposals as to the means of designating and the number of arbitrators, the place of arbitration and the language(s) of the arbitration. 2.4. Upon receipt of the notice of arbitration, the administrator shall communicate with all parties with	3.1. The party initiating recourse to arbitration (hereinafter called the "claimant") shall give to the other party (hereinafter called the "respondent") a notice of arbitration. 3.2. Arbitral proceedings shall be deemed to commence on the date on which the notice of arbitration is received by the respondent. 3.3 The notice of arbitration shall include the following: (a) A demand that the dispute be referred to arbitration; (b) The names and addresses of the parties; (c) A reference to the arbitration clause or the separate arbitration agreement that is invoked; (d) A reference to the contract out of or in relation to which the dispute arises; (e) The general nature of the claim and an indication of the amount involved, if any; (f) The relief or remedy sought; (g) A proposal as to the number of arbitrators (i.e. one	S.12: Power of court to extend time for commencing arbitration. S.13: Application of the Limitation Acts. S.14: Commencement of Arbitration proceedings.

LCIA	ICC	ICDR	UNCITRAL	1996 ACT
(e) if the Arbitration Agreement calls for party nomination of arbitrators, the name, address, telephone, facsimile, telex and e-mail numbers (if known) of the Claimant's nominee; (f) the fee prescribed in the Schedule of Costs (without which the Request shall be treated as not having been received by the Registrar and the arbitration as not having been commenced); and (g) confirmation to the Registrar that copies of the Request (including all accompanying documents) have been or are being served simultaneously on all other parties to the arbitration by one or more means of service to be identified in such confirmation. 1.2 The date of receipt by the Registrar of the Request shall be treated as the date on which the arbitration has commenced for all purposes. The Request (including all accompanying documents) should be submitted to the Registrar in two copies where a sole arbitrator should be appointed, or, if the parties have agreed or the Claimant considers that three arbitrators should be appointed, in four copies.	4.4. Together with the Request, the Claimant shall submit the number of copies thereof required by Article 3(1) and shall make the advance payment on administrative expenses required by Appendix III ("Arbitration Costs and Fees") in force on the date the Request is submitted. In the event that the Claimant fails to comply with either of these requirements, the Secretariat may fix a time limit within which the Claimant must comply, failing which the file shall be closed without prejudice to the right of the Claimant to submit the same claims at a later date in another Request. 4.5. The Secretariat shall send a copy of the Request and the documents annexed thereto to the Respondent for its Answer to the Request once the Secretariat has sufficient copies of the Request and the required advance payment.	respect to the arbitration and shall acknowledge the commencement of the arbitration.	or three), if the parties have not previously agreed thereon. 3.4. The notice of arbitration may also include: (a) The proposals for the appointments of a sole arbitrator and an appointing authority referred to in article 6, paragraph 1; (b) The notification of the appointment of an arbitrator referred to in article 7; (c) The statement of claim referred to in article 18.	

THE RESPONSE/ANSWER, COUNTERCLAIM AND REPLY				
2.1 Within 30 days of service of the Request on the Respondent, (or such lesser period fixed by the LCIA Court), the Respondent shall send to the Registrar a written response to the Request ("the Response"), containing or accompanied by: (a) confirmation or denial of all or part of the claims advanced by the Claimant in the Request; (b) a brief statement describing the nature and circumstances of any counterclaims advanced by the Respondent against the Claimant; (c) comment in response to any statements contained in the Request, as called for under Article 1.1(d), on matters relating to the conduct of the arbitration; (d) if the Arbitration Agreement calls for party nomination of arbitrators, the name, address, telephone, facsimile, telex and e-mail numbers (if known) of the Respondent's nominee; and (e) confirmation to the Registrar that copies of the Response (including all accompanying documents) have been or are being served simultaneously on all other parties to the arbitration by one or more means of service to be identified in such confirmation.	5.1. Within 30 days from the receipt of the Request from the Secretariat, the Respondent shall file an Answer (the "Answer") which shall, *inter alia*, contain the following information: (a) its name in full, description and address; (b) its comments as to the nature and circumstances of the dispute giving rise to the claim(s); (c) its response to the relief sought; (d) any comments concerning the number of arbitrators and their choice in light of the Claimant's proposals and in accordance with the provisions of Articles 8, 9 and 10, and any nomination of an arbitrator required thereby; and (e) any comments as to the place of arbitration, the applicable rules of law and the language of the arbitration. 5.2. The Secretariat may grant the Respondent an extension of the time for filing the Answer, provided the application for such an extension contains the Respondent's comments concerning the number of arbitrators and their choice and, where required by Articles 8, 9 and 10, the nomination of an arbitrator. If the Respondent fails to do so, the Court shall proceed in accordance with these Rules.	3.1. Within 30 days after the commencement of the arbitration, a respondent shall submit a written statement of defense, responding to the issues raised in the notice of arbitration, to the claimant and any other parties, and to the administrator. 3.2. At the time a respondent submits its statement of defense, a respondent may make counterclaims or assert setoffs as to any claim covered by the agreement to arbitrate, as to which the claimant shall within 30 days submit a written statement of defense to the respondent and any other parties and to the administrator. 3.3. A respondent shall respond to the administrator, the claimant and other parties within 30 days after the commencement of the arbitration as to any proposals the claimant may have made as to the number of arbitrators, the place of the arbitration or the language(s) of the arbitration, except to the extent that the parties have previously agreed as to these matters. 3.4. The arbitral tribunal, or the administrator if the arbitral tribunal has not yet been formed, may extend any of the time limits established in this article if it considers such an extension justified.	[There is no provision for an early Response in the UNCITRAL Rules but see the section on Further Written Statements below]	S.79: General power to extend time.

LCIA	ICC	ICDR	UNCITRAL	1996 ACT
2.2 The Response (including all accompanying documents) should be submitted to the Registrar in two copies, or if the parties have agreed or the Respondent considers that three arbitrators should be appointed, in four copies. 2.3 Failure to send a Response shall not preclude the Respondent from denying any claim or from advancing a counterclaim in the arbitration. However, if the Arbitration Agreement calls for party nomination of arbitrators, falure to send a Response or to nominate an arbitrator within time or at all shall constitute an irrevocable waiver of that party's opportunity to nominate an arbitrator.	5.3. The Answer shall be supplied to the Secretariat in the number of copies specified by Article 3(1). 5.4. A copy of the Answer and the documents annexed thereto shall be communicated by the Secretariat to the Claimant. 5.5. Any counterclaim(s) made by the Respondent shall be filed with its Answer and shall provide: (a) a description of the nature and circumstances of the dispute giving rise to the counterclaim(s); and (b) a statement of the relief sought, including, to the extent possible, an indication of any amount(s) counterclaimed. 5.6. The Claimant shall file a reply to any counterclaim within 30 days from the date of receipt of the counterclaim(s) communicated by the Secretariat. The Secretariat may grant the Claimant an extension of time for filing the reply.			
CALCULATION OF TIME, NOTICES AND OTHER COMMUNICATIONS				
4.1 Any notice or other communication that may be or is required to be given by a party under these Rules shall be in writing and shall be delivered by registered postal, or courier service or	3.1. All pleadings and other written communications submitted by any party, as well as all documents annexed thereto, shall be supplied in a number of copies sufficient to provide one copy for each party, plus one for	18.1. Unless otherwise agreed by the parties or ordered by the tribunal, all notices, statements and written communications may be served on a party by air mail, air courier, facsimile transmission, telex, telegram or other	2.1. For the purposes of these Rules, any notice, including a notification, communication or proposal, is deemed to have been received if it is physically delivered to the addressee or if	SS.76–78: Service of notices, documents and reckoning periods of time.

transmitted by facsimile, telex, e-mail or any other means of telecommunication that provide a record of its transmission. 4.2 A party's last-known residence or place of business during the arbitration shall be a valid address for the purpose of any notice or other communication in the absence of any notification of a change to such address by that party to the other parties, the Arbitral Tribunal and the Registrar. 4.3 For the purpose of determining the date of commencement of a time limit, a notice or other communication shall be treated as having been received on the day it is delivered or, in the case of telecommunications, transmitted in accordance with Articles 4.1 and 4.2. 4.4 For the purpose of determining compliance with a time limit, a notice or other communication shall be treated as having been sent, made or transmitted if it is dispatched in accordance with Articles 4.1 and 4.2 prior to or on the date of the expiration of the time-limit. 4.5 Notwithstanding the above, any notice or communication by one party may be addressed to another party in the manner agreed in writing between them or, failing such agreement, according to the practice	each arbitrator, and one for the Secretariat. A copy of any communication from the Arbitral Tribunal to the parties shall be sent to the Secretariat. 3.2. All notifications or communications from the Secretariat and the Arbitral Tribunal shall be made to the last address of the party or its representative for whom the same are intended, as notified either by the party in question or by the other party. Such notification or communication may be made by delivery against receipt, registered post, courier, facsimile transmission, telex, telegram or any other means of telecommunication that provides a record of the sending thereof. 3.3. A notification or communication shall be deemed to have been made on the day it was received by the party itself or by its representative, or would have been received if made in accordance with the preceding paragraph. 3.4. Periods of time specified in or fixed under the present Rules shall start to run on the day following the date a notification or communication is deemed to have been made in accordance with the preceding paragraph. When the day next following such date is an official holiday, or a non-business day in the	written forms of electronic communication addressed to the party or its representative at its last known address or by personal service. 18.2. For the purpose of calculating a period of time under these rules, such period shall begin to run on the day following the day when a notice, statement or written communication is received. If the last day of such period is an official holiday at the place received, the period is extended until the first business day which follows. Official holidays occurring during the running of the period of time are included in calculating the period.	it is delivered at his habitual residence, place of business or mailing address, or, if none of these can be found after making reasonable inquiry, then at the addressee's last-known residence or place of business. Notice shall be deemed to have been received on the day it is so delivered. 2.2. For the purposes of calculating a period of time under these Rules, such period shall begin to run on the day following the day when a notice, notification, communication or proposal is received. If the last day of such period is an official holiday or a non-business day at the residence or place of business of the addressee, the period is extended until the first business day which follows. Official holidays or non-business days occurring during the running of the period of time are included in calculating the period.	

LCIA	ICC	ICDR	UNCITRAL	1996 ACT
followed in the course of their previous dealings or in whatever manner ordered by the Arbitral Tribunal. 4.6 For the purpose of calculating a period of time under these Rules, such period shall begin to run on the day following the day when a notice or other communication is received. If the last day of such period is an official holiday or a non-business day at the residence or place of business of the addressee, the period is extended until the first business day which follows. Official holidays or non-business days occurring during the running of the period of time are included in calculating that period.	country where the notification or communication is deemed to have been made, the period of time shall commence on the first following business day. Official holidays and non-business days are included in the calculation of the period of time. If the last day of the relevant period of time granted is an official holiday or a non-business day in the country where the notification or communication is deemed to have been made, the period of time shall expire at the end of the first following business day.			
EXTENSION OF TIME				
4.7 The Arbitral Tribunal may at any time extend (even where the period of time has expired) or abridge any period of time prescribed under these Rules or under the Arbitration Agreement for the conduct of the arbitration, including any notice or communication to be served by one party on any other party. 22.1 Unless the parties at any time agree otherwise in writing, the Arbitral Tribunal shall have the	32.1. The parties may agree to shorten the various time limits set out in these Rules. Any such agreement entered into subsequent to the constitution of an Arbitral Tribunal shall become effective only upon the approval of the Arbitral Tribunal. 32.2. The Court, on its own initiative, may extend any time limit which has been modified pursuant to Article 32(1) if it decides that it is necessary to do so in order that the Arbitral Tribunal or the Court may fulfil their	17.2 . . . However, the tribunal may extend such time limits [relating to written statements] if it considers such an extension is justified.	23. . . . However, the arbitral tribunal may extend the time-limits relating to written statements if it concludes that an extension is justified.	S.12 and s.79: Power of court to extend time

power, on the application of any party or of its own motion, but in either case only after giving the parties a reasonable opportunity to state their views: (b) to extend or abbreviate any time-limit provided by the Arbitration Agreement or these Rules for the conduct of the arbitration or by the Arbitral Tribunal's own orders;	responsibilities in accordance with these Rules.			
VARIOUS PROVISIONS RELATING TO THE FORMATION OF THE ARBITRAL TRIBUNAL **Independence and Impartiality** 5.2 All arbitrators conducting an arbitration under these Rules shall be and remain at all times impartial and independent of the parties; and none shall act in the arbitration as advocates for any party. No arbitrator, whether before or after appointment, shall advise any party on the merits or outcome of the dispute. 5.3 Before appointment by the LCIA Court, each arbitrator shall furnish to the Registrar a written résumé of his past and present professional positions; he shall agree in writing upon fee rates conforming to the Schedule of Costs; and he shall sign a declaration to the effect	7.1. Every arbitrator must be and remain independent of the parties involved in the arbitration. 7.2. Before appointment or confirmation, a prospective arbitrator shall sign a statement of independence and disclose in writing to the Secretariat any facts or circumstances which might be of such a nature as to call into question the arbitrator's independence in the eyes of the parties. The Secretariat shall provide such information to the parties in writing and fix a time limit for any comments from them. 7.3. An arbitrator shall immediately disclose in writing to the Secretariat and to the parties any facts or	7.1. Arbitrators acting under these rules shall be impartial and independent. Prior to accepting appointment, a prospective arbitrator shall disclose to the administrator any circumstance likely to give rise to justifiable doubts as to the arbitrator's impartiality or independence. If, at any stage during the arbitration, new circumstances arise that may give rise to such doubts, an arbitrator shall promptly disclose such circumstances to the parties and to the administrator. Upon receipt of such information from an arbitrator or a party, the administrator shall communicate it to the other parties and to the tribunal.	9. A prospective arbitrator shall disclose to those who approach him in connexion with his possible appointment any circumstances likely to give rise to justifiable doubts as to his impartiality or independence. An arbitrator, once appointed or chosen, shall disclose such circumstances to the parties unless they have already been informed by him of these circumstances.	S.33: General duty of Tribunal.

LCIA	ICC	ICDR	UNCITRAL	1996 ACT
that there are no circumstances known to him likely to give rise to any justified doubts as to his impartiality or independence, other than any circumstances disclosed by him in the declaration. Each arbitrator shall thereby also assume a continuing duty forthwith to disclose any such circumstances to the LCIA Court, to any other members of the Arbitral Tribunal and to all the parties if such circumstances should arise after the date of such delaration and before the arbitration is concluded.	circumstances of a similar nature which may arise during the arbitration. 7.5. By accepting to serve, every arbitrator undertakes to carry out his responsibilities in accordance with these Rules. [The ICC rules only refer to "independence" and not "independence and impartiality", but in practice this makes no difference.]	7.2. No party or anyone acting on its behalf shall have any *ex parte* communication relating to the case with any arbitrator, or with any candidate for appointment as party-appointed arbitrator except to advise the candidate of the general nature of the controversy and of the anticipated proceedings and to discuss the candidate's qualifications, availability or independence in relation to the parties, or to discuss the suitability of candidates for selection as a third arbitrator where the parties or party designated arbitrators are to participate in that selection. No party or anyone acting on its behalf shall have any *ex parte* communication relating to the case with any candidate for presiding arbitrator.		
Institutional appointment of the arbitrators and procedure 5.4 The LCIA Court shall appoint the Arbitral Tribunal as soon as practicable after receipt by the Registrar of the Response or after the expiry of 30 days following service of the Request upon the Respondent if no Response is received by the Registrar (or such lesser period fixed by the LCIA Court). The LCIA Court may proceed with the formation of the Arbitral Tribunal notwithstanding that the Request is	7.4. The decisions of the Court as to the appointment, confirmation, challenge or replacement of an arbitrator shall be final and the reasons for such decisions shall not be communicated. 7.6. Insofar as the parties have not provided otherwise, the Arbitral Tribunal shall be constituted in accordance with the provisions of Articles 8, 9 and 10.		8.1. When an appointing authority is requested to appoint an arbitrator pursuant to article 6 or article 7, the party which makes the request shall send to the appointing authority a copy of the notice of arbitration, a copy of the contract out of or in relation to which the dispute has arisen and a copy of the arbitration agreement if it is not	S.16: Procedure for appointment of arbitrators.

incomplete or the Response is missing, late or incomplete . . . 5.5 The LCIA Court alone is empowered to appoint arbitrators . . . 5.6 In the case of a three-member Arbitral Tribunal, the chairman (who will not be a party-nominated arbitrator) shall be appointed by the LCIA Court. 7.1 . . . The LCIA Court may refuse to appoint any such nominee if it determines that he is not suitable or independent or impartial.	9.2. The Secretary General may confirm as co-arbitrators, sole arbitrators and chairmen of Arbitral Tribunals persons nominated by the parties or pursuant to their particular agreements, provided they have filed a statement of independence without qualification or a qualified statement of independence has not given rise to objections. Such confirmation shall be reported to the Court at its next session. If the Secretary General considers that a co-arbitrator, sole arbitrator or chairman of an Arbitral Tribunal should not be confirmed, the matter shall be submitted to the Court. 9.3. Where the Court is to appoint a sole arbitrator or the chairman of an Arbitral Tribunal, it shall make the appointment upon a proposal of a National Committee of the ICC that it considers to be appropriate. If the Court does not accept the proposal made, or if the National Committee fails to make the proposal requested within the time limit fixed by the Court, the Court may repeat its request or may request a proposal from another National Committee that it considers to be appropriate. 9.4. Where the Court considers that the circumstances so demand, it may choose the sole arbitrator or the chairman of the Arbitral Tribunal from a country where there is no National		contained in the contract. The appointing authority may require from either party such information as it deems necessary to fulfil its function. [See also pages 213–215 below] 8.2. Where the names of one or more persons are proposed for appointment as arbitrators, their full names, addresses and nationalities shall be indicated, together with a description of their qualifications	

LCIA	ICC	ICDR	UNCITRAL	1996 ACT
	Committee, provided that neither of the parties objects within the time limit fixed by the Court.			
Criteria for appointment				
5.5 . . . The LCIA Court will appoint arbitrators with due regard for any particular method or criteria of selection agreed in writing by the parties. In selecting arbitrators consideration will be given to the nature of the transaction, the nature and circumstances of the dispute, the nationality, location and languages of the parties and (if more than two) the number of parties. 6.1 Where the parties are of different nationalities, a sole arbitrator or chairman of the Arbitral Tribunal shall not have the same nationality as any party unless the parties who are not of the same nationality as the proposed appointee all agree in writing otherwise. 6.2 The nationality of parties shall be understood to include that of controlling shareholders or interests. 6.3 For the purpose of this Article, a person who is a citizen of two or more states shall be treated as a national of each state; and citizens of the European Union shall be treated	9.1. In confirming or appointing arbitrators, the Court shall consider the prospective arbitrator's nationality, residence and other relationships with the countries of which the parties or the other arbitrators are nationals and the prospective arbitrator's availability and ability toconduct the arbitration in accordance with these Rules. The same shall apply where the Secretary General confirms arbitrators pursuant to Article 9(2). 9.5. The sole arbitrator or the chairman of the Arbitral Tribunal shall be of a nationality other than those of the parties. However, in suitable circumstances and provided that neither of the parties objects within the time limit fixed by the Court, the sole arbitrator or the chairman of the Arbitral Tribunal may be chosen from a country of which any of the parties is a national.	6.4. In making such appointments, the administrator, after inviting consultation with the parties, shall endeavor to select suitable arbitrators. At the request of any party or on its own initiative, the administrator may appoint nationals of a country other than that of any of the parties.	6.4. In making the appointment, the appointing authority shall have regard to such considerations as are likely to secure the appointment of an independent and impartial arbitrator and shall take into account as well the advisability of appointing an arbitrator of a nationality other than the nationalities of the parties.	S.19: Criteria for appointment of arbitrators.

as nationals of its different Member States and shall not be treated as having the same nationality.				
Number of arbitrators, party appointments and default appointment by the institution 2.3 . . . However, if the Arbitration Agreement calls for party nomination of arbitrators, failure to send a Response or to nominate an arbitrator within time or at all shall constitute an irrevocable waiver of the party's opportunity to nominate an arbitrator. 5.4 . . . A sole arbitrator shall be appointed unless the parties have agreed in writing otherwise, or unless the LCIA Court determines that in view of all the circumstances of the case a three-member tribunal is appropriate. 7.1 If the parties have agreed that any arbitrator is to be appointed by one or more of them or by any third person, that agreement shall be treated as an agreement to nominate an arbitrator for all purposes. Such nominee may only be appointed by the LCIA Court as arbitrator subject to his prior compliance with Article 5.3. The LCIA Court may refuse to appoint any such nominee if it determines that he is not suitable or independent or impartial.	8.1. The disputes shall be decided by a sole arbitrator or by three arbitrators. 8.2. Where the parties have not agreed upon the number of arbitrators, the Court shall appoint a sole arbitrator, save where it appears to the Court that the dispute is such as to warrant the appointment of three arbitrators. In such case, the Claimant shall nominate an arbitrator within a period of 15 days from the receipt of the notification of the decision of the Court, and the Respondent shall nominate an arbitrator within a period of 15 days from the receipt of the notification of the nomination made by the Claimant. 8.3. Where the parties have agreed that the dispute shall be settled by a sole arbitrator, they may, by agreement, nominate the sole arbitrator for confirmation. If the parties fail to nominate a sole arbitrator within 30 days from the date when the Claimant's Request for Arbitration has been received by the other party, or within such additional time as may be allowed by the	5. If the parties have not agreed on the number of arbitrators, one arbitrator shall be appointed unless the administrator determines in its discretion that three arbitrators are appropriate because of the large size, complexity or other circumstances of the case. 6.1. The parties may mutually agree upon any procedure for appointing arbitrators and shall inform the administrator as to such procedure. 6.2. The parties may mutually designate arbitrators, with or without the assistance of the administrator. When such designations are made, the parties shall notify the administrator so that notice of the appointment can be communicated to the arbitrators, together with a copy of these rules. 6.3. If within 45 days after the commencement of the arbitration, all of the parties have not mutually agreed on a procedure for appointing the arbitrator(s) or have not mutually agreed on the designation of the arbitrator(s), the administrator shall, at	5. If the parties have not previously agreed on the number of arbitrators (i.e. one or three), and if within fifteen days after the receipt by the respondent of the notice of arbitration the parties have not agreed that there shall be only one arbitrator, three arbitrators shall be appointed. 6.1. If a sole arbitrator is to be appointed, either party may propose to the other: (a) The names of one or more persons, one of whom would serve as the sole arbitrator; and (b) If no appointing authority has been agreed upon by the parties, the name or names of one or more institutions or persons, one of whom would serve as appointing authority. 6.2. If within thirty days after receipt by a party of a proposal made in accordance with paragraph 1 the parties	S.12: Limited powers to extend powers for beginning arbitration. SS.15–19: Default provisions in the absence of agreement relating to number of arbitrators, procedure for appointment of arbitrators; and provisions for non-compliance.

LCIA	ICC	ICDR	UNCITRAL	1996 ACT
7.2 Where the parties have howsoever agreed that the Respondent or any third person is to nominate an arbitrator and such nomination is not made within time or at all, the LCIA Court may may appoint an arbitrator not-withstanding the absence of the nomination and without regard to any late nomination. Likewise, if the Request for Arbitration does not contain a nomination by the Claimant where the parties have howsoever agreed that the Claimant or a third person is to nominate an arbitrator, the LCIA Court may appoint an arbitrator not-withstanding the absence of the nomination and without regard to any late nomination.	the Secretariat, the sole arbitrator shall be appointed by the Court. 8.4. Where the dispute is to be referred to three arbitrators, each party shall nominate in the Request and the Answer, respectively, one arbitrator for confirmation. If a party fails to nominate an arbitrator, the appointment shall be made by the Court. The third arbitrator, who will act as chairman of the Arbitral Tribunal, shall be appointed by the Court, unless the parties have agreed upon another procedure for such appointment, in which case the nomination will be subject to confirmation pursuant to Article 9. Should such procedure not result in a nomination within the time limit fixed by the parties or the Court, the third arbitrator shall be appointed by the Court. 9.6. Where the Court is to appoint an arbitrator on behalf of a party which has failed to nominate one, it shall make the appointment upon a proposal of the National Committee of the country of which that party is a national. If the Court does not accept the proposal made, or if the National Committee fails to make the proposal requested within the time limit fixed by the Court, or if the country of which the said party is a national has	the written request of any party, appoint the arbitrator(s) and designate the presiding arbitrator. If all of the parties have mutually agreed upon a procedure for appointing the arbitrator(s), but all appointments have not been made within the time limits provided in that procedure, the administrator shall, at the written request of any party, perform all functions provided for in that procedure that remain to be performed.	have not reached agreement on the choice of a sole arbitrator, the sole arbitrator shall be appointed by the appointing authority agreed upon by the parties. If no appointing authority has been agreed upon by the parties, or if the appointing authority agreed upon refuses to act or fails to appoint the arbitrator within sixty days of the receipt of a party's request therefor, either party may request the Secretary-General of the Permanent Court of Arbitration at The Hague to designate an appointing authority. 6.3. The appointing authority shall, at the request of one of the parties, appoint the sole arbitrator as promptly as possible. In making the appointment the appointing authority shall use the following list-procedure, unless both parties agree that the list-procedure should not be used or unless the appointing authority determines in its discretion that the use of the list-procedure is not appropriate for the case:	

	no National Committee, the Court shall be at liberty to choose any person whom it regards as suitable. The Secretariat shall inform the National Committee, if one exists, of the country of which such person is a national.		(a) At the request of one of the parties the appointing authority shall communicate to both parties an identical list containing at least three names; (b) Within fifteen days after the receipt of this list, each party may return the list to the appointing authority after having deleted the name or names to which he objects and numbered the remaining names on the list in the order of his preference; (c) After the expiration of the above period of time the appointing authority shall appoint the sole arbitrator from among the names approved on the lists returned to it and in accordance with the order of preference indicated by the parties; (d) If for any reason the appointment cannot be made according to this procedure, the appointing authority may exercise its discretion in appointing the sole arbitrator. 7.1. If three arbitrators are to be appointed, each party shall appoint one arbitrator. The two arbitrators thus appointed shall choose the third	

LCIA	ICC	ICDR	UNCITRAL	1996 ACT
			arbitrator who will act as the presiding arbitrator of the tribunal. 7.2. If within thirty days after the receipt of a party's notification of the appointment of an arbitrator the other party has not notified the first party of the arbitrator he has appointed: (a) The first party may request the appointing authority previously designated by the parties to appoint the second arbitrator; or (b) If no such authority has been previously designated by the parties, or if the appointing authority previously designated refuses to act or fails to appoint the arbitrator within thirty days after receipt of a party's request therefor, the first party may request the Secretary-General of the Permanent Court of Arbitration at The Hague to designate the appointing authority. The first party may then request the appointing authority so designated to appoint the second arbitrator. In either case, the appointing authority may exercise its discretion in appointing the arbitrator.	

			7.3. If within thirty days after the appointment of the second arbitrator the two arbitrators have not agreed on the choice of the presiding arbitrator, the presiding arbitrator shall be appointed by an appointing authority in the same way as a sole arbitrator would be appointed under article 6.	
Multiple Parties 8.1 Where the Arbitration Agreement entitles each party howsoever to nominate an arbitrator, the parties to the dispute number more than two and such parties have not all agreed in writing that the disputant parties represent two separate sides for the formation of the Arbitral Tribunal as Claimant and Respondent respectively, the LCIA Court shall appoint the Arbitral Tribunal without regard to any party's nomination. 8.2 In such circumstances, the Arbitration Agreement shall be treated for all purposes as a written agreement by the parties for the appointment of the Arbitral Tribunal by the LCIA Court.	10.1. Where there are multiple parties, whether as Claimant or as Respondent, and where the dispute is to be referred to three arbitrators, the multiple Claimants, jointly, and the multiple Respondents, jointly, shall nominate an arbitrator for confirmation pursuant to Article 9. 10.2. In the absence of such a joint nomination and where all parties are unable to agree to a method for the constitution of the Arbitral Tribunal, the Court may appoint each member of the Arbitral Tribunal and shall designate one of them to act as chairman. In such case, the Court shall be at liberty to choose any person it regards as suitable to act as arbitrator, applying Article 9 when it considers this appropriate.	6.5. Unless the parties have agreed otherwise no later than 45 days after the commencement of the arbitration, if the notice of arbitration names two or more claimants or two or more respondents, the administrator shall appoint all the arbitrators.		SS.16(7) and 18.

LCIA	ICC	ICDR	UNCITRAL	1996 ACT
Expedited formation				
9.1 In exceptional urgency, on or after the commencement of the arbitration, any party may apply to the LCIA Court for the expedited formation of the Arbitral Tribunal, including the appointment of any replacement arbitrator under Articles 10 and 11 of these Rules. 9.2 Such an application shall be made in writing to the LCIA Court, copied to all other parties to the arbitration; and it shall set out the specific grounds for exceptional urgency in the formation of the Arbitral Tribunal. 9.3 The LCIA Court may, in its complete discretion, abridge or curtail any time-limit under these Rules for the formation of the Arbitral Tribunal, including service of the Response and of any matters or documents adjudged to be missing from the Request. The LCIA Court shall not be entitled to abridge or curtail any other time-limit.	[The ICC provides a separate pre-arbitral referee procedure to deal with urgent matters, but the parties have to have made a prior written agreement to use the procedures]	37.1. Unless the parties agree otherwise, the provisions of this Article 37 shall apply to arbitrations conducted under arbitration clauses or agreements entered on or after 1 May 2006. 37.2. A party in need of emergency relief prior to the constitution of the tribunal shall notify the administrator and all other parties in writing of the nature of the relief sought and the reasons why such relief is required on an emergency basis. The application shall also set forth the reasons why the party is entitled to such relief. Such notice may be given by e-mail, facsimile transmission, or other reliable means, but must include a statement certifying that all other parties have been notified or an explanation of the steps taken in good faith to notify other parties. 37.3. Within one business day of receipt of notice as provided in paragraph 2, the administrator shall appoint a single emergency arbitrator from a special panel of emergency arbitrators designated to rule on emergency applications. Prior to accepting appointment, a prospective emergency arbitrator shall disclose to the administrator any circumstance likely to give rise to justifiable doubts		S.44: court's powers prior to formation of tribunal.

		to the arbitrator's impartiality or independence. Any challenge to the appointment of the emergency arbitrator must be made within one business day of the communication by the administrator to the parties of the appointment of the emergency arbitrator and the circumstances disclosed. 37.4. The emergency arbitrator shall as soon as possible, but in any event within two business days of appointment, establish a schedule for consideration of the application for emergency relief. Such schedule shall provide a reasonable opportunity to all parties to be heard, but may provide for proceedings by telephone conference or on written submissions as alternatives to a formal hearing. The emergency arbitrator shall have the authority vested in the tribunal under Article 15, including the authority to rule on her/his own jurisdiction, and shall resolve any disputes over the applicability of this Article 37. 37.5. The emergency arbitrator shall have the power to order or award any interim or conservancy measure the emergency arbitrator deems necessary, including injunctive relief and measures for the protection or conservation of property. Any such measure may take the form of an interim award or of an order. The		

LCIA	ICC	ICDR	UNCITRAL	1996 ACT
		emergency arbitrator shall give reasons in either case. The emergency arbitrator may modify or vacate the interim award or order for good cause shown. 37.6. The emergency arbitrator shall have no further power to act after the tribunal is constituted. Once the tribunal has been constituted, the tribunal may reconsider, modify or vacate the interim award or order of emergency relief issued by the emergency arbitrator. The emergency arbitrator may not serve as a member of the tribunal unless the parties agree otherwise. 37.7. Any interim award or order of emergency relief may be conditioned on provision by the party seeking such relief of appropriate security. 37.8. A request for interim measures addressed by a party to a judicial authority shall not be deemed incompatible with this Article 37 or with the agreement to arbitrate or a waiver of the right to arbitrate. If the administrator is directed by a judicial authority to nominate a special master to consider and report on an application for emergency relief, the administrator shall proceed as in Paragraph 2 of this article and the references to the emergency arbitrator shall be read to mean the special		

		master, except that the special master shall issue a report rather than an interim award. 37.9. The costs associated with applications for emergency relief shall initially be apportioned by the emergency arbitrator or special master, subject to the power of the tribunal to determine finally the apportionment of such costs.		
Fees for arbitrators 5.3 Before appointment by the LCIA Court, each arbitrator . . . shall agree in writing upon fee rates conforming to the Schedule of Costs . . .	Appendix III Article 2(1): Subject to Article 31(2) of the Rules, the Court shall fix the fees of the arbitrator in accordance with the scale set out or, where the sum in dispute is not stated, at its discretion. [Appendix III, Article 2 contains further provisions relating to the fees of arbitrators in different circumstances] 31.2. The Court may fix the fees of the arbitrators at a figure higher or lower than that which would result from the application of the relevant scale should this be deemed necessary due to the exceptional circumstances of the case. . . . [Under the ICC Rules an arbitrator's fees are calculated on a sliding scale according to the amount at stake. Under the LCIA and ICDR rules the fees are calculated on an hourly and/or daily rate.]	32. Arbitrators shall be compensated based upon their amount of service, taking into account their stated rate of compensation and the size and complexity of the case. The administrator shall arrange an appropriate daily or hourly rate, based on such considerations, with the parties and with each of the arbitrators as soon as practicable after the commencement of the arbitration. If the parties fail to agree on the terms of compensation, the administrator shall establish an appropriate rate and communicate it in writing to the parties.	39.1. The fees of the arbitral tribunal shall be reasonable in amount, taking into account the amount in dispute, the complexity of the subject-matter, the time spent by the arbitrators and any other relevant circumstances of the case. 39.2. If an appointing authority has been agreed upon by the parties or designated by the Secretary-General of the Permanent Court of Arbitration at The Hague, and if that authority has issued a schedule of fees for arbitrators in international cases which it administers, the arbitral tribunal in fixing its fees shall take that schedule of fees into account to the extent that it considers appropriate in the circumstances of the case.	S.28: Joint and several liability for fees.

REPLACEMENT OF ARBITRATORS				
10.1 If either (a) any arbitrator gives written notice of his desire to resign as arbitrator to the LCIA Court, to be copied to the parties and the other arbitrators (if any) or (b) any arbitrator dies, falls seriously ill, refuses, or becomes unable or unfit to act, either upon challenge by a party or at the request of the remaining arbitrators, the LCIA Court may revoke that arbitrator's appointment and appoint another arbitrator. The LCIA Court shall decide upon the amount of fees and expenses to be paid for the former arbitrator's services (if any) as it may consider appropriate in all the circumstances. 10.2 If any arbitrator acts in deliberate violation of the Arbitration Agreement (including these Rules) or does not act fairly and impartially as between the parties or does not conduct or participate in the arbitration proceedings with reasonable diligence, avoiding unnecessary delay or expense, that arbitrator may be considered unfit in the opinion of the LCIA Court. 11.1 In the event that the LCIA Court determines that any nominee is not suitable or independent or impartial or if an appointed	12.1. An arbitrator shall be replaced upon his death, upon the acceptance by the Court of the arbitrator's resignation, upon acceptance by the Court of a challenge, or upon the request of all the parties. 12.2. An arbitrator shall also be replaced on the Court's own initiative when it decides that he is prevented *de jure* or *de facto* from fulfilling his functions, or that he is not fulfilling his functions in accordance with the Rules or within the prescribed time limits. 12.3. When, on the basis of information that has come to its attention, the Court considers applying Article 12(2), it shall decide on the matter after the arbitrator concerned, the parties and any other members of the Arbitral Tribunal have had an opportunity to comment in writing within a suitable period of time. Such comments shall be communicated to the parties and to the arbitrators. 12.4. When an arbitrator is to be replaced, the Court has discretion to decide whether or not to follow the original nominating process. Once reconstituted, and after having invited the parties to comment, the Arbitral Tribunal shall determine if and to	10. If an arbitrator withdraws after a challenge, or the administrator sustains the challenge, or the administrator determines that there are sufficient reasons to accept the resignation of an arbitrator, or an arbitrator dies, a substitute arbitrator shall be appointed pursuant to the provisions of Article 6, unless the parties otherwise agree. 11.1 If an arbitrator on a three-person tribunal fails to participate in the arbitration for reasons other than those identified in Article 10 . . . In the event that the two other arbitrators determine not to continue the arbitration without the participation of the third arbitrator, the administrator on proof satisfactory to it shall declare the office vacant, and a substitute arbitrator shall be appointed pursuant to the provisions of Article 6, unless the parties otherwise agree. 11.2. If a substitute arbitrator is appointed under either Article 10 or Article 11, the tribunal shall determine at its sole discretion whether all or part of any prior hearings shall be repeated.	13.1. In the event of the death or resignation of an arbitrator during the course of the arbitral proceedings, a substitute arbitrator shall be appointed or chosen pursuant to the procedure provided for in articles 6 to 9 that was applicable to the appointment or choice of the arbitrator being replaced. 13.2. In the event that an arbitrator fails to act or in the event of the *de jure* or *de facto* impossibility of his performing his functions, the procedure in respect of the challenge and replacement of an arbitrator as provided in the preceding articles shall apply. 14. If under articles 11 to 13 [Party Challenges, see below] the sole or presiding arbitrator is replaced, any hearings held previously shall be repeated; if any other arbitrator is replaced, such prior hearings may be repeated at the discretion of the arbitral tribunal.	SS.23–27: Removal and replacement of arbitrators by the court.

LCIA	ICC	ICDR	UNCITRAL	1996 ACT
arbitrator is to be replaced for any reason, the LCIA Court shall have a complete discretion to decide whether or not to follow the original nominating process. 11.2 If the LCIA Court should so decide, any opportunity given to a party to make a re-nomination shall be waived if not exercised within 15 days (or such lesser time as the LCIA Court may fix), after which the LCIA Court shall appoint the replacement arbitrator.	what extent prior proceedings shall be repeated before the reconstituted Arbitral Tribunal.			
TRUNCATED TRIBUNALS 12.1 If any arbitrator on a three-member Arbitral Tribunal refuses or persistently fails to participate in its deliberations, the two other arbitrators shall have the power, upon their written notice of such refusal or failure to the LCIA Court, the parties and the third arbitrator, to continue the arbitration (including the making of any decision, ruling or award), notwithstanding the absence of the third arbitrator. 12.2 In determining whether to continue the arbitration, the two other arbitrators shall take into account the stage of the arbitration, any explanation made by the third	12.5. Subsequent to the closing of the proceedings, instead of replacing an arbitrator who has died or been removed by the Court pursuant to Articles 12(1) and 12(2), the Court may decide, when it considers it appropriate, that the remaining arbitrators shall continue the arbitration. In making such determination, the Court shall take into account the views of the remaining arbitrators and of the parties and such other matters that it considers appropriate in the circumstances.	11.1. If an arbitrator on a three-person tribunal fails to participate in the arbitration for reasons other than those identified in Article 10, the two other arbitrators shall have the power in their sole discretion to continue the arbitration and to make any decision, ruling or award, notwithstanding the failure of the third arbitrator to participate. In determining whether to continue the arbitration or to render any decision, ruling or award without the participation of an arbitrator, the two other arbitrators shall take into account the stage of the arbitration, the reason, if any, expressed by the third arbitrator for such non-participation, and such other		

arbitrator for his non-participation and such other matters as they consider appropriate in the circumstances of the case. The reasons for such determination shall be stated in any award, order or other decision made by the two arbitrators without the participation of the third arbitrator. 12.3 In the event that the two other arbitrators determine at any time not to continue the arbitration without the participation of the third arbitrator missing from their deliberations, the two arbitrators shall notify in writing the parties and the LCIA Court of such determination; and in that event, the two arbitrators or any party may refer the matter to the LCIA Court for the revocation of that third arbitrator's appointment and his replacement under Article 10.		matters as they consider appropriate in the circumstances of the case. . . .		
PARTY CHALLENGES AND PROCEDURE 10.3 An arbitrator may also be challenged by any party if circumstances exist that give rise to justifiable doubts as to his impartiality or independence. A party may challenge an arbitrator it has nominated, or in whose appointment it has participated, only for reasons of which it becomes aware after the appointment has been made.	11.1. A challenge of an arbitrator, whether for an alleged lack of independence or otherwise, shall be made by the submission to the Secretariat of a written statement specifying the facts and circumstances on which the challenge is based. 11.2. For a challenge to be admissible, it must be sent by a party	8.1. A party may challenge any arbitrator whenever circumstances exist that give rise to justifiable doubts as to the arbitrator's impartiality or independence. A party wishing to challenge an arbitrator shall send notice of the challenge to the administrator within 15 days after being notified of the appointment of the arbitrator or within 15 days after	10.1. Any arbitrator may be challenged if circumstances exist that give rise to justifiable doubts as to the arbitrator's impartiality or independence. 10.2. A party may challenge the arbitrator appointed by him only for reasons of which	S.33: General duty of the tribunal.

LCIA	ICC	ICDR	UNCITRAL	1996 ACT
10.4 A party who intends to challenge an arbitrator shall, within 15 days of the formation of the Arbitral Tribunal or (if later) after becoming aware of any circumstances referred to in Article 10.1, 10.2 or 10.3, send a written statement of the reasons for its challenge to the LCIA Court, the Arbitral Tribunal and all other parties. Unless the challenged arbitrator withdraws or all other parties agree to the challenge within 15 days of receipt of the written statement, the LCIA Court shall decide on the challenge. [See also Article 11.1–2 above under Replacement of Arbitrators]	either within 30 days from receipt by that party of the notification of the appointment or confirmation of the arbitrator, or within 30 days from the date when the party making the challenge was informed of the facts and circumstances on which the challenge is based if such date is subsequent to the receipt of such notification. 11.3. The Court shall decide on the admissibility and, at the same time, if necessary, on the merits of a challenge after the Secretariat has afforded an opportunity for the arbitrator concerned, the other party or parties and any other members of the Arbitral Tribunal to comment in writing within a suitable period of time. Such comments shall be communicated to the parties and to the arbitrators. [See also Article 12 above under Replacement of Arbitrators]	the circumstances giving rise to the challenge become known to that party. 8.2. The challenge shall state in writing the reasons for the challenge. 8.3. Upon receipt of such a challenge, the administrator shall notify the other parties of the challenge. When an arbitrator has been challenged by one party, the other party or parties may agree to the acceptance of the challenge and, if there is agreement, the arbitrator shall withdraw. The challenged arbitrator may also withdraw from office in the absence of such agreement. In neither case does withdrawal imply acceptance of the validity of the grounds for the challenge. 9. If the other party or parties do not agree to the challenge or the challenged arbitrator does not withdraw, the administrator in its sole discretion shall make the decision on the challenge. [See also Article 10 above under Replacement of Arbitrators]	he becomes aware after the appointment has been made. 11.1. A party who intends to challenge an arbitrator shall send notice of his challenge within fifteen days after the appointment of the challenged arbitrator has been notified to the challenging party or within fifteen days after the circumstances mentioned in articles 9 and 10 became known to that party. 11.2. The challenge shall be notified to the other party, to the arbitrator who is challenged and to the other members of the arbitral tribunal. The notification shall be in writing and shall state the reasons for the challenge. 11.3. When an arbitrator has been challenged by one party, the other party may agree to the challenge. The arbitrator may also, after the challenge, withdraw from his office. In neither case does this imply acceptance of the validity of the grounds for the challenge. In both cases the procedure provided in article 6 or 7 shall be used in full for the	

			appointment of the substitute arbitrator, even if during the process of appointing the challenged arbitrator a party had failed to exercise his right to appoint or to participate in the appointment. 12.1. If the other party does not agree to the challenge and the challenged arbitrator does not withdraw, the decision on the challenge will be made: (a) When the initial appointment was made by an appointing authority, by that authority; (b) When the initial appointment was not made by an appointing authority, but an appointing authority has been previously designated, by that authority; (c) In all other cases, by the appointing authority to be designated in accordance with the procedure for designating an appointing authority as provided for in article 6. 12.2. If the appointing authority sustains the challenge, a substitute arbitrator shall be appointed or chosen pursuant to the procedure applicable to the appointment or choice of an	

LCIA	ICC	ICDR	UNCITRAL	1996 ACT
			arbitrator as provided in articles 6 to 9 except that, when this procedure would call for the designation of an appointing authority, the appointment of the arbitrator shall be made by the appointing authority which decided on the challenge. [See also Article 14 above under Replacement of Arbitrators]	
COMMUNICATIONS BETWEEN PARTIES AND THE ARBITRAL TRIBUNAL 13.1 Until the Arbitral Tribunal is formed, all communications between parties and arbitrators shall be made through the Registrar. 13.2 Thereafter, unless and until the Arbitral Tribunal directs that communications shall take place directly between the Arbitral Tribunal and the parties (with simultaneous copies to the Registrar), all written communications between the parties and the Arbitral Tribunal shall continue to be made through the Registrar. 13.3 Where the Registrar sends any written communication to one party	13. The Secretariat shall transmit the file to the Arbitral Tribunal as soon as it has been constituted, provided the advance on costs requested by the Secretariat at this stage has been paid.	12 . . . The names, addresses and telephone numbers of representatives shall be communicated in writing to the other parties and to the administrator. Once the tribunal has been established, the parties or their representatives may communicate in writing directly with the tribunal.	4 . . . The names and addresses of such persons must be communicated in writing to the other party; such communication must specify whether the appointment is being made for purposes of representation or assistance.	

on behalf of the Arbitral Tribunal, he shall send a copy to each of the other parties. Where any party sends to the Registrar any communication (including Written Statements and Documents under Article 15), it shall include a copy for each arbitrator; and it shall also send copies direct to all other parties and confirm to the Registrar in writing that it has done or is doing so.	**TERMS OF REFERENCE AND PROVISIONAL TIMETABLE** 18.1. As soon as it has received the file from the Secretariat, the Arbitral Tribunal shall draw up, on the basis of documents or in the presence of the parties and in the light of their most recent submissions, a document defining its Terms of Reference. This document shall include the following particulars: (a) the full names and descriptions of the parties; (b) the addresses of the parties to which notifications and communications arising in the course of the arbitration may be made; (c) a summary of the parties' respective claims and of the relief sought by each party, with an indication to the extent possible of the amounts claimed or counterclaimed;			

LCIA	ICC	ICDR	UNCITRAL	1996 ACT
	(d) unless the Arbitral Tribunal considers it inappropriate, a list of issues to be determined; (e) the full names, descriptions and addresses of the arbitrators; (f) the place of the arbitration; and (g) particulars of the applicable procedural rules and, if such is the case, reference to the power conferred upon the Arbitral Tribunal to act as *amiable compositeur* or to decide *ex aequo et bono*. 18.2. The Terms of Reference shall be signed by the parties and the Arbitral Tribunal. Within two months of the date on which the file has been transmitted to it, the Arbitral Tribunal shall transmit to the Court the Terms of Reference signed by it and by the parties. The Court may extend this time limit pursuant to a reasoned request from the Arbitral Tribunal or on its own initiative if it decides it is necessary to do so. 18.3. If any of the parties refuses to take part in the drawing up of the Terms of Reference or to sign the same, they shall be submitted to the Court for approval. When the Terms of Reference have been signed in accordance with Article 18(2) or approved by the Court, the arbitration shall proceed.			

	18.4. When drawing up the Terms of Reference, or as soon as possible thereafter, the Arbitral Tribunal, after having consulted the parties, shall establish in a separate document a provisional timetable that it intends to follow for the conduct of the arbitration and shall communicate it to the Court and the parties. Any subsequent modifications of the provisional timetable shall be communicated to the Court and the parties.			
CONDUCT OF THE ARBITRATION				
14.1 The parties may agree on the conduct of their arbitral proceedings and they are encouraged to do so, consistent with the Arbitral Tribunal's general duties at all times: (i) to act fairly and impartially as between all parties, giving each a reasonable opportunity of putting its case and dealing with that of its opponent; and (ii) to adopt procedures suitable to the circumstances of the arbitration, avoiding unnecessary delay or expense, so as to provide a fair and efficient means for the final resolution of the parties' dispute. Such agreements shall be made by the parties in writing or recorded in writing by the Arbitral Tribunal at	15.1. The proceedings before the Arbitral Tribunal shall be governed by these Rules and, where these Rules are silent, by any rules which the parties or, failing them, the Arbitral Tribunal may settle on, whether or not reference is thereby made to the rules of procedure of a national law to be applied to the arbitration. 15.2. In all cases, the Arbitral Tribunal shall act fairly and impartially and ensure that each party has a reasonable opportunity to present its case. 20.1. The Arbitral Tribunal shall proceed within as short a time as possible to establish the facts of the case by all appropriate means.	16.1. Subject to these rules, the tribunal may conduct the arbitration in whatever manner it considers appropriate, provided that the parties are treated with equality and that each party has the right to be heard and is given a fair opportunity to present its case. 16.2. The tribunal, exercising its discretion, shall conduct the proceedings with a view to expediting the resolution of the dispute. It may conduct a preparatory conference with the parties for the purpose of organizing, scheduling and agreeing to procedures to expedite the subsequent proceedings.	15.1. Subject to these Rules, the arbitral tribunal may conduct the arbitration in such manner as it considers appropriate, provided that the parties are treated with equality and that at any stage of the proceedings each party is given a full opportunity of presenting his case. 15.3. All documents or information supplied to the arbitral tribunal by one party shall at the same time be communicated by that party to the other party.	S.33: General Duty of Tribunal. S.34: Procedural and evidential matters.

LCIA	ICC	ICDR	UNCITRAL	1996 ACT
the request of and with the authority of the parties. 14.2 Unless otherwise agreed by the parties under Article 14.1, the Arbitral Tribunal shall have the widest discretion to discharge its duties allowed under such law(s) or rules of law as the Arbitral Tribunal may determine to be applicable; and at all times the parties shall do everything necessary for the fair, efficient and expeditious conduct of the arbitration.		16.3. The tribunal may in its discretion direct the order of proof,bifurcate proceedings, exclude cumulative or irrelevant testimony or other evidence, and direct the parties to focus their presentations on issues the decision of which could dispose of all or part of the case. 16.4. Documents or information supplied to the tribunal by one party shall at the same time be communicated by that party to the other party or parties.		
FURTHER WRITTEN STATEMENTS OR PLEADINGS INCLUDING COUNTERCLAIMS AND SET-OFFS				
15.1 Unless the parties have agreed otherwise under Article 14.1 [parties' entitlement to agree on the conduct of the proceedings] or the Arbitral Tribunal should determine differently, the written stage of the proceedings shall be as set out below. 15.2 Within 30 days of receipt of written notification from the Registrar of the formation of the Arbitral Tribunal, the Claimant shall send to the Registrar a Statement of Case setting out in sufficient detail the facts and any contentions of law on which it relies, together with the	[Directions for these are usually provided for in the Provisional Timetable]	17.1. The tribunal may decide whether the parties shall present any written statements in addition to statements of claims and counterclaims and statements of defense, and it shall fix the periods of time for submitting any such statements. 17.2. The periods of time fixed by the tribunal for the communication of such written statements should not exceed 45 days. However, the tribunal may extend such time limits if it considers such an extension justified.	18.1. Unless the statement of claim was contained in the notice of arbitration, within a period of time to be determined by the arbitral tribunal, the claimant shall communicate his statement of claim in writing to the respondent and to each of the arbitrators. A copy of the contract, and of the arbitration agreement if not contained in the contract, shall be annexed thereto.	

relief claimed against all other parties, save and insofar as such matters have not been set out in its Request. 15.3 Within 30 days of receipt of the Statement of Case or written notice from the Claimant that it elects to treat the Request as its Statement of Case, the Respondent shall send to the Registrar a Statement of Defence setting out in sufficient detail which of the facts and contentions of law in the Statement of Case or Request (as the case may be) it admits or denies, on what grounds and on what other facts and contentions of law it relies. Any counterclaims shall be submitted with the Statement of Defence in the same manner as claims are to be set out in the Statement of Case. 15.4 Within 30 days of receipt of the Statement of Defence, the Claimant shall send to the Registrar a Statement of Reply which, where there are any counterclaims, shall include a Defence to Counterclaim in the same manner as a defence is to be set out in the Statement of Defence. 15.5 If the Statement of Reply contains a Defence to Counterclaim, within 30 days of its receipt the Respondent shall send to the Registrar a Statement of Reply to Counterclaim.			18.2. The statement of claim shall include the following particulars: (a) The names and addresses of the parties; (b) A statement of the facts supporting the claim; (c) The points at issue; (d) The relief or remedy sought. The claimant may annex to his statement of claim all documents he deems relevant or may add a reference to the documents or other evidence he will submit. 19.1. Within a period of time to be determined by the arbitral tribunal, the respondent shall communicate his statement of defence in writing to the claimant and to each of the arbitrators. 19.2. The statement of defence shall reply to the particulars (b), (c) and (d) of the statement of claim (article 18, para. 2). The respondent may annex to his statement the documents on which he relies for his defence or may add a reference to the documents or other evidence he will submit. 19.3. In his statement of defence, or at a later stage in	

LCIA	ICC	ICDR	UNCITRAL	1996 ACT
15.6 All Statements referred to in this Article shall be accompanied by copies (or, if they are especially voluminous, lists) of all essential documents on which the party concerned relies and which have not previously been submitted by any party, and (where appropriate) by any relevant samples and exhibits. 15.7 As soon as practicable following receipt of the Statements specified in this Article, the Arbitral Tribunal shall proceed in such manner as has been agreed in writing by the parties or pursuant to its authority under these Rules.			the arbitral proceedings if the arbitral tribunal decides that the delay was justified under the circumstances, the respondent may make a counter-claim arising out of the same contract or rely on a claim arising out of the same contract for the purpose of a set-off. 19.4. The provisions of article 18, paragraph 2, shall apply to a counter-claim and a claim relied on for the purpose of a set-off. 22. The arbitral tribunal shall decide which further written statements, in addition to the statement of claim and the statement of defence, shall be required from the parties or may be presented by them and shall fix the periods of time for communicating such statements. 23. The periods of time fixed by the arbitral tribunal for the communication of written statements (including the statement of claim and statement of defence) should not exceed forty-five days. However, the arbitral tribunal may extend the time-limits if it concludes that an extension is justified.	

AMENDMENTS AND NEW CLAIMS INCLUDING COUNTERCLAIMS AND SET-OFFS				
22.1 Unless the parties at any time agree otherwise in writing, the Arbitral Tribunal shall have the power, on the application of any party or of its own motion, but in either case only after giving the parties a reasonable opportunity to state their views: (a) to allow any party, upon such terms (as to costs and otherwise) as it shall determine, to amend any claim, counterclaim, defence and reply;	4.6. When a party submits a Request in connection with a legal relationship in respect of which arbitration proceedings between the same parties are already pending under these Rules, the Court may, at the request of a party, decide to include the claims contained in the Request in the pending proceedings provided that the Terms of Reference have not been signed or approved by the Court. Once the Terms of Reference have been signed or approved by the Court, claims may only be included in the pending proceedings subject to the provisions of Article 19. 19. After the Terms of Reference have been signed or approved by the Court, no party shall make new claims or counterclaims which fall outside the limits of the Terms of Reference unless it has been authorized to do so by the Arbitral Tribunal, which shall consider the nature of such new claims or counterclaims, the stage of the arbitration and other relevant circumstances.	4. During the arbitral proceedings, any party may amend or supplement its claim, counterclaim or defense, unless the tribunal considers it inappropriate to allow such amendment or supplement because of the party's delay in making it, prejudice to the other parties or any other circumstances. A party may not amend or supplement a claim or counterclaim if the amendment or supplement would fall outside the scope of the agreement to arbitrate.	20. During the course of the arbitral proceedings either party may amend or supplement his claim or defence unless the arbitral tribunal considers it inappropriate to allow such amendment having regard to the delay in making it or prejudice to the other party or any other circumstances. However, a claim may not be amended in such a manner that the amended claim falls outside the scope of the arbitration clause or separate arbitration agreement.	

LCIA	ICC	ICDR	UNCITRAL	1996 ACT
LANGUAGE OF THE ARBITRATION				
17.1 The initial language of the arbitration shall be the language of the Arbitration Agreement, unless the parties have agreed in writing otherwise and providing always that a non-participating or defaulting party shall have no cause for complaint if communications to and from the Registrar and the arbitration proceedings are conducted in English.	16. In the absence of an agreement by the parties, the Arbitral Tribunal shall determine the language or languages of the arbitration, due regard being given to all relevant circumstances, including the language of the contract.	14. If the parties have not agreed otherwise, the language(s) of the arbitration shall be that of the documents containing the arbitration agreement, subject to the power of the tribunal to determine otherwise based upon the contentions of the parties and the circumstances of the arbitration. The tribunal may order that any documents delivered in another language shall be accompanied by a translation into the language(s) of the arbitration.	17.1. Subject to an agreement by the parties, the arbitral tribunal shall, promptly after its appointment, determine the language or languages to be used in the proceedings. This determination shall apply to the statement of claim, the statement of defence, and any further written statements and, if oral hearings take place, to the language or languages to be used in such hearings.	
17.2 In the event that the Arbitration Agreement is written in more than one language, the LCIA Court may, unless the Arbitration Agreement provides that the arbitration proceedings shall be conducted in more than one language, decide which of those languages shall be the initial language of the arbitration.			17.2. The arbitral tribunal may order that any documents annexed to the statement of claim or statement of defence, and any supplementary documents or exhibits submitted in the course of the proceedings, delivered in their original language, shall be accompanied by a translation into the language or languages agreed upon by the parties or determined by the arbitral tribunal.	
17.3 Upon the formation of the Arbitral Tribunal and unless the parties have agreed upon the language or languages of the arbitration, the Arbitration Tribunal shall decide upon the language(s) of the arbitration, after giving the parties an opportunity to make written comment and taking into account the initial language of the arbitration and any other matter it				

may consider appropriate in all the circumstances of the case. 17.4 If any document is expressed in a language other than the language(s) of the arbitration and no translation of such document is submitted by the party relying upon the document, the Arbitral Tribunal or (if the Arbitral Tribunal has not been formed) the LCIA Court may order that party to submit a translation in a form to be determined by the Arbitral Tribunal or the LCIA Court, as the case may be.				
SEAT AND PLACE OF ARBITRATION 16.1 The parties may agree in writing the seat (or legal place) of their arbitration. Failing such a choice, the seat of arbitration shall be London, unless and until the LCIA Court determines in view of all the circumstances, and after having given the parties an opportunity to make written comment, that another seat is more appropriate. 16.2 The Arbitral Tribunal may hold hearings, meetings and deliberations at any convenient geographical place in its discretion; and if elsewhere than the seat of the arbitration, the arbitration shall be treated as an arbitration conducted at the seat of the arbitration and any award as an	14.1. The place of the arbitration shall be fixed by the Court unless agreed upon by the parties. 14.2. The Arbitral Tribunal may, after consultation with the parties, conduct hearings and meetings at any location it considers appropriate unless otherwise agreed by the parties. 14.3. The Arbitral Tribunal may deliberate at any location it considers appropriate.	13.1. If the parties disagree as to the place of arbitration, the administrator may initially determine the place of arbitration, subject to the power of the tribunal to determine finally the place of arbitration within 60 days after its constitution. All such determinations shall be made having regard for the contentions of the parties and the circumstances of the arbitration. 13.2. The tribunal may hold conferences or hear witnesses or inspect property or documents at any place it deems appropriate. The parties shall be given sufficient written notice to enable them to be present at any such proceedings.	16.1. Unless the parties have agreed upon the place where the arbitration is to be held, such place shall be determined by the arbitral tribunal, having regard to the circumstances of the arbitration. 16.2. The arbitral tribunal may determine the locale of the arbitration within the country agreed upon by the parties. It may hear witnesses and hold meetings for consultation among its members at any place it deems appropriate, having regard to the circumstances of the arbitration.	

LCIA	ICC	ICDR	UNCITRAL	1996 ACT
award made at the seat of the arbitration for all purposes.			16.3. The arbitral tribunal may meet at any place it deems appropriate for the inspection of goods, other property or documents. The parties shall be given sufficient notice to enable them to be present at such inspection. 16.4. The award shall be made at the place of arbitration.	
VARIOUS OTHER PROVISIONS RELATING TO HEARINGS				
Party Representation				
18.1 Any party may be represented by legal practitioners or any other representatives. 18.2 At any time the Arbitral Tribunal may require from any party proof of authority granted to its representative(s) in such form as the Arbitral Tribunal may determine.	21.4. The parties may appear in person or through duly authorized representatives. In addition, they may be assisted by advisers.	12. Any party may be represented in the arbitration . . .	4. The parties may be represented or assisted by persons of their choice . . .	S.36.
Oral Hearings versus decisions on documents alone				
19.1 Any party which expresses a desire to that effect has the right to be heard orally before the Arbitral Tribunal on the merits of the dispute,	20.2. After studying the written submissions of the parties and all documents relied upon, the Arbitral Tribunal shall hear the parties together	20.1. The tribunal shall give the parties at least 30 days advance notice of the date, time and place of the initial oral hearing. The tribunal shall	15.2. If either party so requests at any stage of the proceedings, the arbitral tribunal shall hold hearings for	S.34.

unless the parties have agreed in writing on documents-only arbitration. 19.2 The Arbitral Tribunal shall fix the date, time and physical place of any meetings and hearings in the arbitration, and shall give the parties reasonable notice thereof. 19.5 The Arbitral Tribunal shall have the fullest authority to establish time-limits for meetings and hearings, or for any parts thereof.	in person if any of them so requests or, failing such a request, it may of its own motion decide to hear them. 20.3. The Arbitral Tribunal may decide to hear witnesses, experts appointed by the parties or any other person, in the presence of the parties, or in their absence provided they have been duly summoned. 20.6. The Arbitral Tribunal may decide the case solely on the documents submitted by the parties unless any of the parties requests a hearing. 21.1. When a hearing is to be held, the Arbitral Tribunal, giving reasonable notice, shall summon the parties to appear before it on the day and at the place fixed by it.	give reasonable notice of subsequent hearings. 20.2. At least 15 days before the hearings, each party shall give the tribunal and the other parties the names and addresses of any witnesses it intends to present, the subject of their testimony and the languages in which such witnesses will give their testimony. 20.3. At the request of the tribunal or pursuant to mutual agreement of the parties, the administrator shall make arrangements for the interpretation of oral testimony or for a record of the hearing.	the presentation of evidence by witnesses, including expert witnesses, or for oral argument. In the absence of such a request, the arbitral tribunal shall decide whether to hold such hearings or whether the proceedings shall be conducted on the basis of documents and other materials. 25.1. In the event of an oral hearing, the arbitral tribunal shall give the parties adequate advance notice of the date, time and place thereof. 25.2. If witnesses are to be heard, at least fifteen days before the hearing each party shall communicate to the arbitral tribunal and to the other party the names and addresses of the witnesses he intends to present, the subject upon and the languages in which such witnesses will give their testimony. 25.3. The arbitral tribunal shall make arrangements for the translation of oral statements made at a hearing and for a record of the hearing if either is deemed necessary by the tribunal under the circumstances of the case, or if	

LCIA	ICC	ICDR	UNCITRAL	1996 ACT
			the parties have agreed thereto and have communicated such agreement to the tribunal at least fifteen days before the hearing.	
Burden of Proof		19.1. Each party shall have the burden of proving the facts relied on to support its claim or defense.	24.1. Each party shall have the burden of proving the facts relied on to support his claim or defence.	
Privacy and confidentiality and admission of witnesses				
19.4 All meetings and hearings shall be in private unless the parties agree otherwise in writing or the Arbitral Tribunal directs otherwise. 30.1 Unless the parties expressly agree in writing to the contrary, the parties undertake as a general principle to keep confidential all awards in their arbitration, together with all materials in the proceedings created for the purpose of the arbitration and all other documents produced by another party in the proceedings not otherwise in the public domain—save and to the	21.3. The Arbitral Tribunal shall be in full charge of the hearings, at which all the parties shall be entitled to be present. Save with the approval of the Arbitral Tribunal and the parties, persons not involved in the proceedings shall not be admitted.	20.4. Hearings are private unless the parties agree otherwise or the law provides to the contrary. The tribunal may require any witness or witnesses to retire during the testimony of other witnesses . . . 27.4. An award may be made public only with the consent of all parties or as required by law. 27.8. Unless otherwise agreed by the parties, the administrator may publish or otherwise make publicly available selected awards, decisions and rulings that have been edited to conceal	25.4. Hearings shall be held in camera unless the parties agree otherwise. The arbitral tribunal may require the retirement of any witness or witnesses during the testimony of other witnesses . . . 32.5. The award may be made public only with the consent of both parties.	

extent that disclosure may be required of a party by legal duty, to protect or pursue a legal right or to enforce or challenge an award in bona fide legal proceedings before a state court or other judicial authority. 30.2 The deliberations of the Arbitral Tribunal are likewise confidential to its members, save and to the extent that disclosure of an arbitrator's refusal to participate in the arbitration is required of the other members of the Arbitral Tribunal under Articles 10, 12 and 26. 30.3 The LCIA Court does not publish any award or any part of an award without the prior written consent of all parties and the Arbitral Tribunal.		the names of the parties and other identifying details or that have been made publicly available in the course of enforcement or otherwise. 34. Confidential information disclosed during the proceedings by the parties or by witnesses shall not be divulged by an arbitrator or by the administrator. Except as provided in Article 27, unless otherwise agreed by the parties, or required by applicable law, the members of the tribunal and the administrator shall keep confidential all matters relating to the arbitration or the award		
Evidence: documents, witnesses and other evidence 20.1 Before any hearing, the Arbitral Tribunal may require any party to give notice of the identity of each witness that party wishes to call (including rebuttal witnesses), as well as the subject matter of that witness's testimony, its content and its relevance to the issues in the arbitration.	20.5 At any time during the proceedings, the Arbitral Tribunal may summon any party to provide additional evidence.	19.2. The tribunal may order a party to deliver to the tribunal and to the other parties a summary of the documents and other evidence which that party intends to present in support of its claim, counterclaim or defense.	24.2. The arbitral tribunal may, if it considers it appropriate, require a party to deliver to the tribunal and to the other party, within such a period of time as the arbitral tribunal shall decide, a summary of the documents and other evidence which that	SS.43 and 2(3): Subpoenas of witnesses.

LCIA	ICC	ICDR	UNCITRAL	1996 ACT
20.2 The Arbitral Tribunal may also determine the time, manner and form in which such materials should be exchanged between the parties and presented to the Arbitral Tribunal; and it has a discretion to allow, refuse, or limit the appearance of witnesses (whether witness of fact or expert witness). 20.3 Subject to any order otherwise by the Arbitral Tribunal, the testimony of a witness may be presented by a party in written form, either as a signed statement or as a sworn affidavit. 20.4 Subject to Article 14.1 and 14.2, any party may request that a witness, on whose testimony another party seeks to rely, should attend for oral questioning at a hearing before the Arbitral Tribunal. If the Arbitral Tribunal orders that other party to produce the witness and the witness fails to attend the oral hearing without good cause, the Arbitral Tribunal may place such weight on the written testimony (or exclude the same altogether) as it considers appropriate in the circumstances of the case. 20.5 Any witness who gives oral evidence at a hearing before the Arbitral Tribunal may be questioned		19.3. At any time during the proceedings, the tribunal may order parties to produce other documents, exhibits or other evidence it deems necessary or appropriate. 20.4 . . . The tribunal may determine the manner in which witnesses are examined. 20.5. Evidence of witnesses may also be presented in the form of written statements signed by them. 20.6. The tribunal shall determine the admissibility, relevance, materiality and weight of the evidence offered by any party. The tribunal shall take into account applicable principles of legal privilege, such as those involving the confidentiality of communications between a lawyer and client.	party intends to present in support of the facts in issue set out in his statement of claim or statement of defence. 24.3. At any time during the arbitral proceedings the arbitral tribunal may require the parties to produce documents, exhibits or other evidence within such a period of time as the tribunal shall determine. 25.4 . . . The arbitral tribunal is free to determine the manner in which the witnesses are examined. 25.5. Evidence of witnesses may also be presented in the form of written statements signed by them. 25.6. The arbitral tribunal shall determine the admissibility, relevance, materiality and weight of the evidence offered.	

by each of the parties under the control of the Arbitral Tribunal. The Arbitral Tribunal may put questions at any stage of his evidence. 20.6 Subject to the mandatory provisions of any applicable law, it shall not be improper for any party or its legal representatives to interview any witness or potential witness for the purpose of presenting his testimony in written form or producing him as an oral witness. 20.7 Any individual intending to testify to the Arbitral Tribunal on any issue of fact or expertise shall be treated as a witness under these Rules notwithstanding that the individual is a party to the arbitration or was or is an officer, employee or shareholder of any party. 22.1 Unless the parties at any time agree otherwise in writing, the Arbitral Tribunal shall have the power, on the application of any party or of its own motion, but in either case only after giving the parties a reasonable opportunity to state their views: . . . (e) to order any party to produce to the Arbitral Tribunal, and to the other parties for inspection, and to supply copies of, any documents or classes of documents in their possession, custody or power which the Arbitral Tribunal determines to be relevant;				

LCIA	ICC	ICDR	UNCITRAL	1996 ACT
(f) to decide whether or not to apply any strict rules of evidence (or any other rules) as to the admissibility, relevance or weight of any material tendered by a party on any matter of fact or expert opinion; and to determine the time, manner and form in which such material should be exchanged between the parties and presented to the Arbitral Tribunal;				
Experts				
21.1 Unless otherwise agreed by the parties in writing, the Arbitral Tribunal: (a) may appoint one or more experts to report to the Arbitral Tribunal on specific issues, who shall be and remain impartial and independent of the parties throughout the arbitration proceedings; and (b) may require a party to give any such expert any relevant information or to provide access to any relevant documents, goods, samples, property or site for inspection by the expert. 21.2 Unless otherwise agreed by the parties in writing, if a party so requests or if the Arbitral Tribunal considers it necessary, the expert shall, after delivery of his written or	20.4. The Arbitral Tribunal, after having consulted the parties, may appoint one or more experts, define their terms of reference and receive their reports. At the request of a party, the parties shall be given the opportunity to question at a hearing any such expert appointed by the Tribunal.	22.1. The tribunal may appoint one or more independent experts to report to it, in writing, on specific issues designated by the tribunal and communicated to the parties. 22.2. The parties shall provide such an expert with any relevant information or produce for inspection any relevant documents or goods that the expert may require. Any dispute between a party and the expert as to the relevance of the requested information or goods shall be referred to the tribunal for decision. 22.3. Upon receipt of an expert's report, the tribunal shall send a copy of the report to all parties and shall give the parties an opportunity to express, in writing, their opinion on the report. A party may examine any	27.1. The arbitral tribunal may appoint one or more experts to report to it, in writing, on specific issues to be determined by the tribunal. A copy of the expert's terms of reference, established by the arbitral tribunal, shall be communicated to the parties. 27.2. The parties shall give the expert any relevant information or produce for his inspection any relevant documents or goods that he may require of them. Any dispute between a party and such expert as to the relevance of the required information or production shall be referred to the arbitral tribunal for decision.	S.37.

oral report to the Arbitral Tribunal and the parties, participate in one or more hearings at which the parties shall have the opportunity to question the expert on his report and to present expert witnesses in order to testify on the points at issue. 21.3 The fees and expenses of any expert appointed by the Arbitral Tribunal under this Article shall be paid out of the deposits payable by the parties under Article 24 and shall form part of the costs of the arbitration.		document on which the expert has relied in such a report. 22.4. At the request of any party, the tribunal shall give the parties an opportunity to question the expert at a hearing. At this hearing, parties may present expert witnesses to testify on the points at issue.	27.3. Upon receipt of the expert's report, the arbitral tribunal shall communicate a copy of the report to the parties who shall be given the opportunity to express, in writing, their opinion on the report. A party shall be entitled to examine any document on which the expert has relied in his report. 27.4. At the request of either party the expert, after delivery of the report, may be heard at a hearing where the parties shall have the opportunity to be present and to interrogate the expert. At this hearing either party may present expert witnesses in order to testify on the points at issue. The provisions of article 25 shall be applicable to such proceedings.	
Applicable Rules of Law 16.3 The law applicable to the arbitration (if any) shall be the arbitration law of the seat of arbitration, unless and to the extent that the parties have expressly agreed in writing on the application of another arbitration law and such agreement is not prohibited by the law of the arbitral seat.	17.1. The parties shall be free to agree upon the rules of law to be applied by the Arbitral Tribunal to the merits of the dispute. In the absence of any such agreement, the Arbitral Tribunal shall apply the rules of law which it determines to be appropriate.	28.1. The tribunal shall apply the substantive law(s) or rules of law designated by the parties as applicable to the dispute. Failing such a designation by the parties, the tribunal shall apply such law(s) or rules of law as it determines to be appropriate.	33.1. The arbitral tribunal shall apply the law designated by the parties as applicable to the substance of the dispute. Failing such designation by the parties, the arbitral tribunal shall apply the law determined by the conflict of laws rules which it considers applicable.	S.46.

LCIA	ICC	ICDR	UNCITRAL	1996 ACT
22.3 The Arbitral Tribunal shall decide the parties' dispute in accordance with the law(s) or rules of law chosen by the parties as applicable to the merits of their dispute. If and to the extent that the Arbitral Tribunal determines that the parties have made no such choice, the Arbitral Tribunal shall apply the law(s) or rules of law which it considers appropriate. 22.4 The Arbitral Tribunal shall only apply to the merits of the dispute principles deriving from "*ex aequo et bono*", "amiable composition" or "honourable engagement" where the parties have so agreed expressly in writing.	17.2. In all cases the Arbitral Tribunal shall take account of the provisions of the contract and the relevant trade usages. 17.3. The Arbitral Tribunal shall assume the powers of an *amiable compositeur* or decide *ex aequo et bono* only if the parties have agreed to give it such powers.	28.2. In arbitrations involving the application of contracts, the tribunal shall decide in accordance with the terms of the contract and shall take into account usages of the trade applicable to the contract. 28.3. The tribunal shall not decide as *amiable compositeur* or *ex aequo et bono* unless the parties have expressly authorized it to do so.	33.2. The arbitral tribunal shall decide as *amiable compositeur* or *ex aequo et bono* only if the parties have expressly authorized the arbitral tribunal to do so and if the law applicable to the arbitral procedure permits such arbitration. 33.3. In all cases, the arbitral tribunal shall decide in accordance with the terms of the contract and shall take into account the usages of the trade applicable to the transaction.	
Consolidation and additional parties 22.1 Unless the parties at any time agree otherwise in writing, the Arbitral Tribunal shall have the power, on the application of any party or of its own motion, but in either case only after giving the parties a reasonable opportunity to state their views: . . . (h) to allow, only upon the application of a party, one or more third persons to be joined in the arbitration as a party provided any such third person and the applicant				S.35.

party have consented thereto in writing, and thereafter to make a single final award, or separate awards, in respect of all parties so implicated in the arbitration.				
Additional powers of the Tribunal 19.3 The Arbitral Tribunal may in advance of any hearing submit to the parties a list of questions which it wishes them to answer with special attention. 22.1 Unless the parties at any time agree otherwise in writing, the Arbitral Tribunal shall have the power, on the application of any party or of its own motion, but in either case only after giving the parties a reasonable opportunity to state their views: . . . (c) to conduct such enquiries as may appear to the Arbitral Tribunal to be necessary or expedient, including whether and to what extent the Arbitral Tribunal should itself take the initiative in identifying the issues and ascertaining the relevant facts and the law(s) or rules of law applicable to the arbitration, the merits of the parties' dispute and the Arbitration Agreement; (d) to order any party to make any property, site or thing under its control and relating to the subject	20.7. The Arbitral Tribunal may take measures for protecting trade secrets and confidential information.			S.38: General powers exercisable by the Tribunal.

LCIA	ICC	ICDR	UNCITRAL	1996 ACT
matter of the arbitration available for inspection by the Arbitral Tribunal, any other party, its expert or any expert to the Arbitral Tribunal; (g) to order the correction of any contract between the parties or the Arbitration Agreement, but only to the extent required to rectify any mistake which the Arbitral Tribunal determines to be common to the parties and then only if and to the extent to which the law(s) or rules of law applicable to the contract or Arbitration Agreement permit such correction;				
Procedural Issues				
14.3 In the case of a three-member Arbitral Tribunal the chairman may, with the prior consent of the other two arbitrators, make procedural rulings alone.		26.2. When the parties or the tribunal so authorize, the presiding arbitrator may make decisions or rulings on questions of procedure, subject to revision by the tribunal.	31.2. In the case of questions of procedure, when there is no majority or when the arbitral tribunal so authorizes, the presiding arbitrator may decide on his own, subject to revision, if any, by the arbitral tribunal.	
Default by parties				
15.8 If the Respondent fails to submit a Statement of Defence or the Claimant a Statement of Defence to Counterclaim, or if at any point any party fails to avail itself of the	6.3. If any of the parties refuses or fails to take part in the arbitration or any stage thereof, the arbitration shall proceed notwithstanding such refusal or failure.	23.1. If a party fails to file a statement of defense within the time established by the tribunal without showing sufficient cause for such failure, as determined by the tribunal, the	28.1. If, within the period of time fixed by the arbitral tribunal, the claimant has failed to communicate his claim without showing	S.41: Tribunal's powers in case of default.

opportunity to present its case in the manner determined by Article 15.2 to 15.6 or directed by the Arbitral Tribunal, the Arbitral Tribunal may nevertheless proceed with the arbitration and make an award.	21.2. If any of the parties, although duly summoned, fails to appear without valid excuse, the Arbitral Tribunal shall have the power to proceed with the hearing.	tribunal may proceed with the arbitration. 23.2. If a party, duly notified under these rules, fails to appear at a hearing without showing sufficient cause for such failure, as determined by the tribunal, the tribunal may proceed with the arbitration. 23.3. If a party, duly invited to produce evidence or take any other steps in the proceedings, fails to do so within the time established by the tribunal without showing sufficient cause for such failure, as determined by the tribunal, the tribunal may make the award on the evidence before it.	sufficient cause for such failure, the arbitral tribunal shall issue an order for the termination of the arbitral proceedings. If, within the period of time fixed by the arbitral tribunal, the respondent has failed to communicate his statement of defence without showing sufficient cause for such failure, the arbitral tribunal shall order that the proceedings continue. 28.2. If one of the parties, duly notified under these Rules, fails to appear at a hearing, without showing sufficient cause for such failure, the arbitral tribunal may proceed with the arbitration. 28.3. If one of the parties, duly invited to produce documentary evidence, fails to do so within the established period of time, without showing sufficient cause for such failure, the arbitral tribunal may make the award on the evidence before it.	S.42: Enforcement by the court of Tribunal's peremptory orders.
Closure of proceedings	22.1. When it is satisfied that the parties have had a reasonable	24.1. After asking the parties if they have any further testimony or	29.1. The arbitral tribunal may inquire of the parties if	

LCIA	ICC	ICDR	UNCITRAL	1996 ACT
	opportunity to present their cases, the Arbitral Tribunal shall declare the proceedings closed. Thereafter, no further submissions or argument may be made, or evidence produced, unless requested or authorized by the Arbitral Tribunal. 22.2. When the Arbitral Tribunal has declared the proceedings closed, it shall indicate to the Secretariat an approximate date by which the draft Award will be submitted to the Court for approval pursuant to Article 27. Any postponement of that date shall be communicated to the Secretariat by the Arbitral Tribunal.	evidentiary submissions and upon receiving negative replies or if satisfied that the record is complete, the tribunal may declare the hearings closed. 24.2. The tribunal in its discretion, on its own motion or upon application of a party, may reopen the hearings at any time before the award is made.	they have any further proof to offer or witnesses to be heard or submissions to make and, if there are none, it may declare the hearings closed. 29.2. The arbitral tribunal may, if it considers it necessary owing to exceptional circumstances, decide, on its own motion or upon application of a party, to reopen the hearings at any time before the award is made.	
CONSERVATORY AND INTERIM MEASURES AND SECURITY FOR COSTS 25.1 The Arbitral Tribunal shall have the power, unless otherwise agreed by the parties in writing, on the application of any party: (a) to order any respondent party to a claim or counterclaim to provide security for all or part of the amount in dispute, by way of deposit or bank guarantee or in any other manner and upon such terms as the Arbitral Tribunal considers appropriate. Such terms may include the provision by the claiming or counterclaiming party	23.1. Unless the parties have otherwise agreed, as soon as the file has been transmitted to it, the Arbitral Tribunal may, at the request of a party, order any interim or conservatory measure it deems appropriate. The Arbitral Tribunal may make the granting of any such measure subject to appropriate security being furnished by the requesting party. Any such measure shall take the form of an order, giving reasons, or of an Award, as the	21.1. At the request of any party, the tribunal may take whatever interim measures it deems necessary, including injunctive relief and measures for the protection or conservation of property. 21.2. Such interim measures may take the form of an interim award, and the tribunal may require security for the costs of such measures. 21.3. A request for interim measures addressed by a party to a judicial authority shall not be deemed	26.1. At the request of either party, the arbitral tribunal may take any interim measures it deems necessary in respect of the subject-matter of the dispute, including measures for the conservation of the goods forming the subject-matter in dispute, such as ordering their deposit with a third person or the sale of perishable goods.	SS.44 amd 2(3). S.42: Enforcement of Tribunal's peremptory orders by the court.

of a cross-indemnity, itself secured in such manner as the Arbitral Tribunal considers appropriate, for any costs or losses incurred by such respondent in providing security. The amount of any costs and losses payable under such cross-indemnity may be determined by the Arbitral Tribunal in one or more awards; (b) to order the preservation, storage, sale or other disposal of any property or thing under the control of any party and relating to the subject matter of the arbitration; and (c) to order on a provisional basis, subject to final determination in an award, any relief which the Arbitral Tribunal would have power to grant in an award, including a provisional order for the payment of money or the disposition of property as between any parties. 25.2 The Arbitral Tribunal shall have the power, upon the application of a party, to order any claiming or counterclaiming party to provide security for the legal or other costs of any other party by way of deposit or bank guarantee or in any other manner and upon such terms as the Arbitral Tribunal considers appropriate. Such terms may include the provision by that other party of a cross-indemnity, itself secured in such manner as the Arbitral Tribunal considers appropriate, for any costs	Arbitral Tribunal considers appropriate. 23.2. Before the file is transmitted to the Arbitral Tribunal, and in appropriate circumstances even thereafter, the parties may apply to any competent judicial authority for interim or conservatory measures. The application of a party to a judicial authority for such measures or for the implementation of any such measures ordered by an Arbitral Tribunal shall not be deemed to be an infringement or a waiver of the arbitration agreement and shall not affect the relevant powers reserved to the Arbitral Tribunal. Any such application and any measures taken by the judicial authority must be notified without delay to the Secretariat. The Secretariat shall inform the Arbitral Tribunal thereof.	incompatible with the agreement to arbitrate or a waiver of the right to arbitrate. 21.4. The tribunal may in its discretion apportion costs associated with applications for interim relief in any interim award or in the final award.	26.2. Such interim measures may be established in the form of an interim award. The arbitral tribunal shall be entitled to require security for the costs of such measures. 26.3. A request for interim measures addressed by any party to a judicial authority shall not be deemed incompatible with the agreement to arbitrate, or as a waiver of that agreement.	

LCIA	ICC	ICDR	UNCITRAL	1996 ACT
and losses incurred by such claimant or counterclaimant in providing security. The amount of any costs and losses payable under such cross-indemnity may be determined by the Arbitral Tribunal in one or more awards. In the event that a claiming or counterclaiming party does not comply with any order to provide security, the Arbitral Tribunal may stay that party's claims or counterclaims or dismiss them in an award. 25.3 The power of the Arbitral Tribunal under Article 25.1 shall not prejudice howsoever any party's right to apply to any state court or other judicial authority for interim or conservatory measures before the formation of the Arbitral Tribunal and, in exceptional cases, thereafter. Any application and any order for such measures after the formation of the Arbitral Tribunal shall be promptly communicated by the applicant to the Arbitral Tribunal and all other parties. However, by agreeing to arbitration under these Rules, the parties shall be taken to have agreed not to apply to any state court or other judicial authority for any order for security for its legal or other costs available from the Arbitral Tribunal under Article 25.2.				

JURISDICTION				
23.1 The Arbitral Tribunal shall have the power to rule on its own jurisdiction, including any objection to the initial or continuing existence, validity or effectiveness of the Arbitration Agreement. For that purpose, an arbitration clause which forms or was intended to form part of another agreement shall be treated as an arbitration agreement independent of that other agreement. A decision by the Arbitral Tribunal that such other agreement is non-existent, invalid or ineffective shall not entail *ipso jure* the non-existence, invalidity or ineffectiveness of the arbitration clause. 23.2 A plea by a Respondent that the Arbitral Tribunal does not have jurisdiction shall be treated as having been irrevocably waived unless it is raised not later than the Statement of Defence; and a like plea by a Respondent to Counterclaim shall be similarly treated unless it is raised no later than the Statement of Defence to Counterclaim. A plea that the Arbitral Tribunal is exceeding the scope of its authority shall be raised promptly after the Arbitral Tribunal has indicated its intention to decide on the matter alleged by any party to be beyond the scope of its authority, failing which such plea shall also be treated as having been waived	6.2. If the Respondent does not file an Answer, as provided by Article 5, or if any party raises one or more pleas concerning the existence, validity or scope of the arbitration agreement, the Court may decide, without prejudice to the admissibility or merits of the plea or pleas, that the arbitration shall proceed if it is *prima facie* satisfied that an arbitration agreement under the Rules may exist. In such a case, any decision as to the jurisdiction of the Arbitral Tribunal shall be taken by the Arbitral Tribunal itself. If the Court is not so satisfied, the parties shall be notified that the arbitration cannot proceed. In such a case, any party retains the right to ask any court having jurisdiction whether or not there is a binding arbitration agreement. 6.4. Unless otherwise agreed, the Arbitral Tribunal shall not cease to have jurisdiction by reason of any claim that the contract is null and void or allegation that it is non-existent, provided that the Arbitral Tribunal upholds the validity of the arbitration agreement. The Arbitral Tribunal shall continue to have jurisdiction to determine the respective rights of the parties and to adjudicate their claims and pleas even though the contract itself may be non-existent or null and void.	15.1. The tribunal shall have the power to rule on its own jurisdiction, including any objections with respect to the existence, scope or validity of the arbitration agreement. 15.2. The tribunal shall have the power to determine the existence or validity of a contract of which an arbitration clause forms a part. Such an arbitration clause shall be treated as an agreement independent of the other terms of the contract. A decision by the tribunal that the contract is null and void shall not for that reason alone render invalid the arbitration clause. 15.3. A party must object to the jurisdiction of the tribunal or to the arbitrability of a claim or counterclaim no later than the filing of the statement of defense, as provided in Article 3, to the claim or counterclaim that gives rise to the objection. The tribunal may rule on such objections as a preliminary matter or as part of the final award.	21.1. The arbitral tribunal shall have the power to rule on objections that it has no jurisdiction, including any objections with respect to the existence or validity of the arbitration clause or of the separate arbitration agreement. 21.2. The arbitral tribunal shall have the power to determine the existence or the validity of the contract of which an arbitration clause forms a part. For the purposes of article 21, an arbitration clause which forms part of a contract and which provides for arbitration under these Rules shall be treated as an agreement independent of the other terms of the contract. A decision by the arbitral tribunal that the contract is null and void shall not entail *ipso jure* the invalidity of the arbitration clause. 21.3. A plea that the arbitral tribunal does not have jurisdiction shall be raised not later than in the statement of defence or, with respect to a counter-claim, in the reply to the counter-claim.	SS.30–33 and S.7.

LCIA	ICC	ICDR	UNCITRAL	1996 ACT
irrevocably. In any case, the Arbitral Tribunal may nevertheless admit an untimely plea if it considers the delay justified in the particular circumstances. 23.3 The Arbitral Tribunal may determine the plea to its jurisdiction or authority in an award as to jurisdiction or later in an award on the merits, as it considers appropriate in the circumstances. 23.4 By agreeing to arbitration under these Rules, the parties shall be treated as having agreed not to apply to any state court or other judicial authority for any relief regarding the Arbitral Tribunal's jurisdiction or authority, except with the agreement in writing of all parties to the arbitration or the prior authorisation of the Arbitral Tribunal or following the latter's award ruling on the objection to its jurisdiction or authority.			21.4. In general, the arbitral tribunal should rule on a plea concerning its jurisdiction as a preliminary question. However, the arbitral tribunal may proceed with the arbitration and rule on such a plea in their final award.	
THE AWARD **Form and effect of the award**				
26.1 The Arbitral Tribunal shall make its award in writing and, unless all parties agree in writing otherwise, shall state the reasons upon which its award is based. The award shall also state the date when the award is	25.2. The Award shall state the reasons upon which it is based. 25.3. The Award shall be deemed to be made at the place of the arbitration and on the date stated therein.	27.1. Awards shall be made in writing, promptly by the tribunal, and shall be final and binding on the parties. The parties undertake to carry out any such award without delay.	32.2. The award shall be made in writing and shall be final and binding on the parties. The parties undertake to carry out the award without delay.	SS.52–54 and S.58.

made and the seat of the arbitration; and it shall be signed by the Arbitral Tribunal or those of its members assenting to it. 26.9 All awards shall be final and binding on the parties. By agreeing to arbitration under these Rules, the parties undertake to carry out any award immediately and without any delay (subject only to Article 27); . . .	28.6. Every Award shall be binding on the parties	27.2. The tribunal shall state the reasons upon which the award is based, unless the parties have agreed that no reasons need be given. 27.3. The award shall contain the date and the place where the award was made, which shall be the place designated pursuant to Article 13.	32.3. The arbitral tribunal shall state the reasons upon which the award is based, unless the parties have agreed that no reasons are to be given. 32.4. An award shall be signed by the arbitrators and it shall contain the date on which and the place where the award was made. Where there are three arbitrators and one of them fails to sign, the award shall state the reason for the absence of the signature.	
Arbitrators' duties re awards 26.2 If any arbitrator fails to comply with the mandatory provisions of any applicable law relating to the making of the award, having been given a reasonable opportunity to do so, the remaining arbitrators may proceed in his absence and state in their award the circumstances of the other arbitrator's failure to participate in the making of the award. 26.4 If any arbitrator refuses or fails to sign the award, the signatures of the majority or (failing a majority) of the chairman shall be sufficient, provided that the reason for the omitted signature is stated in the award by the majority or chairman.				

LCIA	ICC	ICDR	UNCITRAL	1996 ACT
26.5 The sole arbitrator or chairman shall be responsible for delivering the award to the LCIA Court . . .				
Majority decisions 26.3 Where there are three arbitrators and the Arbitral Tribunal fails to agree on any issue, the arbitrators shall decide that issue by a majority. Failing a majority decision on any issue, the chairman of the Arbitral Tribunal shall decide that issue.	25.1. When the Arbitral Tribunal is composed of more than one arbitrator, an Award is given by a majority decision. If there be no majority, the Award shall be made by the chairman of the Arbitral Tribunal alone	26.1. When there is more than one arbitrator, any award, decision or ruling of the arbitral tribunal shall be made by a majority of the arbitrators. If any arbitrator fails to sign the award, it shall be accompanied by a statement of the reason for the absence of such signature.	31.1. When there are three arbitrators, any award or other decision of the arbitral tribunal shall be made by a majority of the arbitrators.	
Separate and interim awards 26.7 The Arbitral Tribunal may make separate awards on different issues at different times. Such awards shall have the same status and effect as any other award made by the Arbitral Tribunal.		27.7. In addition to making a final award, the tribunal may make interim, interlocutory or partial orders and awards.	32.1. In addition to making a final award, the arbitral tribunal shall be entitled to make interim, interlocutory, or partial awards.	S.47.
Currency and interest 26.6 An award may be expressed in any currency. The Arbitral Tribunal may order that simple or compound interest shall be paid by any party on any sum awarded at such rates as the Arbitral Tribunal determines to be appropriate, without being bound by legal rates of interest imposed by any state court, in respect of any period		28.4. A monetary award shall be in the currency or currencies of the contract unless the tribunal considers another currency more appropriate, and the tribunal may award such pre-award and post-award interest, simple or compound, as it considers appropriate, taking into consideration the contract and applicable law.		S.49.

which the Arbitral Tribunal determines to be appropriate ending not later than the date upon which the award is complied with.				
Settlement or other reasons for termination 26.8 In the event of a settlement of the parties' dispute, the Arbitral Tribunal may render an award recording the settlement if the parties so request in writing (a "Consent Award"), provided always that such award contains an express statement that it is an award made by the parties' consent. A Consent Award need not contain reasons. If the parties do not require a consent award, then on written confirmation by the parties to the LCIA Court that a settlement has been reached, the Arbitral Tribunal shall be discharged and the arbitration proceedings concluded, subject to payment by the parties of any outstanding costs of the arbitration under Article 28.	26. If the parties reach a settlement after the file has been transmitted to the Arbitral Tribunal in accordance with Article 13, the settlement shall be recorded in the form of an Award made by consent of the parties if so requested by the parties and if the Arbitral Tribunal agrees to do so.	29.1. If the parties settle the dispute before an award is made, the tribunal shall terminate the arbitration and, if requested by all parties, may record the settlement in the form of an award on agreed terms. The tribunal is not obliged to give reasons for such an award. 29.2. If the continuation of the proceedings becomes unnecessary or impossible for any other reason, the tribunal shall inform the parties of its intention to terminate the proceedings. The tribunal shall thereafter issue an order terminating the arbitration, unless a party raises justifiable grounds for objection.	34.1. If, before the award is made, the parties agree on a settlement of the dispute, the arbitral tribunal shall either issue an order for the termination of the arbitral proceedings or, if requested by both parties and accepted by the tribunal, record the settlement in the form of an arbitral award on agreed terms. The arbitral tribunal is not obliged to give reasons for such an award. 34.2. If, before the award is made, the continuation of the arbitral proceedings becomes unnecessary or impossible for any reason not mentioned in paragraph 1, the arbitral tribunal shall inform the parties of its intention to issue an order for the termination of the proceedings. The arbitral tribunal shall have the power to issue such an order unless a party raises justifiable grounds for objection.	S.51.

LCIA	ICC	ICDR	UNCITRAL	1996 ACT
			34.3. Copies of the order for termination of the arbitral proceedings or of the arbitral award on agreed terms, signed by the arbitrators, shall be communicated by the arbitral tribunal to the parties. Where an arbitral award on agreed terms is made, the provisions of article 32, paragraphs 2 and 4 to 7, shall apply.	
Time limits for awards	24.1. The time limit within which the Arbitral Tribunal must render its final Award is six months. Such time limit shall start to run from the date of the last signature by the Arbitral Tribunal or by the parties of the Terms of Reference or, in the case of application of Article 18(3), the date of the notification to the Arbitral Tribunal by the Secretariat of the approval of the Terms of Reference by the Court. 24.2. The Court may extend this time limit pursuant to a reasoned request from the Arbitral Tribunal or on its own initiative if it decides it is necessary to do so.			S.50: Extension of time for making an award
Correction and interpretation of awards and additional awards 27.1 Within 30 days of receipt of any award, or such lesser period as	29.1. On its own initiative, the Arbitral Tribunal may correct a	30.1. Within 30 days after the receipt of an award, any party, with notice to	35.1. Within thirty days after the receipt of the award, either	S.57.

may be agreed in writing by the parties, a party may by written notice to the Registrar (copied to all other parties) request the Arbitral Tribunal to correct in the award any errors in computation, clerical or typographical errors or any errors of a similar nature. If the Arbitral Tribunal considers the request to be justified, it shall make the corrections within 30 days of receipt of the request. Any correction shall take the form of separate memorandum dated and signed by the Arbitral Tribunal or (if three arbitrators) those of its members assenting to it; and such memorandum shall become part of the award for all purposes. 27.2 The Arbitral Tribunal may likewise correct any error of the nature described in Article 27.1 on its own initiative within 30 days of the date of the award, to the same effect. 27.3 Within 30 days of receipt of the final award, a party may by written notice to the Registrar (copied to all other parties), request the Arbitral Tribunal to make an additional award as to claims or counterclaims presented in the arbitration but not determined in any award. If the Arbitral Tribunal considers the request to be justified, it shall make the additional award within 60 days of receipt of the request. The	clerical, computational or typographical error, or any errors of similar nature contained in an Award, provided such correction is submitted for approval to the Court within 30 days of the date of such Award. 29.2 Any application of a party for the correction of an error of the kind referred to in Article 29(1), or for the interpretation of an Award, must be made to the Secretariat within 30 days of the receipt of the Award by such party, in a number of copies as stated in Article 3(1). After transmittal of the application to the Arbitral Tribunal, the latter shall grant the other party a short time limit, normally not exceeding 30 days, from the receipt of the application by that party, to submit any comments thereon. If the Arbitral Tribunal decides to correct or interpret the Award, it shall submit its decision in draft form to the Court not later than 30 days following the expiration of the time limit for the receipt of any comments from the other party or within such other period as the Court may decide. 29.3. The decision to correct or to interpret the Award shall take the form of an addendum and shall constitute part of the Award. The provisions of Articles 25, 27 and 28 shall apply *mutatis mutandis.*	the other parties, may request the tribunal to interpret the award or correct any clerical, typographical or computation errors or make an additional award as to claims presented but omitted from the award. 30.2. If the tribunal considers such a request justified, after considering the contentions of the parties, it shall comply with such a request within 30 days after the request.	party, with notice to the other party, may request that the arbitral tribunal give an interpretation of the award. 35.2. The interpretation shall be given in writing within forty-five days after the receipt of the request. The interpretation shall form part of the award and the provisions of article 32, paragraphs 2 to 7, shall apply 36.1. Within thirty days after the receipt of the award, either party, with notice to the other party, may request the arbitral tribunal to correct in the award any errors in computation, any clerical or typographical errors, or any errors of similar nature. The arbitral tribunal may within thirty days after the communication of the award make such corrections on its own initiative. 36.2. Such corrections shall be in writing, and the provisions of article 32, paragraphs 2 to 7, shall apply. 37.1. Within thirty days after the receipt of the award, either party, with notice to the other party, may request the arbitral tribunal to make an additional	

LCIA	ICC	ICDR	UNCITRAL	1996 ACT
provisions of Article 26 shall apply to any additional award.			award as to claims presented in the arbitral proceedings but omitted from the award. 37.2. If the arbitral tribunal considers the request for an additional award to be justified and considers that the omission can be rectified without any further hearings or evidence, it shall complete its award within sixty days after the receipt of the request. 37.3. When an additional award is made, the provisions of article 32, paragraphs 2 to 7, shall apply.	
Scrutiny of awards				
	27. Before signing any Award, the Arbitral Tribunal shall submit it in draft form to the Court. The Court may lay down modifications as to the form of the Award and, without affecting the Arbitral Tribunal's liberty of decision, may also draw its attention to points of substance. No Award shall be rendered by the Arbitral Tribunal until it has been approved by the Court as to its form.			

Notification of the award				
26.5 . . . [the Court] . . . shall transmit certified copies to the parties provided that the costs of arbitration have been paid to the LCIA in accordance with Article 28.	28.1. Once an Award has been made, the Secretariat shall notify to the parties the text signed by the Arbitral Tribunal, provided always that the costs of the arbitration have been fully paid to the ICC by the parties or by one of them. 28.2. Additional copies certified true by the Secretary General shall be made available on request and at any time to the parties, but to no one else. 28.3. By virtue of the notification made in accordance with Paragraph 1 of this Article, the parties waive any other form of notification or deposit on the part of the Arbitral Tribunal. 28.4. An original of each Award made in accordance with the present Rules shall be deposited with the Secretariat. 28.5. The Arbitral Tribunal and the Secretariat shall assist the parties in complying with whatever further formalities may be necessary.	27.5. Copies of the award shall be communicated to the parties by the administrator. 27.6. If the arbitration law of the country where the award is made requires the award to be filed or registered, the tribunal shall comply with such requirement.	32.6. Copies of the award signed by the arbitrators shall be communicated to the parties by the arbitral tribunal. 32.7. If the arbitration law of the country where the award is made requires that the award be filed or registered by the arbitral tribunal, the tribunal shall comply with this requirement within the period of time required by law.	SS.55–56: Power to withhold awards in case of non-payment.
DEPOSITS AND ADVANCE COSTS				
24.1 The LCIA Court may direct the parties, in such proportions as it thinks appropriate, to make one or several interim or final payments on account of the costs of the arbitration. Such deposits shall be	30.1. After receipt of the Request, the Secretary General may request the Claimant to pay a provisional advance in an amount intended to cover the costs of arbitration until the Terms of Reference have been drawn up.	33.1. When a party files claims, the administrator may request the filing party to deposit appropriate amounts as an advance for the costs referred to in Article 31, paragraphs (a), (b) and (c).	41.1. The arbitral tribunal, on its establishment, may request each party to deposit an equal amount as an advance for the costs referred to in article 38, paragraphs (a), (b) and (c).	

LCIA	ICC	ICDR	UNCITRAL	1996 ACT
made to and held by the LCIA andfrom time to time may be released by the LCIA Court to the arbitrator(s), any expert appointed by the Arbitral Tribunal and the LCIA itself as the arbitration progresses. 24.2 The Arbitral Tribunal shall not proceed with the arbitration without ascertaining at all times from the Registrar or any deputy Registrar that the LCIA is in requisite funds. 24.3 In the event that a party fails or refuses to provide any deposit as directed by the LCIA Court, the LCIA Court may direct the other party or parties to effect a substitute payment to allow the arbitration to proceed (subject to any award on costs). In such circumstances, the party paying the substitute payment shall be entitled to recover that amount as a debt immediately due from the defaulting party. 24 4 Failure by a claimant or counterclaiming party to provide promptly and in full the required deposit may be treated by the LCIA Court and the Arbitral Tribunal as a withdrawal of the claim or counterclaim respectively.	30.2. As soon as practicable, the Court shall fix the advance on costs in an amount likely to cover the fees and expenses of the arbitrators and the ICC administrative costs for the claims and counterclaims which have been referred to it by the parties. This amount may be subject to readjustment at any time during the arbitration. Where, apart from the claims, counterclaims are submitted, the Court may fix separate advances on costs for the claims and the counterclaims. 30.3. The advance on costs fixed by the Court shall be payable in equal shares by the Claimant and the Respondent. Any provisional advance paid on the basis of Article 30(1) will be considered as a partial payment thereof. However, any party shall be free to pay the whole of the advance on costs in respect of the principal claim or the counterclaim should the other party fail to pay its share. When the Court has set separate advances on costs in accordance with Article 30(2), each of the parties shall pay the advance on costs corresponding to its claims. 30.4. When a request for an advance on costs has not been complied with, and after consultation with the Arbitral Tribunal, the Secretary General may direct the Arbitral Tribunal to suspend	33.2. During the course of the arbitral proceedings, the tribunal may request supplementary deposits from the parties. 33.3. If the deposits requested are not paid in full within 30 days after the receipt of the request, the administrator shall so inform the parties, in order that one or the other of them may make the required payment. If such payments are not made, the tribunal may order the suspension or termination of the proceedings. 33.4. After the award has been made, the administrator shall render an accounting to the parties of the deposits received and return any unexpended balance to the parties.	41.2. During the course of the arbitral proceedings the arbitral tribunal may request supplementary deposits from the parties. 41.3. If an appointing authority has been agreed upon by the parties or designated by the Secretary-General of the Permanent Court of Arbitration at The Hague, and when a party so requests and the appointing authority consents to perform the function, the arbitral tribunal shall fix the amounts of any deposits or supplementary deposits only after consultation with the appointing authority which may make any comments to the arbitral tribunal which it deems appropriate concerning the amount of such deposits and supplementary deposits. 41.4. If the required deposits are not paid in full within thirty days after the receipt of the request, the arbitral tribunal shall so inform the parties in order that one or another of them may make the required payment. If such payment is not made, the arbitral tribunal may order the	

	its work and set a time limit, which must be not less than 15 days, on the expiry of which the relevant claims, or counterclaims, shall be considered as withdrawn. Should the party in question wish to object to this measure, it must make a request within the aforementioned period for the matter to be decided by the Court. Such party shall not be prevented, on the ground of such withdrawal, from reintroducing the same claims or counterclaims at a later date in another proceeding. 30.5. If one of the parties claims a right to a set-off with regard to either claims or counterclaims, such set-off shall be taken into account in determining the advance to cover the costs of arbitration in the same way as a separate claim insofar as it may require the Arbitral Tribunal to consider additional matters.		suspension or termination of the arbitral proceedings. 41.5. After the award has been made, the arbitral tribunal shall render an accounting to the parties of the deposits received and return any unexpended balance to the parties.	
ARBITRATION AND LEGAL COSTS 28.1 The costs of the arbitration (other than the legal or other costs incurred by the parties themselves) shall be determined by the LCIA Court in accordance with the Schedule of Costs. The parties shall be jointly and severally liable to the Arbitral Tribunal and the LCIA for such arbitration costs.	31.1. The costs of the arbitration shall include the fees and expenses of the arbitrators and the ICC administrative expenses fixed by the Court, in accordance with the scale in force at the time of the commencement of the arbitral proceedings, as well as the fees and expenses of any experts appointed by the Arbitral Tribunal and the reasonable legal and other costs	31. The tribunal shall fix the costs of arbitration in its award. The tribunal may apportion such costs among the parties if it determines that such apportionment is reasonable, taking into account the circumstances of the case.	38. The arbitral tribunal shall fix the costs of arbitration in its award. The term "costs" includes only: (a) The fees of the arbitral tribunal to be stated separately as to each arbitrator and to be fixed by the tribunal itself in accordance with article 39;	SS.59–62 and S.63: Recoverable costs of the arbitration. SS.64–65. Recoverable fees and expenses of arbitrators and

LCIA	ICC	ICDR	UNCITRAL	1996 ACT
28.2 The Arbitral Tribunal shall specify in the award the total amount of the costs of the arbitration as determined by the LCIA Court. Unless the parties agree otherwise in writing, the Arbitral Tribunal shall determine the proportions in which the parties shall bear all or part of such arbitration costs. If the Arbitral Tribunal has determined that all or any part of the arbitration costs shall be borne by a party other than a party which has already paid them to the LCIA, the latter party shall have the right to recover the appropriate amount from the former party. 28.3 The Arbitral Tribunal shall also have the power to order in its award that all or part of the legal or other costs incurred by a party be paid by another party, unless the parties agree otherwise in writing. The Arbitral Tribunal shall determine and fix the amount of each item comprising such costs on such reasonable basis as it thinks fit. 28.4 Unless the parties otherwise agree in writing, the Arbitral Tribunal shall make its orders on both arbitration and legal costs on the general principle that costs should reflect the parties' relative success and failure in the award or arbitration, except where it appears to the Arbitral Tribunal that in the	incurred by the parties for the arbitration. 31.2. The Court may fix the fees of the arbitrators at a figure higher or lower than that which would result from the application of the relevant scale should this be deemed necessary due to the exceptional circumstances of the case. Decisions on costs other than those fixed by the Court may be taken by the Arbitral Tribunal at any time during the proceedings. 31.3. The final Award shall fix the costs of the arbitration and decide which of the parties shall bear them or in what proportion they shall be borne by the parties.	Such costs may include: (a) the fees and expenses of the arbitrators; (b) the costs of assistance required by the tribunal, including its experts; (c) the fees and expenses of the administrator; (d) the reasonable costs for legal representation of a successful party; and (e) any such costs incurred in connection with an application for interim or emergency relief pursuant to Article 21.	(b) The travel and other expenses incurred by the arbitrators; (c) The costs of expert advice and of other assistance required by the arbitral tribunal; (d) The travel and other expenses of witnesses to the extent such expenses are approved by the arbitral tribunal; (e) The costs for legal representation and assistance of the successful party if such costs were claimed during the arbitral proceedings, and only to the extent that the arbitral tribunal determines that the amount of such costs is reasonable; (f) Any fees and expenses of the appointing authority as well as the expenses of the Secretary-General of the Permanent Court of Arbitration at The Hague. 40.1. Except as provided in paragraph 2, the costs of arbitration shall in principle be borne by the unsuccessful party. However, the arbitral tribunal may apportion each of such costs between the parties if it determines that	limitation thereof.

particular circumstances this general approach is inappropriate. Any order for costs shall be made with reasons in the award containing such order. 28.5 If the arbitration is abandoned, suspended or concluded, by agreement or otherwise, before the final award is made, the parties shall remain jointly and severally liable to pay to the LCIA and the Arbitral Tribunal the costs of the arbitration as determined by the LCIA Court in accordance with the Schedule of Costs. In the event that such arbitration costs are less than the deposits made by the parties, there shall be a refund by the LCIA in such proportion as the parties may agree in writing, or failing such agreement, in the same proportions as the deposits were made by the parties to the LCIA. [See also 24.3 in previous section]			apportionment is reasonable, taking into account the circumstances of the case. 40.2. With respect to the costs of legal representation and assistance referred to in article 38, paragraph (e), the arbitral tribunal, taking into account the circumstances of the case, shall be free to determine which party shall bear such costs or may apportion such costs between the parties if it determines that apportionment is reasonable. 40.3. When the arbitral tribunal issues an order for the termination of the arbitral proceedings or makes an award on agreed terms, it shall fix the costs of arbitration referred to in article 38 and article 39, paragraph 1, in the text of that order or award. 40.4. No additional fees may be charged by an arbitral tribunal for interpretation or correction or completion of its award under articles 35 to 37.	

LCIA	ICC	ICDR	UNCITRAL	1996 ACT
EXCLUSION OF RECOURSE TO THE COURTS 22.2 By agreeing to arbitration under these Rules, the parties shall be treated as having agreed not to apply to any state court or other judicial authority for any order available from the Arbitral Tribunal under Article 22.1, except with the agreement in writing of all parties. 23.4 By agreeing to arbitration under these Rules, the parties shall be treated as having agreed not to apply to any state court or other judicial authority for any relief regarding the Arbitral Tribunal's jurisdiction or authority, except with the agreement in writing of all parties to the arbitration or the prior authorisation of the Arbitral Tribunal or following the latter's award ruling on the objection to its jurisdiction or authority. 26.9 . . . and the parties also waive irrevocably their right to any form of appeal, review or recourse to any state court or other judicial authority, insofar as such waiver may be validly made. 29.2 To the extent permitted by the law of the seat of the arbitration, the parties shall be taken to have waived any right of appeal or review in respect of any such decisions of the	28.6 . . . By submitting the dispute to arbitration under these Rules, the parties undertake to carry out any Award without delay and shall be deemed to have waived their right to any form of recourse insofar as such waiver can validly be made. [See also Article 6.2 under Jurisdiction]			Many sections including SS.45 and 69.

LCIA Court to any state court or other judicial authority. If such appeals or review remain possible due to mandatory provisions of any applicable law, the LCIA Court shall, subject to the provisions of that applicable law, decide whether the arbitral proceedings are to continue, notwithstanding an appeal or review.				
WAIVER OF RULES				
32.1 A party who knows that any provision of the Arbitration Agreement (including these Rules) has not been complied with and yet proceeds with the arbitration without promptly stating its objection to such non-compliance, shall be treated as having irrevocably waived its right to object.	33. A party which proceeds with the arbitration without raising its objection to a failure to comply with any provision of these Rules, or of any other rules applicable to the proceedings, any direction given by the Arbitral Tribunal, or any requirement under the arbitration agreement relating to the constitution of the Arbitral Tribunal, or to the conduct of the proceedings, shall be deemed to have waived its right to object.	25. A party who knows that any provision of the rules or requirement under the rules has not been complied with, but proceeds with the arbitration without promptly stating an objection in writing thereto, shall be deemed to have waived the right to object.	30. A party who knows that any provisions of, or requirement under, these Rules has not been complied with and yet proceeds with the arbitration without promptly stating his objection to such non-compliance, shall be deemed to have waived his right to object.	
EXCLUSION OF LIABILITY				
31.1 None of the LCIA, the LCIA Court (including its President, Vice Presidents and individual members), the Registrar, any deputy Registrar, any arbitrator and any expert to the Arbitral Tribunal shall be liable to any party howsoever for any act or omission in connection with any arbitration conducted by reference to	34. Neither the arbitrators, nor the Court and its members, nor the ICC and its employees, nor the ICC National Committees shall be liable to any person for any act or omission in connection with the arbitration.	35. The members of the tribunal and the administrator shall not be liable to any party for any act or omission in connection with any arbitration conducted under these rules, except that they may be liable for the consequences of conscious and deliberate wrongdoing.		S.29: Immunity of arbitrators. S.74: Immunity of arbitral institutions.

LCIA	ICC	ICDR	UNCITRAL	1996 ACT
these Rules, save where the act or omission is shown by that party to constitute conscious and deliberate wrongdoing committed by the body or person alleged to be liable to that party. 31.2 After the award has been made and the possibilities of correction and additional awards referred to in Article 27 have lapsed or been exhausted, neither the LCIA, the LCIA Court (including its President, Vice Presidents and individual members), the Registrar, any deputy Registrar, any arbitrator or expert to the Arbitral Tribunal shall be under any legal obligation to make anystatement to any person about any matter concerning the arbitration, nor shall any party seek to make any of these persons a witness in any legal or other proceedings arising out of the arbitration.				
PUNITIVE AND EXEMPLARY DAMAGES		28.5. Unless the parties agree otherwise, the parties expressly waive and forego any right to punitive, exemplary or similar damages unless a statute requires that compensatory damages be increased in a specified manner. This provision shall not apply to any award of arbitration costs to a party to compensate for dilatory or bad faith conduct in the arbitration.		

APPENDIX C.1

PART 62: ARBITRATION CLAIMS

CONTENTS OF THIS PART

Scope of this Part and interpretation	Rule 62.1

I—Claims under the 1996 Act

Interpretation	Rule 62.2
Starting the claim	Rule 62.3
Arbitration claim form	Rule 62.4
Service out of the jurisdiction	Rule 62.5
Notice	Rule 62.6
Case management	Rule 62.7
Stay of legal proceedings	Rule 62.8
Variation of time	Rule 62.9
Hearings	Rule 62.10

II—Other Arbitration Claims

Scope of this Section	Rule 62.11
Applications to Judge	Rule 62.12
Starting the claim	Rule 62.13
Claims in District Registries	Rule 62.14
Time limits and other special provisions about arbitration claims	Rule 62.15
Service out of the jurisdiction	Rule 62.16

III—Enforcement

Scope of this Section	Rule 62.17
Enforcement of awards	Rule 62.18
Interest on awards	Rule 62.19
Registration in High Court of foreign awards	Rule 62.20
Registration of awards under the Arbitration (International Investment Disputes) Act 1966	Rule 62.21

Scope of this Part and interpretation

62.1—(1) This Part contains rules about arbitration claims.

(2) In this Part—

(a) "the 1950 Act" means the Arbitration Act 1950[1];

1. 1950 c. 27.

(b) "the 1975 Act" means the Arbitration Act 1975[2];
(c) "the 1979 Act" means the Arbitration Act 1979[3];
(d) "the 1996 Act" means the Arbitration Act 1996[4];
(e) references to—
  (i) the 1996 Act; or
  (ii) any particular section of that Act
include references to that Act or to the particular section of that Act as applied with modifications by the ACAS Arbitration Scheme (England and Wales) Order 2001[5]; and
(f) "arbitration claim form" means a claim form in the form set out in the practice direction.

(3) Part 58 (Commercial Court) applies to arbitration claims in the Commercial Court, Part 59 (Mercantile Court) applies to arbitration claims in the Mercantile Court and Part 60 (Technology and Construction Court claims) applies to arbitration claims in the Technology and Construction Court, except where this Part provides otherwise.

I—CLAIMS UNDER THE 1996 ACT

Interpretation

62.2—(1) In this Section of this Part "arbitration claim" means—
(a) any application to the court under the 1996 Act;
(b) a claim to determine—
  (i) whether there is a valid arbitration agreement;
  (ii) whether an arbitration tribunal is properly constituted; or
what matters have been submitted to arbitration in accordance with an arbitration agreement;
(c) a claim to declare that an award by an arbitral tribunal is not binding on a party; and
(d) any other application affecting—
  (i) arbitration proceedings (whether started or not); or
  (ii) an arbitration agreement.

(2) This Section of this Part does not apply to an arbitration claim to which Sections II or III of this Part apply.

Starting the claim

62.3—(1) Except where paragraph (2) applies an arbitration claim must be started by the issue of an arbitration claim form in accordance with the Part 8 procedure.

(2) An application under section 9 of the 1996 Act to stay legal proceedings must be made by application notice to the court dealing with those proceedings.

2. 1975 c. 3; repealed by the Arbitration Act 1996 (c. 23), section 107(2) and Schedule 4 but continues to apply to claims commenced before 31 January 1997 by virtue of the Arbitration Act 1996 (Commencement No. 1) Order 1996 (S.I. 1996/3146), article 4 and Schedule 2.
3. 1979 c. 42; repealed by the Arbitration Act 1996 (c. 23), section 107(2) and Schedule 4 but continues to apply to claims commenced before 31 January 1997 by virtue of the Arbitration Act 1996 (Commencement No. 1) Order 1996 (S.I. 1996/3146), article 4 and Schedule 2.
4. 1996 c. 23.
5. S.I. 2001/1185.

(3) The courts in which an arbitration claim may be started are set out in the practice direction.

(4) Rule 30.5 applies with the modification that a judge of the Technology and Construction Court may transfer the claim to any other court or specialist list.

Arbitration claim form

62.4—(1) An arbitration claim form must—

(a) include a concise statement of—

(i) the remedy claimed; and

(ii) any questions on which the claimant seeks the decision of the court;

(b) give details of any arbitration award challenged by the claimant, identifying which part or parts of the award are challenged and specifying the grounds for the challenge;

(c) show that any statutory requirements have been met;

(d) specify under which section of the 1996 Act the claim is made;

(e) identify against which (if any) defendants a costs order is sought; and

(f) specify either—

(i) the persons on whom the arbitration claim form is to be served, stating their role in the arbitration and whether they are defendants; or

(ii) that the claim is made without notice under section 44(3) of the 1996 Act and the grounds relied on.

(2) Unless the court orders otherwise an arbitration claim form must be served on the defendant within 1 month from the date of issue and rules 7.5 and 7.6 are modified accordingly.

(3) Where the claimant applies for an order under section 12 of the 1996 Act (extension of time for beginning arbitral proceedings or other dispute resolution procedures), he may include in his arbitration claim form an alternative application for a declaration that such an order is not needed.

Service out of the jurisdiction

62.5—(1) The court may give permission to serve an arbitration claim form out of the jurisdiction if—

(a) the claimant seeks to—

(i) challenge; or

(ii) appeal on a question of law arising out of,

an arbitration award made within the jurisdiction;

(The place where an award is treated as made is determined by section 53 of the 1996 Act.)

(b) the claim is for an order under section 44 of the 1996 Act; or

(c) the claimant—

(i) seeks some other remedy or requires a question to be decided by the court affecting an arbitration (whether started or not), an arbitration agreement or an arbitration award; and

(ii) the seat of the arbitration is or will be within the jurisdiction or the conditions in section 2(4) of the 1996 Act are satisfied.

(2) An application for permission under paragraph (1) must be supported by written evidence—

(a) stating the grounds on which the application is made; and

(b) showing in what place or country the person to be served is, or probably may be found.

(3) Rules 6.24 to 6.29 apply to the service of an arbitration claim form under paragraph (1).

(4) An order giving permission to serve an arbitration claim form out of the jurisdiction must specify the period within which the defendant may file an acknowledgment of service.

Notice

62.6—(1) Where an arbitration claim is made under section 24, 28 or 56 of the 1996 Act, each arbitrator must be a defendant.

(2) Where notice must be given to an arbitrator or any other person it may be given by sending him a copy of—

(a) the arbitration claim form; and

(b) any written evidence in support.

(3) Where the 1996 Act requires an application to the court to be made on notice to any other party to the arbitration, that notice must be given by making that party a defendant.

Case management

62.7—(1) Part 26 and any other rule that requires a party to file an allocation questionnaire does not apply.

(2) Arbitration claims are allocated to the multi-track.

(3) Part 29 does not apply.

(4) The automatic directions set out in the practice direction apply unless the court orders otherwise.

Stay of legal proceedings

62.8—(1) An application notice seeking a stay of legal proceedings under section 9 of the 1996 Act[6] must be served on all parties to those proceedings who have given an address for service.

(2) A copy of an application notice under paragraph (1) must be served on any other party to the legal proceedings (whether or not he is within the jurisdiction) who has not given an address for service, at—

(a) his last known address; or

(b) a place where it is likely to come to his attention.

(3) Where a question arises as to whether—

(a) an arbitration agreement has been concluded; or

(b) the dispute which is the subject-matter of the proceedings falls within the terms of such an agreement,

the court may decide that question or give directions to enable it to be decided and may order the proceedings to be stayed pending its decision.

Variation of time

62.9—(1) The court may vary the period of 28 days fixed by section 70(3) of the 1996 Act for—

(a) challenging the award under section 67 or 68 of the Act; and

(b) appealing against an award under section 69 of the Act.

6. 1996 c. 23.

(2) An application for an order under paragraph (1) may be made without notice being served on any other party before the period of 28 days expires.

(3) After the period of 28 days has expired—

(a) an application for an order extending time under paragraph (1) must—

(i) be made in the arbitration claim form; and

(ii) state the grounds on which the application is made;

(b) any defendant may file written evidence opposing the extension of time within 7 days after service of the arbitration claim form; and

(c) if the court extends the period of 28 days, each defendant's time for acknowledging service and serving evidence shall start to run as if the arbitration claim form had been served on the date when the court's order is served on that defendant.

Hearings

62.10—(1) The court may order that an arbitration claim be heard either in public or in private.

(2) Rule 39.2 does not apply.

(3) Subject to any order made under paragraph (1)—

(a) the determination of—

(i) a preliminary point of law under section 45 of the 1996 Act; or

(ii) an appeal under section 69 of the 1996 Act on a question of law arising out of an award,

will be heard in public; and

(b) all other arbitration claims will be heard in private.

(4) Paragraph (3)(a) does not apply to—

(a) the preliminary question of whether the court is satisfied of the matters set out in section 45(2)(b); or

(b) an application for permission to appeal under section 69(2)(b).

II—OTHER ARBITRATION CLAIMS

Scope of this Section

62.11—(1) This Section of this Part contains rules about arbitration claims to which the old law applies.

(2) In this Section

(a) "the old law" means the enactments specified in Schedules 3 and 4 of the 1996 Act as they were in force before their amendment or repeal by that Act; and

(b) "arbitration claim" means any application to the court under the old law and includes an appeal (or application for permission to appeal) to the High Court under section 1(2) of the 1979 Act.[7]

(3) This Section does not apply to—

(a) a claim to which Section III of this Part applies; or

(b) a claim on the award.

7. 1979 c. 42; repealed by the Arbitration Act 1996 (c. 23), section 107(2) and Schedule 4 but continues to apply to claims commenced before 31 January 1997 by virtue of the Arbitration Act 1996 (Commencement No. 1) Order 1996 (S.I. 1996/3146), article 4 and Schedule 2.

Applications to Judge

62.12—A claim—

(a) seeking permission to appeal under section 1(2) of the 1979 Act;
(b) under section 1(5) of that Act (including any claim seeking permission); or
(c) under section 5 of that Act,

must be made in the High Court and will be heard by a judge of the Commercial Court unless any such judge directs otherwise.

Starting the claim

62.13—(1) Except where paragraph (2) applies an arbitration claim must be started by the issue of an arbitration claim form in accordance with the Part 8 procedure.

(2) Where an arbitration claim is to be made in existing proceedings—

(a) it must be made by way of application notice; and
(b) any reference in this Section of this Part to an arbitration claim form includes a reference to an application notice.

(3) The arbitration claim form in an arbitration claim under section 1(5) of the 1979 Act (including any claim seeking permission) must be served on—

(a) the arbitrator or umpire; and
(b) any other party to the reference.

Claims in District Registries

62.14—If—

(a) a claim is to be made under section 12(4) of the 1950 Act[8] for an order for the issue of a witness summons to compel the attendance of the witness before an arbitrator or umpire; and
(b) the attendance of the witness is required within the district of a District Registry,

the claim may be started in that Registry.

Time limits and other special provisions about arbitration claims

62.15—(1) An arbitration claim to

(a) remit an award under section 22 of the 1950 Act[9];
(b) set aside an award under section 23(2) of that Act[10] or otherwise; or
(c) direct an arbitrator or umpire to state the reasons for an award under section 1(5) of the 1979 Act,

8. 1950 c. 27; section 12(4) was repealed by the Arbitration Act 1996 (c. 23), section 107(2) and Schedule 4 but continues to apply to claims commenced before 31 January 1997 by virtue of the Arbitration Act 1996 (Commencement No. 1) Order 1996 (S.I. 1996/3146), article 4 and Schedule 2.

9. 1950 c. 27; section 22 was repealed by the Arbitration Act 1996 (c. 23), section 107(2) and Schedule 4 but continues to apply to claims commenced before 31 January 1997 by virtue of the Arbitration Act 1996 (Commencement No. 1) Order 1996 (S.I. 1996/3146), article 4 and Schedule 2.

10. 1950 c. 27; section 23(2) was repealed by the Arbitration Act 1996 (c. 23), section 107(2) and Schedule 4 but continues to apply to claims commenced before 31 January 1997 by virtue of the Arbitration Act 1996 (Commencement No. 1) Order 1996 (S.I. 1996/3146), article 4 and Schedule 2.

must be made, and the arbitration claim form served, within 21 days after the award has been made and published to the parties.

(2) An arbitration claim to determine any question of law arising in the course of a reference under section 2(1) of the Arbitration Act 1979 must be made, and the arbitration claim form served, within 14 days after—

(a) the arbitrator or umpire gave his consent in writing to the claim being made; or

(b) the other parties so consented.

(3) An appeal under section 1(2) of the 1979 Act must be filed, and the arbitration claim form served, within 21 days after the award has been made and published to the parties.

(4) Where reasons material to an appeal under section 1(2) of the 1979 Act are given on a date subsequent to the publication of the award, the period of 21 days referred to in paragraph (3) will run from the date on which reasons are given.

(5) In every arbitration claim to which this rule applies—

(a) the arbitration claim form must state the grounds of the claim or appeal;

(b) where the claim or appeal is based on written evidence, a copy of that evidence must be served with the arbitration claim form; and

(c) where the claim or appeal is made with the consent of the arbitrator, the umpire or the other parties, a copy of every written consent must be served with the arbitration claim form.

(6) In an appeal under section 1(2) of the 1979 Act—

(a) a statement of the grounds for the appeal specifying the relevant parts of the award and reasons; and

(b) where permission is required, any written evidence in support of the contention that the question of law concerns—

(i) a term of a contract; or

(ii) an event,

which is not a "one-off" term or event,

must be filed and served with the arbitration claim form.

(7) Any written evidence in reply to written evidence under paragraph (6)(b) must be filed and served on the claimant not less than 2 days before the hearing.

(8) A party to a claim seeking permission to appeal under section 1(2) of the 1979 Act who wishes to contend that the award should be upheld for reasons not expressed or fully expressed in the award and reasons must file and serve on the claimant, a notice specifying the grounds of his contention not less than 2 days before the hearing.

Service out of the jurisdiction

62.16—(1) Subject to paragraph (2)—

(a) any arbitration claim form in an arbitration claim under the 1950 Act or the 1979 Act; or

(b) any order made in such a claim,

may be served out of the jurisdiction with the permission of the court if the arbitration to which the claim relates—

(i) is governed by the law of England and Wales; or

(ii) has been, is being, or will be, held within the jurisdiction.

(2) An arbitration claim form seeking permission to enforce an award may be served out of the jurisdiction with the permission of the court whether or not the arbitration is governed by the law of England and Wales.

(3) An application for permission to serve an arbitration claim form out of the jurisdiction must be supported by written evidence—

(a) stating the grounds on which the application is made; and

(b) showing in what place or country the person to be served is, or probably may be found.

Rules 6.24 to 6.29 apply to the service of an arbitration claim form under paragraph (1).

(4) *Omitted*

(5) An order giving permission to serve an arbitration claim form out of the jurisdiction must specify the period within which the defendant may file an acknowledgment of service.

III—ENFORCEMENT

Scope of this Section

62.17—This Section of this Part applies to all arbitration enforcement proceedings other than by a claim on the award.

Enforcement of awards

62.18—(1) An application for permission under—

(a) section 66 of the 1996 Act[11];

(b) section 101 of the 1996 Act;

(c) section 26 of the 1950 Act[12]; or

(d) section 3(1)(a) of the 1975 Act,[13]

to enforce an award in the same manner as a judgment or order may be made without notice in an arbitration claim form.

(2) The court may specify parties to the arbitration on whom the arbitration claim form must be served.

(3) The parties on whom the arbitration claim form is served must acknowledge service and the enforcement proceedings will continue as if they were an arbitration claim under Section I of this Part.

(4) With the permission of the court the arbitration claim form may be served out of the jurisdiction irrespective of where the award is, or is treated as, made.

(5) Where the applicant applies to enforce an agreed award within the meaning of section 51(2) of the 1996 Act—

(a) the arbitration claim form must state that the award is an agreed award; and

(b) any order made by the court must also contain such a statement.

(6) An application for permission must be supported by written evidence—

(a) exhibiting—

(i) where the application is made under section 66 of the 1996 Act or under section 26 of the 1950 Act, the arbitration agreement and the original award (or copies);

11. 1996 c. 23.

12. 1950 c. 27; section 26 was repealed by the Arbitration Act 1996 (c. 23), section 107(2) and Schedule 4 but continues to apply to claims commenced before 31 January 1997 by virtue of the Arbitration Act 1996 (Commencement No. 1) Order 1996 (S.I. 1996/3146), article 4 and Schedule 2.

13. 1975 c. 3; repealed by the Arbitration Act 1996 (c. 23), section 107(2) and Schedule 4 but continues to apply to claims commenced before 31 January 1997 by virtue of the Arbitration Act 1996 (Commencement No. 1) Order 1996 (S.I. 1996/3146), article 4 and Schedule 2.

(ii) where the application is under section 101 of the 1996 Act, the documents required to be produced by section 102 of that Act; or

(iii) where the application is under section 3(1)(a) of the 1975 Act, the documents required to be produced by section 4 of that Act;

(b) stating the name and the usual or last known place of residence or business of the claimant and of the person against whom it is sought to enforce the award; and

(c) stating either—

(i) that the award has not been complied with; or

(ii) the extent to which it has not been complied with at the date of the application.

(7) An order giving permission must—

(a) be drawn up by the claimant; and

(b) be served on the defendant by—

(i) delivering a copy to him personally; or

(ii) sending a copy to him at his usual or last known place of residence or business.

(8) An order giving permission may be served out of the jurisdiction—

(a) without permission; and

(b) in accordance with rules 6.24 to 6.29 as if the order were an arbitration claim form.

(9) Within 14 days after service of the order or, if the order is to be served out of the jurisdiction, within such other period as the court may set—

(a) the defendant may apply to set aside the order; and

(b) the award must not be enforced until after—

(i) the end of that period; or

(ii) any application made by the defendant within that period has been finally disposed of.

(10) The order must contain a statement of—

(a) the right to make an application to set the order aside; and

(b) the restrictions on enforcement under rule 62.18(9)(b).

(11) Where a body corporate is a party any reference in this rule to place of residence or business shall have effect as if the reference were to the registered or principal address of the body corporate.

Interest on awards

62.19—(1) Where an applicant seeks to enforce an award of interest the whole or any part of which relates to a period after the date of the award, he must file a statement giving the following particulars—

(a) whether simple or compound interest was awarded;

(b) the date from which interest was awarded;

(c) where rests were provided for, specifying them;

(d) the rate of interest awarded; and

(e) a calculation showing—

(i) the total amount claimed up to the date of the statement; and

(ii) any sum which will become due on a daily basis.

(2) A statement under paragraph (1) must be filed whenever the amount of interest has to be quantified for the purpose of—

(a) obtaining a judgment or order under section 66 of the 1996 Act (enforcement of the award); or

(b) enforcing such a judgment or order.

Registration in High Court of foreign awards

62.20—(1) Where—

(a) an award is made in proceedings on an arbitration in any part of a United Kingdom Overseas Territory (within the meaning of rule 6.18(f)) or other territory to which Part I of the Foreign Judgments (Reciprocal Enforcement) Act 1933[14] ("the 1933 Act") extends;

(b) Part II of the Administration of Justice Act 1920[15] extended to that part immediately before Part I of the 1933 Act was extended to that part; and

(c) an award has, under the law in force in the place where it was made, become enforceable in the same manner as a judgment given by a court in that place,

rules 74.1 to 74.7 and 74.9 apply in relation to the award as they apply in relation to a judgment given by the court subject to the modifications in paragraph (2).

(2) The modifications referred to in paragraph (1) are as follows—

(a) for references to the State of origin are substituted references to the place where the award was made; and

(b) the written evidence required by rule 74.4 must state (in addition to the matters required by that rule) that to the best of the information or belief of the maker of the statement the award has, under the law in force in the place where it was made, become enforceable in the same manner as a judgment given by a court in that place.

Registration of awards under the Arbitration (International Investment Disputes) Act 1966

62.21—(1) In this rule—

(a) "the 1966 Act" means the Arbitration (International Investment Disputes) Act 1966[16];

(b) "award" means an award under the Convention;

(c) "the Convention" means the Convention on the settlement of investment disputes between States and nationals of other States which was opened for signature in Washington on 18 March 1965[17];

(d) "judgment creditor" means the person seeking recognition or enforcement of an award; and

(e) "judgment debtor" means the other party to the award.

(2) Subject to the provisions of this rule, the following provisions of Part 74 apply with such modifications as may be necessary in relation to an award as they apply in relation to a judgment to which Part I of the Foreign Judgments (Reciprocal Enforcement) Act 1933[18] applies—

(a) rule 74.1;

(b) rule 74.3;

(c) rule 74.4(1), (2)(a) to (d), and (4);

(d) rule 74.6 (except paragraph (3)(c) to (e)); and

(e) rule 74.9(2).

14. 1933 c. 13 (23 & 24 Geo. 5).

15. 1920 c. 81 (10 & 11 Geo. 5); section 10 of Part II was substituted by the Civil Jurisdiction and Judgments Act 1982 (c. 27), section 35(2) and section 14 of Part II was amended by the Civil Jurisdiction and Judgments Act 1982 (c. 27), section 35(3).

16. 1966 c. 41.

17. The text of the Convention is set out in the Schedule to the Arbitration (International Investment Disputes) Act 1966 (c. 41).

18. 23 & 24 Geo 5 c.13.

(3) An application to have an award registered in the High Court under section 1 of the 1966 Act[19] must be made in accordance with the Part 8 procedure.

(4) The written evidence required by rule 74.4 in support of an application for registration must—

- (a) exhibit the award certified under the Convention instead of the judgment (or a copy of it); and
- (b) in addition to stating the matters referred to in rule 74.4(2)(a) to (d) state whether—
  - (i) at the date of the application the enforcement of the award has been stayed (provisionally or otherwise) under the Convention; and
  - (ii) any, and if so what, application has been made under the Convention, which, if granted, might result in a stay of the enforcement of the award.

(5) Where, on granting permission to register an award or an application made by the judgment debtor after an award has been registered, the court considers—

- (a) that the enforcement of the award has been stayed (whether provisionally or otherwise) under the Convention; or
- (b) that an application has been made under the Convention which, if granted, might result in a stay of the enforcement of the award,

the court may stay the enforcement of the award for such time as it considers appropriate.

19. 1966 c. 41; section 1 was amended by the Administration of Justice Act 1977 (c. 38), sections 4 and 32(4) and Schedule 5, Part I and by the Supreme Court Act 1981 (c. 54), section 152(1) and Schedule 5.

APPENDIX C.2

PRACTICE DIRECTION—ARBITRATION

THIS PRACTICE DIRECTION SUPPLEMENTS PART 62

CONTENTS OF THIS PRACTICE DIRECTION

Section I

62.3—Starting the claim	Para. 2.1
62.4—Arbitration claim form	Para. 3.1
Acknowledgment of service or making representations by arbitrator or ACAS	Para. 4.1
Supply of documents from court records	Para. 5.1
62.7—Case management	Para. 6.1
Securing the attendance of witnesses	Para. 7.1
Interim remedies	Para. 8.1
Applications under sections 32 and 45 of the 1996 Act	Para. 9.1
Decisions without a hearing	Para. 10.1
62.9—Variation of time	Para. 11.1
Applications for permission to appeal	Para. 12.1

Section II

62.13—Starting the claim	Para. 14.1

Section III

62.21—Registration of awards under the Arbitration (International Investment Disputes) Act 1966	Para. 16.1

Section I

1.1 This Section of this Practice Direction applies to arbitration claims to which Section I of Part 62 applies.

1.2 In this Section "the 1996 Act" means the Arbitration Act 1996.

1.3 Where a rule provides for a document to be sent, it may be sent—

(1) by first class post;

(2) through a document exchange; or

(3) by fax, electronic mail or other means of electronic communication.

62.3—Starting the claim

2.1 An arbitration claim under the 1996 Act (other than under section 9) must be started in accordance with the High Court and County Courts (Allocation of Arbitration Proceedings) Order 1996 by the issue of an arbitration claim form.

2.2 An arbitration claim form must be substantially in the form set out in Appendix A to this practice direction.

2.3 Subject to paragraph 2.1, an arbitration claim form—

(1) may be issued at the courts set out in column 1 of the table below and will be entered in the list set out against that court in column 2;

(2) relating to a landlord and tenant or partnership dispute must be issued in the Chancery Division of the High Court.

Court	**List**
Admiralty and Commercial Registry at the Royal Courts of Justice, London	Commercial list
Technology and Construction Court Registry, St. Dunstan's House, London	TCC list
District Registry of the High Court (where mercantile court established)	Mercantile list
District Registry of the High Court (where arbitration claim form marked "Technology and Construction Court" in top right hand corner)	TCC list

2.3A An arbitration claim form must, in the case of an appeal, or application for permission to appeal, from a judge-arbitrator, be issued in the Civil Division of the Court of Appeal. The judge hearing the application may adjourn the matter for oral argument before two judges of that court.

62.4—Arbitration claim form

Service

3.1 The court may exercise its powers under rule 6.8 to permit service of an arbitration claim form at the address of a party's solicitor or representative acting for him in the arbitration.

3.2 Where the arbitration claim form is served by the claimant he must file a certificate of service within 7 days of service of the arbitration claim form.

(Rule 6.10 specifies what a certificate of service must show).

Acknowledgment of service or making representations by arbitrator or ACAS

4.1 Where—

(1) an arbitrator; or

(2) ACAS (in a claim under the 1996 Act as applied with modifications by the ACAS Arbitration Scheme (England and Wales) Order 2001)

is sent a copy of an arbitration claim form (including an arbitration claim form sent under rule 62.6(2)), that arbitrator or ACAS (as the case may be) may—

(a) apply to be made a defendant; or

(b) make representations to the court under paragraph 4.3.

4.2 An application under paragraph 4.1(2)(a) to be made a defendant—

(1) must be served on the claimant; but

(2) need not be served on any other party.

4.3 An arbitrator or ACAS may make representations by filing written evidence or in writing to the court.

Supply of documents from court records

5.1 An arbitration claim form may only be inspected with the permission of the court.

62.7—Case management

6.1 The following directions apply unless the court orders otherwise.

6.2 A defendant who wishes to rely on evidence before the court must file and serve his written evidence—

(1) within 21 days after the date by which he was required to acknowledge service; or,
(2) where a defendant is not required to file an acknowledgement of service, within 21 days after service of the arbitration claim form.

6.3 A claimant who wishes to rely on evidence in reply to written evidence filed under paragraph 6.2 must file and serve his written evidence within 7 days after service of the defendant's evidence.

6.4 Agreed indexed and paginated bundles of all the evidence and other documents to be used at the hearing must be prepared by the claimant.

6.5 Not later than 5 days before the hearing date estimates for the length of the hearing must be filed together with a complete set of the documents to be used.

6.6 Not later than 2 days before the hearing date the claimant must file and serve—

(1) a chronology of the relevant events cross-referenced to the bundle of documents;
(2) (where necessary) a list of the persons involved; and
(3) a skeleton argument which lists succinctly—
  (a) the issues which arise for decision;
  (b) the grounds of relief (or opposing relief) to be relied upon;
  (c) the submissions of fact to be made with the references to the evidence; and
  (d) the submissions of law with references to the relevant authorities.

6.7 Not later than the day before the hearing date the defendant must file and serve a skeleton argument which lists succinctly—

(1) the issues which arise for decision;
(2) the grounds of relief (or opposing relief) to be relied upon;
(3) the submissions of fact to be made with the references to the evidence; and
(4) the submissions of law with references to the relevant authorities.

Securing the attendance of witnesses

7.1 A party to arbitral proceedings being conducted in England or Wales who wishes to rely on section 43 of the 1996 Act to secure the attendance of a witness must apply for a witness summons in accordance with Part 34.

7.2 If the attendance of the witness is required within the district of a district registry, the application may be made at that registry.

7.3 A witness summons will not be issued until the applicant files written evidence showing that the application is made with—

(1) the permission of the tribunal; or
(2) the agreement of the other parties.

Interim remedies

8.1 An application for an interim remedy under section 44 of the 1996 Act must be made in an arbitration claim form.

Applications under sections 32 and 45 of the 1996 Act

9.1 This paragraph applies to arbitration claims for the determination of—

(1) a question as to the substantive jurisdiction of the arbitral tribunal under section 32 of the 1996 Act; and

(2) a preliminary point of law under section 45 of the 1996 Act.

9.2 Where an arbitration claim is made without the agreement in writing of all the other parties to the arbitral proceedings but with the permission of the arbitral tribunal, the written evidence or witness statements filed by the parties must set out any evidence relied on by the parties in support of their contention that the court should, or should not, consider the claim.

9.3 As soon as practicable after the written evidence is filed, the court will decide whether or not it should consider the claim and, unless the court otherwise directs, will so decide without a hearing.

Decisions without a hearing

10.1 Having regard to the overriding objective the court may decide particular issues without a hearing. For example, as set out in paragraph 9.3, the question whether the court is satisfied as to the matters set out in section 32(2)(b) or section 45(2)(b) of the 1996 Act.

10.2 The court will generally decide whether to extend the time limit under section 70(3) of the 1996 Act without a hearing. Where the court makes an order extending the time limit, the defendant must file his written evidence within 21 days from service of the order.

62.9—Variation of time

11.1 An application for an order under rule 62.9(1)—

(1) before the period of 28 days has expired, must be made in a Part 23 application notice; and

(2) after the period of 28 days has expired, must be set out in a separately identified part in the arbitration claim form.

Applications for permission to appeal

12.1 Where a party seeks permission to appeal to the court on a question of law arising out of an arbitration award, the arbitration claim form must—

(1) identify the question of law; and

(2) state the grounds

on which the party alleges that permission should be given.

12.2 The written evidence in support of the application must set out any evidence relied on by the party for the purpose of satisfying the court—

(1) of the matters referred to in section 69(3) of the 1996 Act; and

(2) that permission should be given.

12.3 The written evidence filed by the respondent to the application must—

(1) state the grounds on which the respondent opposes the grant of permission;

(2) set out any evidence relied on by him relating to the matters mentioned in section 69(3) of the 1996 Act; and
(3) specify whether the respondent wishes to contend that the award should be upheld for reasons not expressed (or not fully expressed) in the award and, if so, state those reasons.

12.4 The court will normally determine applications for permission to appeal without an oral hearing.

12.5 Where the court refuses an application for permission to appeal without an oral hearing, it must provide brief reasons.

12.6 Where the court considers that an oral hearing is required, it may give such further directions as are necessary.

SECTION II

13.1 This Section of this Practice Direction applies to arbitration claims to which Section II of Part 62 applies.

62.13—Starting the claim

14.1 An arbitration claim must be started in the Commercial Court and, where required to be heard by a judge, be heard by a judge of that court unless he otherwise directs.

SECTION III

15.1 This Section of this Practice Direction applies to enforcement proceedings to which Section III of Part 62 applies.

62.21—Registration of awards under the Arbitration (International Investment Disputes) Act 1966

16.1 Awards ordered to be registered under the 1966 Act and particulars will be entered in the Register kept for that purpose at the Admiralty and Commercial Registry.

N8 CLAIM FORM (ARBITRATION)

Claim Form
(arbitration)

In the	
	for court use only
Claim No.	
Issue date	

In an arbitration claim between

Claimant

SEAL

Defendant(s)

In the matter of an [intended] arbitration between

Claimant

Respondent(s) *Set out the names and addresses of persons to be served with the claim form stating their role in the arbitration and whether they are defendants.*

Defendant's name and address

☐ This claim will be heard on:

at am/pm

☐ This claim is made without notice.

The court office at

When corresponding with the court, please address forms or letters to the Court Manager and quote the case number.

N8 Claim form (arbitration)

Claim No.	

Remedy claimed and grounds on which claim is made

Claim No.	

The claimant seeks an order for costs against

Statement of Truth
*(I believe)(The Claimant believes) that the facts stated in these particulars of claim are true.
* I am duly authorised by the claimant to sign this statement

Full name ....

Name of claimant's solicitor's firm ....

signed.............................. position or office held ....
*(Claimant)(Claimant's solicitor) (if signing on behalf of firm or company)

delete as appropriate

Claimant's or claimant's solicitor's address to which documents should be sent if different from overleaf. If you are prepared to accept service by DX, fax or e-mail, please add details.

N8A NOTES FOR CLAIMANT

Arbitration Claim - notes for the claimant

Please read these guidance notes before you begin completing the claim form

The arbitration claim form may be used to start proceedings and make an application in existing proceedings. Where an application is being made in existing proceedings, an acknowledgment of service form is not required and the references to an acknowledgment of service form in the Notes for the Defendant should be deleted.

With the exception of:

- applications under section 9 of the Arbitration Act 1996; and
- certain proceedings which may be started only in the High Court or only in a county court - see High Court and County Courts (Allocation of Arbitration Proceedings) Order 1996, arbitration proceedings may be started in the courts set out in the table opposite.

Court	**List**
Admiralty and Commercial Registry at the Royal Courts of Justice, London	Commercial
Technology and Construction Court Registry, St Dunstan's House, London	TCC
District Registry of the High Court *(where Mercantile court established)*	Mercantile
District Registry of the High Court *(where the Claim form marked 'Technology and Construction Court' in top right hand corner)*	TCC
Central London County Court	Mercantile

Heading

You must fill in the heading of the claim form with:

- the name of the court (High Court or county court); and
- if issued in a District Registry, the name of the District Registry

Claimant and defendant details

You must provide your full name and address, including postcode and the full names and addresses of the defendants to be served. If a defendant is to be served outside England and Wales, the court's permission may need to be sought *(see Rule 62.5).*

Remedy claimed and grounds on which claim is made

You must:

- include a concise statement of
  - the remedy claimed; and
  - any questions on which you seek the decision of the court;
- give details of any arbitration award which you challenge, identifying which part or parts of the award are challenged and the grounds for the challenge;
- show that any statutory requirements have been met;
- specify under which section of the Act the claim is made;

Respondents

- if on notice, give the names and addresses of the persons on whom the arbitration claim form is to be served, stating their role in the arbitration and whether they are defendants; or
- state that the claim is made without notice under section 44(3) of the 1966 Act, and the grounds relied on.

Acknowledgment of service form

An acknowledgment of service form N15 must accompany the arbitration claim form. You should complete the heading on this form. Where the claim form is to be served out of the jurisdiction, you must amend the Notes for the Defendant to give the time within which the defendant must acknowledge service and file evidence. The claim form is valid for one month beginning with the date of its issue or, where required to be served out of the jurisdiction, for such period as the court may fix.

Address for documents

You must provide an address for service within England and Wales to which documents should be sent. That address must be either the business address of your solicitor, or your residential or business address.

Statement of Truth

The statement of truth must be signed by you or by your solicitor. Where the statement of truth is not signed by the solicitor and the claimant is a registered company or corporation, the statement of truth must be signed by either a director, the treasurer, secretary, chief executive, manager or other officer of the company and (in the case of a corporation) the mayor, chairman, president or town clerk.

You may rely on the matters set out in the claim form as evidence only if the claim form is verified by a statement of truth. You may also file an affidavit or witness statement in support of the arbitration claim, which must be served with the claim form.

N8A Arbitration claim - notes for claimant (04.06) HMCS

N8B NOTES FOR DEFENDANT

Arbitration Claim - notes for the defendant

Please read these guidance notes carefully before you respond to the arbitration claim form

Court staff can help you with procedures but they cannot give legal advice. If you need legal advice, you should contact a solicitor or a Citizens Advice Bureau immediately.

Responding to the claim

If you are:

- named as a defendant in the claim form; and
- served with a copy of it,

you should respond by completing and returning to the court office the acknowledgment of service form which was enclosed with the claim form, within *(14 days) (   ) of the date it was served on you. At the same time you must serve a copy on the claimant and any other party shown on the claim form.

If the claim form was:

- sent by post, the *(14 days) (   ) starts 2 days from the date of the postmark on the envelope;
- delivered or left at your address, the *(14 days) (   ) starts on the day it was given to you;
- handed to you personally, the *(14 days) (   ) starts on the day it was given to you.

The acknowledgment of service

If you:

- fail to complete and file the acknowledgment of service within the time specified; or
- if you indicate that you do not intend to contest the claim,

If you later change your mind, you will not be entitled to contest the claim without the court's permission.

Evidence

If you wish to rely on evidence before the court, you must file and serve your written evidence within *(21 days) (   ) of the date the claim form was served on you.

Statement of truth

The acknowledgment of service must be signed by you or by your solicitor. Where the acknowledgment of service is not signed by your solicitor and you are a registered company or corporation, it must be signed by either a director, the treasurer, secretary, chief executive, manager or other officer of the company and (in the case of a corporation) the mayor. Chairman, president or town clerk.

Notes for arbitrators

If you are:

- an arbitrator; or
- ACAS (in a claim under the 1996 Act as applied with modification by the ACAS (England and Wales) Order 2001),

who has been named as a defendant in the claim form, the above notes apply to you as they do to any other defendant.

If you were, or are:

- an arbitrator in the arbitration which led to this claim; and
- if you are not named as a defendant;

this claim form is sent to you for information

You may either:

- make a request (with notice only to the claimant) to be made a defendant
- may make representations to the court *(see paragraph 4.3 of practice direction to Part 62)*

**Claimant should alter where appropriate if the claim form is to be served out of the jurisdiction (see CPR Part6)*

N8B Arbitration claim - notes for defendant (03.02)

N15 ACKNOWLEDGEMENT OF SERVICE (ARBITRATION CLAIM)

Acknowledgment of Service
(arbitration claim)

In the	
Claim No.	
Claimant (including ref)	
Defendant	

You should read the 'notes for defendant' attached to the claim form which will tell you how to complete this form, and when and where to send it.

Tick and complete sections A - D as appropriate.
In all cases you must complete sections E and F

Section A

☐ I **do not** intend to contest this claim

Section B

☐ I intend to contest this claim

Give brief details of any different remedy you are seeking.

Section C

☐ I intend to dispute the court's jurisdiction
(Please note, any application must be filed within 14 days of the date on which you file this acknowledgment of service)

The court office at

When corresponding with the court, please address forms or letters to the Court Manager and quote the claim number.

N15 Acknowledgment of Service (arbitration) (03.02)

Claim No.	

Section D

☐ I intend to rely on written evidence

My written evidence:

☐ is filed with this form

☐ will be filed and served within 21 days after the date by which I am required to file this acknowledgment of service.

Section E

Full name of defendant filing this acknowledgment ______________________

Section F

Signed (To be signed by you or by your solicitor)	*(I believe)(The defendant believes) that the facts stated in this form are true. *I am duly authorised by the defendant to sign this statement **delete as appropriate*	**Position or office held** (if signing on behalf of firm or company)	

Date

Give an address in England or Wales to which notices about this case can be sent to you

Postcode

Tel. no.

if applicable	
Ref. no.	
fax no.	
DX no.	
e-mail	

APPENDIX D

THE ADMIRALTY & COMMERCIAL COURTS GUIDE

CONTENTS

. . .

Section F **Applications**
1 Generally
2 Applications without notice
3 Expedited applications
4 Paper applications
5 Ordinary applications
6 Heavy applications
7 Evidence
8 8 Reading time
9 9 Applications disposed of by consent
10 Hearing dates, time estimates and time limits
11 Application bundles
12 Chronologies, indices and *dramatis personae*
13 Authorities
14 Costs
15 Interim injunctions
16 Security for costs

. . .

Section O **Arbitration**
1 Arbitration claims

Claims under the Arbitration Act 1996

2 Starting an arbitration claim
3 The arbitration claim form
4 Service of the arbitration claim form
5 Acknowledgment of service
6 Standard directions
7 Interim remedies
8 Challenging the award
9 Time limits

Claims under the Arbitration Acts 1950–1979

10 Starting an arbitration claim
11 The arbitration claim form
12 Service of the arbitration claim form

13 Acknowledgment of service
14 Standard directions
15 Interim remedies
16 Challenging the award
17 Time limits

Provisions applicable to all arbitrations

18 Enforcement of awards
19 Matters of general application
20 Appointment of a Commercial Judge as arbitrator

. . .

APPENDICES

. . .

5 Forms of freezing injunction and search order

. . .

F. Applications

F1 Generally

F1.1 (a) Applications are governed by CPR Part 23 and PD23 as modified by rule 58 and PD58. As a result
- (i) PD23 §§1 and 2.3–2.6 do not apply;
- (ii) PD23 §§2.8 and 2.10 apply only if the proposed (additional) application will not increase the time estimate already given for the hearing for which a date has been fixed; and
- (iii) PD23 §3 is subject in all cases to the judge's agreeing that the application may proceed without an application notice being served.

(b) An adapted version of practice form N244 (application notice) has been approved for use in the Commercial Court.

F1.2 An application for a consent order must include a draft of the proposed order signed on behalf of all parties to whom it relates: **PD58 §14.1**.

F1.3 The requirement in PD23 §12.1 that a draft order be supplied on disk does not apply in the Commercial Court since orders are generally drawn up by the parties: **PD58 §14.2**.

Service

F1.4 Application notices are served by the parties, not by the court: **PD58 §9**.

Evidence

F1.5 (a) Particular attention is drawn to PD23 §9.1 which points out that even where no specific requirement for evidence is set out in the Rules or Practice Directions the court will in practice often need to be satisfied by evidence of the facts that are relied on in support of, or in opposition to, the application.

(b) Where convenient the written evidence relied on in support of an application may be included in the application notice, which may be lengthened for this purpose.

Time for service of evidence

F1.6 The time allowed for the service of evidence in relation to applications is governed by PD58 §13.

Hearings

F1.7 (a) Applications (other than arbitration applications) will be heard in public in accordance with rule 39.2, save where otherwise ordered.
(b) With certain exceptions, arbitration applications will normally be heard in private: **rule 62.10(3)**. See section O.
(c) An application without notice for a freezing injunction or a search order will normally be heard in private.

F1.8 Parties should pay particular attention to PD23 §2.9 which warns of the need to anticipate the court's wish to review the conduct of the case and give further management directions. The parties should be ready to give the court their assistance and should be able to answer any questions that the court may ask for this purpose.

F1.9 PD23 §§6.1–6.5 and §7 deal with the hearing of applications by telephone (other than an urgent application out of court hours) and the hearing of applications using video-conferencing facilities. These methods may be considered when an application needs to be made before a particular Commercial Judge who is currently on circuit. In most other cases applications are more conveniently dealt with in person.

F2 Applications without notice

F2.1 All applications should be made on notice, even if that notice has to be short, unless

(i) any rule or Practice Direction provides that the application may be made without notice; or
(ii) there are good reasons for making the application without notice, for example, because notice would or might defeat the object of the application.

F2.2 Where an application without notice does not involve the giving of undertakings to the court, it will normally be made and dealt with on paper, as, for example, applications for permission to serve a claim form out of the jurisdiction, and applications for an extension of time in which to serve a claim form.

F2.3 Any application for an interim injunction or similar remedy will require an oral hearing.

F2.4 (a) A party wishing to make an application without notice which requires an oral hearing before a judge should contact the Clerk to the Commercial Court at the earliest opportunity.
(b) If a party wishes to make an application without notice at a time when no commercial judge is available he should apply to the Queen's Bench Judge in Chambers.

F2.5 On all applications without notice it is the duty of the applicant and those representing him to make full and frank disclosure of all matters relevant to the application.

F2.6 The papers lodged for the application should include two copies of a draft of the order sought. Save in exceptional circumstances where time does not permit, all the evidence relied upon in support of the application and any other relevant documents must be lodged in advance with the Clerk to the Commercial Court. If the application is urgent, the Clerk to the Commercial Court should be informed of the fact and of the reasons for the urgency. Counsel's estimate of reading time likely to be required by the court should also be provided.

F3 Expedited applications

F3.1 The Court will expedite the hearing of an application on notice in cases of sufficient urgency and importance.

F3.2 Where a party wishes to make an expedited application a request should be made to the Clerk to the Commercial Court on notice to all other parties.

F4 Paper applications

F4.1 (a) Although contested applications are usually best determined at an oral hearing, some applications may be suitable for determination on paper.

(b) Attention is drawn to the provisions of rule 23.8 and PD23 §11. If the applicant considers that the application is suitable for determination on paper, he should ensure before lodging the papers with the court

(i) that the application notice together with any supporting evidence has been served on the respondent;

(ii) that the respondent has been allowed the appropriate period of time in which to serve evidence in opposition;

(iii) that any evidence in reply has been served on the respondent; and

(iv) that there is included in the papers

(A) the written consent of the respondent to the disposal of the application without a hearing; or

(B) a statement by the applicant of the grounds on which he seeks to have the application disposed of without a hearing, together with confirmation that a copy has been served on the respondent.

(c) Only in exceptional cases will the court dispose of an application without a hearing in the absence of the respondent's consent.

F4.2 (a) Certain applications relating to the management of proceedings may conveniently be made in correspondence without issuing an application notice.

(b) It must be clearly understood that such applications are not applications without notice and the applicant must therefore ensure that a copy of the letter making the application is sent to all other parties to the proceedings.

(c) Accordingly, the following procedure should be followed when making an application of this kind:

(i) the applicant should first ascertain whether the application is opposed by the other parties;

(ii) if it is, the applicant should apply to the court by letter stating the nature of the order which it seeks and the grounds on which the application is made;

(iii) a copy of the letter should be sent (by fax, where possible) to all other parties at the same time as it is sent to the court;

(iv) any other party wishing to make representations should do so by letter within two days (i.e. two clear days) of the date of the applicant's letter of application. The representations should be sent (by fax, where possible) to the applicant and all other parties at the same time as they are sent to the court;

(v) the court will advise its decision by letter to the applicant. The applicant must forthwith copy the court's letter to all other parties, by fax where possible.

F5 Ordinary applications

F5.1 Applications likely to require an oral hearing lasting half a day or less are regarded as "ordinary" applications.

F5.2 Ordinary applications will generally be heard on Fridays, but may be heard on other days. Where possible, the Listing Office will have regard to the availability of advocates when fixing hearing dates.

F5.3 Many ordinary applications, especially those in the non-Counsel list on Fridays, are very short indeed (e.g. applications to extend time). As in the past, it is likely that many, if not most, of such applications can be heard without evidence and on short (i.e. a few days) notice. The parties should however have in mind what is said in section F1.5(a) above.

F5.4 (a) The timetable for ordinary applications is set out in PD58 §13.1 and is as follows:

(i) evidence in support must be filed and served with the application;

(ii) evidence in answer must be filed and served within 14 days thereafter;

(iii) evidence in reply (if any) must be filed and served within 7 days thereafter.

(b) This timetable may be abridged or extended by agreement between the parties provided that any date fixed for the hearing of the application is not affected: **PD58 §13.4**. In appropriate cases, this timetable may be abridged by the Court.

F5.5 An application bundle (see section F11) must be lodged with the Listing Office by 1 p.m. one clear day before the date fixed for the hearing. The case management bundle will also be required on the hearing; this file will be passed by the Listing Office to the judge. Only where it is essential for the court on the hearing of the ordinary application to see the full version of a statement of case that has been summarised in accordance with section C1.4 above should a copy of that statement of case be lodged for the ordinary application.

F5.6 Save in very short and simple cases, skeleton arguments must be provided by all parties. These must be lodged with the Listing Office and served on the advocates for all other parties to the application by 1 p.m. on the day before the date fixed for the hearing (i.e. the immediately preceding day) together with an estimate of the reading time likely to be required by the court. Guidelines on the preparation of skeleton arguments are set out in Part 1 of Appendix 9.

F5.7 Thus, for an application estimated for a half day or less and due to be heard on a Friday:

(i) the application bundle must be lodged by 1 p.m. on Wednesday; and

(ii) skeleton arguments must be lodged by 1 p.m. on Thursday.

If, for reasons outside the reasonable control of the advocate a skeleton argument cannot be delivered to the Listing Office by 1 p.m., it should be delivered direct to the clerk of the judge listed to hear the application and in any event not later than 4 p.m. the day before the hearing.

F5.8 The applicant should, as a matter of course, provide all other parties to the application with a copy of the application bundle at the cost of the receiving party. Further copies should be supplied on request, again at the cost of the receiving party.

F5.9 Problems with the lodging of bundles or skeleton arguments should be notified to the Clerk to the Commercial Court as far in advance as possible. **If the application**

bundle or skeleton argument is not lodged by the time specified, the application may be stood out of the list without further warning.

F6 Heavy applications

F6.1 Applications likely to require an oral hearing lasting more than half a day are regarded as "heavy" applications.

F6.2 Heavy applications normally involve a greater volume of evidence and other documents and more extensive issues. They accordingly require a longer lead-time for preparation and exchange of evidence. Where possible the Listing Office will have regard to the availability of advocates when fixing hearing dates.

F6.3 The timetable for heavy applications is set out in PD58 §13.2 and is as follows:

(i) evidence in support must be filed and served with the application;
(ii) evidence in answer must be filed and served within 28 days thereafter;
(iii) evidence in reply (if any) must be filed and served as soon as possible, and in any event within 14 days of service of the evidence in answer.

F6.4 (a) An application bundle (see section F11) must be lodged with the Listing Office by 4 p.m. two days (i.e. two clear days) before the date fixed for the hearing together with a reading list and an estimate for the reading time likely to be required by the court as agreed between the counsel or other advocates to appear on the application. The case management bundle will also be required on the hearing; this file will be passed by the Listing Office to the judge.

(b) Only where it is essential for the court on the hearing of the application to see the full version of a statement of case that has been summarised in accordance with section C1.4 above should a copy of that statement of case be lodged for the application.

F6.5 Skeleton arguments must be lodged with the Listing Office and served on the advocates for all other parties to the application as follows:

(i) applicant's skeleton argument (with chronology unless one is unnecessary, and with a *dramatis personae* if one is warranted), by 4 p.m. two days (i.e. two clear days) before the hearing;
(ii) respondent's skeleton argument, by 4 p.m. one day (i.e. one clear day) before the hearing.

Guidelines on the preparation of skeleton arguments are set out in Part 1 of Appendix 9.

F6.6 Thus, for an application estimated for more than half a day and due to be heard on a Thursday:

(i) the application bundle and the applicant's skeleton argument must be lodged by 4 p.m. on Monday;
(ii) the respondent's skeleton argument must be lodged by 4 p.m. on Tuesday.

F6.7 The applicant must, as a matter of course, provide all other parties to the application with a copy of the application bundle at the cost of the receiving party. Further copies must be supplied on request, again at the cost of the receiving party.

F6.8 Problems with the lodging of bundles or skeleton arguments should be notified to the Clerk to the Commercial Court as far in advance as possible. **If the application bundle or skeleton argument is not lodged by the time specified, the application may be stood out of the list without further warning.**

F7 Evidence

F7.1 Although evidence may be given by affidavit, it should generally be given by witness statement, except where PD32 requires evidence to be given on affidavit (as, for example, in the case of an application for a freezing injunction or a search order: **PD32 §1.4**). In other cases the Court may order that evidence be given by affidavit: **PD32 §1.4(1) and 1.6**.

F7.2 Witness statements and affidavits must comply with the requirements of PD32, save that photocopy documents should be used unless the court orders otherwise.

F7.3 (a) Witness statements must be verified by a statement of truth signed by the maker of the statement: **rule 22.1**.

(b) At hearings other than trial an applicant may rely on the application notice itself, and a party may rely on his statement of case, if the application notice or statement of case (as the case may be) is verified by a statement of truth: **rule 32.6(2)**.

(c) A statement of truth in an application notice may also be signed as indicated in sections C1.8 and C1.9 above.

F7.4 Proceedings for contempt of court may be brought against a person who makes, or causes to be made, a false statement in a witness statement (or any other document verified by a statement of truth) without an honest belief in its truth: **rule 32.14(1)**.

F8 Reading time

F8 (a) It is essential for the efficient conduct of the court's business that the parties inform the court of the reading required in order to enable the judge to dispose of the application within the time allowed for the hearing and of the time likely to be required for that purpose. Accordingly

(i) in the case of all heavy applications and in the case of other applications, if any advocate considers that the time required for reading is likely to exceed two hours, each party must lodge with the Listing Office not later than 1 p.m. two clear days before the hearing of the application a reading list with an estimate of the time likely to be required by the court for reading;

(ii) in the case of all other applications each party must lodge with the Listing Office by 1 p.m. on the day before the date fixed for the hearing of an application (i.e. the immediately preceding day) a reading list with an estimate of the time required to complete the reading;

(iii) each party's reading list should identify the material on both sides which the court needs to read.

(b) Failure to comply with these requirements may result in the adjournment of the hearing.

F9 Applications disposed of by consent

F9.1 (a) Consent orders may be submitted to the court in draft for approval and initialling without the need for attendance.

(b) Two copies of the draft, one of which (or a counterpart) must be signed on behalf of all parties to whom it relates, should be lodged at the Registry. The copies should be undated. The order will be dated with the date on which the judge initials it, but that does not prevent the parties acting on their agreement immediately if they wish.

(c) The parties should act promptly in lodging the copies at the Registry. If it is important that the orders are made by a particular date, that fact (and the reasons for it) should be notified in writing to the Registry.

F9.2 For the avoidance of doubt, this procedure is not normally available in relation to a case management conference or a pre-trial review. Whether or not the parties are agreed as between themselves on the directions that the court should be asked to consider giving at a case management conference or a pre-trial review, attendance will normally be required.

F9.3 Where an order provides a time by which something is to be done the order should wherever possible state the particular date by which the thing is to be done rather than specify a period of time from a particular date or event: **rule 2.9**.

F10 Hearing dates, time estimates and time limits

F10.1 Dates for the hearing of applications to be attended by advocates are normally fixed after discussion with the counsel's clerks or with the solicitor concerned.

F10.2 The efficient working of the court depends on accurate estimates of the time needed for the oral hearing of an application. Over-estimating can be as wasteful as under-estimating.

F10.3 Subject to section F10.4, the Clerk to the Commercial Court will not accept or act on time estimates for the oral hearing of applications where those estimates exceed the following maxima:

Application to set aside service:	4 hours
Application for summary judgment:	4 hours
Application to set aside or vary interim remedy:	4 hours
Application to set aside or vary default judgment:	2 hours
Application to amend statement of case:	1 hour
Application for specific disclosure:	1 hour
Application for security for costs:	1 hour

F10.4 A longer listing time will only be granted upon application in writing specifying the additional time required and giving reasons why it is required. A copy of the written application should be sent to the advocates for all other parties in the case at the same time as it is sent to the Listing Office.

F10.5 (a) Not later than five days before the date fixed for the hearing the applicant must provide the Listing Office with his current estimate of the time required to dispose of the application.

(b) If at any time either party considers that there is a material risk that the hearing of the application will exceed the time currently allowed it must inform the Listing Office immediately.

F10.6 (a) All time estimates should be given on the assumption that the judge will have read in advance the skeleton arguments and the documents identified in the reading list. In this connection attention is drawn to section F8.

(b) A time estimate for an ordinary application should allow time for judgment and consequential matters; a time estimate for a heavy application should not.

F10.7 Save in the situation referred to at section F10.8, a separate estimate must be given for each application, including any application issued after, but to be heard at the same time as, another application.

F10.8 A separate estimate need not be given for any application issued after, but to be heard at the same time as, another application where the advocate in the case certifies in writing that

(i) the determination of the application first issued will necessarily determine the application issued subsequently; or

(ii) the matters raised in the application issued subsequently are not contested.

F10.9 If it is found at the hearing that the time required for the hearing has been significantly underestimated, the judge hearing the application may adjourn the matter and may make any special costs orders (including orders for the immediate payment of costs and wasted costs orders) as may be appropriate.

F10.10 Failure to comply with the requirements for lodging bundles for the application will normally result in the application not being heard on the date fixed at the expense of the party in default (see further sections F5.9 and F6.8 above). An order for immediate payment of costs may be made.

F11 Application bundles

F11.1 (a) Bundles for use on applications may be compiled in any convenient manner but must contain the following documents (preferably in separate sections in the following order):

(i) a copy of the application notice;
(ii) a draft of the order which the applicant seeks;
(iii) a copy of the statements of case;
(iv) copies of any previous orders which are relevant to the application;
(v) copies of the witness statements and affidavits filed in support of, or in opposition to, the application, together with any exhibits.

(b) Copies of the statements of case and of previous orders in the action should be provided in a separate section of the bundle. They should not be exhibited to witness statements.

(c) Witness statements and affidavits previously filed in the same proceedings should be included in the bundle at a convenient location. They should not be exhibited to witness statements.

(d) Where for the purpose of the application it is likely to be necessary for the court to read in chronological order correspondence or other documents located as exhibits to different affidavits or witness statements, copies of such documents should be filed and paged in chronological order in a separate composite bundle or bundles which should be agreed between the parties. If time does not permit agreement on the contents of the composite bundle, it is the responsibility of the applicant to prepare the composite bundle and to lodge it with the Listing Office by 4 p.m. two clear days before the hearing in the case of heavy applications and one clear day before the hearing in the case of all other applications.

F12 Chronologies, indices and *dramatis personae*

F12.1 For most applications it is of assistance for the applicant to provide a chronology which should be cross-referenced to the documents. *Dramatis personae* are often useful as well.

F12.2 Guidelines on the preparation of chronologies and indices are set out in Part 2 of Appendix 9.

F13 Authorities

F13.1 On some applications there will be key authorities that it would be useful for the judge to read before the oral hearing of the application. Copies of these authorities should be provided with the skeleton arguments.

F13.2 It is also desirable for bundles of the authorities on which the parties wish to rely to be provided to the judge hearing the application as soon as possible after skeleton arguments have been exchanged.

F13.3 Authorities should only be cited when they contain some principle of law relevant to an issue arising on the application and where their substance is not to be found in the decision of a court of higher authority.

F14 Costs

F14.1 Costs are dealt with generally at section J13.

F14.2 Reference should also be made to the rules governing the summary assessment of costs for shorter hearings contained in Parts 43 and 44.

F14.3 In carrying out a summary assessment of costs, the court may have regard amongst other matters to:

(i) advice from a Commercial Costs Judge or from the Chief Costs Judge on costs of specialist solicitors and counsel;
(ii) any survey published by the London Solicitors Litigation Association showing the average hourly expense rate for solicitors in London;
(iii) any information provided to the court at its request by one or more of the specialist associations on average charges by specialist solicitors and counsel.

F15 Interim injunctions

Generally

F15.1 (a) Applications for interim injunctions are governed by CPR Part 25.
(b) Applications must be made on notice in accordance with the procedure set out in CPR Part 23 unless there are good reasons for proceeding without notice.

F15.2 A party who wishes to make an application for an interim injunction must give the Clerk to the Commercial Court as much notice as possible.

F15.3 (a) Except when the application is so urgent that there has not been any opportunity to do so, the applicant must issue his claim form and obtain the evidence on which he wishes to rely in support of the application before making the application.
(b) On applications of any weight, and unless the urgency means that this is not possible, the applicant should provide the court at the earliest opportunity with a skeleton argument.
(c) An affidavit, and not a witness statement, is required on an application for a freezing injunction or a search order: **PD25 §3.1**.

Fortification of undertakings

F15.4 (a) Where the applicant for an interim remedy is not able to show sufficient assets within the jurisdiction of the Court to provide substance to the undertakings given, particularly the undertaking in damages, he may be required to reinforce his undertakings by providing security.
(b) Security will be ordered in such form as the judge decides is appropriate but may, for example, take the form of a payment into court, a bond issued by an insurance company or a first demand guarantee or standby credit issued by a first-class bank.
(c) In an appropriate case the judge may order a payment to be made to the applicant's solicitors to be held by them as officers of the court pending further order. Sometimes the undertaking of a parent company may be acceptable.

Form of order

F15.5 Standard forms of wording for freezing injunctions and search orders are set out in Appendix 5. The forms have been adapted for use in the Commercial Court and should be followed unless the judge hearing a particular application considers there is good reason for adopting a different form.

F15.6 A phrase indicating that an interim remedy is to remain in force until judgment or further order means that it remains in force until the delivery of a final judgment. If an interim remedy continuing after judgment is required, say until judgment has been satisfied, an application to that effect must be made.

F15.7 It is good practice to draft an order for an interim remedy so that it includes a proviso which permits acts which would otherwise be a breach of the order to be done with the written consent of the claimant's solicitors. This enables the parties to agree in effect to variations (or the discharge) of the order without the necessity of coming back to the court.

Freezing injunctions

F15.8 (a) Freezing injunctions made on an application without notice will provide for a return date, unless the judge otherwise orders: **PD25 §5.1(3)**. In the usual course, the return date given will be a Friday (unless a date for a case management conference has already been fixed, in which event the return date given will in the usual course be that date).

(b) If, after service or notification of the injunction, one or more of the parties considers that more than 15 minutes will be required to deal with the matter on the return date the Listing Office should be informed forthwith and in any event no later than 4 p.m. on the Wednesday before the Friday fixed as the return date.

(c) If the parties agree, the return date may be postponed to a later date on which all parties will be ready to deal with any substantive issues. In this event, an agreed form of order continuing the injunction to the postponed return date should be submitted for consideration by a judge and if the order is made in the terms submitted there will be no need for the parties to attend on the day originally fixed as the return date.

(d) In such a case the defendant and any other interested party will continue to have liberty to apply to vary or set aside the order.

F15.9 A provision for the defendant to give notice of any application to discharge or vary the order is usually included as a matter of convenience but it is not proper to attempt to fetter the right of the defendant to apply without notice or on short notice if need be.

F15.10 As regards freezing injunctions in respect of assets outside the jurisdiction, the standard wording in relation to effects on third parties should normally incorporate wording to enable overseas branches of banks or similar institutions which have offices within the jurisdiction to comply with what they reasonably believe to be their obligations under the laws of the country where the assets are located or under the proper law of the relevant banking or other contract relating to such assets.

F15.11 Any bank or third party served with, notified of or affected by a freezing injunction may apply to the court without notice to any party for directions, or notify the court in writing without notice to any party, in the event that the order affects or may affect the position of the bank or third party under legislation, regulations or procedures aimed to prevent money laundering.

Search orders

F15.12 Attention is drawn to the detailed requirements in respect of search orders set out in PD25 §§7.1–8.2. The applicant for the search order will normally be required to undertake not to inform any third party of the search order or of the case until after a specified date.

Applications to discharge or vary freezing injunctions and search orders

F15.13 Applications to discharge or vary freezing injunctions and search orders are treated as matters of urgency for listing purposes. Those representing applicants for discharge or variation should ascertain before a date is fixed for the hearing whether, having regard to the evidence which they wish to adduce, the claimant would wish to adduce further evidence in opposition. If so, all reasonable steps must be taken by all parties to agree upon the earliest practicable date at which they can be ready for the hearing, so as to avoid the last minute need to vacate a fixed date. In cases of difficulty the matter should be referred to a judge who may be able to suggest temporary solutions pending the hearing.

F15.14 If a freezing injunction or search order is discharged on an application to discharge or vary, or on the return date, the judge will consider whether it is appropriate that he should assess damages at once and direct immediate payment by the applicant. Where the judge considers that the hearing for the assessment of damages should be postponed to a future date he will give such case management directions as may be appropriate for the assessment hearing, including, if necessary, disclosure of documents and exchange of witness statements and experts' reports.

Applications under section 25 of the Civil Jurisdiction and Judgments Act 1982

F15.15 A Part 8 claim form (rather than an application notice: cf. rule 25.4(2)) must be used for an application under section 25 of the Civil Jurisdiction and Judgments Act 1982 ("Interim relief in England and Wales and Northern Ireland in the absence of substantive proceedings").

F16 Security for costs

F16.1 Applications for security for costs are governed by rules 25.12–14.
F16.2 The applicable practice is set out in Appendix 16.

O. Arbitration

O1 Arbitration claims

O1.1 (a) Applications to the court under the Arbitration Acts 1950–1996 and other applications relating to arbitrations are known as "arbitration claims".

(b) The procedure applicable to arbitration claims is to be found in Part 62 and its associated practice direction. Separate provision is made

(i) by Section I for claims relating to arbitrations to which the Arbitration Act 1996 applies;

(ii) by Section II for claims relating to arbitrations to which the Arbitration Acts 1950–1979 ("the old law") apply; and

(iii) by Section III for enforcement proceedings.

(c) For a full definition of the expression "arbitration claim" see rule 62.2(1) (claims under the 1996 Act) and rule 62.11(2) (claims under the old law).

(d) Part 58 applies to arbitration claims in the Commercial Court insofar as no specific provision is made by Part 62: **rule 62.1(3)**.

Claims under the Arbitration Act 1996

O2 Starting an arbitration claim

O2.1 Subject to section O2.3 an arbitration claim must be started by the issue of an arbitration claim form in accordance with the Part 8 procedure: **rule 62.3(1)**.

O2.2 The claim form must be substantially in the form set out in Appendix A to practice direction 62: **PD62 §2.2**.

O2.3 An application to stay proceedings under section 9 of the Arbitration Act 1996 must be made by application notice in the proceedings: **rule 62.3(2)**.

O2.4 Where a question arises as to whether an arbitration agreement is null and void, inoperative or incapable of being performed the court may deal with it in the same way as provided by rule 62.8(3) which applies where a question arises as to whether an arbitration agreement has been concluded or the dispute which is the subject matter of the proceedings falls within the terms of such an agreement.

O3 The arbitration claim form

O3.1 The arbitration claim form must contain, among other things, a concise statement of the remedy claimed and, if an award is challenged, the grounds for that challenge: **rule 62.4(1)**.

O3.2 Reference in the arbitration claim form to a witness statement or affidavit filed in support of the claim is not sufficient to comply with the requirements of rule 62.4(1).

O4 Service of the arbitration claim form

O4.1 An arbitration claim form issued in the Admiralty & Commercial Registry must be served by the claimant.

O4.2 (a) The rules governing service of the claim form are set out in Part 6 of the Civil Procedure Rules.

(b) Unless the court orders otherwise an arbitration claim form must be served on the defendant within 1 month from the date of issue: **rule 62.4(2)**.

O4.3 (a) An arbitration claim form may be served out of the jurisdiction with the permission of the court: **rule 62.5(1)**.

(b) Rules 6.24–6.29 apply to the service of an arbitration claim form out of the jurisdiction: **rule 62.5(3)**.

O4.4 The court may exercise its powers under rule 6.8 to permit service of an arbitration claim form on a party at the address of the solicitor or other representative acting for him in the arbitration: **PD62 §3.1**.

O4.5 The claimant must file a certificate of service within 7 days of serving the arbitration claim form: **PD62 §3.2**.

O5 Acknowledgment of service

O5.1 (a) A defendant must file an acknowledgment of service of the arbitration claim form in every case: **rule 58.6(1)**.

(b) An adapted version of practice form N210 (acknowledgment of service of a Part 8 claim form) has been approved for use in the Commercial Court. A copy of this practice form (Form N210(CC)) is included at the end of the Guide, together with adapted versions of the notes for claimants and defendants on completing and replying to an arbitration claim form.

O5.2 The time for filing an acknowledgment of service is calculated from the service of the arbitration claim form.

O6 Standard directions

O6.1 The directions set out in **PD62 §6.2–6.7** apply unless the court orders otherwise.

O6.2 The claimant should apply for a hearing date as soon as possible after issuing an arbitration claim form or (in the case of an appeal) obtaining permission to appeal.

O6.3 A defendant who wishes to rely on evidence in opposition to the claim must file and serve his evidence within 21 days after the date by which he was required to acknowledge service: **PD62 §6.2**.

O6.4 A claimant who wishes to rely on evidence in response to evidence served by the defendant must file and serve his evidence within 7 days after the service of the defendant's evidence: **PD62 §6.3**.

O6.5 An application for directions in a pending arbitration claim should be made by application notice under Part 23. Where an arbitration application involves recognition and/or enforcement of an agreement to arbitrate and that application is challenged on the grounds that the parties to the application were not bound by an agreement to arbitrate, it will usually be necessary for the court to resolve that issue in order to determine the application. For this purpose it may be necessary for there to be disclosure of documents and/or factual and/or expert evidence. In that event, it is the responsibility of those advising the applicant to liaise with the other party and to arrange with the Listing Office for a case management conference to be listed as early as possible to enable the court to give directions as to the steps to be taken before the hearing of the application.

O7 Interim remedies

O7.1 An application for an interim remedy under section 44 of the Arbitration Act 1996 must be made in an arbitration claim form: **PD62 §8.1**.

O8 Challenging the award

Challenge by way of appeal

O8.1 A party wishing to appeal against the award of an arbitrator or umpire must set out in the arbitration claim form

(i) the question of law on which the appeal is based; and
(ii) a succinct statement of the grounds of appeal,

identifying the relevant part(s) of the award and reasons.

O8.2 If the appeal is brought with the agreement of the other parties to the proceedings, a copy of their agreement in writing must be filed with the arbitration claim form.

O8.3 A party seeking permission to appeal must

(i) state in his arbitration claim form the grounds on which he contends that permission to appeal should be given: **PD62 §12.1**; and
(ii) file and serve with the arbitration claim form any written evidence on which he wishes to rely for the purposes of satisfying the court of the matters referred to in section 69(3) of the 1996 Act: **PD62 §12.2**.

O8.4 (a) If the defendant wishes to oppose the claimant's application for permission to appeal he must file a witness statement setting out
(i) the grounds on which he opposes the grant of permission; and
(ii) any evidence on which he relies in relation to the matters mentioned in section 69(3) of the 1996 Act: **PD62 §§12.3(1) & (2)**.

(b) If the defendant wishes to contend that the award should be upheld for reasons other than those expressed in the award, he must set out those reasons in his witness statement: **PD62 §12.3(3)**.

O8.5 The court will normally determine applications for permission to appeal without an oral hearing. If the court considers that an oral hearing is required, it will give further directions as appropriate.

Challenging an award for serious irregularity

O8.6 (a) An arbitration claim challenging an award on the ground of serious irregularity under section 68 of the 1996 Act is appropriate only in cases where there are grounds for thinking
(i) that an irregularity has occurred which
(ii) has caused or will cause **substantial** injustice to the party making the challenge.

(b) An application challenging an award on the ground of serious irregularity should therefore not be regarded as an alternative to, or a means of supporting, an application for permission to appeal.

O8.7 The challenge to the award must be supported by evidence of the circumstances on which the claimant relies as giving rise to the irregularity complained of and the nature of the injustice which has been or will be caused to him.

O8.8 If the nature of the challenge itself or the evidence filed in support of it leads the court to consider that the claim has no real prospect of success, the court may exercise its powers under rule 3.3(4) to dismiss the application summarily. In such cases the applicant will have the right to apply to the court to set aside the order and to seek directions for the hearing of the application.

Multiple claims

O8.9 If the arbitration claim form includes both a challenge to an award by way of appeal and a challenge on the ground of serious irregularity, the applications should be set out in separate sections of the arbitration claim form and the grounds on which they are made separately identified.

O8.10 In such cases the papers will be placed before a judge to consider how the applications may most appropriately be disposed of. It is usually more appropriate to dispose of the application to set aside or remit the award before considering the application for permission to appeal.

O9 Time limits

O9.1 An application to challenge an award under sections 67 or 68 of the 1996 Act or to appeal under section 69 of the Act must be brought within 28 days of the date of the award: **see section 70(3)**.

O9.2 The court has power to vary the period of 28 days fixed by section 70(3) of the 1996 Act: **rule 62.9(1)**. However, it is important that any challenge to an award be pursued without delay and the court will require cogent reasons for extending time.

O9.3 An application to extend time made **before** the expiry of the period of 28 days must be made in a Part 23 application notice, but the application notice need not be served on any other party: **rule 62.9(2)** and **PD62 §11.1(1)**.

O9.4 An application to extend time made **after** the expiry of the period of 28 days must be made in the arbitration claim form in which the applicant is seeking substantive relief: **rule 62.9(3)(a)**.

O9.5 An application to vary the period of 28 days will normally be determined without a hearing and prior to the consideration of the substantive application: **PD62 §10.2**.

Claims under the Arbitration Acts 1950–1979

O10 Starting an arbitration claim

O10.1 Subject to section O10.2 an arbitration claim must be started by the issue of an arbitration claim form in accordance with the Part 8 procedure: **rule 62.13(1)**.

O10.2 The claim form must be substantially in the form set out in Appendix A to PD62 §2.2.

O10.3 An application to stay proceedings on the grounds of an arbitration agreement must be made by application notice in the proceedings: **rule 62.13(2)**.

O11 The arbitration claim form

O11.1 An arbitration claim form must state the grounds of the claim or appeal: **rule 62.15(5)(a)**.

O11.2 Reference in the arbitration claim form to the witness statement or affidavit filed in support of the claim is not sufficient to comply with the requirements of rule 62.15(5)(a).

O12 Service of the arbitration claim form

O12.1 An arbitration claim form issued in the Admiralty & Commercial Registry must be served by the claimant.

O12.2 The rules governing service of the claim form are set out in Part 6 of the Civil Procedure Rules.

O12.3 (a) An arbitration claim form may be served out of the jurisdiction with the permission of the court: **rule 62.16(1)**.

(b) Rules 6.24–6.29 apply to the service of an arbitration claim form out of the jurisdiction: **rule 62.16(4)**.

O12.4 Although not expressly covered by PD62, the court may in an appropriate case exercise its powers under rule 6.8 to permit service of an arbitration claim form on a party at the address of the solicitor or other representative acting for him in the arbitration.

O12.5 The claimant must file a certificate of service within 7 days of serving the claim form.

Acknowledgment of service

O13.1 (a) A defendant must file an acknowledgment of service in every case: **rule 58.6(1)**.

(b) An adapted version of practice form N210 (acknowledgment of service of a Part 8 claim form) has been approved for use in the Commercial Court. A copy of this practice form (Form N210(CC)) is included at the end of the Guide, together with adapted versions of the notes for claimants and defendants on completing and replying to an arbitration claim form.

O13.2 The time for filing an acknowledgment of service is calculated from the service of the arbitration claim form.

O14 Standard directions

O14.1 Where the claim or appeal is based on written evidence, a copy of that evidence must be served with the arbitration claim form: **rule 62.15(5)(b)**.

O14.2 Where the claim or appeal is made with the consent of the arbitrator or umpire or other parties, a copy of every written consent must be served with the arbitration claim form: **rule 62.15(5)(c)**.

O14.3 An application for directions in a pending arbitration claim should be made by application notice under Part 23.

O15 Interim remedies

O15.1 An application for an interim remedy under section 12(6) of the 1950 Act must be made in accordance with Part 25.

O15.2 The application must be made by arbitration claim form.

O15.3 A claim under section 12(4) of the 1950 Act for an order for the issue of a witness summons to compel the attendance of a witness before an arbitrator or umpire where the attendance of the witness is required within the district of a District Registry may be started in that Registry: **rule 62.14**.

O16 Challenging the award

Challenge by way of appeal

O16.1 A party wishing to appeal against the award of an arbitrator or umpire must file and serve with the arbitration claim form a statement of the grounds for the appeal, specifying the relevant part(s) of the award and reasons: **rule 62.15(6)**.

O16.2 A party seeking permission to appeal must also file and serve with the arbitration claim form any written evidence in support of the contention that the question of law concerns a term of the contract or an event which is not "one off": **rule 62.15(6)**.

O16.3 Any written evidence in reply must be filed and served not less than 2 days before the hearing of the application for permission to appeal: **rule 62.15(7)**.

O16.4 A party who wishes to contend that the award should be upheld for reasons other than those set out in the award and reasons must file and serve on the claimant a notice specifying the grounds of his contention not less than 2 days before the hearing of the application for permission to appeal: **rule 62.15(8)**.

O16.5 Applications for permission to appeal will be heard orally, but will not normally be listed for longer than half an hour. Skeleton arguments should be lodged.

Claims to set aside or remit the award

O16.6 A claim to set aside or remit an award on the grounds of misconduct should not be regarded as an alternative to, or a means of supporting, an application for permission to appeal.

O16.7 The directions set out in PD62 §§6.2–6.7 should be followed unless the court orders otherwise.

Multiple claims

O16.8 If the arbitration claim form includes both an appeal and an application to set aside or remit the award, the applications should be set out in separate sections of the arbitration claim form and the grounds on which they are made separately identified.

O16.9 The court may direct that one application be heard before the other or may direct that they be heard together, as may be appropriate. It is usually more appropriate to dispose of the application to set aside or remit the award before considering the application for permission to appeal.

O17 Time limits

O17.1 (a) Time limits governing claims under the 1950 and 1979 Acts are set out in rule 62.15.

(b) Different time limits apply to different claims. **It is important to consult rule 62.15 to ensure that applications are made within the time prescribed.**

(c) The court has power under rule 3.1(2) to vary the time limits prescribed by rule 62.15, but will require cogent reasons for doing so.

Provisions applicable to all arbitrations

Enforcement of awards

O18.1 All applications for permission to enforce awards are governed by Section III of Part 62: **rule 62.17**.

O18.2 An application for permission to enforce an award in the same manner as a judgment may be made without notice, but the court may direct that the arbitration claim form be served, in which case the application will continue as an arbitration claim in accordance with the procedure set out in Section I: **rule 62.18(1)–(3)**.

O18.3 An application for permission to enforce an award in the same manner as a judgment must be supported by written evidence in accordance with rule 62.18(6).

O18.4 (a) Two copies of the draft order must accompany the application.

(b) If the claimant wishes to enter judgment, the form of the judgment must correspond to the terms of the award.

(c) The defendant has the right to apply to the court to set aside an order made without notice giving permission to enforce the award and the order itself must state in terms

(i) that the defendant may apply to set it aside within 14 days after service of the order or, if the order is to be served out of the jurisdiction, within such other period as the court may set; and

(ii) that it may not be enforced until after the end of that period or any application by the defendant to set it aside has been finally disposed of: **rule 62.18(9) & (10)**.

Matters of general application

O19 Transfer of arbitration claims

O19.1 An arbitration claim which raises no significant point of arbitration law or practice will normally be transferred

(i) if a rent-review arbitration, to the Chancery Division;
(ii) if a construction or engineering arbitration, to the Technology and Construction Court;
(iii) if an employment arbitration, to the Central London County Court Mercantile List.

O19.2 Salvage arbitrations will normally be transferred to the Admiralty Court.

O20 Appointment of a Commercial Judge as sole arbitrator or umpire

O20.1 Section 93 of the Arbitration Act 1996 provides for the appointment of a Commercial Judge as sole arbitrator or umpire. The Act limits the circumstances in which a Judge may accept such an appointment.

O20.2 Enquiries should be directed to the Judge in charge of the Commercial List or the Clerk to the Commercial Court.

Appendix 5

Forms of Freezing Injunction and Search Order

adapted for use in the Commercial Court

FREEZING INJUNCTION

IN THE HIGH COURT OF JUSTICE
QUEEN'S BENCH DIVISION
COMMERCIAL COURT

Before The Honourable Mr Justice [ ]

Claim No.

BETWEEN

Claimant(s)

—and—

Defendant(s)

Applicant(s)

Respondent(s)

PENAL NOTICE

If you [ ][1] disobey this order you may be held to be in contempt of court and may be imprisoned, fined or have your assets seized.

Any other person who knows of this order and does anything which helps or permits the Respondent to breach the terms of this order may also be held to be in contempt of court and may be imprisoned, fined or have their assets seized.

THIS ORDER

1. This is a Freezing Injunction made against [ ] ("the Respondent") on [ ] by Mr Justice [ ] on the application of [ ] ("the

1. Insert name of Respondent(s).

Applicant"). The Judge read the Affidavits listed in Schedule A and accepted the undertakings set out in Schedule B at the end of this order.

2. This order was made at a hearing without notice to the Respondent. The Respondent has a right to apply to the court to vary or discharge the order—see paragraph 13 below.
3. There will be a further hearing in respect of this order on [ ] ("the return date").
4. If there is more than one Respondent—
   (a) unless otherwise stated, references in this order to "the Respondent" mean both or all of them; and
   (b) this order is effective against any Respondent on whom it is served or who is given notice of it.

FREEZING INJUNCTION

[For injunction limited to assets in England and Wales]

5. Until the return date or further order of the court, the Respondent must not remove from England and Wales or in any way dispose of, deal with or diminish the value of any of his assets which are in England and Wales up to the value of £ .

[For worldwide injunction]

5. Until the return date or further order of the court, the Respondent must not—
   (1) remove from England and Wales any of his assets which are in England and Wales up to the value of £ ; or
   (2) in any way dispose of, deal with or diminish the value of any of his assets whether they are in or outside England and Wales up to the same value.

[For either form of injunction]

6. Paragraph 5 applies to all the Respondent's assets whether or not they are in his own name and whether they are solely or jointly owned. For the purpose of this order the Respondent's assets include any asset which he has the power, directly or indirectly, to dispose of or deal with as if it were his own. The Respondent is to be regarded as having such power if a third party holds or controls the asset in accordance with his direct or indirect instructions.
7. This prohibition includes the following assets in particular—
   (a) the property known as *[title/address]* or the net sale money after payment of any mortgages if it has been sold;
   (b) the property and assets of the Respondent's business [known as *[name]*] [carried on at *[address]*] or the sale money if any of them have been sold; and
   (c) any money in the account numbered *[account number]* at *[title/address]*.

[For injunction limited to assets in England and Wales]

8. If the total value free of charges or other securities ("unencumbered value") of the Respondent's assets in England and Wales exceeds £ , the Respondent may remove any of those assets from England and Wales or may dispose of or deal with them so long as the total unencumbered value of his assets still in England and Wales remains above £ .

[For worldwide injunction]

8. (1) If the total value free of charges or other securities ("unencumbered value") of the Respondent's assets in England and Wales exceeds £ , the Respondent may remove any of those assets from England and Wales or may dispose of or deal with them so long as the total unencumbered value of the Respondent's assets still in England and Wales remains above £ .

(2) If the total unencumbered value of the Respondent's assets in England and Wales does not exceed £ , the Respondent must not remove any of those assets from England and Wales and must not dispose of or deal with any of them. If the Respondent has other assets outside England and Wales, he may dispose of or deal with those assets outside England and Wales so long as the total unencumbered value of all his assets whether in or outside England and Wales remains above £ .

PROVISION OF INFORMATION

9. (1) Unless paragraph (2) applies, the Respondent must [immediately] [within hours of service of this order] and to the best of his ability inform the Applicant's solicitors of all his assets [in England and Wales] [worldwide] [exceeding £ in value] whether in his own name or not and whether solely or jointly owned, giving the value, location and details of all such assets.
(2) If the provision of any of this information is likely to incriminate the Respondent, he may be entitled to refuse to provide it, but is recommended to take legal advice before refusing to provide the information. Wrongful refusal to provide the information is contempt of court and may render the Respondent liable to be imprisoned, fined or have his assets seized.
10. Within [ ] working days after being served with this order, the Respondent must swear and serve on the Applicant's solicitors an affidavit setting out the above information.

EXCEPTIONS TO THIS ORDER

11.(1) This order does not prohibit the Respondent from spending £ a week towards his ordinary living expenses and also £ [*or* a reasonable sum] on legal advice and representation. [But before spending any money the Respondent must tell the Applicant's legal representatives where the money is to come from.]
[(2) This order does not prohibit the Respondent from dealing with or disposing of any of his assets in the ordinary and proper course of business.]
(3) The Respondent may agree with the Applicant's legal representatives that the above spending limits should be increased or that this order should be varied in any other respect, but any agreement must be in writing.
(4) The order will cease to have effect if the Respondent—
(a) provides security by paying the sum of £ into court, to be held to the order of the court; or
(b) makes provision for security in that sum by another method agreed with the Applicant's legal representatives.

COSTS

12. The costs of this application are reserved to the judge hearing the application on the return date.

VARIATION OR DISCHARGE OF THIS ORDER

13. Anyone served with or notified of this order may apply to the court at any time to vary or discharge this order (or so much of it as affects that person), but they must first inform the Applicant's solicitors. If any evidence is to be relied

upon in support of the application, the substance of it must be communicated in writing to the Applicant's solicitors in advance.

INTERPRETATION OF THIS ORDER

14. A Respondent who is an individual who is ordered not to do something must not do it himself or in any other way. He must not do it through others acting on his behalf or on his instructions or with his encouragement.
15. A Respondent which is not an individual which is ordered not to do something must not do it itself or by its directors, officers, partners, employees or agents or in any other way.

PARTIES OTHER THAN THE APPLICANT AND RESPONDENT

16. **Effect of this order**
    It is a contempt of court for any person notified of this order knowingly to assist in or permit a breach of this order. Any person doing so may be imprisoned, fined or have their assets seized.
17. **Set off by banks**
    This injunction does not prevent any bank from exercising any right of set off it may have in respect of any facility which it gave to the respondent before it was notified of this order.
18. **Withdrawals by the Respondent**
    No bank need enquire as to the application or proposed application of any money withdrawn by the Respondent if the withdrawal appears to be permitted by this order.

[For worldwide injunction]

19. **Persons outside England and Wales**
    (1) Except as provided in paragraph (2) below, the terms of this order do not affect or concern anyone outside the jurisdiction of this court.
    (2) The terms of this order will affect the following persons in a country or state outside the jurisdiction of this court—
        (a) the Respondent or his officer or agent appointed by power of attorney;
        (b) any person who—
            (i) is subject to the jurisdiction of this court;
            (ii) has been given written notice of this order at his residence or place of business within the jurisdiction of this court; and
            (iii) is able to prevent acts or omissions outside the jurisdiction of this court which constitute or assist in a breach of the terms of this order; and
        (c) any other person, only to the extent that this order is declared enforceable by or is enforced by a court in that country or state.

[For worldwide injunction]

20. **Assets located outside England and Wales**
    Nothing in this order shall, in respect of assets located outside England and Wales, prevent any third party from complying with—
    (1) what it reasonably believes to be its obligations, contractual or otherwise, under the laws and obligations of the country or state in which those assets are situated or under the proper law of any contract between itself and the Respondent; and
    (2) any orders of the courts of that country or state, provided that reasonable notice of any application for such an order is given to the Applicant's solicitors.

COMMUNICATIONS WITH THE COURT

All communications to the court about this order should be sent to Room EB09, Royal Courts of Justice, Strand, London WC2A 2LL quoting the case number. The telephone number is 020 7947 6826.

The offices are open between 10 a.m. and 4.30 p.m. Monday to Friday.

SCHEDULE A

AFFIDAVITS

The Applicant relied on the following affidavits—

[name]	[number of affidavit]	[date sworn]	[filed on behalf of]
(1)			
(2)			

SCHEDULE B

UNDERTAKINGS GIVEN TO THE COURT BY THE APPLICANT

(1) If the court later finds that this order has caused loss to the Respondent, and decides that the Respondent should be compensated for that loss, the Applicant will comply with any order the court may make.

[(2) The Applicant will—

(a) on or before *[date]* cause a written guarantee in the sum of £ to be issued from a bank with a place of business within England or Wales, in respect of any order the court may make pursuant to paragraph (1) above; and

(b) immediately upon issue of the guarantee, cause a copy of it to be served on the Respondent.]

(3) As soon as practicable the Applicant will issue and serve a claim form [in the form of the draft produced to the court] [claiming the appropriate relief].

(4) The Applicant will [swear and file an affidavit] [cause an affidavit to be sworn and filed] [substantially in the terms of the draft affidavit produced to the court] [confirming the substance of what was said to the court by the Applicant's counsel/solicitors].

(5) The Applicant will serve upon the Respondent [together with this order] [as soon as practicable]—

(i) copies of the affidavits and exhibits containing the evidence relied upon by the Applicant, and any other documents provided to the court on the making of the application;

(ii) the claim form; and

(iii) an application notice for continuation of the order.

[(6) Anyone notified of this order will be given a copy of it by the Applicant's legal representatives.]

(7) The Applicant will pay the reasonable costs of anyone other than the Respondent which have been incurred as a result of this order including the costs of finding out whether that person holds any of the Respondent's assets and if the court later finds that this order has caused such person loss, and decides that such person should be compensated for that loss, the Applicant will comply with any order the court may make.

(8) If this order ceases to have effect (for example, if the Respondent provides security or the Applicant does not provide a bank guarantee as provided for

above) the Applicant will immediately take all reasonable steps to inform in writing anyone to whom he has given notice of this order, or who he has reasonable grounds for supposing may act upon this order, that it has ceased to have effect.

[(9) The Applicant will not without the permission of the court use any information obtained as a result of this order for the purpose of any civil or criminal proceedings, either in England and Wales or in any other jurisdiction, other than this claim.]

[(10) The Applicant will not without the permission of the court seek to enforce this order in any country outside England and Wales [or seek an order of a similar nature including orders conferring a charge or other security against the Respondent or the Respondent's assets].]

NAME AND ADDRESS OF APPLICANT'S LEGAL REPRESENTATIVES

The Applicant's legal representatives are—

[Name, address, reference, fax and telephone numbers both in and out of office hours and e-mail]

****SEARCH ORDER****

IN THE HIGH COURT OF JUSTICE
QUEEN'S BENCH DIVISION
COMMERCIAL COURT

Before the Honourable Mr Justice [ ]

Claim No.

BETWEEN

Claimant(s)

—and—

Defendant(s)

Applicant(s)

Respondent(s)

PENAL NOTICE

If you [ ][2] disobey this order you may be held to be in contempt of court and may be imprisoned, fined or have your assets seized.

Any other person who knows of this Order and does anything which helps or permits the Respondent to breach the terms of this Order may also be held to be in contempt of court and may be imprisoned, fined or have their assets seized.

2. Insert name of Respondent.

THIS ORDER

1. This is a Search Order made against [ ] ("the Respondent") on [ ] by Mr Justice [ ] on the application of [ ] ("the Applicant"). The Judge read the Affidavits listed in Schedule F and accepted the undertakings set out in Schedules C, D and E at the end of this order.
2. This order was made at a hearing without notice to the Respondent. The Respondent has a right to apply to the court to vary or discharge the order—see paragraph 27 below.
3. There will be a further hearing in respect of this order on [ ] ("the return date").
4. If there is more than one Respondent—
   (a) unless otherwise stated, references in this order to "the Respondent" mean both or all of them; and
   (b) this order is effective against any Respondent on whom it is served or who is given notice of it.
5. This order must be complied with by—
   (a) the Respondent;
   (b) any director, officer, partner or responsible employee of the Respondent; and
   (c) if the Respondent is an individual, any other person having responsible control of the premises to be searched.

THE SEARCH

6. The Respondent must permit the following persons[3]—
   (a) [ ] ("the Supervising Solicitor");
   (b) [ ], a solicitor in the firm of [ ], the Applicant's solicitors; and
   (c) up to [ ] other persons[4] being [*their identity or capacity*] accompanying them,

   (together "the search party"), to enter the premises mentioned in Schedule A to this order and any other premises of the Respondent disclosed under paragraph 18 below and any vehicles under the Respondent's control on or around the premises ("the premises") so that they can search for, inspect, photograph or photocopy, and deliver into the safekeeping of the Applicant's solicitors all the documents and articles which are listed in Schedule B to this order ("the listed items").
7. Having permitted the search party to enter the premises, the Respondent must allow the search party to remain on the premises until the search is complete. In the event that it becomes necessary for any of those persons to leave the premises before the search is complete, the Respondent must allow them to re-enter the premises immediately upon their seeking re-entry on the same or the following day in order to complete the search.

RESTRICTIONS ON SEARCH

8. This order may not be carried out at the same time as a police search warrant.

3. Where the premises are likely to be occupied by an unaccompanied woman and the Supervising Solicitor is a man, at least one of the persons accompanying him should be a woman.

4. None of these persons should be people who could gain personally or commercially from anything they might read or see on the premises, unless their presence is essential.

9. Before the Respondent allows anybody onto the premises to carry out this order, he is entitled to have the Supervising Solicitor explain to him what it means in everyday language.
10. The Respondent is entitled to seek legal advice and to ask the court to vary or discharge this order. Whilst doing so, he may ask the Supervising Solicitor to delay starting the search for up to two hours or such other longer period as the Supervising Solicitor may permit. However, the Respondent must—
 (a) comply with the terms of paragraph 27 below;
 (b) not disturb or remove any listed items; and
 (c) permit the Supervising Solicitor to enter, but not start to search.
11. Before permitting entry to the premises by any person other than the Supervising Solicitor, the Respondent may, for a short time (not to exceed two hours, unless the Supervising Solicitor agrees to a longer period), gather together any documents he believes may be [incriminating or][5] privileged and hand them to the Supervising Solicitor for him to assess whether they are [incriminating or] privileged as claimed. If the Supervising Solicitor decides that any of the documents may be [incriminating or] privileged or is in any doubt as to their status, he will exclude them from the search and retain them in his possession pending further order of the court.
12. If the Respondent wishes to take legal advice and gather documents as permitted, he must first inform the Supervising Solicitor and keep him informed of the steps being taken.
13. No item may be removed from the premises until a list of the items to be removed has been prepared, and a copy of the list has been supplied to the Respondent, and he has been given a reasonable opportunity to check the list.
14. The premises must not be searched, and items must not be removed from them, except in the presence of the Respondent.
15. If the Supervising Solicitor is satisfied that full compliance with paragraphs 13 or 14 is not practicable, he may permit the search to proceed and items to be removed without fully complying with them.

DELIVERY UP OF ARTICLES/DOCUMENTS

16. The Respondent must immediately hand over to the Applicant's solicitors any of the listed items, which are in his possession or under his control, save for any computer or hard disk integral to any computer. Any items the subject of a dispute as to whether they are listed items must immediately be handed over to the Supervising Solicitor for safe keeping pending resolution of the dispute or further order of the court.
17. The Respondent must immediately give the search party effective access to the computers on the premises, with all necessary passwords, to enable the computers to be searched. If they contain any listed items the Respondent must cause the listed items to be displayed so that they can be read and copied.[6] The Respondent must provide the Applicant's Solicitors with copies of all listed items contained in the computers. All reasonable steps shall be taken by the Applicant and the Applicant's solicitors to ensure that no damage

5. References to incriminating documents should be omitted from orders made in intellectual property proceedings, where the privilege against self-incrimination does not apply—see paragraph 8.4 of the practice direction.

6. If it is envisaged that the Respondent's computers are to be imaged (i.e. the hard drives are to be copied wholesale, thereby reproducing listed items and other items indiscriminately), special provision needs to be made and independent computer specialists need to be appointed, who should be required to give undertakings to the court.

is done to any computer or data. The Applicant and his representatives may not themselves search the Respondent's computers unless they have sufficient expertise to do so without damaging the Respondent's system.

PROVISION OF INFORMATION

18. The Respondent must immediately inform the Applicant's Solicitors (in the presence of the Supervising Solicitor) so far as he is aware—
    (a) where all the listed items are;
    (b) the name and address of everyone who has supplied him, or offered to supply him, with listed items;
    (c) the name and address of everyone to whom he has supplied, or offered to supply, listed items; and
    (d) full details of the dates and quantities of every such supply and offer.
19. Within [ ] working days after being served with this order the Respondent must swear and serve an affidavit setting out the above information.[7]

PROHIBITED ACTS

20. Except for the purpose of obtaining legal advice, the Respondent must not directly or indirectly inform anyone of these proceedings or of the contents of this order, or warn anyone that proceedings have been or may be brought against him by the Applicant until 4.30 p.m. on the return date or further order of the court.
21. Until 4.30 p.m. on the return date the Respondent must not destroy, tamper with, cancel or part with possession, power, custody or control of the listed items otherwise than in accordance with the terms of this order.
22. [Insert any negative injunctions.]
23. [Insert any further order.]

COSTS

24. The costs of this application are reserved to the judge hearing the application on the return date.

RESTRICTIONS ON SERVICE

25. This order may only be served between [ ] a.m./p.m. and [ ] a.m./p.m. [and on a weekday].[8]
26. This order must be served by the Supervising Solicitor, and paragraph 6 of the order must be carried out in his presence and under his supervision.

VARIATION AND DISCHARGE OF THIS ORDER

27. Anyone served with or notified of this order may apply to the court at any time to vary or discharge this order (or so much of it as affects that person), but they must first inform the Applicant's solicitors. If any evidence is to be relied

7. The period should ordinarily be longer than the period in paragraph (2) of Schedule D, if any of the information is likely to be included in listed items taken away of which the Respondent does not have copies.

8. Normally, the order should be served in the morning (not before 9.30 a.m.) and on a weekday to enable the Respondent more readily to obtain legal advice.

upon in support of the application, the substance of it must be communicated in writing to the Applicant's solicitors in advance.

INTERPRETATION OF THIS ORDER

28. Any requirement that something shall be done to or in the presence of the Respondent means—
    (a) if there is more than one Respondent, to or in the presence of any one of them; and
    (b) if a Respondent is not an individual, to or in the presence of a director, officer, partner or responsible employee.
29. A Respondent who is an individual who is ordered not to do something must not do it himself or in any other way. He must not do it through others acting on his behalf or on his instructions or with his encouragement.
30. A Respondent which is not an individual which is ordered not to do something must not do it itself or by its directors, officers, partners, employees or agents or in any other way.

COMMUNICATIONS WITH THE COURT

All communications to the court about this order should be sent to Room EB09, Royal Courts of Justice, Strand, London WC2A 2LL quoting the case number. The telephone number is 020 7947 6826.

The offices are open between 10 a.m. and 4.30 p.m. Monday to Friday.

SCHEDULE A

THE PREMISES

SCHEDULE B

THE LISTED ITEMS

SCHEDULE C

UNDERTAKINGS GIVEN TO THE COURT BY THE APPLICANT

(1) If the court later finds that this order or carrying it out has caused loss to the Respondent, and decides that the Respondent should be compensated for that loss, the Applicant will comply with any order the court may make. Further if the carrying out of this order has been in breach of the terms of this order or otherwise in a manner inconsistent with the Applicant's solicitors' duties as officers of the court, the Applicant will comply with any order for damages the court may make.

[(2) As soon as practicable the Applicant will issue a claim form [in the form of the draft produced to the court] [claiming the appropriate relief].]

(3) The Applicant will [swear and file an affidavit] [cause an affidavit to be sworn and filed] [substantially in the terms of the draft affidavit produced to the court] [confirming the substance of what was said to the court by the Applicant's counsel/solicitors].

(4) The Applicant will not, without the permission of the court use any information or documents obtained as a result of carrying out this order nor inform anyone else of these proceedings except for the purposes of these proceedings (including adding further Respondents) or commencing

civil proceedings in relation to the same or related subject matter to these proceedings until after the return date.

[(5) The Applicant will maintain pending further order the sum of £] in an account controlled by the Applicant's solicitors.]

[(6) The Applicant will insure the items removed from the premises.]

SCHEDULE D

UNDERTAKINGS GIVEN BY THE APPLICANT'S SOLICITORS

(1) The Applicant's solicitors will provide to the Supervising Solicitor for service on the Respondent—
  (i) a service copy of this order;
  (ii) the claim form (with defendant's response pack) or, if not issued, the draft produced to the court;
  (iii) an application for hearing on the return date;
  (iv) copies of the affidavits *[or draft affidavits]* and exhibits capable of being copied containing the evidence relied upon by the applicant;
  (v) a note of any allegation of fact made orally to the court where such allegation is not contained in the affidavits or draft affidavits read by the judge; and
  (vi) a copy of the skeleton argument produced to the court by the Applicant's [counsel/solicitors].

(2) The Applicants' solicitors will answer at once to the best of their ability any question whether a particular item is a listed item.

(3) Subject as provided below the Applicant's solicitors will retain in their own safe keeping all items obtained as a result of this order until the court directs otherwise.

(4) The Applicant's solicitors will return the originals of all documents obtained as a result of this order (except original documents which belong to the Applicant) as soon as possible and in any event within [two] working days of their removal.

SCHEDULE E

UNDERTAKINGS GIVEN BY THE SUPERVISING SOLICITOR

(1) The Supervising Solicitor will use his best endeavours to serve this order upon the Respondent and at the same time to serve upon the Respondent the other documents required to be served and referred to in paragraph (1) of Schedule D.

(2) The Supervising Solicitor will offer to explain to the person served with the order its meaning and effect fairly and in everyday language, and to inform him of his right to take legal advice (such advice to include an explanation that the Respondent may be entitled to avail himself of [the privilege against self-incrimination or] [legal professional privilege]) and to apply to vary or discharge this order as mentioned in paragraph 27 above.

(3) The Supervising Solicitor will retain in the safe keeping of his firm all items retained by him as a result of this order until the court directs otherwise.

(4) Within [48] hours of completion of the search the Supervising Solicitor will make and provide to the Applicant's solicitors, the Respondent or his solicitors and to the judge who made this order (for the purposes of the court file) a written report on the carrying out of the order.

SCHEDULE F

AFFIDAVITS

The Applicant relied on the following affidavits—

[name]	[number of affidavit]	[date sworn]	[filed on behalf of]
(1)			
(2)			

NAME AND ADDRESS OF APPLICANT'S SOLICITORS

The Applicant's solicitors are—

[Name, address, reference, fax and telephone numbers both in and out of office hours.]

APPENDIX E

IBA RULES ON THE TAKING OF EVIDENCE IN INTERNATIONAL COMMERCIAL ARBITRATION

Adopted by a resolution of the IBA Council 1 June 1999

PREAMBLE

1. These IBA Rules on the Taking of Evidence in International Commercial Arbitration (the "IBA Rules of Evidence") are intended to govern in an efficient and economical manner the taking of evidence in international commercial arbitrations, particularly those between Parties from different legal traditions. They are designed to supplement the legal provisions and the institutional or *ad hoc* rules according to which the Parties are conducting their arbitration.

2. Parties and Arbitral Tribunals may adopt the IBA Rules of Evidence, in whole or in part, to govern arbitration proceedings, or they may vary them or use them as guidelines in developing their own procedures. The Rules are not intended to limit the flexibility that is inherent in, and an advantage of, international arbitration, and Parties and Arbitral Tribunals are free to adapt them to the particular circumstances of each arbitration.

3. Each Arbitral Tribunal is encouraged to identify to the Parties, as soon as it considers it to be appropriate, the issues that it may regard as relevant and material to the outcome of the case, including issues where a preliminary determination may be appropriate.

4. The taking of evidence shall be conducted on the principle that each Party shall be entitled to know, reasonably in advance of any Evidentiary Hearing, the evidence on which the other Parties rely.

ARTICLE 1 DEFINITIONS

In the IBA Rules of Evidence:

"*Arbitral Tribunal*" means a sole arbitrator or a panel of arbitrators validly deciding by majority or otherwise;

"*Claimant*" means the Party or Parties who commenced the arbitration and any Party who, through joinder or otherwise, becomes aligned with such Party or Parties;

"*Document*" means a writing of any kind, whether recorded on paper, electronic means, audio or visual recordings or any other mechanical or electronic means of storing or recording information;

"*Evidentiary Hearing*" means any hearing, whether or not held on consecutive days, at which the Arbitral Tribunal receives oral evidence;

"*Expert Report*" means a written statement by a Tribunal-Appointed Expert or a Party-Appointed Expert submitted pursuant to the IBA Rules of Evidence;
"*General Rules*" mean the institutional or *ad hoc* rules according to which the Parties are conducting their arbitration;
"*Party*" means a party to the arbitration;
"*Party-Appointed Expert*" means an expert witness presented by a Party;
"*Request to Produce*" means a request by a Party for a procedural order by which the Arbitral Tribunal would direct another Party to produce documents;
"*Respondent*" means the Party or Parties against whom the Claimant made its claim, and any Party who, through joinder or otherwise, becomes aligned with such Party or Parties, and includes a Respondent making a counter-claim;
"*Tribunal-Appointed Expert*" means a person or organization appointed by the Arbitral Tribunal in order to report to it on specific issues determined by the Arbitral Tribunal.

ARTICLE 2 SCOPE OF APPLICATION

1. Whenever the Parties have agreed or the Arbitral Tribunal has determined to apply the IBA Rules of Evidence, the Rules shall govern the taking of evidence, except to the extent that any specific provision of them may be found to be in conflict with any mandatory provision of law determined to be applicable to the case by the Parties or by the Arbitral Tribunal.

2. In case of conflict between any provisions of the IBA Rules of Evidence and the General Rules, the Arbitral Tribunal shall apply the IBA Rules of Evidence in the manner that it determines best in order to accomplish the purposes of both the General Rules and the IBA Rules of Evidence, unless the Parties agree to the contrary.

3. In the event of any dispute regarding the meaning of the IBA Rules of Evidence, the Arbitral Tribunal shall interpret them according to their purpose and in the manner most appropriate for the particular arbitration.

4. Insofar as the IBA Rules of Evidence and the General Rules are silent on any matter concerning the taking of evidence and the Parties have not agreed otherwise, the Arbitral Tribunal may conduct the taking of evidence as it deems appropriate, in accordance with the general principles of the IBA Rules of Evidence.

ARTICLE 3 DOCUMENTS

1. Within the time ordered by the Arbitral Tribunal, each Party shall submit to the Arbitral Tribunal and to the other Parties all documents available to it on which it relies, including public documents and those in the public domain, except for any documents that have already been submitted by another Party.

2. Within the time ordered by the Arbitral Tribunal, any Party may submit to the Arbitral Tribunal a Request to Produce.

3. A Request to Produce shall contain:
   (a) (*i*) a description of a requested document sufficient to identify it, or (*ii*) a description in sufficient detail (including subject matter) of a narrow and specific requested category of documents that are reasonably believed to exist;
   (b) a description of how the documents requested are relevant and material to the outcome of the case; and
   (c) a statement that the documents requested are not in the possession, custody or control of the requesting Party, and of the reason why that Party assumes

the documents requested to be in the possession, custody or control of the other Party.

4. Within the time ordered by the Arbitral Tribunal, the Party to whom the Request to Produce is addressed shall produce to the Arbitral Tribunal and to the other Parties all the documents requested in its possession, custody or control as to which no objection is made.

5. If the Party to whom the Request to Produce is addressed has objections to some or all of the documents requested, it shall state them in writing to the Arbitral Tribunal within the time ordered by the Arbitral Tribunal. The reasons for such objections shall be any of those set forth in Article 9.2

6. The Arbitral Tribunal shall, in consultation with the Parties and in timely fashion, consider the Request to Produce and the objections. The Arbitral Tribunal may order the Party to whom such Request is addressed to produce to the Arbitral Tribunal and to the other Parties those requested documents in its possession, custody or control as to which the Arbitral Tribunal determines that (*i*) the issues that the requesting Party wishes to prove are relevant and material to the outcome of the case, and (*ii*) none of the reasons for objection set forth in Article 9.2 apply.

7. In exceptional circumstances, if the propriety of an objection can only be determined by review of the document, the Arbitral Tribunal may determine that it should not review the document. In that event, the Arbitral Tribunal may, after consultation with the Parties, appoint an independent and impartial expert, bound to confidentiality, to review any such document and to report on the objection. To the extent that the objection is upheld by the Arbitral Tribunal, the expert shall not disclose to the Arbitral Tribunal and to the other Parties the contents of the document reviewed.

8. If a Party wishes to obtain the production of documents from a person or organization who is not a Party to the arbitration and from whom the Party cannot obtain the documents on its own, the Party may, within the time ordered by the Arbitral Tribunal, ask it to take whatever steps are legally available to obtain the requested documents. The Party shall identify the documents in sufficient detail and state why such documents are relevant and material to the outcome of the case. The Arbitral Tribunal shall decide on this request and shall take the necessary steps if in its discretion it determines that the documents would be relevant and material.

9. The Arbitral Tribunal, at any time before the arbitration is concluded, may request a Party to produce to the Arbitral Tribunal and to the other Parties any documents that it believes to be relevant and material to the outcome of the case. A Party may object to such a request based on any of the reasons set forth in Article 9.2. If a Party raises such an objection, the Arbitral Tribunal shall decide whether to order the production of such documents based upon the considerations set forth in Article 3.6 and, if the Arbitral Tribunal considers it appropriate, through the use of the procedures set forth in Article 3.7.

10. Within the time ordered by the Arbitral Tribunal, the Parties may submit to the Arbitral Tribunal and to the other Parties any additional documents which they believe have become relevant and material as a consequence of the issues raised in documents, Witness Statements or Expert Reports submitted or produced by another Party or in other submissions of the Parties.

11. If copies are submitted or produced, they must conform fully to the originals. At the request of the Arbitral Tribunal, any original must be presented for inspection.

12. All documents produced by a Party pursuant to the IBA Rules of Evidence (or by a non-Party pursuant to Article 3.8) shall be kept confidential by the Arbitral Tribunal and by the other Parties, and they shall be used only in connection with the arbitration. The Arbitral Tribunal may issue orders to set forth the terms of this confidentiality. This requirement is without prejudice to all other obligations of confidentiality in arbitration.

ARTICLE 4 WITNESSES OF FACT

1. Within the time ordered by the Arbitral Tribunal, each Party shall identify the witnesses on whose testimony it relies and the subject matter of that testimony.

2. Any person may present evidence as a witness, including a Party or a Party's officer, employee or other representative.

3. It shall not be improper for a Party, its officers, employees, legal advisors or other representatives to interview its witnesses or potential witnesses.

4. The Arbitral Tribunal may order each Party to submit within a specified time to the Arbitral Tribunal and to the other Parties a written statement by each witness on whose testimony it relies, except for those witnesses whose testimony is sought pursuant to Article 4.10 (the "Witness Statement"). If Evidentiary Hearings are organized on separate issues (such as liability and damages), the Arbitral Tribunal or the Parties by agreement may schedule the submission of Witness Statements separately for each Evidentiary Hearing.

5. Each Witness Statement shall contain:

(a) the full name and address of the witness, his or her present and past relationship (if any) with any of the Parties, and a description of his or her background, qualifications, training and experience, if such a description may be relevant and material to the dispute or to the contents of the statement;

(b) a full and detailed description of the facts, and the source of the witness's information as to those facts, sufficient to serve as that witness's evidence in the matter in dispute;

(c) an affirmation of the truth of the statement; and

(d) the signature of the witness and its date and place.

6. If Witness Statements are submitted, any Party may, within the time ordered by the Arbitral Tribunal, submit to the Arbitral Tribunal and to the other Parties revised or additional Witness Statements, including statements from persons not previously named as witnesses, so long as any such revisions or additions only respond to matters contained in another Party's Witness Statement or Expert Report and such matters have not been previously presented in the arbitration.

7. Each witness who has submitted a Witness Statement shall appear for testimony at an Evidentiary Hearing, unless the Parties agree otherwise.

8. If a witness who has submitted a Witness Statement does not appear without a valid reason for testimony at an Evidentiary Hearing, except by agreement of the Parties, the Arbitral Tribunal shall disregard that Witness Statement unless, in exceptional circumstances, the Arbitral Tribunal determines otherwise.

9. If the Parties agree that a witness who has submitted a Witness Statement does not need to appear for testimony at an Evidentiary Hearing, such an agreement shall not be considered to reflect an agreement as to the correctness of the content of the Witness Statement.

10. If a Party wishes to present evidence from a person who will not appear voluntarily at its request, the Party may, within the time ordered by the Arbitral Tribunal, ask it to take whatever steps are legally available to obtain the testimony of that person. The Party shall identify the intended witness, shall describe the subjects on which the witness's testimony is sought and shall state why such subjects are relevant and material to the outcome of the case. The Arbitral Tribunal shall decide on this request and shall take the necessary steps if in its discretion it determines that the testimony of that witness would be relevant and material.

11. The Arbitral Tribunal may, at any time before the arbitration is concluded, order any Party to provide, or to use its best efforts to provide, the appearance for testimony at an Evidentiary Hearing of any person, including one whose testimony has not yet been offered.

ARTICLE 5 PARTY-APPOINTED EXPERTS

1. A Party may rely on a Party-Appointed Expert as a means of evidence on specific issues. Within the time ordered by the Arbitral Tribunal, a Party-Appointed Expert shall submit an Expert Report.

2. The Expert Report shall contain:

(a) the full name and address of the Party-Appointed Expert, his or her present and past relationship (if any) with any of the Parties, and a description of his or her background, qualifications, training and experience;

(b) a statement of the facts on which he or she is basing his or her expert opinions and conclusions;

(c) his or her expert opinions and conclusions, including a description of the method, evidence and information used in arriving at the conclusions;

(d) an affirmation of the truth of the Expert Report; and

(e) the signature of the Party-Appointed Expert and its date and place.

3. The Arbitral Tribunal in its discretion may order that any Party-Appointed Experts who have submitted Expert Reports on the same or related issues meet and confer on such issues. At such meeting, the Party-Appointed Experts shall attempt to reach agreement on those issues as to which they had differences of opinion in their Expert Reports, and they shall record in writing any such issues on which they reach agreement.

4. Each Party-Appointed Expert shall appear for testimony at an Evidentiary Hearing, unless the Parties agree otherwise and the Arbitral Tribunal accepts this agreement.

5. If a Party-Appointed Expert does not appear without a valid reason for testimony at an Evidentiary Hearing, except by agreement of the Parties accepted by the Arbitral Tribunal, the Arbitral Tribunal shall disregard his or her Expert Report unless, in exceptional circumstances, the Arbitral Tribunal determines otherwise.

6. If the Parties agree that a Party-Appointed Expert does not need to appear for testimony at an Evidentiary Hearing, such an agreement shall not be considered to reflect an agreement as to the correctness of the content of the Expert Report.

ARTICLE 6 TRIBUNAL-APPOINTED EXPERTS

1. The Arbitral Tribunal, after having consulted with the Parties, may appoint one or more independent Tribunal-Appointed Experts to report to it on specific issues designated by the Arbitral Tribunal. The Arbitral Tribunal shall establish the terms of reference for any Tribunal-Appointed Expert report after having consulted with the Parties. A copy of the final terms of reference shall be sent by the Arbitral Tribunal to the Parties.

2. The Tribunal-Appointed Expert shall, before accepting appointment, submit to the Arbitral Tribunal and to the Parties a statement of his or her independence from the Parties and the Arbitral Tribunal. Within the time ordered by the Arbitral Tribunal, the Parties shall inform the Arbitral Tribunal whether they have any objections to the Tribunal-Appointed Expert's independence. The Arbitral Tribunal shall decide promptly whether to accept any such objection.

3. Subject to the provisions of Article 9.2, the Tribunal-Appointed Expert may request a Party to provide any relevant and material information or to provide access to any relevant documents, goods, samples, property or site for inspection. The authority of a Tribunal-Appointed Expert to request such information or access shall

be the same as the authority of the Arbitral Tribunal. The Parties and their representatives shall have the right to receive any such information and to attend any such inspection. Any disagreement between a Tribunal-Appointed Expert and a Party as to the relevance, materiality or appropriateness of such a request shall be decided by the Arbitral Tribunal, in the manner provided in Articles 3.5 through 3.7. The Tribunal-Appointed Expert shall record in the report any non-compliance by a Party with an appropriate request or decision by the Arbitral Tribunal and shall describe its effects on the determination of the specific issue.

4. The Tribunal-Appointed Expert shall report in writing to the Arbitral Tribunal. The Tribunal-Appointed Expert shall describe in the report the method, evidence and information used in arriving at the conclusions.

5. The Arbitral Tribunal shall send a copy of such Expert Report to the Parties. The Parties may examine any document that the Tribunal-Appointed Expert has examined and any correspondence between the Arbitral Tribunal and the Tribunal-Appointed Expert. Within the time ordered by the Arbitral Tribunal, any Party shall have the opportunity to respond to the report in a submission by the Party or through an Expert Report by a Party-Appointed Expert. The Arbitral Tribunal shall send the submission or Expert Report to the Tribunal-Appointed Expert and to the other Parties.

6. At the request of a Party or of the Arbitral Tribunal, the Tribunal-Appointed Expert shall be present at an Evidentiary Hearing. The Arbitral Tribunal may question the Tribunal-Appointed Expert, and he or she may be questioned by the Parties or by any Party-Appointed Expert on issues raised in the Parties' submissions or in the Expert Reports made by the Party-Appointed Experts pursuant to Article 6.5.

7. Any Expert-Report made by a Tribunal-Appointed Expert and its conclusions shall be assessed by the Arbitral Tribunal with due regard to all circumstances of the case.

8. The fees and expenses of a Tribunal-Appointed Expert, to be funded in a manner determined by the Arbitral Tribunal, shall form part of the costs of the arbitration.

ARTICLE 7 ON SITE INSPECTION

Subject to the provisions of Article 9.2, the Arbitral Tribunal may, at the request of a Party or on its own motion, inspect or require the inspection by a Tribunal-Appointed Expert of any site, property, machinery or any other goods or process, or documents, as it deems appropriate. The Arbitral Tribunal shall, in consultation with the Parties, determine the timing and arrangement for the inspection. The Parties and their representatives shall have the right to attend any such inspection.

ARTICLE 8 EVIDENTIARY HEARING

1. The Arbitral Tribunal shall at all times have complete control over the Evidentiary Hearing. The Arbitral Tribunal may limit or exclude any question to, answer by or appearance of a witness (which term includes, for the purposes of this Article, witnesses of fact and any Experts), if it considers such question, answer or appearance to be irrelevant, immaterial, burdensome, duplicative or covered by a reason for objection set forth in Article 9.2. Questions to a witness during direct and re-direct testimony may not be unreasonably leading.

2. The Claimant shall ordinarily first present the testimony of its witnesses, followed by the Respondent presenting testimony of its witnesses, and then by the presentation by Claimant of rebuttal witnesses, if any. Following direct testimony, any other Party may question such witness, in an order to be determined by the Arbitral Tribunal. The Party who initially presented the witness shall subsequently have the opportunity to ask additional questions on the matters raised in the other Parties' questioning. The Arbitral Tribunal, upon request of a Party or on its own motion, may vary this order of proceeding, including the arrangement of testimony by particular issues or in such a manner that witnesses presented by different Parties be questioned at the same time and in confrontation with each other. The Arbitral Tribunal may ask questions to a witness at any time.

3. Any witness providing testimony shall first affirm, in a manner determined appropriate by the Arbitral Tribunal, that he or she is telling the truth. If the witness has submitted a Witness Statement or an Expert Report, the witness shall confirm it. The Parties may agree or the Arbitral Tribunal may order that the Witness Statement or Expert Report shall serve as that witness's direct testimony.

4. Subject to the provisions of Article 9.2, the Arbitral Tribunal may request any person to give oral or written evidence on any issue that the Arbitral Tribunal considers to be relevant and material. Any witness called and questioned by the Arbitral Tribunal may also be questioned by the Parties.

ARTICLE 9 ADMISSIBILITY AND ASSESSMENT OF EVIDENCE

1. The Arbitral Tribunal shall determine the admissibility, relevance, materiality and weight of evidence.

2. The Arbitral Tribunal shall, at the request of a Party or on its own motion, exclude from evidence or production any document, statement, oral testimony or inspection for any of the following reasons:

(a) lack of sufficient relevance or materiality;
(b) legal impediment or privilege under the legal or ethical rules determined by the Arbitral Tribunal to be applicable;
(c) unreasonable burden to produce the requested evidence;
(d) loss or destruction of the document that has been reasonably shown to have occurred;
(e) grounds of commercial or technical confidentiality that the Arbitral Tribunal determines to be compelling;
(f) grounds of special political or institutional sensitivity (including evidence that has been classified as secret by a government or a public international institution) that the Arbitral Tribunal determines to be compelling; or
(g) considerations of fairness or equality of the Parties that the Arbitral Tribunal determines to be compelling.

3. The Arbitral Tribunal may, where appropriate, make necessary arrangements to permit evidence to be considered subject to suitable confidentiality protection.

4. If a Party fails without satisfactory explanation to produce any document requested in a Request to Produce to which it has not objected in due time or fails to produce any document ordered to be produced by the Arbitral Tribunal, the Arbitral Tribunal may infer that such document would be adverse to the interests of that Party.

5. If a Party fails without satisfactory explanation to make available any other relevant evidence, including testimony, sought by one Party to which the Party to

whom the request was addressed has not objected in due time or fails to make available any evidence, including testimony, ordered by the Arbitral Tribunal to be produced, the Arbitral Tribunal may infer that such evidence would be adverse to the interests of that Party.

APPENDIX F

THE CHARTERED INSTITUTE OF ARBITRATORS: PROTOCOL FOR THE USE OF PARTY-APPOINTED EXPERT WITNESSES IN INTERNATIONAL ARBITRATION

PREAMBLE

1. This Chartered Institute of Arbitrators Protocol for the Use of Party-Appointed Expert Witnesses in International Arbitration (the **Protocol**) is intended to govern in an efficient and economical manner the preparation and giving of expert evidence in international arbitrations, particularly those between Parties from different legal traditions. It is designed to supplement the legal provisions and the institutional or ad hoc rules according to which the Parties are conducting the Arbitration.

2. Parties and Arbitral Tribunals may adopt the Protocol in whole or in part or may use it as a guideline in developing their own procedures for the preparation and giving of expert evidence. The Protocol is not intended to limit the flexibility that is inherent in, and an advantage of, international arbitration, and Parties and Arbitral Tribunals are free to adapt it to the particular circumstances of each arbitration.

3. Each Arbitral Tribunal is encouraged to identify and establish with the Parties as soon as it is appropriate in the Arbitration, the issues in respect of which it considers expert evidence to be appropriate.

4. The preparation and giving of expert evidence in accordance with this Protocol is intended to give effect to the following principles:

- each Party is entitled to know, reasonably in advance of any Evidentiary Hearing, the expert evidence upon which the other Parties rely;
- experts should provide assistance to the Arbitral Tribunal and not advocate the position of the Party appointing them;
- there should be established before any hearing the greatest possible degree of agreement between experts.

Article 1—Definitions

In the Chartered Institute of Arbitrators Protocol for the Use of Party-Appointed Expert Witnesses in International Arbitration.

"**Arbitral Tribunal**" means a sole arbitrator or a panel of arbitrators validly deciding by majority or otherwise.

"**Arbitration**" means the arbitration in respect of which the Arbitral Tribunal has been appointed.

"**Evidentiary Hearing**" means any hearing in the Arbitration whether or not held on consecutive days, at which the Arbitral Tribunal receives oral evidence.

"**General Rules**" means the institutional or ad hoc rules according to which the Arbitration is being conducted.

"**Party**" means a party to the Arbitration, and "**Parties**" shall be construed accordingly.

"**Protocol**" means this Chartered Institute of Arbitrators Protocol for the Use of Party-Appointed Expert Witnesses in International Arbitration.

Article 2—Use of Protocol

1. Whenever the Parties agree, or the Arbitral Tribunal has directed, that the Protocol shall apply, the Protocol shall govern the preparation and giving of expert evidence.

2. In the event of a conflict between any provision of the Protocol and any mandatory provision of law agreed by the Parties or determined by the Arbitral Tribunal to be applicable to the Arbitration, the mandatory provision of law shall prevail.

3. In the event:
   - (a) of a conflict between the Protocol and the General Rules;
   - (b) that the Protocol and the General Rules are silent on anything concerning the preparation and giving of expert evidence; or
   - (c) that there is a dispute as to the meaning of the Protocol

the Arbitral Tribunal shall, after consultation with the Parties, make any necessary interpretations and shall make any directions appropriate for the preparation and giving of expert evidence in the Arbitration.

Article 3—Permission to Adduce Expert Evidence

1. The Parties shall not be entitled to adduce expert evidence in the Arbitration without the permission of the Arbitral Tribunal.

2. The Arbitral Tribunal shall, in consultation with the Parties and in timely fashion, direct:
   - (a) whether expert evidence shall be adduced in the Arbitration;
   - (b) the issue or issues in the Arbitration in respect of which expert evidence shall be adduced;
   - (c) the number of experts in respect of each issue that shall be permitted to give evidence in the Arbitration;
   - (d) the identity of the experts to give evidence;
   - (e) what tests or analyses shall be required.

3. Expert evidence shall be adduced in the manner provided for in Articles 6 and 7.

Article 4—Independence, Duty and Opinion

1. An expert that gives evidence in the Arbitration shall be independent of the Party which has appointed the expert to give such evidence.

2. Payment by the appointing Party of the expert's reasonable professional fees for the work done in giving such evidence shall not, of itself, vitiate the expert's independence.

3. An expert's duty, in giving evidence in the Arbitration, is to assist the Arbitral Tribunal to decide the issues in respect of which expert evidence is adduced.

4. An expert's opinion shall be independent, objective, unbiased and uninfluenced by the pressures of the dispute resolution process or by any Party.

5. An expert's written opinion should:

(a) contain the full name and address, background, qualifications, training and experience of the expert;
(b) state any past or present relationship with any of the Parties, the Arbitral Tribunal, counsel or other representatives of the Parties, other witnesses and any other person or entity involved in the Arbitration;
(c) contain a statement setting out all instructions the expert has received from the appointing Party and the basis of remuneration of the expert;
(d) only address the issue or issues in respect of which the Arbitral Tribunal has given permission for expert evidence to be adduced.
(e) state which facts, matters and documents, including any assumed facts or other assumptions, have been considered in reaching the opinion;
(f) state which facts, matters and documents, including any assumed facts or other assumptions, the opinion is based upon;
(g) state the opinion(s) and conclusion(s) that have been reached and a description of the method, evidence and information used in reaching the opinion(s) and conclusion(s);
(h) state which matters the expert has been unable to reach an opinion on;
(i) state which matters (if any) are outside the expert's area of expertise;
(j) be as brief as is reasonably possible;
(k) not contain copious extracts from other documents;
(l) adequately reference all documents and sources relied upon;
(m) not annex more than is reasonably necessary to support the opinion;
(n) contain a declaration in the form set out in Article 8; and
(o) be signed by the expert and state its date and place.

Article 5—Privilege

1. All instructions to, and any terms of appointment of, an expert shall not be privileged against disclosure in the Arbitration, but the Arbitral Tribunal, shall not, in relation to the instructions or terms of appointment:
(a) order disclosure of the instructions or appointment or any document relating thereto; or
(b) permit any questioning of the expert about such instructions or appointment

unless it is satisfied that there is good cause.

2. Drafts, working papers or any other documentation created by an expert for the purposes of providing expert evidence in the Arbitration shall be privileged from production and shall not be discloseable in the Arbitration.

Article 6—Expert Evidence

1. Within the time ordered by the Arbitral Tribunal, and save where the Arbitral Tribunal directs to the contrary, expert evidence shall be adduced in the Arbitration using the following procedure:
(a) The experts appointed by the Parties on related expert issues shall hold a discussion for the purpose of:
  (i) identifying and listing the issues upon which they are to provide an opinion;
  (ii) identifying and listing any tests or analyses which need to be conducted; and
  (iii) where possible, reaching agreement on those issues, the tests and analyses which need to be conducted and the manner in which they shall be conducted.

(iv) if the Arbitral Tribunal so directs, the experts shall prepare and exchange draft outline opinions for the purposes of these meetings, which opinions shall be without prejudice to the Parties' respective positions in the Arbitration and privileged from production to the Tribunal.

(b) Following such discussion, the experts shall prepare and send to the Parties and to the Arbitral Tribunal a statement setting out:

(i) those issues upon which they agree and the agreed opinions they have reached on those issues;

(ii) those tests and analyses which they agree need to be conducted and the agreed manner for conducting them;

(iii) those issues upon which they disagree and a summary of their reasons for disagreement; and

(iv) the tests and analyses in respect of which agreement has not been reached as to whether they shall be conducted and/or the manner in which they should be conducted, and a summary of their reasons for disagreement.

(c) Following such statement:

(i) any agreed tests and analyses shall be conducted in the agreed manner;

(ii) any agreed tests and analyses in respect of which the manner of conduct has not been agreed shall be conducted in such manner as each expert considers appropriate in the presence of the other expert(s); and

(iii) any test and analyses which have not been agreed shall be conducted in such manner as the expert requiring them to be conducted considers appropriate in the presence of the other expert(s).

(d) Following such statement, and such tests and analyses (if any), each expert shall produce a written opinion in accordance with the provisions of Article 4 dealing only with those issues upon which there is disagreement.

(e) Such written opinions shall be exchanged simultaneously.

(f) Following such exchange, each expert shall be entitled, should the expert so wish, to produce a further written opinion dealing only with such matters as are raised in the written opinion(s) of the other expert(s).

(g) Such further written opinions shall be exchanged simultaneously.

(h) Each expert who has provided a written opinion in the Arbitration shall give oral testimony at Evidentiary Hearing unless the Parties agree otherwise and the Arbitral Tribunal confirms that agreement.

(i) If an expert who has provided an opinion in the Arbitration does not appear to give testimony at an Evidentiary Hearing without a valid reason then, unless the Parties agree otherwise and the Arbitral Tribunal confirms that agreement, the Arbitral Tribunal shall disregard the expert's written opinion unless, in exceptional circumstances, the Arbitral Tribunal determines otherwise.

2. The contents of the discussion referred to at Article 6.1(a) shall be without prejudice to the Parties' respective positions in the Arbitration and, unless all the Parties agree otherwise, and save as provided in Article 6.1(b), the content of that discussion shall not be communicated to Arbitral Tribunal.

3. Any agreement by the Parties pursuant to Article 6.1(h) that an expert need not give oral testimony at an Evidentiary Hearing shall not constitute agreement with, or acceptance by a Party of, the content of the expert's written opinion.

Article 7—Testimony by Experts

1. The manner in which an expert gives testimony shall be as directed by the Arbitral Tribunal. The expert's testimony shall be given with the purpose of assisting the

Arbitral Tribunal to narrow the issues between the experts and to understand and efficiently to use the expert evidence.

2. The Arbitral Tribunal may at any time, up to and during the hearing, direct the experts to confer further and to provide further written reports to the Arbitral Tribunal either jointly or separately.

3. The Arbitral Tribunal may at any time hold preliminary meetings with the experts.

4. If the Arbitral Tribunal is satisfied that either or both of the written opinion or testimony of an expert is not in accordance with the expert declaration contained in Article 8 of the Protocol the Arbitral Tribunal shall disregard the expert's written opinion and testimony either in whole or in part, as it considers appropriate in all the circumstances.

Article 8—Expert Declaration

1. The expert declaration referred to in Article 4.5(n) shall be in the following form:

"*(a) I understand that my duty in giving evidence in this arbitration is to assist the arbitral tribunal decide the issues in respect of which expert evidence is adduced. I have complied with, and will continue to comply with, that duty.*

(b) I confirm that I am independent of the party which has appointed me.

(c) I confirm that this is my independent, objective, unbiased opinion which has not been influenced by the pressures of the dispute resolution process or by any party to the arbitration.

(d) I confirm that all matters upon which I have expressed an opinion are within my area of expertise.

(e) I confirm that I have referred to all matters which I regard as relevant to the opinions I have expressed and have drawn to the attention of the arbitral tribunal all matters, of which I am aware, which might adversely affect my opinion;

(f) I confirm that, at the time of providing this written opinion, I consider it to be complete and accurate and constitute my true, professional opinion.

(g) I confirm that if, subsequently, I consider this opinion requires any correction, modification or qualification I will notify the parties to this arbitration and the arbitral tribunal forthwith."

APPENDIX G

UNITED NATIONS CONVENTION ON THE RECOGNITION AND ENFORCEMENT OF FOREIGN ARBITRAL AWARDS (NEW YORK, 10 JUNE 1958)

Article I

1. This Convention shall apply to the recognition and enforcement of arbitral awards made in the territory of a State other than the State where the recognition and enforcement of such awards are sought, and arising out of differences between persons, whether physical or legal. It shall also apply to arbitral awards not considered as domestic awards in the State where their recognition and enforcement are sought.

2. The term "arbitral awards" shall include not only awards made by arbitrators appointed for each case but also those made by permanent arbitral bodies to which the parties have submitted.

3. When signing, ratifying or acceding to this Convention, or notifying extension under article X hereof, any State may on the basis of reciprocity declare that it will apply the Convention to the recognition and enforcement of awards made only in the territory of another Contracting State. It may also declare that it will apply the Convention only to differences arising out of legal relationships, whether contractual or not, which are considered as commercial under the national law of the State making such declaration.

Article II

1. Each Contracting State shall recognize an agreement in writing under which the parties undertake to submit to arbitration all or any differences which have arisen or which may arise between them in respect of a defined legal relationship, whether contractual or not, concerning a subject matter capable of settlement by arbitration.

2. The term "agreement in writing" shall include an arbitral clause in a contract or an arbitration agreement, signed by the parties or contained in an exchange of letters or telegrams.

3. The court of a Contracting State, when seized of an action in a matter in respect of which the parties have made an agreement within the meaning of this article, at the request of one of the parties, refer the parties to arbitration, unless it finds that the said agreement is null and void, inoperative or incapable of being performed.

Article III

Each Contracting State shall recognize arbitral awards as binding and enforce them in accordance with the rules of procedure of the territory where the award is relied upon, under the conditions laid down in the following articles. There shall not be imposed substantially more onerous conditions or higher fees or charges on the recognition or enforcement of arbitral awards to which this Convention applies than are imposed on the recognition or enforcement of domestic arbitral awards.

Article IV

1. To obtain the recognition and enforcement mentioned in the preceding article, the party applying for recognition and enforcement shall, at the time of the application, supply:

(a) The duly authenticated original award or a duly certified copy thereof;

(b) The original agreement referred to in article II or a duly certified copy thereof.

2. If the said award or agreement is not made in an official language of the country in which the award is relied upon, the party applying for recognition and enforcement of the award shall produce a translation of these documents into such language. The translation shall be certified by an official or sworn translator or by a diplomatic or consular agent.

Article V

1. Recognition and enforcement of the award may be refused, at the request of the party against whom it is invoked, only if that party furnishes to the competent authority where the recognition and enforcement is sought, proof that:

(a) The parties to the agreement referred to in article II were, under the law applicable to them, under some incapacity, or the said agreement is not valid under the law to which the parties have subjected it or, failing any indication thereon, under the law of the country where the award was made; or

(b) The party against whom the award is invoked was not given proper notice of the appointment of the arbitrator or of the arbitration proceedings or was otherwise unable to present his case; or

(c) The award deals with a difference not contemplated by or not falling within the terms of the submission to arbitration, or it contains decisions on matters beyond the scope of the submission to arbitration, provided that, if the decisions on matters submitted to arbitration can be separated from those not so submitted, that part of the award which contains decisions on matters submitted to arbitration may be recognized and enforced; or

(d) The composition of the arbitral authority or the arbitral procedure was not in accordance with the agreement of the parties, or, failing such agreement, was not in accordance with the law of the country where the arbitration took place; or

(e) The award has not yet become binding on the parties, or has been set aside or suspended by a competent authority of the country in which, or under the law of which, that award was made.

2. Recognition and enforcement of an arbitral award may also be refused if the competent authority in the country where recognition and enforcement is sought finds that:

(a) The subject matter of the difference is not capable of settlement by arbitration under the law of that country; or

(b) The recognition or enforcement of the award would be contrary to the public policy of that country.

Article VI

If an application for the setting aside or suspension of the award has been made to a competent authority referred to in article V(1)(e), the authority before which the award is sought to be relied upon may, if it considers it proper, adjourn the decision on the enforcement of the award and may also, on the application of the party claiming enforcement of the award, order the other party to give suitable security.

Article VII

1. The provisions of the present Convention shall not affect the validity of multilateral or bilateral agreements concerning the recognition and enforcement of arbitral awards entered into by the Contracting States nor deprive any interested party of any right he may have to avail himself of an arbitral award in the manner and to the extent allowed by the law or the treaties of the country where such award is sought to be relied upon.

2. The Geneva Protocol on Arbitration Clauses of 1923 and the Geneva Convention on the Execution of Foreign Arbitral Awards of 1927 shall cease to have effect between Contracting States on their becoming bound and to the extent that they become bound, by this Convention.

Article VIII

1. This Convention shall be open until 31 December 1958 for signature on behalf of any Member of the United Nations and also on behalf of any other State which is or hereafter becomes a member of any specialized agency of the United Nations, or which is or hereafter becomes a party to the Statute of the International Court of Justice, or any other State to which an invitation has been addressed by the General Assembly of the United Nations.

2. This Convention shall be ratified and the instrument of ratification shall be deposited with the Secretary-General of the United Nations.

Article IX

1. This Convention shall be open for accession to all States referred to in article VIII.

2. Accession shall be effected by the deposit of an instrument of accession with the Secretary-General of the United Nations.

Article X

1. Any State may, at the time of signature, ratification or accession, declare that this Convention shall extend to all or any of the territories for the international relations of which it is responsible. Such a declaration shall take effect when the Convention enters into force for the State concerned.

2. At any time thereafter any such extension shall be made by notification addressed to the Secretary-General of the United Nations and shall take effect as from the ninetieth day after the day of receipt by the Secretary-General of the United Nations of this notification, or as from the date of entry into force of the Convention for the State concerned, whichever is the later.

3. With respect to those territories to which this Convention is not extended at the time of signature, ratification or accession, each State concerned shall consider the

possibility of taking the necessary steps in order to extend the application of this Convention to such territories, subject, where necessary for constitutional reasons, to the consent of the Governments of such territories.

Article XI

In the case of a federal or non-unitary State, the following provisions shall apply:

(a) With respect to those articles of this Convention that come within the legislative jurisdiction of the federal authority, the obligations of the federal Government shall to this extent be the same as those of Contracting States which are not federal States;

(b) With respect to those articles of this Convention that come within the legislative jurisdiction of constituent states or provinces which are not, under the constitutional system of the federation, bound to take legislative action, the federal Government shall bring such articles with a favourable recommendation to the notice of the appropriate authorities of constituent states or provinces at the earliest possible moment;

(c) A federal State Party to this Convention shall, at the request of any other Contracting State transmitted through the Secretary-General of the United Nations, supply a statement of the law and practice of the federation and its constituent units in regard to any particular provision of this Convention, showing the extent to which effect has been given to that provision by legislative or other action.

Article XII

1. This Convention shall come into force on the ninetieth day following the date of deposit of the third instrument of ratification or accession.

2. For each State ratifying or acceding to this Convention after the deposit of the third instrument of ratification or accession, this Convention shall enter into force on the ninetieth day after deposit by such State of its instrument of ratification or accession.

Article XIII

1. Any Contracting State may denounce this Convention by a written notification to the Secretary-General of the United Nations. Denunciation shall take effect one year after the date of receipt of the notification by the Secretary-General.

2. Any State which has made a declaration or notification under article X may, at any time thereafter, by notification to the Secretary-General of the United Nations, declare that this Convention shall cease to extend to the territory concerned one year after the date of the receipt of the notification by the Secretary-General.

3. This Convention shall continue to be applicable to arbitral awards in respect of which recognition and enforcement proceedings have been instituted before the denunciation takes effect.

Article XIV

A Contracting State shall not be entitled to avail itself of the present Convention against other Contracting States except to the extent that it is itself bound to apply the Convention.

Article XV

The Secretary-General of the United Nations shall notify the States contemplated in article VIII of the following:

(a) Signatures and ratifications in accordance with article VIII;
(b) Accessions in accordance with article IX;
(c) Declarations and notifications under articles I, X and XI;
(d) The date upon which this Convention enters into force in accordance with article XII;
(e) Denunciations and notifications in accordance with article XIII.

Article XVI

1. This Convention, of which the Chinese, English, French, Russian and Spanish texts shall be equally authentic, shall be deposited in the archives of the United Nations.

2. The Secretary-General of the United Nations shall transmit a certified copy of this Convention to the States contemplated in article VIII.

The New York Convention can be found at www.uncitral.org.

GLOSSARY

Abbreviations

1996 Act	Arbitration Act 1996
CIArb Protocol	Protocol for the Use of Party-Appointed Expert Witnesses in International Arbitration
CPR	Civil Procedure Rules
EC Regulation	Also known as the Brussels Regulation "on jurisdiction and the recognition and enforcement of judgments in civil and commercial matters". It applies to all Member States of the European Community
IBA Rules of Evidence	IBA Rules on the Taking of Evidence in International Commercial Arbitration
ICC	International Chamber of Commerce
ICDR	International Centre for Dispute Resolution
LCIA	London Court of International Arbitration
UNCITRAL	UN Commission on International Trade Law

Other definitions

ADR	Alternative dispute resolution
Ad hoc agreement	One off or submission agreement
Amiable compositeur	Equity clause whereby the tribunal is not constrained by a national law, but can take account of broader considerations in the interest of justice and fairness
Arbitral institutions	Institutions which appoint tribunals and administer arbitration such as the LCIA, ICC and ICDR, but not UNCITRAL
Arbitral rules	Formal sets of rules promulgated by arbitral institutions or other bodies such as the UNCITRAL Rules
Bifurcation	Splitting of the hearing into segments
Curial law	The procedural law
Ex aequo et bono	Equity clause whereby the tribunal is not constrained by a national law, but can take account of broader considerations in the interest of justice and fairness
Functus	Lacking jurisdiction over the matter
Memorial	Brief or written submission
Kompetenz-kompetenz	The entitlement of the tribunal to rule on its own jurisdiction
Lex arbitri	The national supervisory law
New York Convention	The international convention signed by most of the major trading nations in the world relating to recognition and enforcement of arbitral awards
Pathological arbitration clause	A defective clause
Seat	The juridical place of the arbitration
Submission agreement	Ad hoc or one off agreement

INDEX

(All references are to page number)

Acknowledgment of service (N15), copy of, 290–291 (App. C.2)
Additional parties, 12
Ad hoc agreements
- advance payment for fees, 54, 94
- excluding right of appeal and recourse to the court. *See* Mandatory and non-mandatory provisions
- fees and charges, 38, 51
- procedural rules, 5, 17–18
- request for arbitration, 47–48

Administrative secretaries, appointment of, 51
Admiralty and Commercial Courts Guide
- procedure, 81–82
- text, 293–323 (App. D)

Advance payment of costs, 53–54, 98
Advantages and disadvantages of arbitration, 7–14
- additional parties, 12
- arbitrators, choice of, 10
- certainty of result, 12–13
- confidentiality, 9
- costs, 9–10
- delay, 9–10
- enforcement, 7–9
- flexibility of process, 13
- forum shopping, 10–12
- neutrality, 10
- precedent, 12–13
- privacy, 9

Agents, 28, 129–130
Agreement of the parties as to
- arbitral rules as agreement, 17–18
- autonomy over the process, 5
- composition of the tribunal, 19–20
- consolidation and concurrent hearings, 31
- defective arbitration clauses, 24
- directions and timetable, 69–70
- disputes arising after commencement of reference, 27
- flexibility of the process, 13
- procedural rules, 5
- matters which may be agreed, 23–24, 52–53. *See also* Mandatory and non-mandatory provisions

Alter egos, 28–29, 129–130
Alternative dispute resolution (ADR), 13–14, 46, 98–99
Amendments to claims or defence, 93
Anti-arbitration injunctions, 88
Anti-suit injunctions
- breach of arbitration clauses, 6, 44, 87–88
- Brussels Regulation 2001, 88
- claims forms, service of, 83
- EC law, 6, 87–88
- oppressive, unconscionable or vexatious conduct, 88
- procedure, 83
- stay of proceedings, 44, 87

Appeals
- awards, 117, 118–122
- Court of Appeal, 2, 68, 120–122, 126
- delay, 9–10
- enforcement of English or foreign awards, 126
- exclusion of right to appeal, agreements on, 61, 119–120, 122
- jurisdiction, 66, 67–68, 115–117, 124
- leave, 67–68, 83, 117, 118, 119–122
- notice, 120
- permission, 83
- point of law, appeals on, 86–87, 118–121
- procedure, 81–83, 121
- residual jurisdiction, 122
- rules of arbitral institutions, 61, 119
- seat of arbitration, 9–10
- security for costs, 121
- serious irregularity, meaning of, 118–119
- statutory requirements, 115–121
- waiver, 66

Applicable law
- arbitration clauses, 21–23, 63
- conflict of laws, 21–23
- main contract, 22–24, 36–37
- enforcement of English or foreign awards, 129
- expert evidence, 104
- hearings, 104
- jurisdiction, 63
- Rome Convention 1980, 22–23
- seat of arbitration, 20
- states, arbitrations involving, 129

Arbitral institutions
- advantages of using, 18

Arbitral institutions—*cont.*
  rules of. *See* Rules of arbitral institutions
Arbitral tribunals. *See* Arbitrators and arbitral tribunals
Arbitration Act 1996, 4–5
  mandatory and non-mandatory provisions, 5, 52–3
  party autonomy, 5
  text, 133–189 (App. A)
  UNCITRAL Arbitration Rules, 4
Arbitration claims. *See* Procedure
Arbitration clauses, 15–24
  additional exclusions and inclusions, 23–24
  agents, 28
  alter egos, 28–29
  anti-suit injunctions, 87–88
  applicable law, 21–23, 63
  appointing authority, 17
  arbitral tribunals and arbitrators, 19–20, 35, 50
  arbitrators, 19–20
  'arising out of', meaning of, 26
  'arising under', meaning of, 26
  assignees, 29–30
  autonomy and separability of, 63–4
  breach, 6, 87–88
  capacity, 32
  commencement of arbitration, pre-conditions to, 23
  concurrent hearings, 31
  consolidation, 31
  construction, 16, 22, 25–26
  counterclaims, 27, 49
  defective or pathological clauses, 15, 24
  definition, 16–17
  dispute, definition of, 26–27
  election to arbitrate, effect of, 17
  incorporation by reference, 16
  injunctions, 66
  insurers, 29–30
  jurisdiction, 25, 32, 63
  language, 23
  model clauses, 18
  non-signatories and third parties, 28–29
  other forms of dispute resolution clauses compared, 16–17
  parties, 27–28, 29, 32–33
  remedies, 33
  rules of arbitral institution, 17–18
  scope, 25–33
  seat of the arbitration, 20–21
  set-offs, 27
  signatures, 16, 28
  states, arbitrations involving, 30–31
  third parties, 28–29
  time limits, 23
  UNCITRAL Arbitration Rules, 17–18
  validity of agreements, 20, 26, 44–45, 63–4, 66, 124–126
Arbitration clauses—*cont.*
  writing, 16, 28
Arbitrators and arbitral tribunals
  administrative secretaries, appointment of, 51
  appointments, 19, 42, 47–51
  arbitration clauses, 19–20, 35, 50
  availability, 38
  challenges, 51–52
  charges and fees, 38, 51, 54
  civil lawyers versus common law lawyers, 36
  commencement of arbitration, 47–51
  communications between parties and parties and tribunal, 55, 76
  conduct of hearings, 37
  conflicts of interest, 37–38, 50–51
  consolidation, 31
  contract law, applicable law of, 36–37
  criteria for nominating arbitrators, 35–38, 50
  default provisions, 49–50, 52
  delay, 19–20
  efficiency, 38
  emergency arbitrators, appointment of, 42
  English arbitrators, finding out about, 38–39
  evidence, 97
  expertise, 3, 36
  fees, 38, 51, 54
  formation of tribunal, activities and considerations following, 55–61
  independence and impartiality, 50–51
  initiatives from the tribunal, 97
  interviewing arbitrators, guidelines for, 50
  jurisdiction, 65–66
  languages, 38
  London, 3
  mediators, arbitrators as, 99
  nomination of arbitrators, 19, 35–38, 49, 50
  number of arbitrators, 19–20, 35
  qualifications, 35
  reputation, 36
  selection, 10, 19–20, 35–39, 49–50
  sole arbitrators, 19, 35, 42
  tenure, 52
  three person tribunals, advantages of, 19–20
  timescale, 49
  rules of arbitral institutions, 35, 50, 51–52
  umpires, appointment of, 19
  UNCITRAL Model Rules, 51–52
  vacancies, 52
Assignment, 29–30
Awards, 107–113. *See also* Enforcement of English or foreign awards
  appeals, 117, 118–22
  bifurcation of liability and quantum, 110

Awards—*cont.*
challenges to awards, 67–68, 115–122
communication of awards to parties, 111
confidentiality, 111–113
correction, 116, 120
costs, 110–111
courts' powers prior to awards, 66
damages, assessment of, 108–109
disclosure, 112–113
dissenting awards, 109
errors and omissions, 109–110, 116, 118
form and content, 109–110
ICC Court, awards sent to, 109–110
interest, 107–108, 118
investment treaty arbitrations, 132
jurisdiction, 67–68, 115–117
partial or interim awards, 110
privacy and confidentiality, 112–113
provisional awards, 94
registration of awards, 132
remedies, 107–109
remission, 120–121
security for costs, 121
serious irregularity, 117–119
setting aside awards, 120–121
settlements, 111
time limits, 107
variation of awards, 121

Barristers
conflicts of interest, 37–38
court applications, making, 83
instructing, 2–3, 39
solicitors, 2–3
written submissions, 102
Bifurcation of liability and quantum, 57–58, 70, 73–74, 110
Breach of arbitration agreements
anti-suit injunctions, 6, 44, 87–88
EC law, 6
illegality, 44–45
stay of proceedings, 44–45
Briefs. *See* Directions and written submissions
Brussels Regulation 2001, 6, 11–12
anti-suit injunctions, 88
chronological approach to jurisdiction, 11
domicile, 11
enforcement and recognition of judgments, 8
forum non conveniens, 11–12
forum shopping, 11
non-contracting states, defendants and third parties from, 12
parallel proceedings, 12
recognition of judgments, 8
Bundles, 77

Calderbank letters, 98
Capacity, 32
Charges and fees, 38, 51, 53–54, 94
Charging orders, 127–128
Chartered Institute of Arbitrators (CIA)
protocol for use of expert witnesses, 73–74, 333–337 (App. F)
Civil Procedure Rules, 3–4, 81–82
flexibility, 13
overriding objective, 3–4
practice direction, text of, 280–291 (App. C.2)
related claims, 82
relevance to arbitration of, 4
text of Part 62, 269–279 (App. C.1)
Claim forms
anti-suit injunctions, 83
copy, 286–289 (App. C.2)
issue of, 82
practice direction, 286–289 (App. C.2)
service, 83
Commencement of arbitration
activity and considerations prior to, 41–46
advance costs, 53–54
agreement between parties, matters for, 52–53
alternative dispute resolution, 46
arbitration clauses, 23
arbitrators,
appointment of, 42, 47–48, 49–51
challenges to, 51–52
tenure, 52
court applications before tribunal is fully constituted, 42–43
default provisions, 47–48, 53
emergency arbitrators, appointment of, 42
expedited tribunals, 42
fees, deposits for, 53–54
multi-tier clauses, 46
notice, 47–48
pre-conditions, 23
request for arbitration, 47–48
response and replies, 49
rules of arbitral institutions, 48
stay of proceedings, applications for, 44–45
time limits, 47, 48, 49
Commercial Court, 1–2
guide, text of, 293–323 (App. D)
procedure, 83, 293–323 (App. D)
Communications between parties and parties and tribunal, 55, 76
Concurrent hearings, 31
Confidentiality. *See* Privacy and confidentiality
Conflict of laws, 21–23
Conflicts of interest
arbitrators and arbitral tribunals, 37–38, 50–51
barristers 37–38
IBA Rules, 37, 50

Conflicts of interest—*cont.*
traffic lights approach, 37–38, 50
Consolidation, 31
Construction disputes, 2, 83
Costs
advance costs, 53–54, 98
advantages and disadvantages of arbitration, 9–10
amendments to claims or defence, 93
awards, 110–111
Calderbank letters, 98
commencement of arbitration, 53–54
counterclaims, 53–54
cap on recoverable costs, 60, 98
directions, 69
enforcement of English or foreign awards, 126
mediation, 99
open offers, 97–98
peremptory orders, 93
protective measures, 60, 97–98
provisional awards, 94
rules of arbitral institutions, 110
sealed offers, 98
security for costs, 59, 121, 126–127
without prejudice offers, 98
Counterclaims, 27, 49, 53–54
Courts, 42–44, 81–89, 95. *See also* Appeals
aiding foreign arbitrations, 88–89
anti-suit injunctions, 87–88
applications prior to hearings, 81–89
awards, powers prior to, 66
barristers, applications by, 83
ceasing to have effect on order of tribunal, orders, 86
commencement of arbitration, applications before, 42–43
Commercial Court, 1–2, 293–323 (App. D)
court system, 1–2
declarations, 66, 67
exclusion of recourse to the courts, 10–11, 61
freezing injunctions, 85
guides, 81–82, 293–323 (App. D)
injunctions, 84–85
jurisdiction, 10–11, 66–67, 124
ousting jurisdiction of courts, 10–11, 61
preliminary points of law, 86–87
preservation of evidence, 42–43, 59–60, 84–86
procedure, 81–83
provisional measures, 85–86
solicitors, applications by, 83
stay of proceedings, 44–45
Cross-examination, 102–104
Crown, 31
Curial law, 20
Damages
assessment, 57–58, 70, 108–110
awards, 108–109
bifurcation of liability and quantum, 57–58, 70, 73–74, 110
costs, 98
discounted cash flow method of assessment, 108–109
expert evidence, 73–74
factual issues for assessment, 57–58
future loss, 109
injunctions, 85
net asset value or book value, 109
precedent, 12–13
undertakings, 85
Debt orders, 127
Declarations, 66, 67
Defauting parties. *See* Peremptory orders
tribunal's power to continue, 101
Defective or pathological arbitration clauses, 15, 24
Definition of arbitration claims, 82
Delay
advantages and disadvantages of arbitration, 9–10
appeals, 9–10
arbitrators and arbitral tribunals, 38
bifurcation of liability and quantum, 57–58
directions, 69
enforcement, challenging awards to delay, 118–119
extensions of time, 91–92
inordinate and inexcusable delay, 92
jurisdictional issues, raising, 64–65
peremptory orders, 84, 92
sanctions, 92
Terms of Reference, 57
Deposits for costs and fees, 53–54
Directions, 55–56, 69–80, 95–97
allocation of hearing time, 78, 97
briefs, pre-hearing and post-hearing, 78, 79
communications between parties and parties and tribunal, 76
compliance, ensuring, 79–80
costs, 69
delay, 69
disclosure, 71–72, 93
documentation for hearings, 77
evidence, preservation of, 59
expert evidence, 73–75
facilities for the hearing, 96
fixing hearing dates, 76
further procedural hearings, 77
hearings, 69, 77–79
inter-lawyer correspondence, 76
language, 78, 79
oral hearings, 77

Directions—*cont.*
peremptory orders to ensure compliance, 79–80
pre-hearing written material, 78, 97
procedural hearings, 69, 77
rules of arbitral institutions, 75
sanctions for non-compliance, 79–80
timetable, 70, 75, 78–79
UNCITRAL Model Rules, 75
venue for hearings, 77
witnesses of fact, 75, 78
written statements or submissions, 70–71
Disadvantages of arbitration. *See* Advantages and disadvantages of arbitration
Disclosure
awards, 112–113
directions, 71–72
disclosure orders, 93
electronic disclosure, 71
evidence, preservation of, 72
foreign arbitrations, 89
freezing injunctions, 85, 127
IBA Rules of Evidence, 71
injunctions, 85
limits to disclosure, 71
objections, 71–72
privacy and confidentiality, 112–113
reasonable necessity test, 112–113
third parties, 72
Dispute, meaning of, 26–27
Documents
bundles, 77
hearings, for, 77
injunctions, 85
preparation, 96
witness statements, 75, 95–96, 102–103
Domicile, 11

EC law, 6. *See also* Brussels Regulation 2001
anti-suit injunctions, 87–88
applicability to arbitration, 5, 11, 87–88
litigation, 11
Electronic documents, 71, 77
E-mail, 76
Emergency arbitrators, appointment of, 42
Enforcement. *See also* Enforcement of English or foreign awards
Brussels Regulation 2001, 8
interlocutory applications, 59–60
judgments, 8, 124–125
jurisdiction, 66
peremptory orders, 93
personal representatives, 32
Enforcement of English or foreign awards, 123–130
advantages and disadvantages of arbitration, 7–9
ancillary measures, 126–128
appeals, 126

Enforcement of English or foreign awards—*cont.*
applicable law, 129
charging orders, 127–128
costs, 126
delay, 118–119
freezing injunctions, 127
investment treaty arbitrations, 132
jurisdiction, 124
leave, 124, 126
New York Convention 1958, 8–9, 123, 124–127
notice, 126
procedure, 126
seat of arbitration, 20–21
security for costs, 126–127
states, 128–130
sovereign immunity. *See* States
stay of execution, 127
summary enforcement, 124
third party debt orders, 127
English legal system, 1–5
Arbitration Act 1998, 4–5
barristers, 2–3
Civil Procedure Rules, 3–4
court system, 1–2
solicitors, 2–3
split legal profession, 2–3
Errors and omissions in awards, 109–110, 116, 118
Evidence. *See also* Expert evidence
directions, 59
disclosure, 71–72
hearings, 102–103
injunctions, 84–85
oral evidence, 77, 102–103
preservation, 59–60, 72, 84–85
tribunal, initiatives of, 97
written submissions, 102
Expedited tribunals, formation of, 42
Expert evidence
applicable law, 104
bifurcation of liability and quantum, 73–74
CIArb Protocol, 73–74, 333- 337 (App. F)
cross-examination, 104
damages, 73–74
directions, 73–75
hearings, 104
IBA Rules of Evidence, 73, 325–332 (App. E)
meetings, 74
number of experts, 74
oral evidence, presentation of, 74
preparation, 96
reports or statements, 96
third parties, 88–89
timetable, 74
translations, 75
tribunal appointed experts, 74

Expert evidence—*cont.*
  written evidence, presentation of, 74
Exclusion of recourse to the courts, 61

Facilities, preparation of, 96
Fees and charges, 38, 51, 53–54, 94
Fixing dates for hearings, 76
Flexibility of process, 13
Foreign arbitrations. *See also* Enforcement of English or foreign awards
  aiding, 88–89
  disclosure, 89
  injunctions, 89
  letters of request, 89
  service out of the jurisdiction, 89
  third parties, evidence from, 88–89
Foreign judgments, enforcement of. *See* New York Convention on the Recognition and Enforcement of Foreign Arbitral Awards 1958
Foreign lawyers, 3, 39, 83
Freezing orders
  disclosure, 85, 127
  enforcement of English or foreign awards, 127
  guidelines, 85
  worldwide, 85, 127
Forum non conveniens, 11–12
Forum shopping, 10–12
Future loss, damages for, 109

Glossary, 345
Groups of companies, 29

Hearings, 101–105
  allocation of hearing time, 78, 97
  applicable law, 104
  arbitration clauses, 31
  concurrent hearings, 31
  conduct of hearings, 37
  directions for, 69, 77–79
  documentation, 77
  evidence, 102–103
  experts, 104
  failure to attend, 101
  final submissions, 104
  fixing dates, 76
  money laundering, 101–102
  opening statements, 102
  oral hearings, 77, 101
  preparation, 95–97
  privacy and confidentiality, 83, 104–105
  procedural hearings, 69, 77, 97
  public hearings, 83
  representation, 101–102
  time estimates, 78
  venue for hearings, 77
  written submissions, 102

IBA Rules
  conflict of interest, 37, 50
  evidence, taking of, 71, 73, 325–332 (App. E)
  text, 325–332 (App. E)
ICC Rules
  awards, 109–100
  comparison of rules with LCIA, UNCITRAL and ICDR, 191–269 (App. B.1, B.2, B.3)
  ICDR rules, comparison with, 191–269 (App. B.1, B.2, B.3)
  LCIA Rules, comparison with, 191–269 (App. B.1, B.2, B.3)
  Terms of Reference, 57, 70
  timetable, 70
  UNCITRAL Rules, comparison with, 191–269 (App. B.1, B.2, B.3)
ICDR Rules
  comparison of rules with LCIA, UNCITRAL and ICDR, 191–269 (App. B.1, B.2, B.3)
  emergency arbitrators, appointment of, 42
  ICDR rules, comparison with, 191–269 (App. B.1, B.2, B.3)
  LCIA Rules, comparison with, 191–269 (App. B.1, B.2, B.3)
  UNCITRAL Rules, comparison with, 191–269 (App. B.1, B.2, B.3)
ICSID (International Centre for the Settlement of Investment Disputes) Convention Regulations and Rules, 131–132
Impartiality of arbitral tribunals, 36, 37–38, 50–51
Incorporation of arbitration clauses by reference, 29–30
Independence of arbitral tribunals, 37–38, 50–51
Injunctions. *See also* Anti-arbitration and anti-suit injunctions
  damages, undertakings as to, 85
  disclosure, 85
  documentation, accompanying, 85
  evidence, preservation of, 42–43, 84–85
  final injunctions, 84
  foreign arbitrations, 89
  freezing orders, 85, 127
  interim injunctions, 43, 84
  jurisdiction, 66, 67
  urgency, cases of, 84–85
  validity of arbitration agreements, 66
  without notice applications, 85
Initial general communications, 55–56
Insurers, 29–30
Interest, 107–108, 118
Interim awards, 110
Interim or conservatory measures, 42, 43, 60

International Centre for the Settlement of Investment Disputes (ICSID) Convention Regulations and Rules, 131–132
Investment treaty arbitrations, 131–132
enforcement of awards, 132 ICSID
International Centre for the Settlement of Investment Disputes (ICSID) Convention Regulations and Rules, 131–132
justiciability, 131–132
recognition and registration of awards, 132 ICSID
sovereign immunity, 132 ICSID
Issue estoppel, 130

Judgments
enforcement of, 8, 124–125
foreign judgments, enforcement of, 8–9
New York Convention 1958, 124–125
recognition, 8
Jurisdiction, 63–68
appeals, 66, 67–68, 124
applicable law, 20–23, 63
arbitration agreements, autonomy of, 63–64
arbitration clauses, 25, 32
awards, challenges to, 67–68, 115–117
Brussels Regulation 2001, 11
challenges, 32–33, 63–68, 115–117
courts,
applications for determination of preliminary points of, 66–67
powers prior to awards, 66
declarations, 66, 67
delay in raising jurisdictional issues, 64–65
enforcement, 66, 124
injunctions, 66, 67
New York Arbitration Convention 1958, 66
ousting jurisdiction of courts, 10–11
parties, 32
powers of arbitral tribunal, 65–66
service outside the jurisdiction, 82–83, 89
sovereign immunity, 65
states, arbitrations involving, 129–130
stay of proceedings, 65, 66
substantive jurisdiction, challenges on grounds of lack of, 115–117
time limits for challenges, 116
waiver, 33, 116

Kompetenz-kompetenz, 63

Languages, 38, 75, 78, 79
Lawyers. *See* Legal profession
LCIA Rules
comparison of rules, 200–268 (App. B.3)
index, 191–199 (App. B.1)
LCIA Rules—*cont.*
comparison of rules—*cont.*
numerical order, index in, 196–199 (App. B.2)
consolidation hearings, 31
expedited tribunals, 42
fees, 51
ICC Rules, comparison with, 191–269 (App. B.1, B.2, B.3)
ICDR Rules, comparison with, 191–269 (App. B.1, B.2, B.3)
privacy and confidentiality, 112
questions by tribunal, preparation of, 97
UNCITRAL Rules, comparison with, 191–269 (App. B.1, B.2, B.3)
Legal profession
arbitrators and arbitral tribunals, 36
barristers, 2–3, 37–39, 83, 102
civil lawyers and common law lawyers, 36
correspondence, 76
foreign lawyers, 3, 39, 83
selection of legal team, 39
solicitors, 2–3, 83
split legal profession, 2–3
Letters of request, 89
Lex arbitri, 20
Limitation periods. *See* Time limits and timetables

Mandatory and non-mandatory provisions, 5, 52–53
Mediation, 13–14, 46, 98–99
Memorials, 38, 70, 79
Money laundering, 101–102
Multi-tier clauses, 7, 16, 46. *See also* Mediation

Neutrality, 10
New York Convention on the Recognition and Enforcement of Foreign Arbitral Awards 1958
enforcement under, 8–9, 123–127
grounds for refusal of enforcement, 125–126
judgments, enforcement of, 8–9, 124–125
jurisdiction, 66
procedure, 126
public policy, refusal on grounds of, 125–126
recognition of awards, 124–125
security for costs, 126–127
text, 339–343 (App. G)
writing, 16
Non-participating parties, communication with, 56
Non-signatories and third parties, 28–29
Novation, 32

Oaths, 103
Ongoing issues, 91–95
  amendments of claims or defence, 93
  costs and charges, 94
  court applications, 95
  delay, 91–92
  disclosure, 93
  failure to participate, 93
  orders, non-compliance with tribunal's, 92
  peremptory orders, 92–93
  procedural orders and hearings, 93–94
  provisional awards, 94
Opening statements, 102
Oppressive, unconscionable or vexatious conduct, 88
Ousting jurisdiction of courts, 10–11
Overriding objective, 3–4

Parallel proceedings, 12
Pathological arbitration clauses, 15, 24
Partial awards, 110
Parties
  additional parties, 12
  agreement between. *See also* Mandatory and non-mandatory provisions, 5, 52–53
  arbitration clauses, 27–28, 29, 32–33
  assignees and insurers, 29
  autonomy of parties, 5
  communications between parties and parties and tribunal, 76
  companies/single economic unit doctrine, 29
  failure to participate, 93
  groups of companies, 29
  identification, 27–28, 29, 32
  jurisdiction, 32
  non-participating parties, 56
  non-signatories, 28–29
  novation, 32
  personal representatives, 32
  trustees in bankruptcy, 32
Peremptory orders
  delay, 84, 92
  directions, ensuring compliance with, 79–80
  enforcement, 93
  expiry of, tribunal's powers on, 92–93
  failure to comply with, 59–60
  notice, 60, 93
  sanctions, 59–60
Personal representatives, 32
Practice directions (PDs)
  acknowledgment of service (N15), copy of, 290–291 (App. C.2)
  Civil Procedure Rules Part 62, text of PD supplementing, 280–291 (App. C.2)
  claim forms, 286–289 (App. C.2)
  procedure, 81
Precedent, 12–13
Preliminary points of law, 86–87
Preliminary issues, 58
Preparation, 96
Privacy and confidentiality
  advantages and disadvantages of arbitration, 9
  awards, 111–113
  disclosure, reasonable necessity test for, 112–113
  express agreement, 24, 53, 106
  hearings, 83, 104–105
  LCIA Rules, 112
  rules of arbitral institutions, 53, 105–106
  written agreements, 106
Procedure
  arbitration claims, definition of, 82
  Civil Procedure Rules, 81–82
  claim forms, issue of, 82
  court guides, 81–82, 293–323 (App. D)
  enforcement of English or foreign awards, 126
  hearings, 69, 77, 79, 93–94, 97
  orders, 93–94
  practice directions, 81
  private or public hearings, 83
  service out of the jurisdiction, 82–83
  stay of proceedings, 83
Protective measures, 60, 84–85, 97–98
Provisional awards, 94
Provisional measures, 85–86

Queen's Counsel, 2, 35, 39

Recognition of awards, 124–125
Recognition of judgments, 8, 132
Remedies, 33, 107–109. *See* Damages, injunctions
Request for arbitration, 47–48
Responses and replies, 49
Rome Convention on the Law Applicable to Contractual Obligations 1980, 22–23
Rules of arbitral institutions. *See also* LCIA Rules, UNCITRAL Arbitration Rules
  advantages of using institutional rules, 18
  appeals, 61, 119
  arbitration clauses, 17–18
  arbitrators and arbitral tribunals, 35, 50, 51–52
  changing institutions, 53
  commencement of arbitration, 48
  comparison of rules of LCIA, ICC, ICDR and UNCITRAL, 200–268 (App. B.3)
    index, 191–199 (App. B.1)
    numerical order, index in, 196–199 (App. B.2)
  confidentiality, 53
  costs, 110
  counterclaims, 27

Rules of arbitral institutions—*cont.*
directions, 75
exclusion of recourse to courts, 61
ICC Rules,
awards, 109–110
comparison with LCIA, ICDR and UNCITRAL Rules of, 191–269 (App. B.1, B.2, B.3)
provisional timetable, 70
Terms of Reference, 57, 70
ICDR Rules
comparison with ICC, ICDR and UNCITRAL Rules of, 191–269 (App. B.1, B.2, B.3)
emergency arbitrators, appointment of, 42
ICSID Convention Regulations and Rules, 131–132
privacy and confidentiality, 105–106
set-off, 27
Swiss Rules of International Arbitration, 31
time limits, 23, 49

Scott v *Avery* clauses, 46
Sealed offers, 98
Seat of arbitration
appeals, 9–10
applicable law, 20
arbitration clauses, 20–21
enforcement of arbitration awards, 20–21, 123, 124–126
juridical seat or location, 20
location of proceedings, 20
outside the jurisdiction, 20
Security for costs, 59, 121, 126–127
Serious irregularity as grounds for appeal, 117–119
Service
anti-suit injunctions, 83
claim forms, 83
in the EC, 83
outside the jurisdiction, 82–83, 89
Set-offs, 27
Settlements, 99, 111
Signatures, 16, 38
Skeleton arguments, 83
Solicitors
barristers, 2–3
court applications, making, 83
London, 3
partnerships, 3
Sovereign immunity, 30, 65, 128–130, 132
Start of arbitration. *See* Commencement of arbitration
States, arbitration involving
alter egos or agents of state, 129–130
applicable law, 129
arbitration clauses, 30–31

States, arbitration involving—*cont.*
central bank or other monetary authority, property of, 130
Crown, 31
enforcement of English or foreign awards, 128–130
investment treaty arbitrations, 132
issue estoppel, 130
jurisdiction, 65, 129–130
sovereign immunity, 30, 65, 128–130, 132
waiver, 129, 130
Stay of proceedings
anti-suit injunctions, 87
applications for, 44–45
breach of arbitration agreements, proceedings brought in, 44–45
enforcement of English or foreign awards, 127
illegality, 44–45
jurisdiction, 65, 66
notice, 83
procedure, 83
Swiss Rules of International Arbitration, 31

Technology and Construction Court, 2, 83
Terms of Reference, 57, 70
Third parties
arbitration clauses, 28–29
Brussels Regulation 2001, 12
consolidation, 31
debt orders, 127
disclosure, 72
evidence, 88–89
foreign arbitrations, 88–89
Time limits and timetables
arbitration clauses, 23
arbitrators and arbitral tribunals, appointment of, 35, 50, 51–52
awards, 107
bifurcation of liability and quantum, 70
commencement of arbitration, 47, 48, 49
delay, 91–92
directions, 70, 75, 78–79
expert evidence, 74
extension, 23, 49, 91–92
hearings, time estimates for, 78
ICC Rules, 70
jurisdiction, challenging, 116
rules of arbitral institutions, 23, 49, 70
Translations, 75
Tribunals. *See* Arbitrators and arbitral tribunals
Trustees in bankruptcy, 32

Umpires, appointment of, 19
UNCITRAL Arbitration Rules
Arbitration Act 1996, 4
arbitration clauses, 17–18

UNCITRAL Arbitration Rules—*cont.*
arbitrators and arbitral tribunals, challenges to, 51–52
comparison of rules with LCIA, UNCITRAL and ICDR, 191–269 (App. B.1, B.2, B.3)
directions, 75
ICDR rules, comparison with, 191–269 (App. B.1, B.2, B.3)
LCIA Rules, comparison with, 191–269 (App. B.1, B.2, B.3)
UNCITRAL Rules, comparison with, 191–269 (App. B.1, B.2, B.3)

Venue for hearings, 20, 77

Without notice applications, 60, 85
Witnesses
cross-examination, 102–103, 104
directions, 75, 78
fact, of, 75, 78, 102–103
further written statements or submissions, 70–71
oaths, 103
preparation of statements, 95–96
statements, 75, 95–96, 102–103
Written statements or submissions, 70–71, 102
Writing, need for, 16, 28